Emotional Intelligence Matters

R. S. Mekhala

Emotional Intelligence Matters

A Machine-Generated Literature Overview

palgrave
macmillan

R. S. Mekhala
Vellore Institute of Technology
Chennai, Tamil Nadu, India

ISBN 978-981-99-7726-0   ISBN 978-981-99-7727-7 (eBook)
https://doi.org/10.1007/978-981-99-7727-7

© The Editor(s) (if applicable) and The Author(s), under exclusive license to Springer Nature Singapore Pte Ltd. 2024

This work is subject to copyright. All rights are solely and exclusively licensed by the Publisher, whether the whole or part of the material is concerned, specifically the rights of translation, reprinting, reuse of illustrations, recitation, broadcasting, reproduction on microfilms or in any other physical way, and transmission or information storage and retrieval, electronic adaptation, computer software, or by similar or dissimilar methodology now known or hereafter developed.
The use of general descriptive names, registered names, trademarks, service marks, etc. in this publication does not imply, even in the absence of a specific statement, that such names are exempt from the relevant protective laws and regulations and therefore free for general use.
The publisher, the authors and the editors are safe to assume that the advice and information in this book are believed to be true and accurate at the date of publication. Neither the publisher nor the authors or the editors give a warranty, expressed or implied, with respect to the material contained herein or for any errors or omissions that may have been made. The publisher remains neutral with regard to jurisdictional claims in published maps and institutional affiliations.

This Palgrave Macmillan imprint is published by the registered company Springer Nature Singapore Pte Ltd.
The registered company address is: 152 Beach Road, #21-01/04 Gateway East, Singapore 189721, Singapore

If disposing of this product, please recycle the paper.

Preface

Auto-summaries can be generated by either an abstractive or extractive auto-summarization:

- An extraction-based summarizer identifies the most important sentences of a text and uses the original sentences to create the summary.
- An abstraction-based summarizer creates new text based on deep learning. New phrases are created to summarize the content.

The auto-summaries you will find in this book have been generated via an extractive summarization approach.

Each chapter was carefully edited by [name of editor]. The editors selected the papers which were then auto-summarized. The editors have not edited the auto-summaries due to the extraction-based approach, and have not changed the original sentences. You will find the editors' reviews and guidance on the auto-summaries in their chapter introductions.

In machine-generated books, editors are defined as those who curate the content for the book by selecting the papers to be auto-summarized and by organizing the output into a meaningful order. Next to the thoughtful curation of the papers, editors should guide the readers through the auto-summaries and make transparent why they selected the papers.

The ultimate goal is to provide a current literature review of Springer Nature publications on a given topic in order to support readers in overcoming information overload and to help them dive into a topic faster; to identify interdisciplinary overlaps; and to present papers which might not have been on the readers' radar.

Please note, that the selected papers are not used to train a LLM while the auto-summaries are created.

Chennai, India   R. S. Mekhala

Contents

1 **Emotional Intellience—It Matters** 1
   Introduction by the Author 1
   Machine Generated Summaries 2
      When Feeling Poorly at Work Does Not Mean Acting Poorly
      at Work: The Moderating Role of Work-Related Emotional
      Intelligence [62] 3
      The Way to Improve Organizational Citizenship Behavior
      for the Employees Who Lack Emotional Intelligence [63] 5
      Limitations and Future Research 9
      Do Agile Managed Information Systems Projects Fail Due
      to a Lack of Emotional Intelligence? [64] 9
      The Impact of Psychological Capital on Project Success
      Mediating Role of Emotional Intelligence in Construction
      Organizations of Pakistan [65] 14
      A Contingency Model of Emotional Intelligence in Professional
      Selling [66] 16
      Effectiveness of Emotional Fitness Training in Police [67] 19
      How Does Authentic Leadership Influence Employee Voice?
      From the Perspective of the Theory of Planned Behavior [68] 22
      To Share or Not to Share: How Perceived Institutional
      Empowerment Shapes Employee Perceived Shared Leadership
      [69] 25
   Bibliography 28

2 **Emotional Intelligence and Job Performance** 33
   Introduction by the Author 33
   Machine Generated Summaries 35
      Development of Workplace Emotional Health Scale [170] 36
      Group Leader Emotional Intelligence and Group Performance:
      A Multilevel Perspective [171] 39

The Effects of Emotional Intelligence on Job Performance
and Life Satisfaction for the Research and Development
Scientists in China [172] 42
Other-Caring or Other-Critical? A Contagious Effect of Leaders'
Emotional Triads on Subordinates' Performance [173] 46
Does Emotional Intelligence Moderate the Relationship
Between Workplace Bullying and Job Performance? [174] 49
Effects of Perceptions on LMX and Work Performance:
Effects of Supervisors' Perception of Subordinates'
Emotional Intelligence and Subordinates' Perception of Trust
in the Supervisor on LMX and, Consequently, Performance [175] ... 56
Brand Managers' Mindful Self-Management of Their
Professional Experience: Consequences for Pay, Self-Efficacy
and Job Performance [176] 58
Psychological Capital and Employee Engagement as Predictors
of Organisational Citizenship Behaviour in the Industrial
Revolution 4.0 Era: Transfer of Training as a Mediator [177] 64
Effect of Employee Recognition, Employee Engagement
on Their Productivity: The Role of Transformational Leadership
Style at Ghana Health Service [178] 66
Display Rule Perceptions and Job Performance in a Chinese
Retail Firm: The Moderating Role of Employees' Affect
at Work [179] 70
How Authentic Leadership Influences Employee Proactivity:
The Sequential Mediating Effects of Psychological
Empowerment and Core Self-Evaluations and the Moderating
Role of Employee Political Skill [180] 73
How Does the Needs-Supplies Fit of Developmental Job
Experience Affect Employees' Proactive Behavior? [181] 76
The Effects of Job Involvement and Supervisor Developmental
Feedback on Employee Creativity: A Polynomial Regression
with Response Surface Analysis [182] 79
You Are "Insisting", or You Want to "Withdraw"? Research
on the Negative Effect of Ethical Leadership on Leaders
Themselves [183] 83
Emotional Intelligence as a Moderator of Affectivity/
Emotional Labor and Emotional Labor/Psychological Distress
Relationships [184] 87
Bibliography 90

**3 The Role of Emotional Intelligence in Propelling Productivity
at Workplace** 101
Introduction by the Author 101
Machine Generated Summaries 103
   Are Self-sacrificing Employees Liked by Their Supervisor? [86] 103

Contents

      Mediating Effect of Social Support between the Emotional
      Intelligence and Job Satisfaction of Chinese Employees [87] 107
      Why and When can CSR toward Employees Lead
      to Cyberloafing? The Role of Workplace Boredom and Moral
      Disengagement [88] 109
      The Effects of Emotional Display Rules on Flight Attendants'
      Emotional Labor Strategy, Job Burnout and Performance [89] 112
      Service Employee Burnout and Engagement: The Moderating
      Role of Power Distance Orientation [90] 115
      A Morphological Analyses of the Literature on Employee
      Work-life Balance [91] 119
      How Quality of Work-life Influence Employee Job Satisfaction
      in a Gas Processing Plant in Ghana [92] 123
      The Effect of Servant Leadership on Employee Outcomes: Does
      Endogeneity Matter? [93] 126
      Is Transformational Leadership Always Good for Employee
      Task Performance? Examining Curvilinear and Moderated
      Relationships [94] 129
      The Antecedents of Corporate Reputation and Image and Their
      Impacts on Employee Commitment and Performance: The
      Moderating Role of CSR [95] 134
   Bibliography 138

4 Stress and Emotional Intelligence 143
   Introduction by the Author 143
   Machine Generated Summaries 145
      The Effects of Culture Shock on Foreign Employees
      in the Service Industry [51] 145
      The Impact of Emotional Self-management on Benefit Offerings
      and Employment Growth: An Analysis of the Fastest Growing
      Businesses in the United States [52] 148
      Alleviating Job Stress to Improve Service Employee Work
      Affect: The Influence of Rewarding [53] 151
      To Drink or Not to Drink; That is the Question! Antecedents
      and Consequences of Employee Business Drinking [54] 154
      Research on the Influence Mechanism of Emotional Intelligence
      and Psychological Empowerment on Customers' Repurchase
      Intention Under the Situation of Online Shopping Service
      Recovery [55] 157
      An Empirical Study on the Impact of Employee Voice
      and Silence on Destructive Leadership and Organizational
      Culture [56] 160
      Relationship Between Emotional Labor and Job Satisfaction:
      Testing Mediating Role of Emotional Intelligence on South
      Korean Public Service Employees [57] 163

How Spiritual Leadership Leads to Employee Followership Behavior: The Role of Relational Identification and Spiritual Intelligence [58] 166
It Takes a Village: Examining How and When Brand-specific Transformational Leadership Affects Employees in Internal Brand Management [59] 169
Bibliography 173

5 Emotional Intelligence and Leadership 177
Introduction by the Author 177
Machine Generated Summaries 178
    Correctional Executives' Leadership Self-Efficacy and Their Perceptions of Emotional Intelligence [189] 179
    A Multi-level Study of Emergent Group Leadership: Effects of Emotional Stability and Group Conflict [190] 182
    An Adaptive Leadership Approach: The Impact of Reasoning and Emotional Intelligence (EI) Abilities on Leader Adaptability [191] 185
    Recovering Troubled IT Projects: The Roles of Transformational Leadership and Project Complexity [192] 187
    Leading in the Paradoxical World of Crises: How Leaders Navigate Through Crises [193] 190
    Impact of Abusive Supervision on Intention to Leave: A Moderated Mediation Model of Organizational-Based Self Esteem and Emotional Exhaustion [194] 194
    Transformational Leadership, Innovative Work Behavior, and Employee Well-Being [195] 197
    Ethical Leadership and Ambidexterity in Young Firms: Examining the CEO-TMT Interface [196] 200
    Learning Value-Based Leadership in Teams: The Moderation of Emotional Regulation [197] 203
    The Impact of Emotional Leadership on Chinese Subordinates' Work Engagement: Role of Intrinsic Motivation and Traditionality [198] 205
    Impact of Self-leadership on Employee Voice Behavior: A Moderated Mediating Model [199] 209
    Longitudinal Effects of Job Insecurity on Employee Outcomes: The Moderating Role of Emotional Intelligence and the Leader-member Exchange [200] 212
    Does Transformational Leadership Facilitate Technological Innovation? The Moderating Roles of Innovative Culture and Incentive Compensation [201] 215
    The Role of Transformational Leadership and Institutional Entrepreneurship in Organizational Change in Indian Public Organizations [202] 218

How Can Managers, Acting as Brokers, Be Ambidextrous? The Effect of Trust Brokerage on Managers' Ambidexterity [203]	221
A Critical Analysis of Elon Musk's Leadership in Tesla Motors [204]	225
Cultural Congruence or Compensation? A Meta-Analytic Test of Transformational and Transactional Leadership Effects Across Cultures [205]	228
The Relationship Between Ethical Leadership and Unethical Pro-Organizational Behavior: Linear or Curvilinear Effects? [206]	232
The Effect of Organizational Citizenship Behavior and Leadership Effectiveness on Public Sectors Organizational Performance: Study in the Department of Education, Youth and Sports in Maluku Province, Indonesia [207]	237
Machiavellianism and Task-Orientated Leadership: Moderating Effect of Job Autonomy [208]	240
Transformational Leadership and Follower Task Performance: The Role of Susceptibility to Positive Emotions and Follower Positive Emotions [209]	243
Heightening Citizenship Behaviours of Academicians Through Transformational Leadership: Evidence Based Interventions [210]	246
Bibliography	250

6 Emotional Intelligence in Human Resource Management ... 261

Introduction by the Author	261
Machine Generated Summaries	262
Investigating the Serial Psychological Processes of Workplace COVID-19 Infection Risk and Employees' Performance [58]	263
Does Perfectionism Influence Individual Financial Risk Tolerance and Financial Well-Being? Evidence From an Online Survey Data From the US [59]	266
How Do Job Insecurity and Perceived Well-Being Affect Expatriate Employees' Willingness to Share or Hide Knowledge? [60]	270
Moving Crisis to Opportunities: A Corporate Perspective on the Impact of Compassionate Empathic Behaviour on the Well-Being of Employees [61]	273
The Perceived Well-Being and Health Costs of Exiting Self-Employment [62]	276
Corporate Philanthropy and Employee Wellbeing: Do Types of Corporate Philanthropy Matter? [63]	280
Employee Mindfulness, Innovative Work Behaviour, and IT Project Success: The Role of Inclusive Leadership [64]	283

How Servant Leadership Predicts Employee Resilience in Public
Organizations: A Social Identity Perspective [65] 286
Relationship Conflict and Counterproductive Work Behavior:
The Roles of Affective Well-Being and Emotional Intelligence
[66] 288
Engaging With Intelligent Voice Assistants for Wellbeing
and Brand Attachment [67] 291
Bibliography 295

7 Impact of Emotional Intelligence on Employees Performance 299
Introduction by the Author 299
Machine Generated Summaries 300
How Emotional Intelligence Promotes Leadership
and Management Practices [131] 301
Exploring the Relationship Between the Emotional Labor
and Performance in the Jordanian Insurance Industry [132] 304
Conclusion 308
Managers' Conflict Management Styles and Employee
Attitudinal Outcomes: The Mediating Role of Trust [133] 308
Building Emotional Principal–Teacher Relationships in Chinese
Schools: Reflecting on Paternalistic Leadership [134] 313
The Value of a Smile: Does Emotional Performance Matter
More in Familiar or Unfamiliar Exchanges? [135] 316
An Exploration of the Relationship Between Emotional
Intelligence and Job Performance in Police Organizations [136] 320
The Emotional Machiavellian: Interactions Between Leaders
and Employees [137] 322
Impact of Emotional Intelligence and Personality Traits
on Managing Team Performance in Virtual Interface [138] 327
Bosses Without a Heart: Socio-Demographic and Cross-Cultural
Determinants of Attitude Toward Emotional AI in the Workplace
[139] 330
The Joint Influence of Supervisor and Subordinate Emotional
Intelligence on Leader–Member Exchange [140] 334
A Thematic Analysis on "Employee Engagement in IT
Companies from the Perspective of Holistic Well-being
Initiatives" [141] 336
Paying Close Attention to Strengths Mindset: The Relationship
of Employee Strengths Mindset with Job Performance [142] 340
The Effects of Perceived Supervisor Incivility on Child-Care
Workers' Job Performance: The Mediating Role of Emotional
Exhaustion and Intrinsic Motivation [143] 344
Bibliography 347

8 Emotional Intelligence on Customer Experience in Service Domain 355
Introduction by the Author 355
Machine Generated Summaries 356
   Emotional Intelligence and Consumer Ethics: The Mediating Role of Personal Moral Philosophies [86] 357
   Enhancing International Buyer–Seller Relationship Quality and Long-Term Orientation Using Emotional Intelligence: The Moderating Role of Foreign Culture [87] 362
   Consumer Emotional Intelligence and Its Effects on Responses to Transgressions [88] 366
   Modeling Brand Immunity: The Moderating Role of Generational Cohort Membership [89] 368
   Emotional Intelligence and Service Quality: A Meta-Analysis with Initial Evidence on Cross-Cultural Factors and Future Research Directions [90] 371
   When Does Customer CSR Perception Lead to Customer Extra-Role Behaviors? The Roles of Customer Spirituality and Emotional Brand Attachment [91] 374
   How Does Topic Consistency Affect Online Review Helpfulness? The Role of Review Emotional Intensity [92] 377
   Want to Make Me Emotional? The Influence of Emotional Advertisements on Women's Consumption Behavior [93] 380
   Artificial Empathy in Marketing Interactions: Bridging the Human-AI Gap in Affective and Social Customer Experience [94] 384
Bibliography 387

About the Author

Dr. R.S. Mekhala is an Assistant professor in the arena of OB & HRM in Vellore Institute of Technology, Chennai Campus. She has completed her Master's in Business Administration from Institute of Management, University Campus Kerala. She has extensive corporate experience as a Technical recruiter for engineers in Oil and Gas Industry with organizations like TECHNIP, chiyoda, CCC etc. Later she transformed her career to teaching in Anna University affiliated colleges and meanwhile pursued research in Anna University. She has 15 years of broad experience in teaching and research activities. Her area of research involves Emotional Intelligence, Perception of Organizational Politics, Organizational Commitment and other work outcomes. And she started exploring the impact of personalities in predicting and prescribing diseases, especially with Coronary Artery Diseases in individuals. She has been awarded with Best faculty award, Best paper awards, published several research papers and attended several conferences and workshops especially in the subject of Emotional Intelligence.

Chapter 1
Emotional Intelligence—It Matters

Introduction by the Author

Emotions are a part of our biological makeup, and they follow us and influence how we act every day. Emotional Intelligence (EI) is a set of characteristics and abilities that includes a wide range of individual skills as well as dispositions, also known as interpersonal abilities or inter and intra-personal competencies, that extend beyond the boundaries of specific knowledge, broad cognitive ability, and scientific or professional skills. The five categories of emotional intelligence are knowing one's own feelings, controlling emotions, motivating oneself, recognising emotions in others, and coping with relationships. Emotion refers to a feeling/state (including physical responses and perceptions) that conveys information about relationships. For example, happiness is a state of feeling that also carries details about relationships—typically, that one would like to socialize with others. Similarly, fear is a state of feeling that corresponds to a relationship—the need to take away others. Intelligence refers to the ability to analyse the validity about information. This usage of the term emotional intelligence in this way is rational with scientific literature in the areas of intelligence, personality psychology, and emotions.

It's easy to push your feelings about the encounter to the back burner during the day. However, taking the time to identify how you feel about situations is critical for improving EI. If sensations are disregarded, crucial information is transmitted that has a significant impact on one's mind-set and behaviour. Begin paying greater attention to your sentiments and relating them to your experiences. Instead of dismissing physical manifestations of emotions, start paying attention to them. Our thoughts and body are not different; they are inextricably linked. In a study conducted by Krishna Kumar et al., 2016 demonstrated that higher level of emotional intelligence has a strong association with work outcomes like job satisfaction, team effectiveness, leadership and task performance. There are ways to improve emotional intelligence emphasized in a study by Kim et al., 2020 shows that employees with higher emotional intelligence increases organizational citizenship behaviour or employees with low EI can be driven better by emotionally intelligent managers. When compared to talent management approaches, EI training imparts an immediate effect in productivity. EI can be increased by acquiring the ability to read physical signs that indicate emotions. The trait emotional intelligence plays a vital role in maintaining self-efficacy, optimism and resilience. It is the ability to understand between change of emotional states from progression of anger and then to grief. The one who have these trait will clearly discriminate between negative emotions and stress. Moreover the negative effects will be effectively managed.

The ability to recognise the emotional sequence that may end up in negative behavioural outcomes and environmental stressors can positively affect improved performance. Emotional fitness training may enhance cognitive flexibility and well-being. The framework of planned behaviour gives a more comprehensive mediation to comprehend leadership qualities. A contingency model developed by Mc Farland establishes that emotional intelligence mediates harmful effects of role stress on emotional exhaustion and sales performance. Training provided in such skills are effective in managing sales team. Emotional Fitness training workshops helps to enhance resilience, positive emotions, cognitive and emotional flexibility. Practising this skill not only enhances the cognitive and behavioural skills but also improve their motivation. The theory of planned behaviour examines how authentic leadership influences employees speaking out towards the superior. This theory investigates the psychological mechanism by which authentic leadership influences speaking out. There are theories and study done to prove that emotional intelligence has a directly proportional connection with leadership skills.

Examine the relationship between emotions and behaviours. When a person experiences intense emotions, discover the gut reactions to everyday events rather than simply reacting without reflection. The concept of perceived institutional empowerment may have a positive impact on leadership mechanism. Traditionality moderated the indirect effects of authentic leadership through psychological safety and psychological ownership, a subset of emotional intelligence. The highest level of counter productive work behaviour can be observed in employees with high emotional intelligence. All emotions, including unpleasant ones, are genuine. If someone incorrectly interprets emotions, it makes it harder to employ them productively. Each feeling is an additional source of useful knowledge related to anything going on in the world. Let's look at several areas where emotional intelligence might be useful.

Machine Generated Summaries

Disclaimer: The summaries in this chapter were generated from Springer Nature publications using extractive AI auto-summarization: An extraction-based summarizer aims to identify the most important sentences of a text using an algorithm and uses those original sentences to create the auto-summary (unlike generative AI). As the constituted sentences are machine selected, they may not fully reflect the body of the work, so we strongly advise that the original content is read and cited. The auto generated summaries were curated by the editor to meet Springer Nature publication standards. To cite this content, please refer to the original papers.

Machine generated keywords: project, training, resilience, success, leadership, OCB, psychological capital, psychological, voice, police, mayer, share, capital, emotional intelligence, empowerment.

When Feeling Poorly at Work Does Not Mean Acting Poorly at Work: The Moderating Role of Work-Related Emotional Intelligence [62]

This is a machine-generated summary of:
Krishnakumar, Sukumarakurup; Hopkins, Kay; Robinson, Michael D.: When feeling poorly at work does not mean acting poorly at work: The moderating role of work-related emotional intelligence [62]
Published in: Motivation and Emotion (2016)
Link to original: https://doi.org/10.1007/s11031-016-9588-0
Copyright of the summarized publication:
Springer Science+Business Media New York 2016
All rights reserved.
If you want to cite the papers, please refer to the original.
For technical reasons we could not place the page where the original quote is coming from.

Abstract-Summary

"That such behaviors are more likely to be exhibited by unhappy employees (i.e., those high in job negative affect), but this should be particularly true for individuals low in work-related emotional intelligence."

"The two predictors interacted for all five outcomes such that the highest levels of counterproductive work behavior were observed among employees who were high in job negative affect and low in emotional intelligence."

"The discussion focuses on implications for understanding counterproductive work behaviors and on the value of assessing work-related emotional intelligence as an ability that differs by employees."

Introduction

"The relationship between JNA and CWBs should become attenuated at higher, relative to lower, levels of work-related emotional intelligence (W-EI)."

"People high in EI have emotions as well as the knowledge required to control their influence (Mayer & Salovey [2])."

"Because CWBs are often if not typically impulsive reactions to feeling upset (Spector [3]; Spector & others [4]), people higher in W-EI should be less prone to CWBs even when a job is stressful or frustrating."

"Such considerations led to key predictions for the study: Hypothesis 2, in other words, predicts that W-EI and JNA will interact, with the most frequent CWBs exhibited by employees high in JNA and low in W-EI."

"Negative feelings will positively predict CWBs at lower levels of W-EI, but JNA will be a weaker predictor at higher levels of W-EI."

"W-EI will be a strong inverse predictor of CWBs among employees with high levels of JNA."

Method

"Higher levels of EI, as assessed by the NEAT, predict a number of work-related outcomes, including satisfaction with interpersonal features of a job, teamwork effectiveness, leadership performance, and task performance, even after controlling for personality traits and cognitive ability."

"Correlations among the branches were substantial (perception and understanding: $r = .66$, $p < .001$; perception and management: $r = .63$, $p < .001$; understanding and management: $r = .57$, $p < .001$), indicating that people receiving high W-EI scores for one facet received high W-EI scores for the other facets as well."

"Employees were asked to indicate how frequently ($1 =$ never; $5 =$ extremely often) they felt 15 markers of negative affect (e.g., angry, frustrated, disgusted) while at work and these frequency ratings were averaged ($M = 2.43$; $SD = .74$; $\alpha = .91$)."

Results

"Consistent with this idea, there was a significant yet modest inverse relationship between work-related EI (i.e., NEAT scores) and job negative affect ($r = -.22$, $p = .041$)."

"In these multiple regressions, JNA was a consistent predictor of CWBs (βs ranging from .25 for theft to .41 for abuse) with levels of W-EI controlled."

"JNA was a significant and strong predictor of CWBs at the low level of W-EI (βs ranging from .53 for abuse to .43 for theft)."

"In an analysis of log-transformed total CWB scores, for example, the JNA by W-EI interaction was significant, $t = -2.23$, $p = .028$, $\beta = -.16$, and JNA was a stronger predictor at low (-1 SD), $t = 5.39$, $p < .001$, $\beta = .54$, relative to high ($+1$ SD), $t = 1.68$, $p = .096$, $\beta = .22$, levels of the W-EI continuum."

Discussion

"To suggesting that the pernicious effects of JNA are not inevitable, our results suggest that W-EI might be a particularly important set of abilities for jobs that are very stressful, such as law enforcement or emergency management."

"There tended to be modest relationships between W-EI and the CWB measures among employees lucky enough to experience low levels of negative affect at their jobs."

"Such results make sense and again suggest that W-EI might be particularly important for stressful jobs or those associated with high JNA."

"This perspective on the results comports with other suggestions that EI may be particularly important for certain jobs (e.g., those in which emotion labor is expected: Joseph & Newman [5]) relative to others."

"We suggest that low W-EI workers should be prone to CWBs when they experience JNA regardless of whether that JNA is caused by objective features of the job or not."

Conclusions

"Job negative affect is a potent predictor of counterproductive work behaviors."

"We hypothesized that this would be less true at higher levels of work-related emotional intelligence than at lower levels."

"Interactions of this type were found for CWBs as diverse as abusive behaviors, production deviance, and withdrawal."

"Feeling poorly at work translates to acting poorly at work, these results suggest, primarily among people who lack the ability to make correct emotion-related inferences in the workplace."

The Way to Improve Organizational Citizenship Behavior for the Employees Who Lack Emotional Intelligence [63]

This is a machine-generated summary of:
Kim, Dongyoup; Park, Jungkun: The way to improve organizational citizenship behavior for the employees who lack emotional intelligence [63]
Published in: Current Psychology (2020)
Link to original: https://doi.org/10.1007/s12144-020-01104-5
Copyright of the summarized publication:
Springer Science+Business Media, LLC, part of Springer Nature 2020
All rights reserved.
If you want to cite the papers, please refer to the original.

For technical reasons we could not place the page where the original quote is coming from.

Abstract-Summary

"Previous literature on organizational citizenship behavior (OCB) has emphasized that service employees' emotional intelligence (EI) is an essential antecedent to perform OCB."

"The malleability of EI is not always guaranteed, so it is necessary for the success of the organization to make the employee who lacks the EI perform OCB."

"The results of the present study reassured that service employees' EI is positively related to their OCB, which is consistent with previous literature."

"This study showed that managers' EI and service employees' perseverance increase employee's OCB, especially for the employee low in EI compared to those high in EI."

"The results also showed that the effects of service employees' EI and perseverance on OCB are mediated by deep acting strategy among emotional labor acting strategies."

"This paper initially found that service employees low in EI can perform beneficial extra-role behaviors with supervisors' or own support."

Introduction

"The current study looks for the answer from the nature of the organism of individuals and organizations to increase service employee's OCB when their EI lacks."

"This study suggests employee's perseverance and manager's EI as the supporting variables to the employee's lack of EI to perform OCB."

"The support of managers with high EI will have a greater positive impact on OCB performance of employees with low EI."

"This study examines the relationship between employee's EI, perseverance, manager's EI and OCB by investigating organizational members of the premium hair salon franchise in Korea."

"This study examines whether employee's perseverance and manager's EI moderates the effect of employee's EI on OCB."

"This study analyzes the role of employee's emotional acting strategies in the relationship between employee's EI, perseverance, manager's EI and employee's OCB."

Literature Review and Hypotheses

"If employees engage in momentary emotional labor, EI also have a positive impact on the use of surface acting strategy because individuals high in EI use the right one to suit their situations (Yin & others [11])."

"While EI contributes to OCB through the emotional self-regulation by helping employees appraise and control their emotions well in emotional labor situations, perseverance positively affects OCB through motivation in behavioral domain as well as motivation in emotional dimensions."

"Service employees' perseverance is more positively related to organizational citizenship behavior for themselves with low emotional intelligence than those with high emotional intelligence."

"Service employee's perseverance is more positively related to the use of surface and deep acting strategies for themselves with low emotional intelligence than those with high emotional intelligence."

"Service employees' use of deep acting strategies mediates the effect of emotional intelligence and perseverance on OCB."

Methodology

"To test the hypotheses proposed in this study, we collected data for employees and managers in a major franchise of premium hair salon in Korea; twenty salons were randomly selected and asked to respond to the questionnaire."

"Each hair salon in franchise consisted of several service employees and fewer managers, making it easy to check the influence of each other's emotional intelligence."

"Surface acting and deep acting were measured on a 7-point Likert scale for an employee's agreement on attitude toward customers or colleagues, which was adopted by Jeon [12]."

"The indirect effect of emotional acting strategies in the relationship between employee's EI, manager's EI, employee's perseverance and OCB was tested by bootstrapping method."

"For the analysis, the manager's EI was aggregated by hair salon with the assumption that each manager have the same influence on the service employees who work together."

Results

"When controlling for the effects of demographic variables, employees' EI and perseverance were positively related to OCB ($\beta = .47$, $p < .001$; $\beta = .29$, $p < .001$), and incremental effects were significant ($\Delta R^2 = .49$, $p < .001$), thus hypothesis 1 and 3 were supported."

"Employees' EI is positively related to both surface and deep acting regardless of whom they interact with ($\beta = .31$; $\beta = .56$; $\beta = .32$; $\beta = .52$, all p-values $< .001$), supporting hypotheses 4 and 5."

"Unlike EI, perseverance was positively related to deep acting ($\beta = .24$, $p < .001$; $\beta = .21$, $p = .001$), but not related to surface acting ($\beta = .12$, $p = .12$; $\beta = .09$, $p = .24$), so only hypothesis 6 was supported."

"Perseverance was more positively related to emotional labor acting strategies for employees low in EI, so hypothesis 9 was partially supported."

Discussion

"The service employees high in EI were shown to have the capability to diagnose and manage positive and negative emotions in their workplace, so they tend to perform more OCB."

"The result that EI increases use of both surface acting and deep acting strategies implies that employees high in EI use emotions effectively and efficiently by considering their emotional resources."

"The results showed that employees with low EI tend to perform less OCB than employees with high EI despite high manager's EI."

"The results of moderated mediation test showed that employees high in EI can effectively use both surface and deep acting, but they are more likely to perform OCB only with the use of deep acting strategy."

"Managers' EI, however, has no relationship to employees' emotional labor acting strategies, which had a direct impact on the performing OCB rather than emotional display."

Implication

"As the research by Wong and Law [13], employees high in EI have a greater tendency to drive OCB as emotional labor becomes stronger."

"To the emotional competence of service employees, this study also extends the influence of character strength, called perseverance, to OCB in the emotional labor work environment."

"Distinct from previous research, this research proposes that employees low in EI can benefit an organization if they are assisted by another competence (i.e., perseverance) or emotionally intelligent managers."

"While the previous literature on OCB emphasized the training of employee's EI, the results of this study implies that organizations can suggest another way to make-up to the employees who lack EI."

"Organizations should consider multi-dimensional competencies for OCB when hiring new employees, and recommend assessment of EI in promotions to managers."

Limitations and Future Research

"Many studies examining the impact of employee EI on OCB have measured the personality of an employee through the Big Five personality model to control for the impact on OCB (e.g., Modassir & Singh [14])."

"The nested data structure where employees and managers coexist for each hair salon could better capture the effect of manager's EI on employee's OCB by using multi-level modeling rather than multiple linear regression (Aguinis & others [15])."

"Our current study revealed that emotional labor partially mediated the relationships among EI, perseverance, and OCB."

"Kim and others [16] showed that EI is negatively related to surface acting, but positively related to deep acting, in a study of frontline hotel employees."

"Identifying which contextual differences in the two studies cause the opposite effect of EI on surface acting and defining the causal variables will be an important topic in future research exploring the emotional labor area."

Do Agile Managed Information Systems Projects Fail Due to a Lack of Emotional Intelligence? [64]

This is a machine-generated summary of:

Luong, Tan Trung; Sivarajah, Uthayasankar; Weerakkody, Vishanth: Do Agile Managed Information Systems Projects Fail Due to a Lack of Emotional Intelligence? [64]

Published in: Information Systems Frontiers (2019)

Link to original: https://doi.org/10.1007/s10796-019-09962-6

Copyright of the summarized publication:

The Author(s) 2019

License: OpenAccess CC BY 4.0

This article is distributed under the terms of the Creative Commons Attribution 4.0 International License (http://creativecommons.org/licenses/by/4.0/), which permits unrestricted use, distribution, and reproduction in any medium, provided you give appropriate credit to the original author(s) and the source, provide a link to the Creative Commons license, and indicate if changes were made.

If you want to cite the papers, please refer to the original.

For technical reasons we could not place the page where the original quote is coming from.

Abstract-Summary

"The purpose of this study is therefore to examine if these human related challenges are related to a lack of Emotional Intelligence (EI) by means of a quantitative approach."

"From a sample of 194 agile practitioners, EI was found to be significantly correlated to human related challenges in agile teams in terms of anxiety, motivation, mutual trust and communication competence."

"These findings offer important new knowledge for IS-scholars, project managers and human resource practitioners, about the vital role of EI for staffing and training of agile managed IS-projects."

Introduction

"The importance of the people factor for the success of ADM projects has been constantly highlighted in the scholarly literature (Cockburn & Highsmith [17]; Boehm & Turner [18]; Moe & others [19]; Fortmann [20]; Cram [21]) and it has been repeatedly identified as critical success factor for ADM managed projects (Lindvall & others [22]; Chow & Cao [23]; Pedersen [24]; Kalenda & others [25])."

"Recognizing the importance of the people factor, scholars have made considerable effort to examine human related challenges that occur in agile teams."

"A construct that might be related to these reported challenges and that has been neglected so far is Emotional Intelligence (EI)."

"The purpose of this study is to examine how the EI of IS-professionals influences the success of ADM-projects."

"The research question it endeavors to answer is whether human related challenges that IS-professionals perceive when working in agile managed teams are related to a lack of their EI."

"This study contributes to information systems, project management, organizational, psychology and human resources research."

"It introduces EI as so far neglected critical success factor to the ADM literature."

Literature Review

"Ability-based models have their origin in the Four-Branch model of EI conceptualized by Mayer and Salovey [26], including the branches: perceiving emotions, facilitating thought by using emotions, understanding emotions and managing emotions in oneself and others."

"To ability-based models, mixed-based models of EI include in addition to emotional abilities, a constellation of non-cognitive competencies, such as motivation, personality, temperament or character and social skills (Schutte & others [27]; Cho & others [28])."

"Some scholars argue that that EI is best measured as ability, because people are poor at estimating their own levels of intelligence and therefore they estimate their abilities based on other bases, such as self-confidence or self-esteem (Mayer & others [29]; Schlegel & Mortillaro [30])."

"The Mayer-Salovey-Caruso Emotional Intelligence Test (MSCEIT) is still the only performance-based ability assessment tool (Macht & others [31])."

"One of the most frequently administered ability EI self-report assessment tools is the Wong and Law Emotional Intelligence Scale (WLEIS)."

Conceptual Model and Hypotheses Development

"The ability to regulate one's own emotions is negatively associated with anxiety perceived by agile team members."

"Another aspect has been highlighted by Lalsing and others [32], who reported that agile team members might suffer from motivation issues, when tasks are assigned to them that they do not perceive as challenging enough."

"The ability to use emotions is negatively associated with motivation challenges of agile team members."

"The ability to regulate emotions is negatively associated with motivation challenges of agile team members."

"As stated by Barczak and others [33] team trust is mainly build on both, emotional bonds and perceived competencies of individual team members."

"They argued that when team members manage their own emotions and those of their peers, they are more likely to be trusted and relied on for their competence and ability."

Research Methodology

"PSA can thus only provide consistent estimates, if the researcher has sufficient knowledge about covariates that predict whether an individual would have received the treatment or not (Antonakis & others [34])."

"Covariates omitted are controlled for the extent that they correlate with the covariates included in the propensity score and therefore from a theoretic perspective, the inclusion of only those covariates that effect the treatment assignment is sufficient and thus covariates related to the outcome can be neglected (Austin [35])."

"EI has thus been dichotomized, in a way that participants, with a score in the upper third of the population in the examined EI dimension have been assigned to the treatment group and respectively, participants with a score in the lower third have been assigned to the control group."

"As recent research indicated that these kind of trainings indeed can increase EI for adults (Schutte & others [27]; Lopes [36]; Mattingly and Kraiger [37]), these participants were also excluded."

Data Analysis

"Hypothesis 1, proposing a negative association between ROE and ANX was not supported (p = 0.106)."

"Hypothesis 2a and 2b, suggesting a negative association between MOT and UOE, as well as ROE were both fully supported with statistical significance (p ≤ 0.01)."

"Hypothesis 3a and 3c, suggesting a negative association between COM and SEA as well as ROE were also both fully supported with statistical significance (p ≤ 0.001)."

"Hypothesis 3b proposing a negative association between COM and OEA was also supported with statistical significance (p ≤ 0.05)."

"Hypothesis 4a and 4c, suggesting a negative association between TRU and ROE, as well as OEA were both fully supported with statistical significance (p ≤ 0.01)."

"Hypothesis 4b, proposing a negative association between TRU and SEA was not supported (p = 0.150)."

"COM and UOE were also statistically significant negatively associated (p ≤ 0.001)."

Discussion and Findings

"The purpose of this research was to examine if a lack of EI has a negative impact on perceived human related challenges in agile teams within the dimensions of anxiety, motivation, communication competence and mutual trust."

"The results showed that anxiety in agile teams is negatively related to the abilities of self-emotional appraisal and use of emotions."

"The results of this study have found that the abilities to use emotions and to regulate emotions are both negatively related to agile team members perceiving challenges in regard to motivation."

"The results have revealed that all four dimensions of EI, self-emotional appraisal, others' emotional appraisal, use of emotions and regulation of emotions are significantly related to communication challenges occurring in agile teams."

"The results provide preliminary evidence that mutual trust challenges in agile teams are negative related to the ability to appraise others' emotions and the ability to regulate one's own emotions."

Contribution

"This study has provided preliminary evidence that EI plays an important role in agile teams and thus extends the research on critical success factors in ADM-projects."

"This research also contributes to research efforts on the vital role of EI in the workplace."

"This study therefore provides support for researchers who have argued that prior research has focusing on technical skills of software developers on project outcome, yet underestimated social and emotional skills (Rezvani & Khosravi [38]) or who advocated that employers should select employees not only based on their technical skills, but also if they can express their expertise with the use of positive EI and communication effectiveness (Hendon & others [39])."

"Training of agile team members should go beyond improving only their technical skills but also include special EI awareness and development training."

"Compared to more long-term or costly talent management approaches, EI training programs can provide a more immediate benefit to organizations, such as improved performance and affective outcomes (Mattingly & Kraiger [37])."

Limitations and Future Research

"Both HRACI, as well as WLEIS are self-report measures and therefore are prone to self-enhancement and socially desirable responses (Lopes [36])."

"Scholars have raised concerns, if EI assessed by self- report measures, actually measures an actual ability rather than a trait (Mayer & others [40]; Brannick & others [41]; Joseph & Newman [5])."

"Contrariwise, self-report EI measures are more efficient to assess EI in cross-cultural settings, because they tap into typical attributes of the individual's thoughts, feelings, and behaviors in certain situations (Li & others [42])."

"The authors acknowledge that the sample only includes IS-professionals and thus limits the generalizability of the research findings."

Conclusions

"Prior work has only focused on reporting various human related challenges, without providing insights about their origins."

"The findings of this study provide preliminary evidence that these challenges are negatively related to specific dimensions of EI."

"Recent research suggests that AI might assist human programmers in coding, e.g. AI could act as pair programming partner or humans could focus on writing test cases and AI would create the corresponding code."

"With the increasing use of AI, the human role in ADM might shift from coding into primarily focusing on unstructured tasks, such as organizing and collaboration, which then might result in more human related challenges."

The Impact of Psychological Capital on Project Success Mediating Role of Emotional Intelligence in Construction Organizations of Pakistan [65]

This is a machine-generated summary of:
Sarwar, Huma; Nadeem, Kashif; Aftab, Junaid: The impact of psychological capital on project success mediating role of emotional intelligence in construction organizations of Pakistan [65]
Published in: Journal of Global Entrepreneurship Research (2017)
Link to original: https://doi.org/10.1186/s40497-017-0080-4
Copyright of the summarized publication:
The Author(s). 2017
License: OpenAccess CC BY 4.0
This article is distributed under the terms of the Creative Commons Attribution 4.0 International License (http://creativecommons.org/licenses/by/4.0/), which permits unrestricted use, distribution, and reproduction in any medium, provided you give appropriate credit to the original author(s) and the source, provide a link to the Creative Commons license, and indicate if changes were made.

If you want to cite the papers, please refer to the original.

For technical reasons we could not place the page where the original quote is coming from.

Abstract-Summary

"The current study aims to examine the mediating effect of emotional intelligence in the relationship between psychological capital and project success."

"The findings of the research revealed that psychological capital has significant relationship with emotional intelligence and emotional intelligence has also positive relationship with project success."

"Emotional intelligence mediated the relationship between three dimensions of psychological capital (self-efficacy, resilience and optimism) and project success whereas no mediation found between hope and project success."

"The results also indicated that three dimensions of psychological capital (self-efficacy, optimism and resilience) have positive significant relationship with project success and significant mediating effect of emotional intelligence."

Background

"This study attempted to integrate the psychological capital (PsyCap), emotional intelligence and project success."

"Emotional intelligence is set to mediate the relationship and association between psychological capital and project success in construction organizations of Pakistan."

"This research is considered as the first systematic research by its nature because of the unavailability of this research to explore the relationship between psychological capital and project success in construction organizations especially from Pakistan."

"The main aim of current study is to investigate the relationship among psychological capital and its impact on success of project with mediation effect of emotional intelligence."

"According to the researcher's knowledge, no prior study has investigated the mediation role emotional intelligence among the relationship of psychological capital (hope, self-efficacy, resilience and optimism) and project success, so, this current study examines mediating role of emotional intelligence among the relationship of psychological capital (hope, self-efficacy, resilience and optimism) and project success among construction sector employees in Pakistan."

Methods

"Data collected through questionnaires which were designed in such a way to get the desire information."

"Close ended questions of 5 points Likert scale were used to acquire data about respondent's level of affirmation to investigate and uncover the effect of psychological factors on project success."

"Structured questionnaire has been developed to collect data from respondents."

"A questionnaire having all measurement scales were distributed to 500 employees of construction organizations."

"To measure the project success, a scale developed by (Aga & others [43]) having 13 items was used in this study."

"These 13 items scale demonstrated adequate internal reliability with 0.896."

"Psychological capital was measured thorough the 24 items instrument developed by Luthans and others [44]."

"This instrument of psychological capital includes 6 items for each of these four dimensions."

Results and Discussion

"It has been examined that 2 item of emotional intelligence, 2 items of project success and 1 item of PsyCap was removed due to less factor loading <0.40 and all ratios such as CMIN/DF, GFI, CFI, NFI and RMSEA shows good model fitness."

"It was proved that hope does not affect project success significantly both directly ($\beta = .10$, p-value > 0.01) and indirectly ($\beta = .35$ p-value > 0.01), Thus, there is no mediation of emotional intelligence found between project success and hope and hypothesis 5 is rejected."

"The main aim of current study was to carry out an empirical exploration of association between hope, resilience, efficacy, optimism with project success and the mediating effect of emotional intelligence on all the dimensions of psychological capital and project success among the employees of construction organizations of Pakistan."

Conclusion

"It is also noted that leaders who have high emotional intelligence can often lead their projects toward success and effect the psychological capital also."

"The main objective of current study was to examine the role of psychological capital and its implication on project success while emotional intelligence mediating the effect between them in the construction organizations of Pakistan."

"The results depicted that there is strong association exists among all three variables and three dimensions (self-efficacy, resilience and optimism) of psychological capital significant relationship with project success except H_1 where there is no significant relationship exists between hope and project success."

"The results of mediation showed that there is partial mediation exist between psychological capital dimensions (self-efficacy optimism and resilience) and project success."

"When the individuals feel positive about psychological capital than it increased their performance and hence it helps the organizations to make the project successful."

A Contingency Model of Emotional Intelligence in Professional Selling [66]

This is a machine-generated summary of:
McFarland, Richard G.; Rode, Joseph C.; Shervani, Tasadduq A.: A contingency model of emotional intelligence in professional selling [66]
Published in: Journal of the Academy of Marketing Science (2015)
Link to original: https://doi.org/10.1007/s11747-015-0435-8
Copyright of the summarized publication:
Academy of Marketing Science 2015
All rights reserved.
If you want to cite the papers, please refer to the original.
For technical reasons we could not place the page where the original quote is coming from.

Abstract-Summary

"Despite significant attention from practitioners and broad claims of the importance of Emotional Intelligence (EI), empirical support for its incremental direct effects on outcomes relevant to professional selling has been disappointing."

"Drawing on the appraisal theory of emotions, the authors develop a contingency model, which proposes that salesperson EI moderates the harmful effects of role stress on three work outcomes—emotional exhaustion, customer-oriented selling, and sales performance."

"Using three matched data sources from multiple professional selling workgroups in a business-to-business sales setting, the authors find that EI moderates the relationship between role ambiguity and all three outcome variables."

Emotional Intelligence (EI) in Professional Selling

"Our conceptual model integrates EI theory and the appraisal theory of emotions in order to offer new theory explaining the mechanisms by which EI serves to buffer the harmful effects of role stress (e.g., role conflict and role ambiguity) on our outcome variables."

"EI is defined as the ability to recognize and manage emotional cues and information (Mayer & Salovey [45])."

"The ability to perceive emotions means that one can better identify emotions in oneself and in others (Mayer & Salovey [45])."

"Understanding emotions refers to the ability to determine likely transitions between emotional states such as a progression of denial to anger and then to grief (Mayer & Salovey [45])."

"This ability can enable salespeople to disconnect from negative affective states when needed and to adopt the appropriate emotions for a specific situation, customer, or role partner."

Theory and Hypotheses

"Salespeople with higher EI are better able to strategically detach from negative emotions and they have more accurate appraisals and reappraisals, which helps to reduce stress over the long term (Kahn & others [46]) and helps to interrupt potentially escalating cycles of stress."

"Higher EI should enable the salesperson to appraise extant role stressors from a more realistic and productive perspective and to more effectively manage the negative emotions that result from role stress through the appraisal process."

"In regard to primary and secondary appraisals, higher EI should enable salespeople to more effectively reduce and refocus the negative emotions associated with role stress."

"The ability to recognize the emotional sequences that commonly result from the initial appraisal process can help reduce the negative behavioral responses one may have to the normal progression of experienced emotions resulting from environmental stressors, which in turn can also positively affect the ongoing reappraisal process and thereby improve performance."

Methods

"These include data from an ability-based, objective EI instrument (i.e., the MSCEIT), supervisor ratings of salespeople, and self-reported responses by salespeople."

"Each sales manager also completed an online questionnaire for each salesperson; we received ratings for a total of 190 salespeople."

"Managing emotions is measured by sections that ask respondents to evaluate the effectiveness of a character's response with respect to managing specific emotions (emotional management task), and to rate the usefulness of several actions, given specific interpersonal relationship objectives (emotional relations task)."

"We estimated one confirmatory factor analysis (CFA) model that included all six multi-item measures reported by sales managers and salespeople, using ML estimation with LISREL 8.80."

"We did not include the EI score in the CFA given it is not a latent factor and is based on the number of correct responses given by respondents."

Results

"That while role ambiguity did have a significant main effect on each dependent variable, role conflict had a significant main effect only on emotional exhaustion amongst the three main effects–only models."

"We included the interactions of both role conflict and role ambiguity in the emotional exhaustion model, but only the role ambiguity interaction in the customer orientation and interactional sales performance models because there were no significant main effects of role conflict in these two models."

"The interaction of EI x role ambiguity was significantly associated with customer-oriented selling ($\gamma = .008$, $p < .01$), providing support for H2."

"The interaction of EI x role ambiguity was significantly related to sales performance ($\gamma = .006$, $p < .01$), providing support for H3."

"EI reduced the harmful effects of role ambiguity in all models."

Discussion

"Empirical findings in professional sales research (e.g., Kidwell & others [47]) and in organizational behavior research (e.g., Rode & others [48]), including several meta-analyses (e.g., Joseph & Newman [5]; O'Boyle & others [49]), demonstrate support for the moderating effects of EI, but not for the direct effects of EI on sales outcomes."

"While our study is not a direct test of appraisal theory, our results are consistent with the theory's main propositions and suggest that appraisal theory could be used to identify and test other environmental factors that may be relevant to EI sales research."

"Research on role stress typically suggests that managers should seek to reduce role stress given its harmful impact on important sales outcomes such as emotional exhaustion and sales performance."

"The results of our study, combined with the results of previous research, suggest that claims of EI as a silver bullet that results in positive outcomes for virtually all salespeople are overblown, but that EI interventions are likely to be beneficial when high levels of role stress (and role ambiguity in particular) are present."

[Section 6]

"Extant research has predominantly viewed EI as having a direct effect on outcomes, such as sales performance, yet recent indications clearly suggest that EI is better viewed as a moderator."

"While it may be intuitively obvious that EI should have a direct effect on sales performance and other sales outcomes, in fact research suggests that these direct effects do not exist or are at best quite small (Cron & others [50])."

"A long research tradition has demonstrated the negative effects of role stress on a number of sales outcomes, including emotional exhaustion, customer-oriented behaviors, and sales performance (e.g., Siguaw & others [51]; Singh & others [52]; Verbeke & others [53])."

"We examine the moderating effects of EI on the relationship between role stress and emotional exhaustion, customer-oriented selling, and interactional sales performance."

"The results of this study have important theoretical implications regarding how to best model the effects of EI in future research as well as practical implications regarding the use of EI tools in sales management practice."

Effectiveness of Emotional Fitness Training in Police [67]

This is a machine-generated summary of:
Au, Wing Tung; Wong, Yuet Yi; Leung, Ka Mei; Chiu, Sau Mee: Effectiveness of Emotional Fitness Training in Police [67]
Published in: Journal of Police and Criminal Psychology (2018)
Link to original: https://doi.org/10.1007/s11896-018-9252-6
Copyright of the summarized publication:

Society for Police and Criminal Psychology 2018
All rights reserved.
If you want to cite the papers, please refer to the original.
For technical reasons we could not place the page where the original quote is coming from.

Abstract-Summary

"The Emotional Fitness Training workshops evaluated were conducted in three phases."

"Phase 2 workshops were offered to supervisory staff with train-the-trainer purposes."

"Phase 3 workshops were also offered to supervisory staff, but as a regular training-day activity to let the staff learn to deliver training packages."

"We measured professional pride and organizational commitment 1 year after the workshop and found that workshop participants reported greater pride and commitment compared with nonparticipants of the same rank."

"Among workshop participants, those with better emotional fitness also reported greater pride and commitment."

"The findings provide strong evidence supporting the effectiveness of emotional fitness training to enhance resilience, positive emotions, cognitive flexibility, and emotional well-being, and more importantly, they strengthen professional pride and organizational commitment even 1 year after training."

Introduction

"The major purpose of this study is to evaluate to what extent the HKPF training is effective in improving emotional fitness of the police force and how emotional fitness can in turn promote professional pride and organizational commitment."

"We anticipate that emotional fitness training may enhance professional pride through increases in resilience, positive emotions, cognitive flexibility, and emotional well-being."

"We hypothesize that increases in resilience, positive emotions, cognitive flexibility, and emotional well-being as a result of the HKPF emotional fitness training program may enhance professional pride."

"In relation to the components of Emotional Fitness Training, we expect police officers with strong cognitive flexibility will develop strong organizational commitment, because they are able to constructively interpret feedback, have resilience against negative experiences, and are able to maintain positive emotions."

"We hypothesized that increases in resilience, positive emotions, cognitive flexibility, and emotional well-being as a result of the HKPF emotional fitness training program may enhance organizational commitment."

Method

"A total of 300 respondents out of 717 workshop participants participated in this program evaluation study across the three phases, and of this number, 168 respondents provided measurements of professional pride and organizational commitment at least 1 year after workshop completion."

"In 2016, at least 1 year after completion of all three workshop phases, in conjunction with an internal organizational campaign, the 210 respondents participating in the phase 2 and 3 program evaluation studies were invited to provide ratings of professional pride and organizational commitment."

"At about the same time riding on the same internal organizational campaign, a separate sample of 413 police officers also provided ratings on pride and commitment, 69 of which indicated they had participated in one of the Emotional Fitness Training workshops."

Results

"Participants who attended the training reported stronger resilience coping as measured by BRCS in both the posttest immediately after workshops ($M = 4.23$, $F(1, 40) = 12.43$, $p < .05$) and the posttest 10 weeks after the workshops ($M = 4.35$, $F(1, 40) = 22.58$, $p < .05$) as compared to the pretest measured at the beginning of the workshops ($M = 3.94$)."

"Regarding resilience, compared to the pretest measure ($M = 4.10$), respondents reported statistically significant improvement in the first posttest only ($M = 4.20$, $F(1, 82) = 3.99$, $p < .05$), but statistically nonsignificant improvement in the second posttest ($M = 4.23$, $F(1, 82) = 3.13$, n.s.)."

Discussion

"Phase 1 workshops registering the most training effectiveness across all seven measures of psychological well-being could be attributed to the higher motivation of phase 1 participants."

"The purpose of spreading the sessions 1 week apart in phase 1 was to allow time for participants to practice skills learned."

"Phase 3 workshops did not strongly demand participants do practice, so training effectiveness was found to be moderated by the amount voluntary practice engaged in."

"The weaker training effects in phase 2 compared to phase 1 workshops may also be attributed to not having time for practice between sessions."

"Practicing the skills not only allowed participants to better learn the cognitive and behavioral skills, but also be able to experience the positive effects from exercising the skills and thus enhanced their motivation to learn beyond workshop teaching."

Limitations

"The collection of pride and commitment measures was riding on a campaign unrelated to emotional fitness training that participants should have no motivation to affirm their learning from the workshop in reporting their pride and commitment."

"In phases 2 and 3, we were simply measuring effectiveness in pretest and posttest differences of workshop participants without comparing with a control group."

"Phase 1 is close to a randomized control study that participants in the later workshops served as a time-lag control group."

"Participants in Emotional Fitness Training sessions reported significantly higher professional pride and organizational commitment when compared to nonparticipants matched in rank."

"The effect of emotional fitness training on pride and commitment was small, perhaps because the extent of improvement in emotional fitness was different across participants."

Conclusion

"Evaluation of the three phases of Emotional Fitness Training sessions conducted by HKPF demonstrated that the workshops in general were effective in enhancing resilience, positive emotions, cognitive flexibility, and emotional well-being of police officers."

"When controlling pretraining psychological states, participants who learned from the training to become better in resilience coping, cognitive flexibility, subjective happiness, and satisfaction with life reported stronger pride and commitment 1 year later."

"Continuous refinement in workshop design enhances the development of emotional fitness in the police force in three aspects."

"In order to enhance the development of emotional fitness training, the police force could consider continuous refinement in workshop design like incorporating skills practice and improvements in program evaluation like implementing a randomized control design and incorporating job outcomes and other ratings as training effectiveness measures."

How Does Authentic Leadership Influence Employee Voice? From the Perspective of the Theory of Planned Behavior [68]

This is a machine-generated summary of:
 Xu, Zhihua; Yang, Fu; Peng, Jianfeng: How does authentic leadership influence employee voice? From the perspective of the theory of planned behavior [68]
 Published in: Current Psychology (2021)

Link to original: https://doi.org/10.1007/s12144-021-01464-6
Copyright of the summarized publication:
The Author(s), under exclusive licence to Springer Science+Business Media, LLC part of Springer Nature 2021
All rights reserved.
If you want to cite the papers, please refer to the original.
For technical reasons we could not place the page where the original quote is coming from.

Abstract-Summary

"Drawing on the theory of planned behavior, this study examines how and when authentic leadership influences employees speaking out (voice toward peers) and speaking up (voice toward the supervisor) by demonstrating psychological safety, psychological ownership, and voice efficacy as key mediating mechanisms, and Chinese traditionality as a crucial boundary condition."

"A total effect moderation model analysis found that traditionality moderated the direct effects of psychological safety on speaking out, psychological ownership on speaking out, voice efficacy on speaking out, and authentic leadership on voice efficacy."

"Traditionality moderated the indirect effects of authentic leadership on speaking up and speaking out through voice efficacy and on speaking out through psychological safety and psychological ownership as well, suggesting that these effects were stronger for employees who were high, rather than low, in traditionality."

Introduction

"Because current research has not drawn on a systematic theoretical framework to explain the psychological mechanisms underlying the effect of authentic leadership on employee voice, we suggest that the conceptual model built in the current research may not comprehensively explain the psychological process of how authentic leadership influences employee voice."

"Consistent with our view, Luo and Zhao [56] called on future researchers to build an improved conceptual model to elucidate the psychological mechanisms through which authentic leadership influences employee voice."

"Using the systematic theoretical framework of planned behavior as the theoretical underpinning, this study develops and tests a more comprehensive mediation model to depict the psychological mechanisms and thereby deepen our understanding of how authentic leadership influences employee voice."

"Given previous research on how authentic leadership influences employee voice has examined the mediating effect of PS, PO, and VE in isolation (Luo & Zhao [56]; Zou & Yang [57]), we know little about the unique mediating effect of each of the mediators."

Literature Review and Hypotheses

"The following moderated mediation hypotheses are posited: Hypothesis 8a Chinese traditionality moderates the indirect effect of authentic leadership on speaking up mediated by PS, such that this mediation effect is stronger for those high, rather than low, in traditionality."

"Hypothesis 8b Chinese traditionality moderates the indirect effect of authentic leadership on speaking out mediated by PS, such that this mediation effect is stronger for those high, rather than low, in traditionality."

"Hypothesis 9b Chinese traditionality moderates the indirect effect of authentic leadership on speaking out mediated by PO, such that this mediation effect is stronger for those high, rather than low, in traditionality."

"Hypothesis 10b Chinese traditionality moderates the indirect effect of authentic leadership on speaking out mediated by VE, such that this mediation effect is stronger for those high, rather than low, in traditionality."

Methods

"To address the potentially negative effects on the study results caused by common method variance, this study adopted a research design of investigating employee-supervisor dyads, in which each supervisor rated one to three of their immediate employees in terms of speaking up and speaking out, while each employee rated their immediate supervisor's authentic leadership and their own PS, PO, VE, and Chinese traditionality."

"All variables in this study were measured using Chinese versions of scales used in previous studies."

"Chinese traditionality was measured with the 5-item simplified version that has been used in the Farh and others [58] study."

"Voice behavior was measured with the scale developed by Liu and others [59], nine items of which were used to measure speaking up (e.g., "This person speaks up and influences the supervisor regarding issues that affect the organization") and six items were used to measure speaking out (e.g., "This person speaks out and encourages colleagues to get involved in issues that affect the organization")."

Results

"The mediation model of PS as a single mediator fit the data well ($\chi^2 = 407.07$, df $= 102$, RMSEA $= .098$, NNFI $= .87$, CFI $= .90$, IFI $= .91$), and the paths from authentic leadership to PS ($\beta = .80$, p $< .001$) and from PS to both speaking up ($\beta = .40$, p $< .001$) and speaking out ($\beta = .46$, p $< .001$) were all significant, indicating that PS as a single mediator mediated the relationships between authentic leadership and speaking up and speaking out."

"The mediation model of PO as a single mediator had a good fit to the data (χ^2 = 373.99, df = 102, RMSEA = .092, NNFI = .88, CFI = .91, IFI = .91), and the paths from authentic leadership to PO (β = .75, p < .001) and from PO to both speaking up (β = .50, p < .001) and speaking out (β = .51, p < .001) were all significant, indicating that PO as a single mediator mediated the relationships between authentic leadership and speaking up and speaking out."

Discussion

"Using the theory of planned behavior as the theoretical underpinning, this study posited PS, PO, and VE as the mediators to comprehensively investigate the psychological mechanisms by which authentic leadership influences speaking up and speaking out."

"This study draws on the theory of planned behavior as a complete theoretical model to propose PS, PO, and VE as the appropriate psychological mechanisms and, thus, comprehensively investigates how authentic leadership impacts employee voice."

"By drawing on the fundamental theory of planned behavior, this study proposes and empirically tests the three mechanisms (i.e., PS, PO, and VE) to depict a more complete picture of how authentic leadership influences employee voice."

"Authentic leadership has a unique influence on employee voice through VE after controlling the mediation effects of PS and PO."

To Share or Not to Share: How Perceived Institutional Empowerment Shapes Employee Perceived Shared Leadership [69]

This is a machine-generated summary of:

Mi, Yaping; Zhang, Xue; Liang, Liang; Tian, Guyang; Tian, Yezhuang: To share or not to share: How perceived institutional empowerment shapes employee perceived shared leadership [69]

Published in: Current Psychology (2023)

Link to original: https://doi.org/10.1007/s12144-023-04701-2

Copyright of the summarized publication:

The Author(s), under exclusive licence to Springer Science+Business Media, LLC, part of Springer Nature 2023

Copyright comment: Springer Nature or its licensor (e.g. a society or other partner) holds exclusive rights to this article under a publishing agreement with the author(s) or other rightsholder(s); author self-archiving of the accepted manuscript version of this article is solely governed by the terms of such publishing agreement and applicable law.

All rights reserved.
If you want to cite the papers, please refer to the original.
For technical reasons we could not place the page where the original quote is coming from.

Abstract-Summary

"The present study aims to expand the existing research by uncovering the overlooked role of situational factors in shaping employee perceived shared leadership."

"To further advance this field of research, our study introduces a novel situational phenomenon called perceived institutional empowerment."

"Based on social information processing theory and adaptive leadership theory, we assume that perceived institutional empowerment may have a positive impact on perceived shared leadership via a chain mediating mechanism of perceived organizational support (POS) and psychological safety."

Introduction

"To advance this field of research, the present study introduces a new phenomenon, institutional empowerment, to explain how to enhance the perceived shared leadership from the situational perspective."

"To further explore how perceived institutional empowerment affects perceived shared leadership, our study introduces two vital internal psychological resources as mediating variables: perceived organizational support (POS) and psychological safety."

"Our study contributes to the existing literature by revealing the overlooked role of the situational factor (i.e., perceived institutional empowerment) in shaping employee perceived shared leadership."

"While prior studies have extensively investigated internal factors such as ability and motivational factors, our study highlights perceived institutional empowerment as a situational cue in shaping employee perceived shared leadership."

"Our study provides a novel perspective for exploring the mechanism through which perceived institutional empowerment affects employee perceived shared leadership."

Theory and Hypotheses

"Based on social information processing theory, we propose that perceived institutional empowerment can enhance employees' perceived shared leadership by legalizing leadership enacting behaviors."

"The higher the perceived level of institutional empowerment, the more likely employees are to participate in leadership-sharing, and correspondingly, the higher their perceived level of shared leadership."

"We propose the following hypothesis: Psychological safety mediates the positive relationship between perceived institutional empowerment and perceived shared leadership."

"We further assume that perceived institutional empowerment can enhance employees' psychological safety by improving POS in the workplace, ultimately enhancing employees' perception of shared leadership."

"We propose that POS and psychological safety play a chain mediating role in the relationship between perceived institutional empowerment and perceived shared leadership."

"We propose the following hypothesis: POS and psychological safety sequentially mediate the positive relationship between perceived institutional empowerment and perceived shared leadership."

Method

"We used a four-dimensional scale to measure perceived institutional empowerment, including employees' perceived: (a) enhancement of work meaningfulness (three items, $\alpha = 0.92$; e.g., "The company's institution helps me understand the importance of my work to the overall effectiveness of the company"), (b) facilitation of participation in decision-making (three items, $\alpha = 0.88$; e.g., "The company's institution allows me to participate in major decisions of the company"), (c) expression of confidence in high performance (three items, $\alpha = 0.84$; e.g., "The company's institution believes in my ability to improve even when I make mistakes"), and (d) provision of autonomy from bureaucratic constraints (three items, $\alpha = 0.82$; e.g., "The company's institution allows me to do my job my way")."

Results

"The hypotheses, we conducted a CFA to examine construct validity by using Amos 21.0."

"We examined VIF, which is a widely applied indicator to detect collinearity (García & others [60])."

"If VIF is less than 10, indicating that there is no excessive or serious collinearity."

"The maximum VIF was 1.56, indicating no potentially confounding collinearity problems among the variables (Hair & others [61])."

Discussion

"The present study investigates the mechanism by which perceived institutional empowerment promotes employee perceived shared leadership."

"We find that perceived institutional empowerment can enhance perceived shared leadership by the following three ways: (a) by enhancing employees' POS, they can promptly compensate for the energy consumed during the process of implementing shared leadership, enabling them to continuously participate in leadership-claiming and leadership-maintaining activities; (b) by improving employees' psychological safety when they engage in informal leadership, thereby making them realize that they are allowed and encouraged to share power; (c) on the basis of (a) and (b), employees' enhanced POS through perceived institutional empowerment leads to a gain spiral effect, which further activates their psychological safety and ultimately promotes perceived shared leadership."

"Our study suggest that perceived institutional empowerment increases employees' perceived shared leadership."

"Our findings suggest that perceived institutional empowerment positively influences employees' POS and psychological safety, ultimately enhancing perceived shared leadership."

Bibliography

1. Fox, S., Spector, P. E., & Miles, D. (2001). Counterproductive work Behavior (CWB) in response to job stressors and organizational justice: Some mediator and moderator tests for autonomy and emotions. *Journal of Vocational Behavior, 59*, 291–309.
2. Mayer, J. D., & Salovey, P. (1997). *What is emotional intelligence?* Basic Books.
3. Spector, P. E. (2011). The relationship of personality to counterproductive work behavior (CWB): An integration of perspectives. *Human Resource Management Review, 21*, 342–352.
4. Spector, P. E., Fox, S., & Domagalski, T. (2006). Emotions, violence, and counterproductive work behavior. In E. K. Kelloway, J. Barling, & J. J. Hurrell (Eds.), *Handbook of workplace violence* (pp. 29–46). Sage Publications.
5. Joseph, D. L., & Newman, D. A. (2010). Emotional intelligence: An integrative meta-analysis and cascading model. *Journal of Applied Psychology, 95*, 54–78.
6. Hayes, A. F. (2017). *Introduction to mediation, moderation, and conditional process analysis: A regression-based approach.* Guilford Publications.
7. Miao, C., Humphrey, R. H., & Qian, S. (2017). Are the emotionally intelligent good citizens or counterproductive? A meta-analysis of emotional intelligence and its relationships with organizational citizenship behavior and counterproductive work behavior. *Personality and Individual Differences, 116*, 144–156.
8. Turnipseed, D. L. (2018). Emotional intelligence and OCB: The moderating role of work locus of control. *The Journal of Social Psychology, 158*(3), 322–336.
9. Turnipseed, D. L., & Vandewaa, E. A. (2012). Relationship between emotional intelligence and organizational citizenship behavior. *Psychological Reports, 110*(3), 899–914.
10. Ölçer, F., Florescu, M. S., & Nastase, M. (2014). The effects of transformational leadership and emotional intelligence of managers on organizational citizenship behaviors of employees. *Revista de Management Comparat International, 15*(4), 385–401.

Bibliography

11. Yin, H. B., Lee, J. C. K., & Zhang, Z. H. (2013). Exploring the relationship among teachers' emotional intelligence, emotional labor strategies and teaching satisfaction. *Teaching and Teacher Education, 35,* 137–145.
12. Jeon, A. (2016). The effect of pre-flight attendants' emotional intelligence, emotional labor, and emotional exhaustion on commitment to customer service. *Service Business, 10*(2), 345–367.
13. Wong, C. S., & Law, K. S. (2002). The effects of leader and follower emotional intelligence on performance and attitude: An exploratory study. *The Leadership Quarterly, 13*(3), 243–274.
14. Modassir, A., & Singh, T. (2008). Relationship of emotional intelligence with transformational leadership and organizational citizenship behavior. *International Journal of Leadership Studies, 4,* 3–21.
15. Aguinis, H., Gottfredson, R. K., & Culpepper, S. A. (2013). Best-practice recommendations for estimating cross-level interaction effects using multilevel modeling. *Journal of Management, 39*(6), 1490–1528.
16. Kim, T. T., Yoo, J. J. E., Lee, G., & Kim, J. (2012). Emotional intelligence and emotional labor acting strategies among frontline hotel employees. *International Journal of Contemporary Hospitality Management, 24*(7), 1029–1046.
17. Cockburn, A., & Highsmith, J. (2001). Agile software development, the people factor. *Computer, 34*(11), 131–133. https://doi.org/10.1109/2.963450
18. Boehm, B., & Turner, R. (2005). Management challenges to implementing agile processes in traditional development organizations. *IEEE Software, 22*(5), 30–39. https://doi.org/10.1109/MS.2005.129
19. Moe, N. B., Aurum, A., & Dybå, T. (2012). Challenges of shared decision-making: A multiple case study of agile software development. *Information and Software Technology, 54*(8), 853–865. https://doi.org/10.1016/j.infsof.2011.11.006
20. Fortmann, L. (2018). *Agile or fragile?—The depleting effects of agile methodologies for software developers.* In ECIS.
21. Cram, W. A. (2019). Agile development in practice: Lessons from the trenches. *Information Systems Management, 36*(1), 2–14. https://doi.org/10.1080/10580530.2018.1553645
22. Lindvall, M., Basili, V., Boehm, B., Costa, P., Dangle, K., Shull, F., Tesoriero, R., Williams, L., & Zelkowitz (2002). Empirical findings in agile methods. In *Proceedings of Extreme Programming and Agile Methods—XP/Agile Universe.* Springer.
23. Chow, T., & Cao, D.-B. (2008). A survey study of critical success factors in agile software projects. *Journal of Systems and Software, 81*(6), 961–971. https://doi.org/10.1016/j.jss.2007.08.020
24. Pedersen, M. (2013). *A quantitative examination of critical success factors comparing agile and waterfall project management methodologies.* ProQuest Dissertations Publishing.
25. Kalenda, M., Hyna, P., & Rossi, B. (2018). Scaling agile in large organizations: Practices, challenges, and success factors. *Journal of Software: Evolution and Process, 30*(10), e1954. https://doi.org/10.1002/smr.1954
26. Mayer, J., & Salovey, P. (1997). *What is emotional intelligence? Emotional development and emotional intelligence: Educational implications* (pp. 3–34). Basic Book.
27. Schutte, N. S., Malouff, J. M., & Thorsteinsson, E. B. (2013). Increasing emotional intelligence through training: Current status and future directions. *International Journal of Emotional Education, 5*(1), 56–72.
28. Cho, S., Drasgow, F., & Cao, M. (2015). An investigation of emotional intelligence measures using item response theory. *Psychological Assessment, 27*(4), 1241.
29. Mayer, J. D., Caruso, D. R., & Salovey, P. (2016). The ability model of emotional intelligence: Principles and updates. *Emotion Review, 8*(4), 290–300. https://doi.org/10.1177/1754073916639667
30. Schlegel, K., & Mortillaro, M. (2019). The Geneva emotional competence test (GECo): An ability measure of workplace emotional intelligence. *The Journal of Applied Psychology, 104*(4), 559–580. https://doi.org/10.1037/apl0000365
31. Macht, G. A., Nembhard, D. A., & Leicht, R. M. (2019). Operationalizing emotional intelligence for team performance. *International Journal of Industrial Ergonomics, 71,* 57–63. https://doi.org/10.1016/j.ergon.2019.02.007

32. Lalsing, V., Kishnah, S., & Pudaruth, S. (2012). People factors in agile software development and project management. *International Journal of Software Engineering & Applications, 3*(1), 117–137.
33. Barczak, G., Lassk, F., & Mulki, J. (2010). Antecedents of team creativity: An examination of team emotional intelligence, team trust and collaborative culture. *Creativity and Innovation Management, 19*(4), 332. https://doi.org/10.1111/j.1467-8691.2010.00574.x
34. Antonakis, J., Bendahan, S., Jacquart, P., & Lalive, R. (2010). On making causal claims: A review and recommendations. *The Leadership Quarterly, 21*(6), 1086–1120. https://doi.org/10.1016/j.leaqua.2010.10.010
35. Austin, P. C. (2011). An introduction to propensity score methods for reducing the effects of confounding in observational studies. *Multivariate Behavioral Research, 46*(3), 399–424. https://doi.org/10.1080/00273171.2011.568786
36. Lopes, P. N. (2016). Emotional intelligence in organizations: Bridging research and practice. *Emotion Review, 8*(4), 316–321. https://doi.org/10.1177/1754073916650496
37. Mattingly, V., & Kraiger, K. (2019). Can emotional intelligence be trained? A meta-analytical investigation. *Human Resource Management Review, 29*(2), 140–155.
38. Rezvani, A., & Khosravi, P. (2019). Emotional intelligence: The key to mitigating stress and fostering trust among software developers working on information system projects. *International Journal of Information Management, 48*, 139–150. https://doi.org/10.1016/j.ijinfomgt.2019.02.007
39. Hendon, M., Powell, L., & Wimmer, H. (2017). Emotional intelligence and communication levels in information technology professionals. *Computers in Human Behavior, 71*, 165–171. https://doi.org/10.1016/j.chb.2017.01.048
40. Mayer, J. D., Salovey, P., & Caruso, D. R. (2008). Emotional intelligence—New ability or eclectic traits? *American Psychologist, 63*, 503–517.
41. Brannick, M. T., Wahi, M. M., Arce, M., Johnson, H.-A., Nazian, S., & Goldin, S. B. (2009). Comparison of trait and ability measures of emotional intelligence in medical students. *Medical Education, 43*(11), 1062–1068. https://doi.org/10.1111/j.1365-2923.2009.03430.x
42. Li, T., Saklofske, D. H., Bowden, S. C., Yan, G., & Fung, T. S. (2012). The measurement invariance of the Wong and Law emotional intelligence scale (WLEIS) across three Chinese University student groups from Canada and China. *Journal of Psychoeducational Assessment, 30*(4), 439–452. https://doi.org/10.1177/0734282912449449
43. Aga, D. A., Noorderhaven, N., & Vallejo, B. (2016). Transformational leadership and project success: The mediating role of team-building. *International Journal of Project Management, 34*(5), 806–818.
44. Luthans, F., Youssef, C. M., & Avolio, B. J. (2007). *Psychological capital: Developing the human competitive edge* (p. 3). Oxford University Press.
45. Mayer, J. D., & Salovey, P. (1997). What is emotional intelligence? In P. Salovey & D. Sluyter (Eds.), *Emotional development and emotional intelligence: Implications for educators* (pp. 3–31). Basic Books.
46. Kahn, R. L., Wolfe, D. M., Quinn, R. P., Snoek, J. D., & Rosenthal, R. A. (1964). *Organizational stress: Studies in role conflict and ambiguity*. Wiley.
47. Kidwell, B., McFarland, R. G., & Avila, R. A. (2007). Perceiving emotion in the buyer–seller interchange: The moderated impact on performance. *Journal of Personal Selling & Sales Management, 27*, 119–132.
48. Rode, J. C., Mooney, C. H., Arthaud-Day, M. L., Near, J. P., Rubin, R. S., Baldwin, R. S., & Bommer, W. H. (2008). An examination of the structural, discriminant, nomological, and incremental predictive validity of the MSCEIT© V2.0. *Intelligence, 36*, 350–366.
49. O'Boyle, E. H., Humphrey, R. H., Pollack, J. M., Hawver, T. H., & Story, P. A. (2011). The relation between emotional intelligence and job performance: A meta-analysis. *Journal of Organizational Behavior, 32*, 788–818.
50. Cron, W. L., Marshall, G. W., Singh, J., Spiro, R. L., & Sujan, H. (2005). Salesperson selection, training, and development: Trends, implications, and research opportunities. *Journal of Personal Selling & Sales Management, 25*, 123–136.

Bibliography

51. Siguaw, J. A., Brown, G., & Widing, R. E. (1994). The influence of the market orientation of the firm on sales force behavior and attitudes. *Journal of Marketing Research, 31*, 106–116.
52. Singh, J., Goolsby, J., & Rhoads, G. (1994). Behavioral and psychological consequences of boundary spanning burnout for customer service representatives. *Journal of Marketing Research, 31*(31), 558–569.
53. Verbeke, W., Dietz, B., & Verwaal, E. (2011). Drivers of sales performance: A contemporary meta-analysis. Have salespeople become knowledge brokers? *Journal of the Academy of Marketing Science, 39*, 404–428.
54. Beck, A. T., & Clark, D. A. (1997). An information processing model of anxiety: Automatic and strategic processes. *Behaviour Research and Therapy, 35*(1), 49–58. https://doi.org/10.1016/s0005-7967(96)00069-1
55. Bernard, M. E. (2009). Dispute irrational beliefs and teach rational beliefs: An interview with Albert Ellis. *Journal of Rational-Emotive & Cognitive-Behavior Therapy, 27*(1), 66–76. https://doi.org/10.1007/s10942-009-0089-x
56. Luo, J., & Zhao, J. (2013). A study about the influential mechanism of authentic leadership on employee voice behavior. *Soft Science, 27*(12), 41–44.
57. Zou, Z., & Yang, Z. (2013). The effect of authentic leadership on employee voice behavior: Mediated by voice efficacy and moderated by leadership-member exchange. *Human Resources Development of China, 21*, 41–45.
58. Farh, J. L., Earley, P. C., & Lin, S. C. (1997). Impetus for action: A cultural analysis of justice and organizational citizenship behavior in Chinese society. *Administrative Science Quarterly, 42*(3), 421–444.
59. Liu, W., Zhu, R. H., & Yang, Y. K. (2010). I warn you because I like you: Voice behavior, employee identifications, and transformational leadership. *Leadership Quarterly, 21*(1), 189–202.
60. García, C. B., García, J., López Martín, M. M., & Salmerón, R. (2015). Collinearity: Revisiting the variance inflation factor in ridge regression. *Journal of Applied Statistics, 42*(3), 648–661. https://doi.org/10.1080/02664763.2014.980789
61. Hair, J. F., Black, W. C., Babin, B. J., Anderson, R. E., & Tatham, R. L. (1998). *Multivariate data analysis* (Vol. 5, No. 3, pp. 207–219). Upper Saddle River.
62. Krishnakumar, S., Hopkins, K., & Robinson, M. D. (2017). When feeling poorly at work does not mean acting poorly at work: The moderating role of work-related emotional intelligence. *Motivation and Emotion, 41*, 122–134. https://doi.org/10.1007/s11031-016-9588-0
63. Kim, D., & Park, J. (2022). The way to improve organizational citizenship behavior for the employees who lack emotional intelligence. *Current Psychology, 41*(9), 6078–6092. https://doi.org/10.1007/s12144-020-01104-5
64. Luong, T. T., Sivarajah, U., & Weerakkody, V. (2021). Do agile managed information systems projects fail due to a lack of emotional intelligence? *Information Systems Frontiers, 23*, 415–433. https://doi.org/10.1007/s10796-019-09962-6
65. Sarwar, H., Nadeem, K., & Aftab, J. (2017). The impact of psychological capital on project success mediating role of emotional intelligence in construction organizations of Pakistan. *Journal of Global Entrepreneurship Research, 7*, 1–13. https://doi.org/10.1186/s40497-017-0080-4
66. McFarland, R. G., Rode, J. C., & Shervani, T. A. (2016). A contingency model of emotional intelligence in professional selling. *Journal of the Academy of Marketing Science, 44*, 108–118. https://doi.org/10.1007/s11747-015-0435-8
67. Au, W. T., Wong, Y. Y., Leung, K. M., & Chiu, S. M. (2019). Effectiveness of emotional fitness training in police. *Journal of Police and Criminal Psychology, 34*, 199–214. https://doi.org/10.1007/s11896-018-9252-6
68. Xu, Z., Yang, F., & Peng, J. (2023). How does authentic leadership influence employee voice? From the perspective of the theory of planned behavior. *Current Psychology, 42*(3), 1851–1869. https://doi.org/10.1007/s12144-021-01464-6
69. Mi, Y., Zhang, X., Liang, L., Tian, G., & Tian, Y. (2024). To share or not to share: How perceived institutional empowerment shapes employee perceived shared leadership. *Current Psychology, 43*(6), 4918–4929. https://doi.org/10.1007/s12144-023-04701-2

Chapter 2
Emotional Intelligence and Job Performance

Introduction by the Author

Workplace emotional health plays a vital role in managing stress and maintaining strong interpersonal relationship in the workplace. Workplace emotional health is regulated by mainly four factors namely work load, emotional intelligence, emotional blackmail and emotional labour. A study undergone by Chin yen et al., in 2023 states that workplace emotional health can be measured by four factors emotional expression strategies, emotional awareness, interpersonal adaptation and work load. Stress is crucial to academic and industrial jobs, which should be regulated in a productive way. The results of this study revealed that workplace emotional health can be regulated by three factors emotional control, interpersonal relationship management and self-motivation. The same way a manager's emotional quotient also affects the subordinate's productivity. Zhang et al., adopted a multilevel framework investigation in 2020 to find out the link between group leader's emotional intelligence with group performance, came out with a reliable result of two factors group cohesion and person-group fit. A good match between job match and group member's characteristics may help in addressing these issues in advance.

Emotional intelligence, which is a subset of social intelligence, according to Mayer and Salovey is the ability to monitor one's own and other's feeling and emotion. Since EI is defined as an interpersonal and intrapersonal related human skillsets, it should have direct impact on predicting personal and social outcomes. The improvement of EI skills are learned, to equip yourself with the team to excel in business growth. Developing emotional intelligence is highly essential for the human resource, since they constantly communicate with each other in organization. There are many factors which determine the job satisfaction of employees such as career upliftment, recognition, involvement towards completion of work. The absence of even the simplest factor may lead to job dissatisfaction. But when an individual have high emotional intelligence, they work towards attainment of organizational goal irrespective of all threats. As a result positive communication and in-depth relationship will be developed. Many research results shows that EI is the strongest predictor of job performance. EI is responsible for more than 80% of the competencies that distinguish high performers. You may ask these three simple questions to yourself to find out how emotionally aware you are?

1. What are your current feelings towards your job or your co-workers?
2. How do your emotions effect those around you?
3. Are you allowing negative emotions to influence how you interact with co-workers or accomplish your job?

Chin Yin Che in 2023 conducted a study on Emotional health scale of employees pointing the stress and burnout faced in work place. It depend on the capacity to evaluate and express emotions and relieve stress and burnout by the employees in workplace. The study concluded that scale has eight subscales and can be evaluated in terms of emotional expression strategies, emotional awareness, interpersonal adaptation and workload. Emotional intelligence trait play a vital role in job performance and life satisfaction. There are several scales available to measure emotional intelligence like Emotional Quotient Inventory (EQ-I; Bar-On [11]), the Trait Meta-Mood Scale (TMM; Salovey and others), Wong and Law Emotional Intelligence Scale, WLEIS) and the list goes on. When tested the Chinese workers life satisfaction WLEIS has a better predictive power than MSCEIT (Mayor and Salovey emotional Intelligence Test). Life satisfaction of the employees significantly related to the two factors in MSEIT scale while in WLEIS the factors were emotional regulation and utilisation of emotion. Wong and Law suggested that emotional intelligence measured was distinct from personal dimensions with desired outcomes like life satisfaction and positive job performance.

A study conducted by Li et al., in 2019 evaluated two factors of emotional triads among superiors and subordinators, the CAD factors which comprises Contempt, Anger, and Disgust (CAD) and ESP factor and empathy, sympathy, and pity (ESP). According to emotional contagion theory, the contagious effect has a higher chance of incurring from superiors to subordinates and the effect of superiors empathy, sympathy and pity has a positive effect on subordinate's positive performance outcomes. The study explored why leader's emotions affect employee's performance by focusing on emotional triads and emotional contagion, a process that naturally endure over time. Emotional intelligence trait soothes the negative effect of work place bullying. Although bullying has a negative impact on job performance, the harmful impact was lower for those with higher emotional intelligence. Workplace bullying is manifested as the act of belittlement, intimidation and humiliation of abilities and invention of mistakes. As a result the bullied individuals will perform less, it may be reasoned that the employees with high EI may experience less stress or threat.

Organisations with significant amounts of EI in their executives are more likely to be highly profitable. EI is an important aspect in job performance because it allows people to make better choices, create and maintain effective connections, cope without stress more efficiently, and deal with frequent change. People must be aware to watch themselves and understand how their moods effect their actions. Being aware of their own emotion is a fantastic first step, but the next stage is to find out how to manage it and recreate the desired response. For example, we can all recall a supervisor or co-worker acting impulsively or unreasonably due to lack of self-management or regulation. These activities often create an unfavourable environment in which employees are unable to work to their full potential. They frequently produce emotionally charged workplaces that are riddled with unresolved conflict and animosity; for example, employees may be distracted by badly managed arguments and unable to work together or create for fear of repercussions. The purpose of self-management is for you to recognise emotional responses but not allow them to hijack your behaviour or govern your ability to handle relationships.

The role of mindfulness in professional experience assess the impact of brand management, self-direction and self-efficacy. Self-management, a subset of emotional intelligence plays a vital role in occupational self-efficacy. The mechanism whereby career progression been a subject of investigation. Over a 20 years research revealed that self-efficacy have a strong and positive relationship with job performance. The study revealed that the more the manager's self-efficacy, the more will be the initiative taken, tasks improved and problem persistence. Studies based on the interplay between personal resources and job resources through JD-R theory (Job demands-resources model) and KTEM theory (represented by cognitively dominant PsyCap) has shed light on the cruciality on influencing resources handled by employees.

Self-awareness in the work environment assists employees in tracking their emotions and determining how this affect their performance at work as well as, when it may rub off on their co-workers. A leader in charge of a struggling team is an example of strong EI plays in the workplace. While less emotionally intelligent people may search for extenuating circumstances outside their control as the reason for the circumstances, leaders with high EI see it as a chance to demonstrate their value and turn the group around. People with great social awareness can sense their colleague's feelings, relate to them, perceive the issue through their eyes, and use this information to make unbiased choices. Putting all of this together to improve social abilities and relationship management is the fourth pillar of emotional intelligence. Being pleasant and personable is not enough. It entails taking into account everyone's feelings in order to efficiently manage social interactions.

Machine Generated Summaries

Disclaimer: The summaries in this chapter were generated from Springer Nature publications using extractive AI auto-summarization: An extraction-based summarizer aims to identify the most important sentences of a text using an algorithm and uses those original sentences to create the auto-summary (unlike generative AI). As the constituted sentences are machine selected, they may not fully reflect the body of the work, so we strongly advise that the original content is read and cited. The auto generated summaries were curated by the editor to meet Springer Nature publication standards. To cite this content, please refer to the original papers.

Machine generated keywords: leader, leader emotional, proactive, supervisor, fit, appraisal, job performance, training, performance, subordinate, person, developmental, transfer, process, health.

Development of Workplace Emotional Health Scale [170]

This is a machine-generated summary of:

Chen, Yin-Che; Tseng, Yu; Chu, Hui-Chuang: Development of Workplace Emotional Health Scale [170]

Published in: Employee Responsibilities and Rights Journal (2023)

Link to original: https://doi.org/10.1007/s10672-023-09446-5

Copyright of the summarized publication:

The Author(s), under exclusive licence to Springer Science+Business Media, LLC, part of Springer Nature 2023

Copyright comment: Springer Nature or its licensor (e.g. a society or other partner) holds exclusive rights to this article under a publishing agreement with the author(s) or other rightsholder(s); author self-archiving of the accepted manuscript version of this article is solely governed by the terms of such publishing agreement and applicable law.

All rights reserved.

If you want to cite the papers, please refer to the original.

For technical reasons we could not place the page where the original quote is coming from.

Abstract-Summary

"Workplace emotional health refers to employees' emotional stability and ability to express their emotions, adapt to stressful events, and develop and maintain strong interpersonal relationships in the workplace."

"This study identified four factors, namely workload, emotional intelligence, emotional blackmail, and emotional labor, and integrated them into the concept of workplace emotional health to explore emotional health from a comprehensive perspective."

"This study also developed a workplace emotional health scale comprising four dimensions: emotional expression strategies, emotional awareness, interpersonal adaptation, and workload."

"For the formal scale, the overall internal consistency reliability was .813, and that of the subscales was .879, .897, .764, and .854, respectively."

"The average variance extracted were between .470 and .671."

"The square root of the average variance extracted were between .685 and .819."

"These results indicated that the proposed scale exhibited favorable reliability and validity."

Introduction

"Numerous factors in the workplace affect the emotional health of employees, including (1) stress caused by workload; (2) emotional labor, which affects workplace health and has generated considerable discussion (Goodwin & others [1]); and (3) emotional blackmail, which creates interpersonal stress."

"This study employed workload, emotional labor, emotional blackmail, and emotional intelligence as the four dimensions of emotional health."

"Emotional health depends on the ability to evaluate emotions, express emotions appropriately, and relieve stress, and negative feelings by adapting and managing emotions (Chang-Lee & others, 2020)."

"This study used workload, emotional blackmail, emotional labor, and emotional intelligence to comprehensively analyze emotional health."

"The scale can be used to provide preliminary screenings of workplace emotional health and reference for evaluating workplace emotional health in employees."

"The literature on workload, emotional intelligence, emotional blackmail, and emotional labor were reviewed to determine their effects on workplace emotional health and the dimensions and preliminary items of the workplace emotional health scale."

Literature Review

"This study referenced Chang-Lee (2020), Liao (2011), and Scriven [2] and defined workplace emotional health as follows: the ability for workers to recognize and express personal emotions, adapt to and manage stressful events at work, develop positive interpersonal relationships, and maintain stable and healthy emotions."

"We explored emotional health by using four dimensions, namely workload, emotional awareness, emotional expression strategy, and interpersonal adaptation, and four variables, namely workload, emotional intelligence, emotional labor, and emotional blackmail."

"The finding that workload generates work stress is crucial to both academia and various industries; therefore, we included workload in the workplace emotional health scale as an independent dimension."

"The study defined emotional intelligence as a combination of self-management, the ability to manage interpersonal relationships, and the ability to offer knowledge to an organization and explored how these abilities affect organizational performance."

Research Methods

"The items were reviewed and evaluated by experts, who proposed suggestions for revisions before the preliminary questionnaires were distributed."

"The remaining items were used on the formal questionnaire."

"After the formal questionnaires were retrieved, an additional analysis was performed to determine the scale's reliability, validity, and measurement effect."

"We invited four experts from state-owned enterprises, science and technology industries, and the field of education to determine the validity of the scale, ensure the framework of the preliminary scale was correct, and indicate whether the scale required adjustment or improvement."

"We modified the wording of some items and removed others to ensure the validity of the preliminary questionnaire before distribution."

Results

"The results revealed that the correlation coefficient of the items in the emotional expression strategy, emotional awareness, interpersonal adaptation, and workload subscales ranged between 0.382 and 0.641, 0.292 and 0.589, 0.399 and 0.616, and 0.709 and 0.774, respectively."

"The total correlation analysis results indicated that the correlation coefficients of the subscales were greater than 0.4, suggesting a moderate to high positive correlation between each item and the overall scores and that all items should be retained."

"The comparison between the high-scoring and low-scoring groups and the corrected item total correlation analysis indicated that all items in the formal workplace emotional health scale exhibited discrimination."

"The emotional expression strategy, emotional awareness, interpersonal adaptation, and workload subscales consisted of eight, nine, four, and three items, respectively; the Cronbach's α of the scales was 0.879, 0.897, 0.764, and 0.854, respectively."

Conclusion

"These indicators were employed to develop the workplace emotional health scale."

"The proposed scale can be used to examine the emotional health of employees in the workplace in several dimensions."

"The results of the formal scale item analysis revealed that the CRs of each subscale satisfied suggested standards; this indicates that the subscale items could be used to determine workplace emotional health."

"On the basis of the results of confirmatory factor analysis, the goodness-of-fit test indicated that the corrected four-dimension model was more favorable than the single-dimension model."

"The internal consistency reliability analysis of the corrected formal scale revealed that the workplace emotional health scale had a Cronbach's α of 0.813 and that the subscales had a Cronbach's α between 0.764 and 0.897."

"This suggests that both the overall scale and the subscales of the corrected workplace emotional health scale have favorable internal consistency reliability."

Discussion and Suggestions

"These studies ascertained that in addition to evaluating workplace emotional health in terms of the effects of negative emotions (e.g., depression, anxiety, and stress), workplace emotional health can be evaluated in terms of emotional expression strategies, emotional awareness, interpersonal adaptation, and workload."

"The results of our analysis suggest that workplace emotional health is affected by emotional awareness through three channels, namely emotional control, interpersonal relationship management, and self-motivation."

"The results of analysis demonstrated that the scale has outstanding reliability and construct validity, indicating that workplace emotional health is a combination of emotional expression strategy, emotional awareness, interpersonal adaptation, and workload."

"Subsequent studies should conduct dynamic longitudinal research to explore changes in workplace emotional health in the context of societal changes and organizations' programs to assist workers; the findings of such research may provide corporations with reference to evaluate the outcomes of training courses and employee care programs."

Group Leader Emotional Intelligence and Group Performance: A Multilevel Perspective [171]

This is a machine-generated summary of:

Zhang, Yucheng; Zhang, Long; Zhu, Jingtao; Liu, Chih-Hsing; Yang, Mengxi; Liu, Guangjian: Group leader emotional intelligence and group performance: a multilevel perspective [171]

Published in: Asian Business & Management (2020)
Link to original: https://doi.org/10.1057/s41291-020-00123-1
Copyright of the summarized publication:
Springer Nature Limited 2020
Copyright comment: corrected publication 2020
All rights reserved.
If you want to cite the papers, please refer to the original.
For technical reasons we could not place the page where the original quote is coming from.

Abstract-Summary

"Drawing from the IPO (Input–Process–Output) model, this study adopted a multi-level framework to investigate the dynamic mediating mechanisms that link group leader emotional intelligence (EI) with group performance."

"Based on a sample of 64 group leaders and 194 group members, this research applied multilevel structural equation modeling (SEM) and explored two mechanisms, namely group cohesion at the group level and person–group fit at the individual level in the relationship."

"The paper utilized and expanded the IPO framework to explain the relationship between group leader EI and group performance from a multilevel perspective."

Introduction

"Our study joins the conversation by exploring how leader EI could build high-performing groups."

"Studies that focus on the mechanisms linking leader EI with group performance are largely unsystematic, such that the theoretical argument often lacks an overarching theoretical framework."

"Given the dearth of cross-level research on how leaders recognize and manage emotions in themselves and in others in the group context, this study aims to contribute to closing the void."

"This research explores the underlying dynamic mechanisms as the group processes linking group inputs (group leader EI) and group outcomes (group performance)."

"Our study takes a first step in investigating how specific leader quality, EI, has cross-level influence in the team process and thus promises to provide important implications for leadership literature."

Theory and Hypotheses Development

"At the individual level, leader EI reflects leaders' ability to understand and managing the nature of both job requirements and group members' traits, which jointly comprise the P-G fit (Hollenbeck & others [3])."

"Group leaders with high EI can improve the group performance through improving P-G fit because they can use positive emotions to promote the realization of group functions, accurately evaluate employees' feelings, and use this information to affect employees' emotions so that they understand and support the group goals (Cavazotte & others [4])."

"Group leaders with high EI are more likely to deeply understand and effectively manage group members' emotional traits and abilities as well as the emotional traits and abilities that the job position requires, and therefore to deliver not only a good fit between group members and the group in traits and abilities, but also a good match between the job requirements and the group members' characteristics (Wong & Law [5])."

Method

"The hypotheses were tested by collecting data from 64 groups in different organizations from various industries using a convenience sampling method in the region of Taiwan."

"Based on convenient sampling, we received 64 group leaders and 197 subordinates' responses (yielding a response rate of 64% and 39.4% respectively)."

"The sample consisted of 67.9% male group leaders and 52.4% male subordinates."

"Supervisors report data on group performance and group information, including group size and leaders' group tenure."

"Subordinates report data on P-G fit, group cohesion and group leader EI."

"The subordinates of the group rated their agreements with these statements."

"A sample item is "How well do members of your group get along with each other?""

"Our control variables include group size and leaders' group tenure based on previous research about group performance (Zhang & others [6])."

Results

"All factor loadings of were all statistically significant and of considerable magnitude (Group performance, range from 0.80 to 0.93; Group cohesion, range from 0.76 to 0.89; P-G fit, range from 0.74 to 0.87; Group leader EI, range from 0.74 to 0.93)."

"For hypothesis 2 and 4, we hypothesized group cohesion (H2) and P-G fit (H4) mediated the relationship between group leader EI and group performance at the individual and the group level respectively."

"At the group level, the mediation effect from group leader EI on group performance through group cohesion was $\gamma = 0.16$ ($\beta = 0.14$, $p = 0.049$) with a 95% bias-corrected bootstrap confidence interval that was entirely above zero (0.001, 0.37)."

"The mediation effect from group leader EI on group performance through P-G fit was $\gamma = 0.35$ ($\beta = 0.31$, $p = 0.162$) with a 95% bias-corrected bootstrap confidence interval that contained zero (− 0.11, 0.98)."

Discussion

"Two mediating mechanisms—group cohesion (at the group level) and P-G fit (at the individual level)—that link group leader EI to group performance were examined."

"Applying the IPO framework, by differentiating the two-level group process of group-level cohesion and individual level P-G fit, this study depicted a complete picture of how the effects of group leader EI transfer to the group members, and eventually to the group performance."

"At the individual level, finding a positive relationship between group leader EI and P-G fit suggests organizations, in the staffing process, to consider and develop group managers' abilities and skills of emotional management, so that the interpersonal compatibility between the individuals and their work groups can be improve, and group members' capacity and traits can be maximally utilized in the role (Pieterse & others [7])."

"The present research failed to find the individual-level mediating role of P-G fit underlying the relationships between group leader EI and group performance."

Conclusion

"Given the increasing work complexity and interdependency in contemporary organizations, group leader EI that fosters effective group management becomes crucial."

"We adopted a multilevel SEM analysis to explore the dynamic mechanisms linking group leader EI and group performance from a multilevel perspective using the IPO model."

"The findings extend prior research on group cohesion by exploring its function as a group-level facilitator that connects group supervisor and group outcomes."

The Effects of Emotional Intelligence on Job Performance and Life Satisfaction for the Research and Development Scientists in China [172]

This is a machine-generated summary of:
Law, Kenneth S.; Wong, Chi-Sum; Huang, Guo-Hua; Li, Xiaoxuan: The effects of emotional intelligence on job performance and life satisfaction for the research and development scientists in China [172]
Published in: Asia Pacific Journal of Management (2007)
Link to original: https://doi.org/10.1007/s10490-007-9062-3
Copyright of the summarized publication:
Springer Science+Business Media, LLC 2007
All rights reserved.
If you want to cite the papers, please refer to the original.
For technical reasons we could not place the page where the original quote is coming from.

Abstract-Summary

"To demonstrate the utility of the emotional intelligence (EI) construct in organizational studies, this study focuses on the effect of EI on job performance among research and development scientists in China."

"This predictor effect is supported by results on a study of research and development scientists working for a large computer company in China."

A Review of Emotional Intelligence: Its Nature, Domain and Development

"Salovey and Mayer [8, p. 189] gave their first definition of EI as "the subset of social intelligence that involves the ability to monitor one's own and others' feelings and emotions, to discriminate among them and to use this information to guide one's thinking and actions"."

"The four EI dimensions proposed by Davies and others are: (1) Appraisal and expression of emotion in one's self, which relates to an individual's ability to understand his/her deep emotions and to be able to express emotions naturally."

"Since EI is defined as a set of interpersonally and intrapersonally related human abilities, it should have the ability to predict various personal and social outcomes."

"The reason is that a person with high EI is able to understand his/her own and others' emotions and to draw upon this understanding to improve behaviors and attitudes for positive results."

EI, GMA, and Job Performance

"Although it seems clear that EI can affect job performance, it is important to establish its unique contribution to job performance when compared with other established constructs, especially traditional intelligence measures, such as the General Mental Ability (GMA) battery, which has been shown to be a valid predictor of performance."

"We echo this view and argue that EI is an additional factor that makes an incremental contribution to predicting job performance and work success on top of GMA."

"Since all three parts of the human mind are related to human performance, it is logical that both GMA and EI make their own unique contributions to job performance."

"Discussion, it seems clear that even for jobs that require high GMA, EI may still play an important role so far as the MOT job determinant is important for job performance."

Measurement: Self-Reported Versus Ability Testing

"Scholars in favor of task-based tests stated that EI can be assessed most directly by asking a person to solve an emotional problem (Mayer, Caruso, & Salovey [9]; Salovey & others [10])."

"Compared with the limited number of task-based tests, many self-reported EI scales have been developed, such as the Emotional Quotient Inventory (EQ-I; Bar-On [11]), the Trait Meta-Mood Scale (TMM; Salovey & others [12]) (see Salovey & others [10] for an extensive review of available measures)."

"As the self-reported WLEIS has been shown to be an EI measure with acceptable reliability and validity for Chinese samples while some of the MSCEIT items may be culturally specific, we predict that: Emotional intelligence as measured by the WLEIS developed from Chinese samples has better predictive power for Chinese workers' job performance than does the MSCEIT, which was developed from U.S. samples."

"We test the following hypothesis: Emotional intelligence as measured by the WLEIS developed from Chinese samples has better predictive power for Chinese workers' life satisfaction than does the MSCEIT, which was developed from U.S. samples."

Materials and Methods

"The data used in this study were collected from employees in the research laboratory of a large Chinese computer company in Beijing."

"We sent out invitations to all research laboratory employees to participate in the study."

"The company's formal appraisal of the employees' performance was used as the measure of job performance."

"The exceptionally high mean Wonderlic score of 37.5 confirmed our argument that GMA was well above average in our sample of research and development employees."

"We controlled for four demographic variables: age, measured by the actual number of years; gender dummy (1 for male, 2 for female); educational level (with 1 to 5 indicating degree from low to high: two-year college graduate, four-year university graduate, master, doctoral, and post-doctoral), and job tenure, measured by the number of years that an employee has been in his/her current position in the company."

Results

"Life satisfaction is significantly related to two dimensions of the MSCEIT (r = .24 and .31, respectively, for using emotions and managing emotions) and two dimensions of the WLEIS (r = .35 and .23, respectively, for emotional regulation and utilization of emotion)."

"To test the incremental predictive validity of EI measured by the MSCEIT and the WLEIS, we ran a hierarchical linear regression using job performance and life satisfaction as dependent variables."

"When the WLEIS indicators are dropped, the fit of the two-factor (i.e., the MSCEIT and life satisfaction) model is acceptable (CFI = .95; TLI = .92; RMSEA = .08)."

"When the MSCEIT indicators are dropped, the fit of the two-factor (i.e., the WLEIS and life satisfaction) model is acceptable (CFI = .97; TLI = .95; RMSEA = .06)."

Discussion

"Personnel psychologists have argued that when any other personnel measure, such as the integrity test or the conscientiousness test, is used, one question must be asked; that is, "...how much will each of these measures increase the predictive validity for job performance over the .51 that can be obtained by using only GMA?" (Schmidt & Hunter [13, p. 266]) Results from this study demonstrate that on top of GMA, EI still accounts for about 10% of overall job performance."

"An ideal research design to test the proposed model of the relationships among human mind, EI, GMA, and job performance is to use performance measures that fit Campbell's performance model, that is, to use measures of the three components of performance."

"Given the results that the MSCEIT is not able to predict job performance and its relatively low scores for this highly educated Chinese sample, more validation evidence appears to be necessary before the MSCEIT can be used to measure the levels of EI among Chinese respondents."

[Section 7]

"Law, Wong and Song [14] demonstrated that when defined and measured properly, EI was distinct from personality dimensions, and was a significant predictor of a bundle of desired outcomes, such as life satisfaction and supervisory ratings of job performance."

"EI was found to be positively related to leadership effectiveness, employee job satisfaction, and job performance (see, e.g., Rosete & Ciarrochi [15]; Wong & Law [5])."

"Although there is some evidence that EI is related to job satisfaction in Chinese samples (e.g., Wong, Wong & Law [16]), there is little evidence concerning the effect of EI on job performance among Chinese employees."

"We develop the hypotheses of this study, i.e., on the validity of EI to predict job performance beyond the effect of GMA, and the comparability of the two EI measures in predicting job performance."

Other-Caring or Other-Critical? A Contagious Effect of Leaders' Emotional Triads on Subordinates' Performance [173]

This is a machine-generated summary of:

Li, Yolanda N.; Law, Kenneth S.; Yan, Ming: Other-caring or other-critical? A contagious effect of leaders' emotional triads on subordinates' performance [173]

Published in: Asia Pacific Journal of Management (2019)

Link to original: https://doi.org/10.1007/s10490-018-9617-5

Copyright of the summarized publication:
Springer Science+Business Media, LLC, part of Springer Nature 2019

All rights reserved.

If you want to cite the papers, please refer to the original.

For technical reasons we could not place the page where the original quote is coming from.

Abstract-Summary

"We focus on two other-focus emotional triads: contempt, anger, and disgust (CAD) and empathy, sympathy, and pity (ESP) to investigate how supervisors' CAD and ESP affect their subordinates' performance, including task proficiency, adaptivity, proactivity, and counterproductive work behaviors (CWBs)."

"Based on emotional contagion theory, we argue that supervisors' CAD and ESP are contagious to subordinates by stimulating their CAD and ESP, respectively, and then influence their performance, an effect contingent on leader prototypicality."

"We find that the effect of supervisors' CAD on subordinates' performance only works through subordinates' CAD, while the effect of supervisors' ESP on subordinates' performance only works through subordinates' ESP."

Theoretical Background and Hypotheses

"When a supervisor with high ESP, an other-caring emotional triad, frequently and constantly emphasizes his or her consideration and caring for others (e.g., Rozin & others [17]; Wispé [18]), and displays to others kindness such as a smile or a hug, subordinates could be aware of such a supervisor's action tendency and view ESP emotions as appropriate standards in their team context."

"High sensitivity and perspective-taking tendency of subordinates with ESP emotions also motivate them to be supportive and responsive to colleagues' and supervisors' needs (e.g., George [19]; Hendriks & Vingerhoets [20])."

"According to emotional contagion theory, the contagious effect is more likely to incur from superior ones to others such as from supervisors to subordinates rather than the reverse (e.g., Bono & Ilies [21]; Johnson [22]; Visser & others [23])."

Methods

"Consistent with some previous studies using supervisor-subordinate dyads to examine emotional contagion (e.g., Hsee & others [24]; Sullins [25]), we asked supervisors to nominate one of their corresponding subordinates for our following surveys."

"At Time 3, supervisors were asked to rate subordinates' performance, including proficiency, adaptivity, proactivity, and CWBs."

"Following Mathieu and Taylor [26], we first tested a full mediation model where supervisors' CAD and ESP triads only related to subordinates' CAD and ESP triads, while subordinates' CAD and ESP triads only related to subordinates' proficiency, adaptivity, proactivity, and CWBs."

"We tested a partial mediation model by evaluating the change in chi-square ($\Delta \chi^2$) and model fit indices when the paths from supervisors' CAD and ESP triads to subordinates' proficiency, adaptivity, proactivity, and CWBs were freely estimated."

Results

"A similar result is found for supervisors' four-factor model of CAD, ESP, NA, and PA ($\chi^2(48) = 113.63$, $p < .01$; CFI $= .97$, TLI $= .96$, RMSEA $= .07$)."

"In support of Hypotheses 3 and 4a-4c, we found that subordinates' CAD was significantly and positively related to subordinates' CWBs ($\beta = .57$, SE $= .06$, $p < .01$), and subordinates' ESP was significantly and positively related to subordinates' proficiency ($\beta = .32$, SE $= .05$, $p < .01$), adaptivity ($\beta = .36$, SE $= .06$, $p < .01$), and proactivity ($\beta = .35$, SE $= .06$, $p < .01$)."

"In support of Hypotheses 6a-6c, subordinates' ESP mediated the effect of supervisors' ESP on subordinates' positive performance outcomes, with significant indirect effects emerging for proficiency (indirect effect = .09, SE = .02, 95% CI of [.06, .14]), adaptivity (indirect effect = .11, SE = .02, 95% CI of [.07, .16]) and proactivity (indirect effect = .10, SE = .02, 95% CI of [.06, .15])."

General Discussion

"In exploration of the impacts of supervisors' trait-like emotions on employees' performance, we adopt an emotional triad approach and unfold the effects of supervisors' CAD and ESP on subordinates' proficiency, adaptivity, proactivity, and CWBs from the lens of conscious emotional contagion."

"We rely on emotional contagion theory, especially conscious emotional contagion, to explore the effects of supervisors' trait-like emotional triads on subordinates' performance in real work settings from an Asian context."

"Extend current studies on the effects of leaders on subordinate performance to an emotional triad perspective and unfold its specific mechanism by emotional contagion effects."

"Our findings that supervisors' two different emotional triads, CAD and ESP, effectuate through contagious mechanisms to influence subordinates' performance empirically support the application of the emotional triad approach to the performance literature and other relevant literature related to emotions."

[Section 5]

"It was found that leaders' positive emotions (e.g., enthusiasm and happiness) and negative emotions (e.g., anger and sadness) were related to employees' performance (e.g., Damen, Van Knippenberg, & Van Knippenberg [27]; Gaddis, Connelly, & Mumford [28]; Glomb & Hulin [29])."

"In explaining why leaders' emotions could influence employees' performance, one significant mechanism was suggested to be emotional contagion, which refers to the transfer of one's emotion (s) to another (e.g., Hatfield, Cacioppo, & Rapson, [30])."

"Consistent with the conscious cognitive processes of emotional contagion (e.g., Hatfield & others [30, p. 7]), during which people use others' emotional sentiments as one type of social information to determine appropriate feelings for their particular situations (e.g., Barsade [31]), we posit that supervisors' emotions manifest appropriateness and are contagious to subordinates."

"We explore why leaders' emotions affect employees' performance by focusing on the more stable trait-like emotional triads and on the conscious cognitive process of emotional contagion, a process that is more likely to incur in naturally leader-follower relationships and endure over time."

Does Emotional Intelligence Moderate the Relationship Between Workplace Bullying and Job Performance? [174]

This is a machine-generated summary of:
Ashraf, Fatima; Khan, Muhammad Asif: Does emotional intelligence moderate the relationship between workplace bullying and job performance? [174]
Published in: Asian Business & Management (2013)
Link to original: https://doi.org/10.1057/abm.2013.5
Copyright of the summarized publication:
Palgrave Macmillan, a division of Macmillan Publishers Ltd 2013
All rights reserved.
If you want to cite the papers, please refer to the original.
For technical reasons we could not place the page where the original quote is coming from.

Abstract-Summary

"The present investigation mainly premised an undesirable impact of (supervisor) workplace bullying on (employee) job performance and that emotional intelligence (EI) of the bullied would moderate the negative impact."

"Although bullying negatively impacted job performance, the harmful impact was lower for those high on EI and higher for those low on EI."

"The study mainly highlights the need to eliminate workplace bullying from organisations and also emphasises the importance of EI to cope with bullying, for those bullied at work."

Literature Review

"Certain scholars [32–36] have categorised workplace bullying using various terms, for example, mobbing, emotional abuse, occupational stress, workplace violence, workplace abuse and workplace harassment."

"Workplace bullying is essentially psychological violence [37] that is manifest in targeted acts of belittlement, such as intimidation and humiliation, criticism of abilities and competence [38] and invention of mistakes [39]."

"Workplace bullying also includes acts that undermine targets' work, such as refusing relevant information, coercing work and setting difficult goals [38, 40]."

"Throughout this study, we refer to the study variable as workplace bullying and operationalise it as inclusive of the stated negative acts.'"

"Managers may resort to bullying as a means to achieve results, as they are pressurised to attain organisational goals [33] using whatever means [41]."

Workplace Bullying and Job Performance

"The consequences of bullying on those targeted are invariably destructive [42]."

"Past research has associated workplace bullying with serious detrimental outcomes for targets and indicates that it jeopardises individual [37] and organisational performance [32, 43, 44]."

"In such cases, the bullied individuals will perform less well at their jobs because of the bullying they experience."

"Building on arguments presented in past literature, a negative impact of workplace bullying on job performance is expected."

Job Performance

"As a job-related consequence, job performance concerns appraisal of the tasks that relate to an employee's job and aims at achieving organisational goals [45]."

"A traditional perspective is that enhanced job performance will contribute to firm success."

"Organisations should aim to maximise factors that are expected to boost job performance and eliminate factors that threaten it."

Emotional Intelligence

"The EI construct has permeated modern academic as well as popular literature [43, 46, 47]."

"In the domain of work performance, EI essentially represents an ability that precedes enhanced work performance [48]."

"One might thus anticipate organisations to be specifically interested in the EI construct, as it may be developed and enhanced for individual and organisational gain [48, 49], especially because people differ in their ability to focus on, manage and suitably apply emotions that pertain to themselves and others [50]."

"Several empirical studies have confirmed the utility of trait EI for desirable outcomes [50–53], which makes it a valid and robust concept for the work domain."

How Emotional Intelligence May Moderate the Workplace Bullying/Job Performance Relationship

"Emotions play an important role in performance [54], it may be reasoned that individuals with high EI will not experience stress or threat when faced with a perpetrator, and will control their performance at work by regulating their emotions positively, not allowing bullying behaviour to influence their job performance, at least not in the short run."

"For those with high EI, detrimental effects on job performance due to bullying experienced at work are less likely, but may be anticipated among those low on EI."

"It is this effective use of emotions that may conceivably moderate the damaging impact of bullying on work performance."

"The impact of bullying on job performance will be less for those high on EI than for those low on EI."

"Our framework posits that emotionally intelligent persons are better able to cope with bullying and thus weaken its negative consequences on their job performance."

Research Hypotheses

"This study will test the following hypotheses: Workplace bullying negatively impacts on employee job performance."

"Belittlement negatively impacts on job performance."

"Workplace exclusion negatively impacts on job performance."

Methods and Materials

"A total of 400 questionnaires were distributed, and 242 usable replies were received, yielding a response rate of 60.5 per cent."

"The study sample comprised 132 men and 110 women."

"A total of 132 respondents were under 30 years of age, whereas 110 respondents were 30 years or older."

"As for work experience, 125 respondents had less than 5 years, while 117 respondents had 5 years or more."

Measures

"We measured workplace bullying using 38 instrument, which originally contained 43 items."

"Discrepancies were revised and it was ensured that all items represented the main theme of the construct and corresponded to cultural settings."

"Six items measured belittlement, five items work undermined, six items verbal abuse, and two items workplace exclusion."

"Job performance was measured using 55 overall job-performance instrument that uses five items to assess task performance, adaptive performance and job dedication."

"To these, we developed items to measure interpersonal facilitation and innovation aspects of job performance."

Data Collection

"Junior doctors were identified as trainees/medical students from Years 1 to 5 of medical studies, whereas senior doctors were identified as heads of departments."

"We distributed a total of 400 questionnaires to doctors working at five hospitals and six clinics in Islamabad and Rawalpindi and received 252 replies; ten contained a majority of blank responses and were dropped, resulting in 242 usable replies."

"The effective response rate was thus 60.5 per cent."

Analyses of Data and Results

"We analysed demographic variables first, followed by descriptive statistics, reliability and correlation analysis."

"Multicollinearity indicates a strong relationship between two or more independent variables, and one way to test it is by examining the variance inflation factor and tolerance statistics."

"Workplace bullying and its dimensions positively correlated, as expected."

"It was also expected that job performance would correlate negatively with workplace bullying (r=−0.532)."

"Job performance correlates negatively with workplace bullying dimensions of belittlement (r=−0.63), work undermined (r=−0.05), verbal abuse (r=−0.54) and workplace exclusion (r=−0.23)."

"EI correlates negatively with workplace bullying (r=−0.46) and its four dimensions of belittlement (r=−0.50), work undermined (r=−0.4), verbal abuse (r=−0.44) and workplace exclusion (r=−0.20)."

Control Variables

"To control for the effects of demographic variables of age, gender and years of work experience on job performance, we entered these in the first step of forced-entry multiple regression."

"An R^2 value of 0.0071 and F statistic of 0.21 (p<0.76) showing the relation between control variables and job performance suggests that the controls had no significant relation with job performance."

Hypotheses Testing

"Observing the regression coefficients of workplace bullying dimensions, we see that belittlement (β=−0.67, p<0.000) has a significant negative impact on job performance, which confirms Hypothesis 1a."

"We added workplace bullying (predictor) and EI (hypothesised moderator) to see their impact on job performance."

Machine Generated Summaries 53

"In the last step, an interaction term created as a product of standardised variables [56] of workplace bullying and EI was added to examine the potential moderating effect of EI on workplace bullying and job performance."

"Following [57] procedure to test the moderation effect, we added the predictor (workplace bullying) and hypothesised moderator (EI) in the second step, with job performance as the criterion variable."

"The moderating effect of EI on the relationship between workplace bullying and job performance is confirmed, as their product term (interaction term) is significant (R^2=0.841, F statistic=34.91, p<0.000)."

Discussion

"One, whether workplace bullying in doctors negatively impacts on their job performance; two, which workplace bullying dimension impacts most on job performance; three, whether EI plays a moderating role in the relationship between workplace bullying and job performance, such that the negative impact of workplace bullying is lower for those who are high on EI and high for those who are low on EI."

"This study found that workplace bullying indeed negatively impacts on job performance among doctors."

"This study also found that employee EI indeed moderates the relationship between workplace bullying and job performance, such that the performance of those who are high on EI is not as negatively impacted by bullying behaviour as performance of those who are low on EI, where it is more strongly negative."

Theoretical Implications

"Results of this study clearly indicate that workplace bullying has adverse effects on employee job performance."

"Contrary to what was hypothesised, verbal abuse and work undermined did not exert negative impact, suggesting that when a supervisor verbally abuses employees or undermines an employee's work, such bullying acts do not necessarily impede the employee's performance at work."

"As medical hospitals typically have a hierarchical organisational culture, verbal abuse and undermining may be perceived as acceptable, rather than as bullying behaviour."

"Doctors encountering acts that involve verbal abuse and work undermining do not identify them as bullying behaviour, but as accepted components of that culture."

"Their job performance is not negatively impacted because they do not perceive themselves to have been bullied."

"An interesting finding of this research is that the negative impact of workplace bullying is weaker for highly emotionally intelligent individuals, and stronger for individuals low on EI."

Contribution to Literature

"To the best of our knowledge, this study is the first to examine EI as a moderator to cope with workplace bullying for those who experience it."

"A novel contribution of this study is that it emphasises the role of both organisational and societal culture in the perception and outcomes related to workplace bullying."

"This study has examined the workplace bullying construct in Asian settings, where such research is lacking, as most studies related to bullying have been conducted in Western settings [58]."

Managerial and Organisational Implications

"Organisations must work towards removing bullying from the work environment."

"We reassert the need for leadership to create an anti-bullying climate in organisations based on trust and integrity [36]."

"An anti-bullying climate will lead to lower stress and anxiety levels among employees, higher commitment, reduced turnover, better employee health and consequently better job performance."

"Organisations may introduce anti-bullying policies to encourage an anti-bullying climate."

"Such remedial actions would ensure the emotional and physical health of employees; healthier, happier employees working in a bullying-free environment are expected to be more productive and their contribution to enhanced organisational performance would be an added benefit."

"Workplace bullying is destructive in the emotional sense to the individual, and in the financial sense to the organisation [59, 60]."

"Workloads increase for such employees as a result of global pressure and organisational change, in addition to bullying at work."

Limitations

"It is possible that the short-term effects of bullying may not impact on job performance for emotionally intelligent persons, but the results might change over time."

"After all, bullying is repetitive and insulting behaviour [61] and the emotional 'strength' of those who are targeted may be presumed to wear down over time."

"Another weakness of this study is that it has relied on employee perception of bullying behaviour, which overlooks whether such behaviour was intentional."

"Since the nature of the bullying construct is based on the victim's perception, it evidently excludes the intent of the alleged bully."

"Further, as some scholars [62] have criticised the moderated multiple regression method, a limitation of this study may be its use of the product-term method to test moderation effects."

Future Research Direction

"As bullying behaviour may be directed towards an individual or group, as indicated earlier, we suggest group-level analysis in future research."

"Future research may examine gender differences with regard to emotional responses within the studied relationship for a more holistic framework and theory-building."

"After all, women and men may differ in their reasons for going out to work, and this might affect how bullying behaviour affects their job performance."

"As this research has proven that workplace bullying negatively impacts job performance, a similar adverse effect is likely on other aspects of work, such as turnover intentions, employee stress, workplace conflict, workplace climate and so on."

[Section 19]

"Workplace bullying is an important issue, as it occurs globally in organisations [61, 63]."

"Workplace bullying is particularly deleterious for staff, patients and outcomes [64] in health-care organisations."

"It is important to investigate factors that may lessen the expected adverse impact of bullying behaviour at work, with the aim of enhancing job performance and subsequently organisational performance."

"Using one's emotional ability to cope with bullying perpetrated by managers is likely to reduce the negative effects that workplace bullying might have on employee job performance."

"The present study is unique in that it focuses on the EI of those bullied at work."

"Whether the EI of those bullied at work impacts their job performance is currently unknown; this is an important gap the present study aims to bridge."

"This study empirically examines the possible moderating role of EI in the relationship between workplace bullying and job performance."

Effects of Perceptions on LMX and Work Performance: Effects of Supervisors' Perception of Subordinates' Emotional Intelligence and Subordinates' Perception of Trust in the Supervisor on LMX and, Consequently, Performance [175]

This is a machine-generated summary of:
Chen, Ziguang; Lam, Wing; Zhong, Jian An: Effects of perceptions on LMX and work performance: Effects of supervisors' perception of subordinates' emotional intelligence and subordinates' perception of trust in the supervisor on LMX and, consequently, performance [175]
Published in: Asia Pacific Journal of Management (2010)
Link to original: https://doi.org/10.1007/s10490-010-9210-z
Copyright of the summarized publication:
Springer Science+Business Media, LLC 2010
All rights reserved.
If you want to cite the papers, please refer to the original.
For technical reasons we could not place the page where the original quote is coming from.

Abstract-Summary

"The trust perception may interact with supervisor-rated emotional intelligence to influence the quality of LMX, and, consequently, work performance."

"Using a longitudinal study on a sample of 285 supervisor-subordinate dyads from a manufacturing firm in China, we found that (1) supervisor-rated emotional intelligence of subordinates (Time 1) positively predicts the quality of LMX (Time 2); (2) this relationship is stronger when subordinates highly trust their supervisors (Time 1); (3) LMX (Time 2) positively predicts work performance (Time 3); and (4) LMX (Time 2) fully mediates the interactive effect of emotional intelligence (Time 1) and trust in the supervisor (Time 1) on work performance (Time 3)."

Theory and Hypotheses

"In having a high level of trust in the supervisor, subordinates may actively perform the beneficial risk-taking behaviors by sharing information and cooperating with their supervisors, further facilitating the positive relationship between emotional intelligence and LMX, as discussed in Hypothesis 1."

"The interaction of subordinates' emotional intelligence and trust in the supervisor may not directly influence work performance; rather, this interaction relationship may be mediated by LMX."

"Taking the above arguments together, investigating whether LMX may facilitate the exchange process (i.e., to mediate the interactive effect of supervisor-rated emotional intelligence and trust in the supervisor on the work performance of subordinates) would be of great interest in the field."

Method

"In administering questionnaire for Wave 1, 312 usable supervisor-subordinate dyad questionnaires out of 328 were returned, giving a usable response rate of 95.1%."

"The supervisor-rated emotional intelligence (Time 1) and the work performance (Time 3) of the subordinates were rated by their immediate supervisors, while trust in the supervisor (Time 1) and LMX (Time 2) were rated by the subordinates."

"The scale consists of seven items that characterize the trust of subordinates in their immediate supervisors."

"The scale consists of seven items that characterize the overall effectiveness of the relationship between supervisor and subordinate."

"A three-item seven-point scale performance rating developed by Van Scotter and Motowidlo [65] was used to measure how the supervisors perceive the overall work performance of their subordinates (1 = very unsatisfactory; 7 = excellent)."

Findings

"Since the ICCs of the three variables (performance, trust in the supervisor, and emotional intelligence) in this study were less than .05 and one variable (LMX) was below .09, we concluded that the group variances of these variables are small."

"The results of the entire model test show that the direct path coefficients of the relationship between emotional intelligence and performance, between trust in the supervisor and performance, and the interaction of emotional intelligence and trust in the supervisor on performance were not significant."

"Although Mplus 5.1 has often been used to test for moderation, it does not produce traditional model fit statistics when calculating latent variable interactions."

"We concluded that LMX (Time 2) fully mediates the interaction of emotional intelligence (Time 1) and trust in the supervisor (Time 1) on work performance (Time 3)."

Discussion

"While many studies have examined how the perception of the competence of a subordinate by a supervisor (assessed by work performance) affects the quality of LMX (e.g., Deluga & Perry [66]; Dockery & Steiner [67]), there has been little discussion regarding the cognitive ability of members to process emotional information (i.e., the ability that predicts one's success in relationship building in the current environment with its intensive social interactions)."

"Our findings show that the emotional intelligence of subordinates, as perceived by supervisors, is strongly positively related to high-quality LMX and work performance."

"Although there are insufficient empirical data to support the research on emotional intelligence, our findings provide new insights into the effect of the additional predictability of perceived emotional intelligence on the supervisor-subordinate relationship as well as on the work performance of subordinates."

[Section 5]

"The perception of supervisors regarding the competency of their subordinates is a critical antecedent of high-quality LMX."

"Our study allows us to speculate on the process of how the perceptions of both supervisor and subordinate toward the other party contribute to high-quality LMX."

"Since emotional intelligence is recognized as an essential cognitive competence in dealing with emotions (Wong & others [16]), it is important to investigate if and how the rating of a subordinate's emotional intelligence by a supervisor help predict high-quality LMX."

"There appears a lack of research on how the perception of supervisors by their subordinates contributes to high-quality LMX."

"The present study thus adds value to the LMX literature by investigating whether the trust perception of supervisors by their subordinates can help explain the development of high-quality LMX."

Brand Managers' Mindful Self-Management of Their Professional Experience: Consequences for Pay, Self-Efficacy and Job Performance [176]

This is a machine-generated summary of:
Bennett, Roger: Brand managers' mindful self-management of their professional experience: Consequences for pay, self-efficacy and job performance [176]
Published in: Journal of Brand Management (2011)
Link to original: https://doi.org/10.1057/bm.2010.55
Copyright of the summarized publication:
Palgrave Macmillan, a division of Macmillan Publishers Ltd 2011
All rights reserved.
If you want to cite the papers, please refer to the original.
For technical reasons we could not place the page where the original quote is coming from.

Abstract-Summary

"This article examines the role of 'mindfulness' in a brand manager's self-direction of his or her professional experience, and assesses the impacts of experience of brand management, general marketing, general management and financial analysis on the person's self-perceived mastery of the brand management role."

"It explores the effects of a high level of 'self-efficacy' as a brand manager on an individual's pay, status within the brand management hierarchy and operational performance."

"It emerged that 'mindful' self-management of a brand manager's previous work experience significantly moderated the effects of all kinds of past experience on an individual's feelings of self-efficacy as a brand manager."

"The duration of a person's experience of brand management had a significant direct influence on pay, but not on professional status or self-assessed on-job performance."

"The outcomes to the study imply the need for brand managers to fashion and learn from their work experience in particular ways."

"A number of antecedents of self-efficacy vis-à-vis brand management and general management roles were identified in the course of the research."

"The outcomes shed light on the previously unexplored question of how professional experience of general managerial and marketing work can translate into successful career advancement for brand managers."

Introduction

"The mechanisms whereby experience of marketing work (general and specifically in the area of brand management) can translate into better pay and career progression have not (to the very best of the author's knowledge) been the subject of investigation."

"The study described below attempted to help fill this lacuna in knowledge about the consequences of experience of general marketing, general management and brand management for the development and career advancement of brand managers via an empirical investigation of possible links between (i) various types of marketing and management work experience and an individual brand manager's feelings of self-efficacy in his or her present position, and (ii) self-efficacy and pay, occupational status as a brand manager, and self-assessments of performance."

"Its purpose was to demonstrate how the self-management of professional experience in specific ways (for example, by obtaining training in, familiarity with and first-hand experience of particular aspects of business associated with brand management) can improve a person's career prospects."

Nature and Possible Benefits of Occupational Experience

"The occupancy of previous brand management jobs that involved work activities similar in nature to those required in a more senior branding position might be expected to enhance performance in the new role to greater extents than work experience in other marketing functions."

"Experience of non-marketing functions might make an individual a better marketing manager through giving the person useful all-round business skills that can be applied within a marketing role [68] plus the capacities to appreciate how marketing fits into corporate strategy and operations as a whole [69], and how it contributes to the creation of shareholder (as well as customer) value [70, 71]."

"Brand managers who have acquired (non-trivial) experience of, for example, financial marketing planning and financial control, financial modelling, financial market analysis and financial forecasting should be better able to understand critical 'bottom line financial considerations' (cf [72, p. 30]) relevant to their work."

"Knowledge and experience of financial management exposes a brand manager to a whole series of metrics and issues relating to shareholder value [73], accountability [74], profitability and cash inflows [70, 75], and other 'hard' aspects of the marketing function."

Consequences of Experience for Self-Efficacy

"In a managerial context, occupational self-efficacy involves executives' beliefs in their being able to accomplish specific managerial tasks [76], to 'execute the behaviours required for effective job performance' [77, p. 586], to fulfil competently all the demands attached to a job role [78] and, in the words of [79], to 'mobilise cognitive resources and courses of action needed to successfully execute a specific task within a given context' (p. 379)."

"Through experience, people learn how to perform more difficult tasks, and this leads to greater self-efficacy [80]."

"[81] observed how experience created information about a manager's capabilities and that the 'weighing, integrating and evaluation' of this information affected assessments of self-efficacy (p. 35)."

"The longer the period of a person's experience of something (for example, a business function or an industry sector) the heavier the impact on the individual's feelings of self-efficacy in relation to (say) the function or sector concerned [82–84]."

Consequences of Self-Efficacy for Performance

"[79] reported that 'over 20 years of research has revealed a strong positive relationship between self-efficacy and managerial performance' (p. 379)."

"A meta analysis undertaken by 85 found that, on average, published studies have reported a 28 per cent improvement in performance among employees with high self-efficacy."

"Studies have shown (see [79]) that the higher a manager's self-efficacy the more likely that the person will 'initiate tasks, sustain effort towards task improvement, and persist when problems are encountered' (p. 379)."

"Highly self-efficacious people expect to succeed [80], and hence are willing to 'do what is necessary' to make things happen [86, p. 119]."

Self-Management of Experience

"[87–90] and others have argued that experience improves a person's occupational ability and self-confidence when the individual exercises forethought in relation to lessons learned from experience, reflects deliberately and thoughtfully on past events, and proactively seeks to improve his or her knowledge and skills in consequence of having had the experience."

"Such individuals are said to use experience in 'mindful' ways [89, 90]."

"Mindfulness has been defined as an individual's ability to pay complete and careful attention to current experiences affecting both the person him or herself and the person's environment [91]."

"Mindful reflection on a work experience creates awareness of the context and essence of the experience [92] and of how methods and procedures that succeeded in the past might be extrapolated from one job to another [93]."

"[92] observed that, in fact, 'most' people in organisations are not mindful due to their being overloaded with tasks and not having the time needed to pay proper attention to the nature and content of an experience when or shortly after it occurs (p. 1)."

Other Possible Influences on Pay, Status and Performance

"Gender, education, firm size, location and industry sector are routinely reported to exert important impacts on marketers' salaries (see [94, 95])."

"Gender has consistently been found to affect the salaries of marketing managers."

"[96] reported an average pay gap of around £10 000 per annum between men and women in many types of marketing management position."

"Education level may impact on performance and salary through managers with higher overall levels of education (undergraduate, postgraduate and so on) possessing greater capabilities for information processing [97] and abilities to devise more creative solutions to complex problems (see [98]), thus helping them to attain more senior positions within companies (see [99])."

A Suggested Model

"Mindfulness is posited to represent a (positive) moderator of suggested links between various types of experience (brand management, sector, non-marketing, financial) and occupational self-efficacy as a brand marketer and as a marketing manager in general."

"Self-efficacy is then regarded as exerting a significant influence on a person's occupational status, self-assessed quality of current performance, and level of pay having controlled for the individual's gender, education and training, geographical location, the size of an employing firm and the firm's industry sector."

"[77, 100] and [86] also argued the case for the presence of a positive and significant relationship between education and/or training and improved self-efficacy."

Measurement of Variables

"Mindfulness was assessed through 12 items adapted mainly from the Freiburg Mindfulness Scale [101], the Kentucky Inventory of Mindfulness Skills [102] and [90] 'inventory of inventories' of mindfulness questionnaire items."

"The strength of an individual's self-efficacy was assessed twice: first in relation to the person's functional role (as a brand manager); second vis-à-vis his or her work as a marketing manager in general."

"80 stressed the need to tailor the assessment of self-efficacy to the specific function(s) involved, and it is possible that high self-efficacy in respect of a particular function is not always matched by high self-efficacy concerning an individual's collateral role as a general marketing manager."

"Three dependent variables were included in the model: status, pay and self-assessed on-job performance."

"According to [103], attributes deemed important for financial performance are normally self-evaluated with satisfactory levels of accuracy, provided managers fully understand what precisely they need to self-assess."

The Sample

"The sets of items for the three constructs addressed in the course of the study (mindfulness, marketing self-efficacy and performance) were individually subjected to principal components factor analyses."

"Only item B(g) of the mindfulness construct migrated (to the self-efficacy factor), and just two items (C(f) and (h)) of the self-efficacy construct moved to the performance factor."

"None of the performance items shifted. (This relative stability of the factor structure was anticipated a priori, given that self-efficacy concerns feelings, whereas the performance measure involves cognitive assessments, and as the mindfulness items are quite different in character to the items reflecting the other two constructs.) The mean values of each of the three composites fell within the central region for the measures, and standard deviations displayed a reasonably wide range of responses."

Results

"Certain variables consistently failed to exert significant influences on any of the dependent variables, irrespective of the model estimated (functional self-efficacy in brand management or self-efficacy as a general marketing manager) or the configurations of the sets of other regressors used in particular estimations."

"Periods of experience spent in particular sectors failed to exert a significant influence on self-efficacy."

"Nor did experience of this type exert any direct significant influences on pay, status as a brand manager or self-assessed performance in a branding position."

"Although length of experience of non-marketing functions did not significantly affect a person's self-efficacy as a brand manager, the proportion of this experience that involved financial management most certainly did."

"Experience of non-marketing functions (for example human resources or production) did not of itself contribute significantly to a person's self-efficacy as a brand manager, only when the experience had a substantial financial content."

Conclusion

"Theoretical contributions of the research extend to the development of the constructs of self-efficacy and mindfulness for use in a specific occupational context (brand management), the composition of measures of these constructs in relation to marketing management, and the establishment of the mediating role played by self-efficacy in the connection between experience of marketing work and on-job self-assessed performance, pay and professional status."

"They suggest strongly the need for businesses to provide their brand management employees with (i) guidance to regarding how they should consciously self-manage experience gained in the early stages of a career (that is, by approaching their experiences mindfully), (ii) training, particularly in the area of financial management, and (iii) information on certain factors that appear to be associated with progression to higher status marketing positions."

Psychological Capital and Employee Engagement as Predictors of Organisational Citizenship Behaviour in the Industrial Revolution 4.0 Era: Transfer of Training as a Mediator [177]

This is a machine-generated summary of:

Ting, Qian Hui; Lew, Tek Yew; Goi, Chai Lee; Sim, Adriel K.S.; Gim, Gabriel C.W.: Psychological capital and employee engagement as predictors of organisational citizenship behaviour in the industrial revolution 4.0 era: transfer of training as a mediator [177]

Published in: Current Psychology (2023)

Link to original: https://doi.org/10.1007/s12144-023-04595-0

Copyright of the summarized publication:

The Author(s), under exclusive licence to Springer Science+Business Media, LLC, part of Springer Nature 2023

Copyright comment: Springer Nature or its licensor (e.g. a society or other partner) holds exclusive rights to this article under a publishing agreement with the author(s) or other rightsholder(s); author self-archiving of the accepted manuscript version of this article is solely governed by the terms of such publishing agreement and applicable law.

All rights reserved.

If you want to cite the papers, please refer to the original.

For technical reasons we could not place the page where the original quote is coming from.

Abstract-Summary

"This study seeks to examine the relationships between psychological capital (PsyCap), employee engagement (EE), transfer of training (TOT), and organizational citizenship behaviour (OCB) among youth participants of IR4.0 in Sarawak."

"Results revealed that PsyCap was positively related to EE, TOT, and OCB."

"EE and TOT were also found to be positively influence OCB."

"TOT was found to mediate the relationship between PsyCap and OCB."

"Besides, the model reflects the interplay between personal resource (PsyCap) and job resource (TOT) to influence effective organisational functioning (represented by OCB) through a motivational process."

"Findings suggest practical implications whereby organisations should engage pre-training psychological capital intervention to increase rate of training transfer whilst developing digital competencies of the workforce."

Introduction

"Malaysian employers hesitate to provide training opportunities and found trainings beyond employees' current work-scope to be unnecessary (Training Workforce [104])."

"Extant literature attributed the lack of personal motivations as the reason why employees failed to transfer training outcomes to work (Elliott & others [105])."

"Grover and others [106] and Bruning and Campion [107] collectively raised concerns on the vague understanding of the influence of personal resources (represented by psychological capital) on job-resources (represented by transfer of training) and the pathway resulting organisational citizenship behaviour which is a favourable outcome that benefits employing organisations."

"Following the theoretical gaps in the extant literature, the research objectives of this study are: a) To examine the relationships between psychological capital (PsyCap), employee engagement (EE) and transfer of training (TOT) respectively."

"b) To examine the relationships between psychological capital (PsyCap), employee engagement (EE), transfer of training (TOT) and organisational citizenship behaviour (OCB) respectively."

Literature Review

"This study shall integrate JD-R theory and the KTEM theory to examine the role of individual's personal resources (represented by the cognitively dominant PsyCap) on job resources (represented by TOT) through positive affect and how the interplay between personal resources and job resources will subsequently result in OCB."

"Sharing similar grounds that proposes EE as a predictor of TOT, this study seeks to examine the influence of motivation on TOT through PsyCap- a personal resource that demonstrates an individual's motivated efforts and resilience to positively appraise circumstances and increase the likelihood of success (Luthans & others [108, 109]; Luthans & Youssef-Morgan [110]) suggested that PsyCap resources are state-like constructs which are relatively flexible than personality traits, yet comparatively stable against moods and emotions."

"Examining the influence of the positively fuelled EE on OCB will validate theoretical claims that positive emotions lead to social resources, while the potentially mediating role of TOT substantiates theoretical understanding on how positive emotions will advance social and work role expansion when essential job resources are acquired."

Discussion

"The KTEM model falls short of identifying individual factors that enhance training effectiveness Based on the findings of this study, personal resources were found to exert positive influence on the generation of job resources, manifested through TOT to mitigate job demands."

"This study has shed light on the cruciality of cognition at influencing resources experienced by employees- an area that has been widely debated within the domains of job crafting (Zhang & Parker [111]; Lazazzara & others [112]) through the positive relationships of PsyCap and TOT, PsyCap and OCB, as well as the mediating effect of TOT in the relationship between PsyCap and OCB."

"This study has shed light on the cruciality of cognition at influencing resources experienced by employees - an area that has been widely debated within the domains of job crafting through the positive relationships of PsyCap and TOT, PsyCap and OCB, as well as the mediating effect of TOT in the relationship between PsyCap and OCB."

Effect of Employee Recognition, Employee Engagement on Their Productivity: The Role of Transformational Leadership Style at Ghana Health Service [178]

This is a machine-generated summary of:

Kwarteng, Samuel; Frimpong, Samuel Oti; Asare, Richard; Wiredu, Twumasi Jacob Nana: Effect of employee recognition, employee engagement on their productivity: the role of transformational leadership style at Ghana Health Service [178]

Published in: Current Psychology (2023)

Link to original: https://doi.org/10.1007/s12144-023-04708-9

Copyright of the summarized publication:

The Author(s), under exclusive licence to Springer Science+Business Media, LLC, part of Springer Nature 2023

Copyright comment: Springer Nature or its licensor (e.g. a society or other partner) holds exclusive rights to this article under a publishing agreement with the author(s) or other rightsholder(s); author self-archiving of the accepted manuscript version of this article is solely governed by the terms of such publishing agreement and applicable law.

All rights reserved.

If you want to cite the papers, please refer to the original.

For technical reasons we could not place the page where the original quote is coming from.

Abstract-Summary

"The main aim of the study was to assess the effect of employee recognition and employee engagement on their productivity: the moderating role of transformational leadership style at Ghana Health Service."

"The population of the study consisted of 258 employees who have worked for Ghana Health Service in Kumasi for at least 5 years and had complete contact information were chosen using random sampling technique."

"From the present study, employee recognition program motivates and influence employees positively to improve their productivity."

"The present study depicts that employee engagement is a strong predictor of employee productivity in the health sector in Ghana."

"Transformational leaders boost their followers' motivation and self-efficacy which aims at increasing their productivity."

"Close-ended questionnaire was used for the study to get responses from respondents."

Introduction

"Recent studies have shown that a transformational leadership style can positively influence employee engagement, employee recognition which enhances their productivity and make an organization become more stable and effective (Osborne and others, 2017; Turner, 2020)."

"Employee engagement, employee recognition and productivity are directly impacted by incorporating their measurements into a transformational leadership style (Boyd, 2019; Popli & others, 2017; Williams & others, 2019)."

"Transformational leadership in a company has a favorable impact on the relationship between employee recognition and productivity, as well as the relationship between employee engagement and productivity (Kalimuthu, 2019)."

"The present study extends the existing literature by including how transformational leadership affects employee's recognition and engagement positively to determine employee productivity at Ghana Health Service."

"The purpose of the present study is to determine how employee recognition, transformational leadership style, and employee engagement affect employee productivity in the Ghana Health Service."

Theoretical and Literature Review

"Employee recognition can help employees feel the communication and interaction with leaders, as well as understand their job responsibilities and roles, in order to improve the quality of trust and relationship with leaders, better integrate employees into the organization, and perceive organizational support, as an effective feedback behavior (Manoj, 2015; Yao & others [113])."

"Through recognizing employees' production at work in a variety of ways, transformational leadership improves job performance, which is a huge organizational advantage (Zheng, 2014; Fayzhall & others [114])."

"A transformative leader recognizes their employees in a variety of ways, which increases their productivity (Hutagalung & others [115])."

"Transformational leadership positively moderates the relationship between employee recognition and employee productivity."

"The relationship between employee engagement and employee productivity is positively moderated by transformational leadership."

"The relationship between employee recognition and employee productivity, as well as the relationship between employee engagement and employee productivity, is positively moderated by transformational leadership style."

Research Methodology

"258 employees who have worked for the Ghana Health Service for at least 5 years and had complete contact information were chosen using simple random sampling technique since the total number of the health workers is large."

"Section A presented the demographic characteristics of the study; Section B presented questions on employee recognition; Section C presented questions on employee engagement; Section D addressed questions on employee productivity; and Section E also had questions relating to transformational leadership style."

"The present study controlled for five variables that might have impact on employee productivity."

"There were four latent variables, which were employee recognition (ER), employee engagement (EE), transformational leadership style (TL) and employee productivity (EP)."

"Employee recognition had 4 measurement items, employee engagement had 7 measurement items, transformational leadership style had 4 measurement items and employee productivity had 4 measurement items."

Results

"Employee performance was negatively impacted by level of qualification and years of experience; however, age had a positive and significant impact."

"Under the model 2 and 3, both employee engagement and transformational leadership style had a positive significant effect."

"According to model 4 to 5, the relationship between employee recognition and transformational leadership style, as well as the relationship between employee engagement and transformational leadership style, had a negative impact on employee productivity."

"This means that the relationship between employee recognition and employee productivity is negatively moderated by transformational leadership style."

"The relationship between employee engagement and employee productivity was negatively moderated by transformational leadership style."

Discussion

"We hypothesized (H2) that employee engagement had a significant effect on employee productivity, which the data supported."

"Transformational leadership style has a significant effect on employee productivity which was also confirmed by the analysis."

"We hypothesized that, transformational leadership style significantly moderates the relationship between employee recognition and employee productivity."

"This also shows that transformational leadership style significantly reduces the relationship between employee recognition on employee productivity due to differences in the employees' interests and the organization's culture (Smith & others, 2002; Mixdorf & others [116])."

"We hypothesized that, transformational leadership style significantly moderates the relationship between employee engagement and employee productivity."

"This implies that when transformational leadership style is included as a moderator, the significant relationship between employee engagement and employee productivity is weakened based on the coefficient of the interaction term."

Conclusion and Contributions

"Employee recognition, employee engagement and transformational leadership style individually had a positive significant effect on employee productivity."

"The relationship between employee recognition and employee productivity, as well as the relationship between employee engagement and employee productivity was negatively influenced by transformational leadership style."

"Employee engagement has a significant effect on employee productivity, according to the study."

"Transformational leadership has a significant influence on employee recognition and engagement which directly affect their productivity in an organization (Holten & Carneiro [117])."

"Employee recognition, employee engagement and transformational leadership style are the main goal of every business if the organization wants to optimize employee productivity which was confirmed from the analysis (Khan [118])."

"It is therefore recommended that organizations should come out with measures that will fully induce employee recognition, employee engagement and transformational leadership style to increase employee productivity."

Limitations and Future Research Suggestions

"The questionnaires in this study were made up of closed-ended questions and used a basic random sample technique."

"While this study concentrated on Ghana's health sector, more research is needed in a variety of sectors both within and outside of Ghana, notably among government and private hospitals."

"Future research should also consider more factors that can influence employee productivity rather than considering only transformational leadership, employee recognition and engagement (Rich & others, 2010)."

"To begin, the study contributes to the body of knowledge by examining the effects of employee recognition and employee engagement on employee productivity, as well as testing the moderating effects of transformational leadership style in the relationships between employee recognition and employee productivity and employee engagement and employee productivity."

Display Rule Perceptions and Job Performance in a Chinese Retail Firm: The Moderating Role of Employees' Affect at Work [179]

This is a machine-generated summary of:

Lam, Catherine K.; Walter, Frank; Ouyang, Kan: Display rule perceptions and job performance in a Chinese retail firm: The moderating role of employees' affect at work [179]

Published in: Asia Pacific Journal of Management (2013)
Link to original: https://doi.org/10.1007/s10490-013-9348-6
Copyright of the summarized publication:
Springer Science+Business Media New York 2013
All rights reserved.
If you want to cite the papers, please refer to the original.
For technical reasons we could not place the page where the original quote is coming from.

Abstract-Summary

"Results obtained in a sample of 245 frontline service employees and their 63 immediate supervisors from a retail firm in China demonstrate that display rule perceptions were positively related with task and contextual performance among employees experiencing little positive affective states at work, but not among employees experiencing highly positive affect."

"Display rule perceptions were positively associated with one aspect of contextual performance (voluntary learning) among employees with little negative affect, whereas highly negative affect buffered this linkage."

"This study highlights performance consequences of employees' display rule perceptions and uncovers key boundary conditions for these relationships."

Theory and Hypotheses

"If employees experience strong negative affective states at work, we therefore expect integrative display rule perceptions to diminish their willingness for contextual performance behaviors that extend beyond immediate job tasks, such as organizational citizenship and voluntary learning."

"Hypothesis 1 Employees' negative affect at work moderates the relationships of perceived display rules with (a) task performance and (b) contextual performance (organizational citizenship and voluntary learning behavior)."

"Integrative display requirements that encourage positive emotion expressions may promote rather than deteriorate work motivation among employees experiencing little positive affect, contributing to their willingness to engage in discretionary, contextual performance behaviors (e.g., organizational citizenship and voluntary learning)."

"Hypothesis 2 Employees' positive affect at work moderates the relationships of perceived display rules with (a) task performance and (b) contextual performance (organizational citizenship and voluntary learning behavior)."

Methods

"Employees reported their display rule perceptions and affective states at work, whereas supervisors rated each of their direct subordinates' performance."

"Each supervisor rated the performance of four employees within his or her store."

"The items focused on integrative display requirements that mandate expression of positive and suppression of negative emotions (e.g., "Your job requires you to only show positive emotions to customers;" 1 = strongly disagree, 5 = strongly agree; α = .79)."

"Supervisors rated each of their subordinates on 16 organizational citizenship behavior items from Lee and Allen [119], assessing beneficial, discretionary behaviors directed toward the organization (OCBO; e.g., "Offers ideas to improve the functioning of the organization") and coworkers (OCBI; e.g., "Assists others with their duties;" 1 = strongly disagree, 7 = strongly agree)."

"However, employees were nested within 63 stores (Level-2), with the respective stores' supervisors rating multiple employees' performance."

Results

"Hypotheses 1a and 1b, in particular, predicted negative affect to moderate the role of display rule perceptions."

"Display rule perceptions were unrelated (not negatively related) with voluntary learning ($\beta = -.02$, ns) when negative affect was high (+1 SD)."

"Hypotheses 2a and 2b predicted positive affect to moderate the display rule perception—job performance linkage."

"When positive affect was low (but not when it was high), display rule perceptions were positively related with task performance ($\beta = .23$, $p < .01$; vs. $\beta = -.07$, ns), organizational citizenship ($\beta = .22$, $p < .001$; vs. $\beta = -.02$, ns) and voluntary learning behavior ($\beta = .09$, $p < .01$; vs. $\beta = -.03$, ns)."

Discussion

"The impetus for this research was to reconcile opposing theoretical predictions on the role of display rule perceptions for service employees' job performance and to clarify prior, inconsistent findings."

"This study demonstrates the affect employees experience at work as an important, heretofore neglected moderator for the performance consequences of display rule perceptions."

"Another interesting aspect of our findings is that display rule perceptions only facilitated job performance among service employees experiencing low-intensity affective states at work."

"Strong positive affect may enable high job performance among service employees even if they fail to perceive relevant display rules."

"Our results intimate that display rule perceptions may broadly stimulate job performance among employees experiencing little positive affect and promote voluntary learning among employees experiencing little negative affect at work."

[Section 5]

"Display rules are an important element of most emotional labor theories, and employees' perceptions of such rules have been suggested to critically shape both individually and organizationally relevant outcomes—potentially exhibiting pronounced impacts on a service organization's bottom-line (Diefendorff & Gosserand [120]; Morris & Feldman [121]; Zapf [122])."

"Display rule perceptions may positively relate with job performance, enabling employees to express appropriate emotions and, thereby, to fulfill important performance criteria (Ashforth & Humphrey [123])."

"Given these opposing predictions, consideration of moderating factors appears crucial to uncover conditions under which display rule perceptions may help or hinder employee performance (Gosserand & Diefendorff [124])."

"The current study advances existing knowledge by investigating the interplay of employees' display rule perceptions and affect at work as performance antecedents in a Chinese service environment."

How Authentic Leadership Influences Employee Proactivity: The Sequential Mediating Effects of Psychological Empowerment and Core Self-Evaluations and the Moderating Role of Employee Political Skill [180]

This is a machine-generated summary of:
Zhang, Jing; Song, Lynda J.; Wang, Yue; Liu, Guangjian: How authentic leadership influences employee proactivity: the sequential mediating effects of psychological empowerment and core self-evaluations and the moderating role of employee political skill [180]

Published in: Frontiers of Business Research in China (2018)
Link to original: https://doi.org/10.1186/s11782-018-0026-x
Copyright of the summarized publication:
The Author(s). 2018
License: OpenAccess CC BY 4.0
This article is distributed under the terms of the Creative Commons Attribution 4.0 International License (http://creativecommons.org/licenses/by/4.0/), which permits unrestricted use, distribution, and reproduction in any medium, provided you give appropriate credit to the original author(s) and the source, provide a link to the Creative Commons license, and indicate if changes were made.

If you want to cite the papers, please refer to the original.

For technical reasons we could not place the page where the original quote is coming from.

Abstract-Summary

"This study aims to examine the relationship between authentic leadership and employee proactive behavior."

"Based on self-determination theory, we argue that such a relationship is sequentially mediated by psychological empowerment and core self-evaluations."

"Results show that authentic leadership (Time 1) influences employees' proactive behavior (Time 3) through the psychological empowerment (Time 1) and core self-evaluations of employees (Time 2), and the relationship between core self-evaluations and proactive behavior is positively moderated by employees' political skill."

"Bootstrapping results also verify the moderating role played by employees' political skill in the indirect relationship between authentic leadership and proactive behavior through core self-evaluations."

Introduction

"According to SDT, authentic leadership might affect proactive behavior by causing some changes in employees' psychological outcomes (Rosen & others [125])."

"Research pertaining to the psychological mechanism through which authentic leadership influences employee proactive behavior is scarce."

"We infer that psychological empowerment and core self-evaluations can be used as mediating variables linking authentic leadership and employees' proactive behaviors."

"We are the first to propose and test the positive relationship between authentic leadership and employee proactive behavior."

"Drawing on SDT, we locate the sequential mediating effect of psychological empowerment and core self-evaluations in the relationship between authentic leadership and employee proactive behavior, which can help people to get a better understanding of its internal mechanisms."

"Employees' political skill is demonstrated in this research to serve as an important boundary condition influencing the indirect linkage between authentic leadership and employee proactive behaviors through core self-evaluations."

Theory and Hypothesis

"We expect that employees with high core self-evaluations are more likely to engage in proactive behavior, thus strengthening the relationship between authentic leadership and proactive behavior."

"We hypothesize the following: Hypothesis 2: Employees' core self-evaluations mediate the relationship between authentic leadership and employees' proactive behavior."

"We propose the following hypothesis: Hypothesis 5: Employees' psychological empowerment and core self-evaluations sequentially mediate the relationship between authentic leadership and employees' proactive behavior."

"We propose a third-stage, indirect moderating effect of political skill in the relationship between authentic leadership and proactive behavior as follows: Hypothesis 7: Political skill moderates the indirect relationships between authentic leadership and proactive behavior through core self-evaluations, such that the indirect effects of authentic leadership will be stronger under conditions of high political skill."

Methods

"In the first survey (Time 1), team members were asked to evaluate authentic leadership of their team supervisor and their own perception of psychological empowerment."

"This scale contains four items for each of the four components of authentic leadership: self-awareness, relational transparency, moral perspective and balanced processing."

"We measure psychological empowerment with Spreitzer [126]'s scale, which consists of 12 items used to assess the extent to which individuals experience four components of psychological empowerment: meaning, competence, self-determination, and impact."

"We use a 12-item scale from the Core Self-Evaluations Scale (Judge & others [127]) to assess personal core self-evaluations."

"To measure proactive behavior, we use the 8-item scale that Yang and others [128] revised to measure proactive behavior in China, with team leader evaluating their team subordinates."

"We use an 18-item scale adapted from Ferris and others [129]'s to measure follower political skill."

Results

"When core self-evaluations are included in regression analyses, core self-evaluations are significantly and positively related to proactive behavior (Model 3, $\beta = 0.12$, $p < 0.10$), but the significant effect of authentic leadership and proactive behavior become insignificant (Model 3, $\beta = 0.10$, n.s)."

"In order to test the hypothesis of whether psychological empowerment and core self-evaluations sequentially mediate the impact of authentic leadership on employee proactive behavior, we performed a sequential mediation analyses (Model 6 as described in PROCESS, 10,000) with bootstrapping methods."

"While testing for sequential multiple mediation, the specific indirect effect of authentic leadership on employee proactive behavior through both psychological empowerment and core self-evaluations is found to be significant with a point estimate of 0.0076 and a 95% confidence interval between 0.0004 and 0.0251, providing full support for Hypothesis 5."

Discussion

"Analysis of data from 275 subordinate-supervisor dyads at two private companies in China shows that the seven hypotheses about the influence of authentic leadership on employee proactive behavior through the sequential mediating effects of psychological empowerment and core-self evaluations, and the moderating effect of political skill are verified."

"The results indicate that psychological empowerment and core self-evaluations not only exert a mediating role, but also sequentially mediate the relationship between authentic leadership and employee proactive behavior."

"In order to gain a better understanding of the boundary conditions by which authentic leadership exerts its influence, we explore the moderating role of employee political skill and find that political skill positively moderates the relation between core self-evaluations and proactive behavior."

"From the perspective of SDT, this study finds that psychological empowerment and core self-evaluations play a sequential mediating role in the relationship between authentic leadership and proactive behavior."

Conclusion

"Based on SDT, this research excavates the psychological mechanism through which authentic leadership is positively related to employee proactive behavior, and we find that psychological empowerment and core self-evaluations play a mediating role respectively and sequentially."

"Empirical evidence also indicates the moderating effect of employee political skill in the relationship between core self-evaluations and proactive behavior."

"Despite the limitations of this paper, we offer some valuable contributions to the discussion on authentic leadership and proactive behavior."

How Does the Needs-Supplies Fit of Developmental Job Experience Affect Employees' Proactive Behavior? [181]

This is a machine-generated summary of:

Chen, Qishan; Li, Miaosi; Fan, Honglan: How does the needs-supplies fit of developmental job experience affect employees' proactive behavior? [181]

Published in: Asia Pacific Journal of Management (2023)

Link to original: https://doi.org/10.1007/s10490-023-09894-5

Copyright of the summarized publication:

The Author(s), under exclusive licence to Springer Science+Business Media, LLC, part of Springer Nature 2023

Copyright comment: Springer Nature or its licensor (e.g. a society or other partner) holds exclusive rights to this article under a publishing agreement with the author(s) or other rightsholder(s); author self-archiving of the accepted manuscript version of this article is solely governed by the terms of such publishing agreement and applicable law.

All rights reserved.

If you want to cite the papers, please refer to the original.

For technical reasons we could not place the page where the original quote is coming from.

Abstract-Summary

"Based on person-organization fit and social exchange theory, this study investigates the effect of the needs-supplies fit of developmental job experience (DJE) on proactive behavior and explores the mediating role of affective organizational commitment (AOC)."

"The results show that different fit combinations between individuals' needs for DJE and organizations' supplies affect proactive behavior."

"The effect of the needs-supplies fit of DJE on the different foci of proactive behavior is different."

"As hypothesized, the relationship between the needs-supplies fit of DJE and proactive behavior is mediated by AOC."

Theoretical Background and Hypothesis Development

"According to social exchange theory (Cropanzano & Mitchell [130]), employees who receive what they need in the workplace become satisfied with their work and feel obligated to help the organization that has benefited them, which means that the match between the supply and need of DJE can promote the motivational behavior of employees."

"Based on POF theory (Kristof-Brown & others [131]) and social exchange theory (Cropanzano & Mitchell [130]), we argue that the needs-supplies fit of DJE influences employees' proactive behavior through their attitudes toward the organization, i.e., AOC."

"We propose the following hypothesis: The relationship between the needs-supplies fit of DJE and proactive behavior is mediated by employees' AOC."

"We propose the following hypothesis: The relationship between the needs-supplies fit of DJE and (a) organizational proactive behavior and (b) interpersonal proactive behavior is mediated by employees' AOC."

Methods

"We surveyed participants about their demographic variables (e.g., age and education) and the supply of and need for DJE at Time (1)."

"The Cronbach's alpha coefficients on the needs and supplies of the scale in this study were 0.82 and 0.74, respectively."

"We created a polynomial regression model according to the following equations: where Z represents proactive behavior and S and N represent the supplies and needs of DJE."

"If the slope of the fit line ($b_1 + b_2$) is significantly positive, the dependent variables are higher when the supplies and needs are both at high levels than when they are at low levels."

"If the slope of the misfit line (b_1-b_2) is significantly positive, it indicates that high supplies and low needs have a better level of dependent variables than low supplies and high needs."

Results

"The slope of the N = S fit line ($b_1 + b_2$) is significantly positive (slope = 0.37, p < 0.01), and proactive behavior is higher when supplies and needs are both at a high level than when they are at a low level."

"The slope of the N = -S misfit line (b_1-b_2) is significantly negative (slope = -0.46, p < 0.01), indicating that employees show more proactive behavior when their needs exceed supplies than when supplies exceed needs."

"The results showed that AOC mediated the positive relationship between the needs-supplies fit of DJE and organizational proactive behavior ($\beta 1 = 0.18$, p < 0.001; $\beta 2 = 0.54$, p < 0.001; mediated effect = 0.10; 95% CI: [0.04, 0.18]), interpersonal proactive behavior ($\beta 1 = 0.20$, p < 0.001; $\beta 2 = 0.55$, p < 0.001; mediated effect = 0.11; 95% CI: [0.05, 0.18])."

Discussion

"From the POF perspective, this study examined the impact of the needs-supplies fit of DJE on employees' proactive behavior based on social exchange theory and explored the role of AOC."

"The results showed that different combinations of fit between individuals' needs and organizations' supplies of DJE affect proactive behavior through AOC, and this effect depends on the different foci of proactive behavior."

"When supplies cannot satisfy their needs, employees may actively participate in more proactive behavior, hoping that organizations see their contributions and return more supplies of DJE."

"As the first study to explore the relationship between the needs-supplies fit of DJE and proactive behavior, the results of this study contribute to our understanding of the positive effect of DJE."

"Our findings show that the needs-supplies fit of DJE influences employees' organizational proactive behavior and interpersonal proactive behavior through AOC, which are other-oriented outcomes that mainly benefit organizations."

[Section 5]

"This study also aims to explore how the needs-supplies fit of DJE affects employees' proactive behavior."

"Based on social exchange theory (Cook & others [132]; Cropanzano & Mitchell [130]), this study proposes a mediating model to test the role of affective organizational commitment (AOC) between the needs-supplies fit of DJE and proactive behavior."

"This study adopts needs-supplies fit perspective to systematically examine the effects of different fitting situations between the individual's needs of DJE and what is supplied by organizations."

"We introduce AOC into the research framework as a mediator to explain the motivational process of the needs-supplies fit of DJE on proactive behavior based on social exchange theory and to further clarify the motivation behind different proactive behaviors."

"AOC relies on individuals' perceptions of the exchange relationship between themselves and the organization and can serve as a bridge between the needs-supplies fit of DJE and different foci of proactive behaviors."

The Effects of Job Involvement and Supervisor Developmental Feedback on Employee Creativity: A Polynomial Regression with Response Surface Analysis [182]

This is a machine-generated summary of:

Li, Guangping; Xie, Lei: The effects of job involvement and supervisor developmental feedback on employee creativity: A polynomial regression with response surface analysis [182]

Published in: Current Psychology (2022)

Link to original: https://doi.org/10.1007/s12144-022-02901-w

Copyright of the summarized publication:

The Author(s), under exclusive licence to Springer Science+Business Media, LLC, part of Springer Nature 2022

All rights reserved.

If you want to cite the papers, please refer to the original.

For technical reasons we could not place the page where the original quote is coming from.

Abstract-Summary

"This paper aims to explore how job involvement and supervisor developmental feedback (SDF) interact to affect employee creativity."

"The two studies confirmed a dynamic relationship among these three variables (i.e., job involvement, SDF, and creativity)."

"The polynomial regression results indicated that employee creativity peaks when job involvement and SDF are both high."

"When job involvement is low but SDF is high, or vice versa, employee creativity is at a high level as well."

Introduction

"Further, during the novelty seeking process, SDF helps employees develop and improve their creativity-relevant ideas and thus facilitate employees' creative behavior (Hon [134])."

"In a fit environment, employees may feel empowered and take advantage of SDF to improve their creative processes."

"We provided a brief literature review to substantiate our argument regarding the connections between job involvement, SDF, and employee creativity, and here we explain why we choose to use the method of polynomial regression analysis with response surface by examining the effect of the interaction term of job involvement and SDF on creativity."

"Different from traditional moderation studies, by which the researcher attempts to explain in what condition the focus predictor demonstrates a statistical relationship with the outcome variable (Aiken & others [135]; Wu & Zumbo [136]), we treat the effect of job involvement and SDF on creativity indiscriminately."

Theoretical Background and Hypothesis Development

"Based on the tenets of P-S fit theory, we argue that a fit between supervisors and employees (i.e., job involvement and perceived SDF are both high) is needed to achieve optimal creativity and that a misfit would produce inferior performance."

"When SDF and job involvement are both low, meaning that the employees are not psychologically attached to the organization, and the supervisor pays less attention to the development of the employee, creativity is less likely to be high because novelty seeking needs motivation and a clear guidance (Zhou [137])."

"In the other P-S misfit situation, when SDF is high and job involvement is low, employees may demonstrate inferior performance."

"H4: When the discrepancy between the ratings of job involvement and supervisor developmental feedback increase (job involvement is high but SDF is low or SDF is high but job involvement is low), employee creativity decreases."

Methods

"Our polynomial regression model is as follows: The outcome variable Z represents employee creativity, X is the predictor job involvement, and Y is the employee's perception of SDF."

"For the response surface analysis, we specifically focused on interpreting two lines (X = Y, line of congruence; X = -Y, line of incongruence) to investigate the dynamic relationship among job involvement, SDF, and creativity."

"Job involvement is also moderately correlated with SDF as predicted (r = 0.37, p < 0.01), justifying the use of polynomial regression analysis to test curvilinear effects (Dawson [138])."

"Confirmatory factor analysis was conducted and the results revealed that the four-factor measurement model ($\chi^2/62 = 259.61$ p < 0.001, RMSEA = 0.09 CFI = 0.94, TLI = 0.93, SRMR = 0.06) did not show a better fit to the data than the three-factor (job involvement, SDF, and creativity) measurement model."

Discussion

"Study 1 demonstrated that both job involvement and SDF interact with creativity in the workplace such that when job involvement and SDF are high and congruent (on the X = Y line), employee creativity is high, and when there is a discrepancy between job involvement and SDF (P-E misfit; on the X = -Y line), employee creativity increases more sharply as the discrepancy increases (on a convex surface)."

"If the results from Study 2 generate a similar pattern among these three variables, the contribution to the field of creativity is substantial given the multi-study research design examining the dynamic relationships among job involvement, SDF, and employee creativity."

"The results were the same as Study 1: job involvement and SDF were positively correlated (r = 0.25, p < 0.01); job involvement was positively connected with employee creativity (r = 0.24 p < 0.01)."

General Discussion

"The regression results also showed that employee creativity increases when there is a misfit between employees' job involvement and SDF."

"Previous research has confirmed the important role of each variable (i.e., job involvement and SDF) in creativity separately, but our work integrated the two aspects of employees' organizational life and connected them with their creative on-the-job behavior."

"From the two studies, we found that job involvement and supervisor support together exert an influence on employee creativity."

"This particular finding indicated that job involvement and SDF are strong positive predictors of employee creativity respectively, which is in line with previous research (Koberg & Chusmir [139]; Zhou [137])."

"When the supervisor offers candid and frequent developmental feedback, employee creativity increases, in spite of one's decrease in degree of involvement (level of involvement does not moderate the effect of SDF on creativity)."

Theoretical Implications

"Following Shanock and others's [133] suggestions, we built on P-S fit theory to connect job involvement and SDF with creativity."

"Our findings demonstrate that when job involvement and SDF are not in congruence (P-S misfit), employee creativity increases and incongruence enlarges."

"In a complex organizational environment, employees' personal attitude (job involvement) and external environment (SDF in this case) both significantly impact the outcome for employees (creativity in this study)."

"Despite the strong effect of job involvement or SDF on creativity, when they are in congruence (P-E fit), employee creativity peaks."

Practical Implication

"And foremost, job involvement and SDF are both important to employee creativity in the high-technology industry."

"Employees need to work in a fit environment to achieve high creativity with supervisor support."

"For high-technology companies, the best strategy to increase employee creativity is to identify self-motived employees and encourage them by offering developmental feedback from their supervisors simultaneously."

"Analyzing data from two distinct samples, the results suggest that, if possible, a balance between job involvement and supervisor feedback generates the best results in terms of employees' creative behavior."

Limitations

"Although the data did not suffer from a serious CMV issue, the data were collected at the same point in time in each study."

"Future data could be obtained using a longitudinal study design."

"This data collection method would increase the accuracy of the complete view of the dynamic relationship between employees and their supervisors."

"Future research could consider replicating this study in a non-Eastern cultural society."

You Are "Insisting", or You Want to "Withdraw"? Research on the Negative Effect of Ethical Leadership on Leaders Themselves [183]

This is a machine-generated summary of:
Qi, He; Jingtao, Fu; Wenhao, Wu; Pervaiz, Sabeeh: You are "insisting", or you want to "withdraw"? Research on the negative effect of ethical leadership on leaders themselves [183]
Published in: Current Psychology (2022)
Link to original: https://doi.org/10.1007/s12144-022-03433-z
Copyright of the summarized publication:
The Author(s), under exclusive licence to Springer Science+Business Media, LLC, part of Springer Nature 2022.
Copyright comment: Springer Nature or its licensor holds exclusive rights to this article under a publishing agreement with the author(s) or other rightsholder(s); author self-archiving of the accepted manuscript version of this article is solely governed by the terms of such publishing agreement and applicable law.
All rights reserved.
If you want to cite the papers, please refer to the original.
For technical reasons we could not place the page where the original quote is coming from.

Abstract-Summary

"Based on resource conservation theory and implicit leadership theory, this research instead focuses on the negative effect of ethical leadership on leaders themselves through leader emotional exhaustion under the condition of employee followership, therefore leader psychological withdrawal (resource loss spiral)."

"The results of the stuy are: (1) Ethical leadership links to growing leader emotional exhaustion; (2) Leader emotional exhaustion associates with intensified leader psychological withdrawal; (3) Leader emotional exhaustion mediates the relation between ethical leadership and leader psychological withdrawal; (4) Employee followership reversely moderates the effect of ethical leadership on leader emotional exhaustion; (5) Employee followership reversely moderates the effect of ethical leadership on leader psychological withdrawal through leader emotional exhaustion."

"This research interpretates the mechanism and boundary condition for the negative effects of ethical leadership on leaders themselves."

Introduction

"In order to further expand the empirical and theoretical research of ethical leadership, this research aims to answer these following questions: (1) Does ethical leadership have a negative effect on leaders themselves due to resource loss spiral? (2) Are there any boundary conditions for ethical leadership negatively affecting leaders themselves?"

"Although some scholars have shifted the research focus of ethical leadership from employees to leaders (Lin & others [140]), they ignored employees' cognitive process and the fact that leadership effectiveness requires employees' support to achieve goals (Shkoler & others [141])."

"Based on resource conservation theory and implicit leadership theory, this research will examine the effect of resource acquisition spiral generated by employee followership on ethical leadership, and explore the role of employee followership in the process of ethical leadership negatively affecting leaders themselves."

"It has been verified by previous researches that leader characteristic moderates the effect of ethical leadership (Presbitero & others [142])."

"Different from previous research that focused on the interpersonal effects of ethical leadership (Zhong & others [143]), this research will examine the negative effect of ethical leadership on leaders themselves and fits the nature of resource loss spiral in resource conservation theory (Kammeyer-Mueller & others [144])."

Literature Review

"Employees regard ethical leaders as models and voluntarily assume responsibilities and obligations, even contribute more to the organizational development by extending their area of responsibility (Liang [145])."

"Based on the framework of self-determination theory (Ryan & others [146]), the above research findings are dissected by social learning theory (Bandura [80]), social exchange theory (Law & others [147]), social identity theory (Tajfel [148]), and other mechanisms to explain the positive effect of ethical leadership on employees: (1) By delivering ethical values and relevant behavioral rules, ethical leaders awaken employees' ethical thinking, cultivate their positive self-view and ethical realm (Koopman & others [149]), satisfying employees' essential requirements for self-realization. (2) Ethical leaders believe in virtues and abide by ethical guidelines (Li & others [150]), emphasize the importance of accomplishing tasks to achieve organizational goals, forming a strong appeal to employees from both rational and perceptual aspects (Haller & others [151]), as well as acquiesce rights and obligations on the basis of mutual benefit, endue employees work interest to stimulate their spiritual needs and intrinsic motivation. (3) In addition, ethical leaders bravely promote their true inner feelings and ideas."

"Ethical managers show ethical courage and legitimate beliefs out of the self-concept of justice and kindness, setting an example of ethical sentiment and personality charm, then exert their role in the process of contacting with employees, such as enrich employees' psychological needs and spiritual gains, inspire their ethical awareness and work intentions (Jordan & others [152])."

Theoretical Hypothesis

"The research discussed the relation among ethical leadership (ethical character, ethical drive, ethical sentiment, and ethical vision), leader emotional exhaustion, leader psychological withdrawal through leader's resource loss spiral, as well as the moderating role of employees' followership from the perspective of leader's resource acquisition spiral."

"If leaders cannot prevent resource loss because of ethical leadership, they are prone to generate low emotional states, such as emotional exhaustion, strengthen negative resource processing strategies rather than the motivation to obtain effective compensation, which will induce slack awareness and declining work attitude away from workplace (Chi & others [153]) to alleviate the discomfort caused by threatening environment through hidden psychological activities."

"This research proposes following hypothesis: Employee followership moderates the positive effect of ethical leadership on leader emotional exhaustion."

"This research proposes following hypothesis: Employee followership moderates the indirect positive effect of ethical leadership on leader psychological withdrawal through leader emotional exhaustion."

Research Method

"In order to avoid leaders' report of their ethical leadership willingness or over-evaluation of their ethical leadership level, this research asked them to rate the ethical leadership style they have actually demonstrated, and the Cronbach's alpha reliability coefficient is 0.87."

"This research mainly referred to the Job Burnout Scale compiled by Maslach and others [154], 6 items of emotional exhaustion dimension with a Cronbach's alpha reliability coefficient of 0.90 was selected to reflect leader's perception of his own emotional exhaustion state at work."

"This research used 4 items of psychological withdrawal dimension reserved by Yu and others [155] with a Cronbach's alpha reliability coefficient of 0.91, reflecting leader's work withdrawal from psychological perspective."

"This research followed Deng's [156] recommendation and required the leaders to report the overall perception of employees' followership based on the aforementioned 5 items, then obtained a Cronbach's alpha reliability coefficient of 0.76."

Hypothesis Testing

"Significance level of chi-square test is greater than 0.05 in terms of gender, position, and industry for ethical leadership, leader emotional exhaustion, leader psychological withdrawal, and employee followerhip."

"Significance level of one-way analysis of variance is greater than 0.05 in terms of age and tenure for ethical leadership, leader emotional exhaustion, leader psychological withdrawal, and employee followerhip, which indicates no significant differences."

"Before conducting hypothesis testing, confirmatory factor analysis of ethical leadership, leader emotional exhaustion, leader psychological withdrawal, and employee followership was carried out to evaluate the fitting effect."

"From Model 4, the interactive item of ethical leadership and employee followership has a negative and significant effect on leader emotional exhaustion (β=-0.15, p < .05), while ethical leadership has a positive and significant effect on leader emotional exhaustion ($\beta = 0.25$, p < .001)."

"Employee followership moderates the indirect positive effect of ethical leadership on leader psychological withdrawal through leader emotional exhaustion."

Results Discussion

"Based on resource conservation theory, this research explores the negative effect of ethical leadership on leaders themselves, revealing that ethical leadership can cause leader emotional exhaustion and psychological withdrawal."

"Based on implicit leadership theory, this research explores the boundary role of employee followership in the negative effect of ethical leadership on leaders themselves."

"This research explores the negative effect of ethical leadership on leaders themselves by introducing employee followership as a boundary condition."

"This research focuses on exploring the negative effect of ethical leadership on leaders themselves, and takes employee followership as the moderating variable to include both leader and employees in the theoretical model."

"This research differentiate itself by exploring the negative effect of ethical leadership on leaders themselves rather than on the interpersonal influence on employees."

Conclusions

"Although ethical leadership has widely recognized positive significance, based on resource conservation theory and implicit leadership theory, this research reveals that ethical leadership will also bring resource loss spiral to leaders themselves, and the occurrence of its negative effects depends on the reconciliation degree between the leader's demostration and the employee's expectation."

"The results of this research not only break the conventional ethical leadership thinking and the weak thinking of employees, but also inspire future scholars to weigh the advantages and disadvantages of ethical leadership, also gradually form a management awareness of the complementary relationship between leaders and employees."

Emotional Intelligence as a Moderator of Affectivity/ Emotional Labor and Emotional Labor/Psychological Distress Relationships [184]

This is a machine-generated summary of:
Karim, Jahanvash; Weisz, Robert: Emotional Intelligence as a Moderator of Affectivity/Emotional Labor and Emotional Labor/Psychological Distress Relationships [184]
Published in: Psychological Studies (2011)
Link to original: https://doi.org/10.1007/s12646-011-0107-9
Copyright of the summarized publication:
National Academy of Psychology (NAOP) India 2011
All rights reserved.
If you want to cite the papers, please refer to the original.
For technical reasons we could not place the page where the original quote is coming from.

Abstract-Summary

"Emotional labor refers to effort, planning, and control required to display organizationally desired emotions during interpersonal transactions and performed by individuals either through deep acting or surface acting."

"We found that (a) regulation of emotion was a particularly important emotional intelligence dimension in influencing the use of deep acting, both directly and indirectly through the interaction with negative affectivity; (b) positive affectivity emerged as an important affectivity dimension in influencing the use of deep acting both directly and indirectly through the interaction with self-emotional appraisal; (c) negative affectivity was a particularly important affectivity dimension in influencing the use of surface acting, both directly and indirectly through its interaction with emotional intelligence dimensions of self-emotional appraisal and use of emotion; and finally (d) regulation of emotion interacted with deep acting to influence the psychological distress arising from EL requirements."

Objectives of Study

"Because of the previously mentioned findings regarding EI and EL, it is expected that one or more of these components provide an individual the ability to the use of SA or DA."

"Because of the previously mentioned findings regarding EI and strain, burnout, or psychological distress, it is expected that one or more of these components provide an individual the ability to evade psychological distress related to one's perceptions of EL."

"We describe the research design and methodology of the study we have undertaken to examine the relationships among EI, EL, affectivity, and psychological distress."

"We analyze the findings of our study, and in the final section we discuss the implications of considering the relationship among EI, EL, affectivity, and psychological distress."

Conceptual Framework

"According to Liu and others [157], people low in emotional resources (as indicated by high NA), when required to perform EL, are likely to use strategies associated with lower immediate resource investment, which is SA."

"According to Liu and others [157], employees rich in (emotional) resources (indicated by high EI and low NA) are likely to use strategies associated with potential gain (i.e., D.A), "both because they can afford the loss if it occurs, and because they are less likely to incur resource loss and more likely to ensure resource gain" (p. 2417)."

"Hypothesis 1a: The individual components of EI (self-emotional appraisal, others' emotional appraisal, use of emotion, and regulation of emotion) will moderate the relationship between PA and EL."

"Hypothesis 1b: The individual components of EI (self-emotional appraisal, others' emotional appraisal, use of emotion, and regulation of emotion) will moderate the relationship between NA and SA."

Method

"Affectivity was measured by 20 items Positive and Negative Affect Schedule (PANAS) (Watson & others [158])."

"PANAS is composed of two ten-item mood scales; one to measure positive affectivity and the other to measure negativity affectivity."

"Psychological distress was measured by Chan's [159] 20 items scale."

"Respondents were requested to rate each symptom statement on a 5-point scale (not at all to extremely) by comparing themselves during the past 2 weeks with their 'usual selves'."

"SA was measured by three items adopted from Grandey's [160] emotional labor scale."

"The sample items include, "I just pretend to have the emotions I need to display for my job"."

"DA was measured by three items adopted from Brotheridgen and Lee [161] emotional labor scale."

"The sample items include, "I make an effort to actually feel the emotions that I need to display to others"."

Results

"EI dimensions of UOE and ROE, and PA were negatively related to psychological distress, whereas SA and NA correlated positively with Psychological distress."

"When predicting EL strategies (i.e., DA and SA), affectivity (PA and NA) and the four EI dimensions were entered into the equation first (step 1)."

"Eight interaction terms (four EI dimensions * PA and NA) were entered into the second step."

"Significant correlates of DA included the ROE dimension of EI, the PA dimension of affectivity, the interaction between SEA and PA, the interaction between OEA and NA, and the interaction between ROE and NA."

"Significant correlates of SA included the NA dimension of affectivity, the interaction between SEA and NA, and the interaction between UOE and NA."

"Significant correlates of psychological distress included the UOE dimension of EI, SA, the interaction between ROE and DA, and the interaction between SEA and SA."

Discussion

"The results of this study provide evidence to represent some EI dimensions moderating the relationship between affectivity and EL strategies (DA and SA), as well as a positive influence in alleviating strain resulting from the use of EL strategies."

"Correlation results indicated that, university teachers high on PA are more likely to engage in DA, because these individuals are predisposed to positive emotions and they can easily change their internal feelings via DA strategy than to suppress/fake emotions through SA (e.g., Brotheridge & Grandey [162]; Brotheridge & Lee [163]; Johnson [164])."

"The significant relationship between PA and DA in regression analysis suggests that university teachers high on PA prefer to use DA because they are usually predisposed to experience positive emotions, so on the occasions when they experience negative emotions (e.g., handling a difficult student) that conflict with class/organizational display rules, they are more likely to transform their feelings via deep acting than to provide fake expression via surface acting."

"We found that university teachers high on emotional resources (EI and PA) are more likely to use DA."

[Section 6]

"Further to this, there is a paucity of studies that examine the extent to which individual components of EI construct (such as, perception of emotion, understanding of emotion, and regulation of emotion) are related to different EL strategies (i.e., DA and SA) and whether EI components moderate the relationship between affectivity and EL strategies."

"Although, previous studies have suggested that EI may moderate the relationship between EL and various organizational behavior outcomes (e.g., Abraham [165]; Giardini & Frese [166]; Jordan & others [167]; Morris & Feldman [168]; Rubin & others [169]) but there is a paucity of studies that examine the extent to which different dimensions of the EI construct independently may serve to alleviate negative outcomes (i.e., psychological distress) associated with perceptions of EL."

Bibliography

1. Goodwin, R. E., Groth, M., & Frenkel, S. J. (2011). Relationships between emotional labor, job performance, and turnover. *Journal of Vocational Behavior, 79*(2), 538–548. https://doi.org/10.1016/j.jvb.2011.03.001
2. Scriven, A. (2017). *Promoting health: A practical guide-e-book: Ewles & Simnett*. Elsevier Health Sciences.
3. Hollenbeck, J. R., Moon, H., Ellis, A. P. J., West, B. J., Ilgen, D. R., Sheppard, L., et al. (2002). Structural contingency theory and individual differences: Examination of external and internal person-team fit. *Journal of Applied Psychology, 87*(3), 599–606.
4. Cavazotte, F., Moreno, V., & Hickmann, M. (2012). Effects of leader intelligence, personality and emotional intelligence on transformational leadership and managerial performance. *The Leadership Quarterly, 23*(3), 443–455.
5. Wong, C. S., & Law, K. S. (2002). The effects of leader and follower emotional intelligence on performance and attitude: An exploratory study. *The Leadership Quarterly, 13*(3), 243–274.
6. Zhang, Z., Wang, M., & Shi, J. (2012). Leader-follower congruence in proactive personality and work outcomes: The mediating role of leader-member exchange. *Academy of Management Journal, 55*(1), 111–130.
7. Pieterse, A. N., Van Knippenberg, D., & Van Dierendonck, D. (2013). Cultural diversity and team performance: The role of team member goal orientation. *Academy of Management Journal, 56*(3), 782–804.
8. Salovey, P., & Mayer, J. D. (1990). Emotional intelligence. *Imagination, Cognition and Personality, 9*(3), 185–211.
9. Mayer, J. D., Caruso, D. R., & Salovey, P. (1999). Emotional intelligence meets traditional standards for an intelligence. *Intelligence, 27,* 267–298.
10. Salovey, P., Woolery, A., & Mayer, J. D. (2001). Emotional intelligence: Conceptualization and measurement. In G. J. O. Fletcher & M. S. Clark (Eds.), *Blackwell Handbook of Social Psychology: Interpersonal Processes* (pp. 279–307). Blackwell.
11. Bar-On, R. (1997). *Bar-On emotional quotient inventory: A measure of emotional intelligence.* Multi-Health Systems Inc.

Bibliography

12. Salovey, P., Mayer, J. D., Goldman, S. L., Turvey, C., & Palfai, T. (1995). Emotional attention, clarity and repair: Exploring emotional intelligence using the Trait Meta-Mood Scale. In J. W. Pennebacker (Eds.), *Emotion, disclosure, and health*. American Psychological Association.
13. Schmidt, F. L., & Hunter, J. E. (1998). The validity and utility of selection methods in personnel psychology: Practical and theoretical implications of 85 years of research findings. *Psychological Bulletin, 124*, 262–274.
14. Law, K. S., Wong, C.-S., & Song, L. J. (2004). The construct and criterion validity of emotional intelligence and its potential utility for management studies. *Journal of Applied Psychology, 89*(3), 483–496. https://doi.org/10.1037/0021-9010.89.3.483
15. Rosete, D., & Ciarrochi, J. (2005). Emotional intelligence and its relationship to workplace performance outcomes of leadership effectiveness. *Leadership & Organization Development Journal, 26*(5), 388–399. https://doi.org/10.1108/01437730510607871
16. Wong, C. S., Wong, P. M., & Law, K. S. (2007). Evidence on the practical utility of Wong's emotional intelligence scale in Hong Kong and Mainland China. *Asia Pacific Journal of Management, 24*(1), 43–60.
17. Rozin, P., Lowery, L., Imada, S., & Haidt, J. (1999). The CAD triad hypothesis: A mapping between three moral emotions (contempt, anger, disgust) and three moral codes (community, autonomy, divinity). *Journal of Personality and Social Psychology, 76*(4), 574–586.
18. Wispé, L. (1986). The distinction between sympathy and empathy: To call forth a concept, a word is needed. *Journal of Personality and Social Psychology, 50*(2), 314–321.
19. George, J. M. (1991). State or trait: Effects of positive mood on prosocial behaviors at work. *Journal of Applied Psychology, 76*(2), 299–307.
20. Hendriks, M., & Vingerhoets, A. (2006). Social messages of crying faces: Their influence on anticipated person perception, emotions and behavioral responses. *Cognition and Emotion, 20*(6), 878–886.
21. Bono, J. E., & Ilies, R. (2006). Charisma, positive emotions and mood contagion. *The Leadership Quarterly, 17*(4), 317–334.
22. Johnson, S. K. (2008). I second that emotion: Effects of emotional contagion and affect at work on leader and follower outcomes. *The Leadership Quarterly, 19*(1), 1–19.
23. Visser, V. A., Van Knippenberg, D., Van Kleef, G. A., & Wisse, B. (2013). How leader displays of happiness and sadness influence follower performance: Emotional contagion and creative versus analytical performance. *The Leadership Quarterly, 24*(1), 172–188.
24. Hsee, C. K., Hatfield, E., Carlson, J. G., & Chemtob, C. (1990). The effect of power on susceptibility to emotional contagion. *Cognition and Emotion, 4*(4), 327–340.
25. Sullins, E. S. (1991). Emotional contagion revisited: Effects of social comparison and expressive style on mood convergence. *Personality and Social Psychology Bulletin, 17*(2), 166–174.
26. Mathieu, J. E., & Taylor, S. R. (2006). Clarifying conditions and decision points for mediational type inferences in organizational behavior. *Journal of Organizational Behavior, 27*(8), 1031–1056.
27. Damen, F., Van Knippenberg, B., & Van Knippenberg, D. (2008). Affective match in leadership: Leader emotional displays, follower positive affect, and follower performance. *Journal of Applied Social Psychology, 38*(4), 868–902.
28. Gaddis, B., Connelly, S., & Mumford, M. D. (2004). Failure feedback as an affective event: Influences of leader affect on subordinate attitudes and performance. *The Leadership Quarterly, 15*(5), 663–686.
29. Glomb, T. M., & Hulin, C. L. (1997). Anger and gender effects in observed supervisor-subordinate dyadic interactions. *Organizational Behavior and Human Decision Processes, 72*(3), 281–307.
30. Hatfield, E., Cacioppo, J., & Rapson, R. L. (1994). *Emotional contagion*. Cambridge University Press.
31. Barsade, S. G. (2002). The ripple effect: Emotional contagion and its influence on group behavior. *Administrative Science Quarterly, 47*(4), 644–675.

32. McMahon, L. (2000). Bullying and harassment in the workplace. *International Journal of Contemporary Hospitality Management, 12*(6), 384–397.
33. Sheehan, M., & Jordan, P. J. (2000, November 16–17). *The antecedents and implications of workplace bullying: A bounded emotionality analysis.* Paper presented at the Annual Conference of the Association Francophone de Gestion des Ressources Humaines (AGRH).
34. Lindy, C., & Schaefer, F. (2010). Negative workplace behaviours: An ethical dilemma for nurse managers. *Journal of Nursing Management, 18*(3), 285–292.
35. Pate, J., & Beaumont, P. (2010). Bullying and harassment: A case of success? *Employee Relations, 32*(2), 171–183.
36. Stogstad, A., Torsheim, T., Einarsen, S., & Hauge, L. J. (2011). Testing the work environment hypothesis of bullying on a group level of analysis: Psychological factors as precursors of observed workplace bullying. *Applied Psychology, 60*(3), 475–495.
37. Namie, G., & Namie, R. (2009). *The bully at work: What you can do to stop the hurt and reclaim your dignity on the job.* Sourcebooks.
38. Brotheridge, C. M., & Lee, R. T. (2010). Restless and confused: Emotional responses to workplace bullying in men and women. *Career Development International, 15*(7), 687–707.
39. Namie, G. (2003). Workplace bullying: Escalated incivility. *Ivey Business Journal, 68*(2), 1–6.
40. Cheema, S., Ahmad, K., Naqvi, S. A., Giri, S. K., & Kaliaperumal, V. K. (2005). Bullying of junior doctors prevails in Irish health system: A bitter reality. *Irish Medical Journal, 98*(9), 274–275.
41. Sheehan, M. (1999). Workplace bullying: Responding with some emotional intelligence. *International Journal of Manpower, 20*(1/2), 57–69.
42. Vickers, M. H. (2009). Bullying, disability and work: A case study of workplace bullying. *Qualitative Research in Organisations and Management, 4*(3), 255–272.
43. Fernández-Berrocal, P., & Extremera, N. (2006). Special issue on emotional intelligence: An overview. *Psicothema, 18*(Supplement), 1–6.
44. Townend, A. (2008). Understanding and addressing bullying in the workplace. *Industrial and Commercial Training, 40*(5), 270–273.
45. Sharma, D., Borna, S., & Stearns, J. M. (2009). An investigation of the effects of corporate ethical values on employee commitment and performance: Examining the moderating role of perceived fairness. *Journal of Business Ethics, 89*(2), 251–260.
46. Petrides, K. V., & Furnham, A. (2001). Trait emotional intelligence: Psychometric investigation with reference to established trait taxonomies. *European Journal of Personality, 15*(6), 425–448. https://doi.org/10.1002/per.416
47. Bar-On, R. (2005). The Bar-On model of emotional-social intelligence. Special issue on emotional intelligence. *Psicothema, 18*(Supplement), 13–25.
48. Boyatzis, R. E., & Saatcioglu, A. (2008). A 20-year view of trying to develop emotional, social and cognitive intelligence competencies in graduate management education. *Journal of Management Development, 27*(1), 92–108.
49. Jordan, P. J. (2005). Dealing with organisational change: Can emotional intelligence enhance organisational learning? *International Journal of Organisational Behaviour, 8*(1), 456–471.
50. Petrides, K. V., & Furnham, A. (2006). The role of trait emotional intelligence in a gender-specific model of organisational variables. *Journal of Applied Psychology, 36*(2), 552–569.
51. Petrides, K. V., Frederickson, N., & Furnham, A. (2004). The role of trait emotional intelligence in academic performance and deviant behaviour at school. *Personality and Individual Differences, 36*(2), 277–293.
52. Mavroveli, S., Petrides, K. V., Reiffe, C., & Bakker, F. (2007). Trait emotional intelligence, psychological well-being and peer-rated social competence in adolescence. *British Journal of Developmental Psychology, 25*(2), 263–275.
53. Petrides, K. V., Vernon, P. A., Schermer, J. A., Ligthart, L., Boomsma, D. I., & Vesellca, L. (2010). Relationships between trait emotional intelligence and the big five in the Netherlands. *Personality and Individual Differences, 48*, 906–910.

54. Wagner, D. T., & Ilies, R. (2008). Affective influences on employee satisfaction and performance. In N. M. Ashkanasy & C. L. Cooper (Eds.), *Research Companion to Emotion in Organisations* (pp. 152–169). Edward Elgar.
55. Blickle, G., et al. (2009). Job demands as a moderator of the political skill-job performance relationship. *Career Development International, 14*(4), 333–350.
56. Aiken, L. S., & West, S. G. (1991). *Multiple regression: Testing and interpreting interactions.* Sage.
57. Baron, R. M., & Kenny, D. A. (1986). The moderator–mediator variable distinction in social psychological research: Conceptual, strategic, and statistical considerations. *Journal of Personality and Social Psychology, 51*(6), 1173–1182.
58. Giorgi, G. (2010). Workplace bullying partially mediates the climate–health relationship. *Journal of Managerial Psychology, 25*(7), 727–740.
59. Carbo, J., & Hughes, A. (2010). Workplace bullying: Developing a human rights definition from the perspective and experiences of targets. *Working USA: The Journal of Labor and Society, 13*(3), 387–403.
60. Boddy, C. R. (2011). Corporate psychopaths, bullying and supervision in the workplace. *Journal of Business Ethics, 100*(3), 367–379.
61. Saam, N. J. (2010). Interventions in workplace bullying: A multilevel approach. *European Journal of Work and Organisational Psychology, 19*(1), 51–75.
62. Aguinis, H. (1995). Statistical power problems with moderated multiple regression in management research. *Journal of Management, 21*(6), 1141–1158.
63. Mathisen, G. E., Einarsen, S., & Reidar, M. (2011). The relationship between supervisor personality, supervisor's perceived stress and workplace bullying. *Journal of Business Ethics, 99*(4), 637–651.
64. Michelle, J., Phylavanh, P., & Brenda, J. (2010). The bullying aspect of workplace violence in nursing. *JONA's Healthcare Law, Ethics and Regulation, 12*(2), 36–42.
65. Van Scotter, J. R., & Motowidlo, S. J. (1996). Interpersonal facilitation and job dedication as separate facets of contextual performance. *Journal of Applied Psychology, 81*, 525–531.
66. Deluga, R. J., & Perry, J. T. (1994). The role of subordinate performance and ingratiation in leader-member exchanges. *Group and Organization Management, 19*, 67–86.
67. Dockery, T. M., & Steiner, D. D. (1990). The role of the initial interaction in leader-member exchange. *Group and Organization Studies, 15*, 395–413.
68. Simms, J. (2003, November 20). How to make it to the board. *Marketing*, pp. 27–28.
69. Baker, S., & Holt, S. (2004). Making marketers accountable: A failure of marketing education. *Marketing Intelligence and Planning, 22*(5), 557–567.
70. Doyle, P. (2000). Valuing marketing's contribution. *European Management Journal, 18*(2), 233–245.
71. Fisk, P. (2003, October 16). Be 'hard-edged' to impress CEOs. *Marketing*, p. 15.
72. Hadden, N., & Duckworth, G. (2005, December 7). What have they got that you haven't? *Marketing*, pp. 30–32.
73. Ambler, T. (2000). Marketing metrics. *Business Strategy Review, 11*, 59–66.
74. Campbell, L. (2000, February 25). New survey shows marketing is still undervalued. *Campaign*, p. 12.
75. McDonald, M. (2006). How to get marketing back in the boardroom. *Marketing Intelligence and Planning, 24*, 426–431.
76. Lu, C., Siu, O., & Cooper, C. (2005). Managers' occupational stress in China: The role of self-efficacy. *Personality and Individual Differences, 38*(4), 569–578.
77. Robbins, S. (1993). *Organisational Behaviour* (6th ed.). Prentice Hall International.
78. Rigotti, T., Schyns, B., & Mohr, G. (2008). A short version of the occupational self-efficacy scale: Structural and construct validity across five countries. *Journal of Career Assessment, 16*(2), 238–255.
79. Luthans, F., & Peterson, S. (2002). Employee engagement and manager self-efficacy. *Journal of Management Development, 21*(5), 376–387.

80. Bandura, A. (1977). Self-efficacy: Toward a unifying theory of behavioural change. *Psychological Review, 84*(2), 191–215.
81. Appelbaum, S., & Hare, A. (1996). Self-efficacy as a mediator of goal setting and performance: Some human resource implications. *Journal of Managerial Psychology, 11*(3), 33–47.
82. Barron, D. (1982). Extending managerial skills: A case from a telecommunications company. *Journal of Management Development, 1*(4), 61–67.
83. Bowman, C. (1999). Action-led strategy and managerial self-confidence. *Journal of Managerial Psychology, 14*(7/8), 558–568.
84. Gundlach, M., Martinko, M., & Douglas, S. (2003). Emotional intelligence, casual reasoning, and the self-efficacy development process. *International Journal of Organisational Analysis, 11*(3), 229–246.
85. Stajkovic, A., & Luthans, F. (1998). Social cognition theory and self-efficacy: Going beyond traditional motivational and behavioural approaches. *Organisational Dynamics, 26*(1), 62–74.
86. Orpen, C. (1999). The impact of self-efficacy on the effectiveness of employee training. *Journal of Workplace Learning, 11*(4), 119–122.
87. Bandura, A. (1991). Social cognitive theory of self-regulation. *Organisational Behaviour and Human Decision Processes, 50*(2), 248–287.
88. Mumford, A. (1994). Four approaches to learning from experience. *The Learning Organisation, 1*(1), 4–10.
89. Brown, K., & Ryan, R. (2004). Perils and promise in defining and measuring mindfulness: Observations from experience. *Clinical Psychology: Science and Practice, 11*, 242–248.
90. Baer, R., Smith, G., Hopkins, J., Krietemeyer, J., & Toney, L. (2006). Using self-report assessment methods to explore facets of mindfulness. *Assessment, 13*(1), 27–45.
91. Bishop, S., Lau, M., Shapiro, S., Carlson, L., Anderson, N., & Carmody, J. (2004). Mindfulness: A proposed operational definition. *Clinical Psychology: Science and Practice, 11*(3), 230–242.
92. Heuerman, T., & Olson, D. (2009). Organisational mindfulness. *Self Help*, pp. 1–5. http://selfhelpmagazine.com/article/node/825
93. Schenström, A., Rönnberg, S., & Bodlund, O. (2006). Mindfulness-based cognitive attitude training for primary care staff: A pilot study. *Complementary Health Practice Review, 11*(3), 144–152.
94. Marketing Magazine. (2007a, July 4). Careers: Salary snapshots, pp. 17–19.
95. Marketing Magazine. (2007b, October 30). Remembering that first job in marketing, pp. 1–2.
96. Marketing Week. (2009, January 16). The marketing week/ball and Hoolahan marketing salary survey 2009, pp. 2–12.
97. Hambrick, D., & Mason, P. (1984). Upper echelons: The organisation as a reflection of its top management. *Academy of Management Review, 9*(2), 193–206.
98. Geletkanycz, M., & Black, S. (2001). Bound by the past? Experience-based effects on commitment to the strategic status quo. *Journal of Management, 27*(1), 3–21.
99. Bennett, R. (2009). Reaching the board: Factors facilitating the progression of marketing executives to senior positions in British companies. *British Journal of Management, 20*(1), 30–54.
100. Robertson, I., & Sadri, G. (1993). Managerial self-efficacy and managerial performance. *British Journal of Management, 4*(1), 37–45.
101. Buchheld, N., Grossman, P., & Walach, H. (2001). Measuring mindfulness in insight meditation: The development of the Freiburg Mindfulness Inventory. *Journal for Meditation Research, 1*(1), 11–34.
102. Baer, R., Smith, G., & Allen, K. (2004). Assessment of mindfulness by self-report: The Kentucky inventory of mindfulness skills. *Assessment, 11*(3), 191–206.
103. Pehrsson, A. (2006). Business relatedness measurements: State of the art and a proposal. *European Business Review, 18*(5), 350–363.
104. Training Workforce. (2017, July 17). Training the workforce for industry 4.0. *The Star Online.* https://www.thestar.com.my/metro/smebiz/news/2017/07/17/training-the-workforce-for-industry-40. Accessed 11 December 2019.

Bibliography

105. Elliott, M., Dawson, R., & Edwards, J. (2009). Providing demonstrable return-on-investment for organisational learning and training. *Journal of European Industrial Training, 33*(7), 657–670. https://doi.org/10.1108/03090590910985408
106. Grover, S. L., Teo, S. T. T., Pick, D., Roche, M., & Newton, C. J. (2018). Psychological capital as a personal resource in the JD-R model. *Personnel Review, 47*(4), 968–984. https://doi.org/10.1108/PR-08-2016-0213
107. Bruning, P. F., & Campion, M. A. (2018). A role-resource approach-avoidance model of job crafting: A multimethod integration and extension of job crafting theory. *Academy of Management Journal, 61*(2), 499–522. https://doi.org/10.5465/amj.2015.0604
108. Luthans, F., Youssef, C. M., & Avolio, B. J. (2007). *Psychological capital: Developing the human competitive edge*. Oxford University Press.
109. Luthans, F., Avey, J. B., Avolio, B. J., & Peterson, S. J. (2010). The development and resulting performance impact of positive psychological capital. *Human Resource Development Quarterly, 21*(1), 41–67. https://doi.org/10.1002/hrdq.20034
110. Luthans, F., & Youssef-Morgan, C. M. (2017). Psychological Capital: An Evidence-Based Positive Approach. *In SSRN*. https://doi.org/10.1146/annurev-orgpsych-032516-113324
111. Zhang, F., & Parker, S. K. (2018). Reorienting job crafting research: A hierarchical structure of job crafting concepts and integrative review. *Journal of Organizational Behavior, 40*(2), 126–146. https://doi.org/10.1002/job.2332
112. Lazazzara, A., Tims, M., & de Gennaro, D. (2020). The process of reinventing a job: A meta-synthesis of qualitative job crafting research. *Journal of Vocational Behavior*, 116. https://doi.org/10.1016/j.jvb.2019.01.001
113. Yao, J., Qiu, X., Yang, L., Han, X., & Li, Y. (2022). The relationship between work engagement and job performance: Psychological capital as a moderating factor. *Frontiers in Psychology, 13*, 729131. https://doi.org/10.3389/fpsyg.2022.729131
114. Fayzhall, M., Asbari, M., Purwanto, A., Goestjahjanti, F. S., Yuwono, T., Radita, F. R., Yulia, Y., Cahyono, Y., & Suryani, P. (2020). Transformational versus Transactional Leadership: Manakah yang Mempengaruhi Kepuasan Kerja Guru? *EduPsyCouns: Journal of Education, Psychology and Counseling, 2*(1), 256–275. https://ummaspul.e-journal.id/Edupsycouns/article/view/463
115. Hutagalung, D., Asbari, M., Fayzhall, M., Ariyanto, E., Agistiawati, E., Sudiyono, R. N., Waruwu, H., Goestjahjanti, F. S., Winanti, & Yuwono, T. (2020). Peran Religiusitas, Kepemimpinan Transformasional, Kepuasan Kerja dan Mediasi Organizational Citizenship Behavior terhadap Kinerja Guru. *EduPsyCouns: Journal of Education, Psychology and Counseling, 2*(1), 311–326.
116. Mixdorf, J. C., Murali, D., Xin, Y., DiFilippo, A. H., Aluicio-Sarduy, E., Barnhart, T. E., Engle, J. W., Ellison, P. A., & Christian, B. T. (2021). Alternative strategies for the synthesis of [11C]ER176 for PET imaging of neuroinflammation. *Applied Radiation and Isotopes, 178*, 109954. https://doi.org/10.1016/j.apradiso.2021.109954
117. Holten, A. L., & Carneiro, L. G. (2018). A within-country study of leadership perceptions and outcomes across native and immigrant employees: Questioning the universality of transformational leadership. *Journal of Management & Organization, 24*(1), 145–162.
118. Khan, M. A. (2010). Effects of human resource management practices on organizational performance: An empirical study of oil and gas industry in Pakistan. *European Journal of Economics, Finance and Administrative Science, 24*(157–174), 6.
119. Li, Y. (2011). Emotions and new venture judgment in China. *Asia Pacific Journal of Management, 28*(2), 277–298.
120. Diefendorff, J. M., & Gosserand, R. H. (2003). Understanding the emotional labor process: A control theory perspective. *Journal of Organizational Behavior, 24*(8), 945–959.
121. Muraven, M., & Baumeister, R. F. (2000). Self-regulation and depletion of limited resources: Does self-control resemble a muscle? *Psychological Bulletin, 126*(2), 247–259.
122. Zapf, D., & Holz, M. (2006). On the positive and negative effects of emotion work in organizations. *European Journal of Work and Organizational Psychology, 15*(1), 1–28.

123. Ashforth, B. E., & Humphrey, R. H. (1993). Emotional labor in service roles: The influence of identity. *Academy of Management Review, 18*(1), 88–115.
124. Gosserand, R. H., & Diefendorff, J. M. (2005). Emotional display rules and emotional labor: The moderating role of commitment. *Journal of Applied Psychology, 90*(6), 1256–1264.
125. Rosen, C. C., Ferris, D. L., Brown, D. J., Chen, Y., & Yan, M. (2014). Perceptions of organizational politics: A need satisfaction paradigm. *Organization Science, 25*(4), 1026–1055.
126. Spreitzer, G. M. (1995). Psychological empowerment in the workplace: Dimensions, measurement, and validation. *Academy of Management Journal, 38*(5), 1442–1465.
127. Judge, T. A., Erez, A., Bono, J. E., & Thoresen, C. J. (2003). The core self-evaluations scale: Development of a measure. *Personnel Psychology, 56*(2), 303–331.
128. Yang, Z., Chen, Q., Zhu, Y., & Zeng, B. (2016). Is spiritual leadership one of the drivers of proactive behavior? Testing of a multiple mediating effects model. *Management Review, 28*(11), 191–202.
129. Ferris, G. R., Treadway, D. C., Kolodinsky, R. W., Hochwarter, W. A., Kacmar, C. J., Douglas, C., & Frink, D. D. (2005). Development and validation of the political skill inventory. *Journal of Management Official Journal of the Southern Management Association, 31*(1), 126–152.
130. Cropanzano, R., & Mitchell, M. S. (2005). Social exchange theory: An interdisciplinary review. *Journal of Management, 31*(6), 874–900.
131. Kristof-Brown, A. L., Zimmerman, R. D., & Johnson, E. C. (2005). Consequences of individual's fit at work: A meta-analysis of person-job, person-organization, person-group, and person-supervisor fit. *Personnel psychology, 58*(2), 281–342.
132. Cook, K. S., Cheshire, C., Rice, E. R., & Nakagawa, S. (2013). Social exchange theory. In J. Delamater & A. Ward (Eds.), *Handbook of social psychology* (pp. 61–88). Springer Science & Business Media.
133. Shanock, L. R., Baran, B. E., Gentry, W. A., Pattison, S. C., & Heggestad, E. D. (2010). Polynomial regression with response surface analysis: A powerful approach for examining moderation and overcoming limitations of difference scores. *Journal of Business and Psychology, 25*(4), 543–554.
134. Hon, A. H. (2012). Shaping environments conductive to creativity: The role of intrinsic motivation. *Cornell Hospitality Quarterly, 53*(1), 53–64.
135. Aiken, L. S., West, S. G., & Reno, R. R. (1991). *Multiple regression: Testing and interpreting interactions*. Sage.
136. Wu, A. D., & Zumbo, B. D. (2008). Understanding and using mediators and moderators. *Social Indicators Research, 87*(3), 367–392.
137. Zhou, J. (2003). When the presence of creative coworkers is related to creativity: Role of supervisor close monitoring, developmental feedback, and creative personality. *Journal of Applied Psychology, 88*(3), 413–422.
138. Dawson, J. F. (2014). Moderation in management research: What, why, when, and how. *Journal of Business and Psychology, 29*(1), 1–19.
139. Koberg, C. S., & Chusmir, L. H. (1987). Organizational culture relationships with creativity and other job-related variables. *Journal of Business Research, 15*(5), 397–409.
140. Lin, S. H., Ma, J., & Johnson, R. E. (2016). When ethical leader behavior breaks bad: How ethical leader behavior can turn abusive via ego depletion and moral licensing. *Journal of Applied Psychology, 101*(6), 815–830.
141. Shkoler, O., Tziner, A., Vasiliu, C., & Ghinea, C. N. (2021). Are positive and negative outcomes of organizational justice conditioned by leader-member exchange? *Amfiteatru Economic, 23*, 240–258.
142. Presbitero, A., & Teng-Calleja, M. (2019). Ethical leadership, team leader's cultural intelligence and ethical behavior of team members: Implications for managing human resources in global teams. *Personnel Review, 48*(5), 1381–1392.
143. Zhong, L. F., Meng, J., & Gao, L. (2019). The influence of moral leadership on employee innovation performance: The mediating role of social exchange and the moderating role of power distance orientation. *Management World, 35*(5), 149–160.

144. Kammeyer-Mueller, J. D., Simon, L. S., & Judge, T. A. (2016). A head start or a step behind? Understanding how dispositional and motivational resources influence emotional exhaustion. *Journal of Management, 42*(3), 561–581.
145. Liang, J. (2014). Ethical leadership and employee voice: Examining a moderated-mediation model. *Acta Psychologica Sinica, 46*(1), 1–13.
146. Ryan, R. M., & Deci, E. L. (2000). Self-determination theory and the facilitation of intrinsic motivation, social development, and well-being. *American Psychologist, 55*(1), 68–78.
147. Law, K. S., & Hackett, R. D. (2005). Leader-member exchange as a mediator of the relationship between transformational leadership and followers' performance and organizational citizenship behavior. *Academy of Management Journal, 48*(3), 420–432.
148. Tajfel, H. (1986). The social identity theory of intergroup behavior. *Political Psychology, 13*(3), 7–24.
149. Koopman, J., Scott, B. A., Matta, F. K., Conlon, D. E., & Dennerlein, T. (2019). Ethical leadership as a substitute for justice enactment: An information-processing perspective. *Journal of Applied Psychology, 104*(9), 1103–1116.
150. Li, C., & Bao, Y. (2020). Ethical leadership and positive work behaviors: A conditional process model. *Journal of Managerial Psychology, 35*(3), 155–168.
151. Haller, D. K., Peter, F., & Dieter, F. (2018). The power of good: A leader's personal power as a mediator of the ethical leadership-follower outcomes link. *Frontiers in Psychology, 9*, 1–21.
152. Jordan, J., Brown, M. E., Trevino, L. K., & Finkelstein, S. (2013). Someone to look up to: Executive-follower ethical reasoning and perceptions of ethical leadership. *Journal of Management, 39*(3), 660–683.
153. Chi, S. C. S., & Liang, S. G. (2013). When do subordinates' emotion-regulation strategies matter? Abusive supervision, subordinates' emotional exhaustion, and work withdrawal. *Leadership Quarterly, 24*(1), 125–137.
154. Maslach, C., Schaufeli, W. B., & Leiter, M. P. (2003). Job burnout. *Annual Review of Psychology, 52*(1), 397–422.
155. Yu, X. T., Chen, X., & Wang, H. (2019). Why does perceived dirty work lead to work withdrawal behavior? The mediating role of negative emotion and work alienation. *Human Resources Development of China, 36*(6), 33–47.
156. Deng, S. M. (2017). *The influence of followship on employee work engagement: The mediating role of affective commitment and the moderating role of supervisor's organization embodiment.* Jiangxi University of Finance and Economics.
157. Liu, Y., Prati, L. M., Perrewé, P. L., & Ferris, G. R. (2008). The relationship between emotional resources and emotional labor: An exploratory study. *Journal of Applied Social Psychology, 38*, 2410–2439.
158. Watson, D., Clark, L. A., & Tellegen, A. (1988). Development and validation of brief measures of positive and negative affect: The PANAS scales. *Journal of Personality and Social Psychology, 54*(6), 1063–1070.
159. Chan, D. W. (2005). Emotional intelligence, social coping, and psychological distress among Chinese gifted students in Hong Kong. *High Ability Studies, 16*(2), 163–178.
160. Grandey, A. A. (2003). When 'the show must go on'. Surface acting and deep acting as determinants of emotional exhaustion and peer-rated service delivery. *Academy of Management Journal, 46*(1): 86–96.
161. Brotheridgen, C. M. & Lee, R. E. (1998). *On the dimensionality of emotional labor: Development and validation of the emotional labor scale.* Paper presented at the first conference on emotions in organizational life. San Diego.
162. Brotheridge, C. M., & Grandey, A. A. (2002). Emotional labor and burnout: Comparing two perspectives of "people work." *Journal of Vocational Behavior, 60*(1), 17–39.
163. Brotheridge, C. M., & Lee, R. T. (2002). Testing a conservation of resources model of the dynamics of emotional labor. *Journal of Occupational Health Psychology, 7*(1), 57–67.
164. Johnson, H. M. (2007). *Service with a smile: Antecedents and consequences of emotional labor strategies.* Unpublished doctoral dissertation. University of South Florida.

165. Abraham, R. (1999). The impact of emotional dissonance on organizational commitment and intention to turnover. *Journal of Psychology, 133*, 441–455.
166. Giardini, A., & Frese, M. (2006). Reducing the negative effects of emotion work in service occupations: Emotional competence as a psychological resource. *Journal of Occupational Health Psychology, 11*, 63–75.
167. Jordan, P. J., Ashkanasy, N. M., & Hartel, C. E. J. (2002). Emotional intelligence as a moderator of emotional and behavioral reactions to job insecurity. *Academy of Management Review, 27*, 361–372.
168. Morris, J. A., & Feldman, D. C. (1996). The dimensions, antecedents, and consequences of emotional labor. *Academy of Management Review, 21*, 986–1010.
169. Rubin, R. S., Tardino, V. M. S., Daus, C. S., & Munz, D. C. (2005). A reconceptualization of the emotional labor construct: On the development of an integrated theory of perceived emotional dissonance and emotional labor. In C. E. J. Hartel, W. J. Zerbe, & N. M. Ashkanasy (Eds.), *Emotions in organizational behavior* (pp. 189–211). Erlbaum.
170. Chen, Y. C., Tseng, Y., & Chu, H. C. (2023). Development of Workplace Emotional Health Scale. *Employee Responsibilities and Rights Journal*, 1–28.https://doi.org/10.1007/s10672-023-09446-5
171. Zhang, Y., Zhang, L., Zhu, J., Liu, C.-H., Yang, M., & Liu, G. (2020). Group leader emotional intelligence and group performance: A multilevel perspective. *Asian Business & Management*, 1–23.https://doi.org/10.1057/s41291-020-00123-1
172. Law, K. S., Wong, C. S., Huang, G. H., & Li, X. (2008). The effects of emotional intelligence on job performance and life satisfaction for the research and development scientists in China. *Asia Pacific Journal of Management, 25*(1), 51–69. https://doi.org/10.1007/s10490-007-9062-3
173. Li, Y. N., Law, K. S., & Yan, M. (2019). Other-caring or other-critical? A contagious effect of leaders' emotional triads on subordinates' performance. *Asia Pacific Journal of Management, 36*(4), 995–1021. https://doi.org/10.1007/s10490-018-9617-5
174. Ashraf, F., & Khan, M. A. (2014). Does emotional intelligence moderate the relationship between workplace bullying and job performance? *Asian Business & Management, 13*(2), 171–190. https://doi.org/10.1057/abm.2013.5
175. Chen, Z., Lam, W., & Zhong, J. A. (2012). Effects of perceptions on LMX and work performance: Effects of supervisors' perception of subordinates' emotional intelligence and subordinates' perception of trust in the supervisor on LMX and consequently, performance. *Asia Pacific journal of management, 29*(3), 597–616. https://doi.org/10.1007/s10490-010-9210-z
176. Bennett, R. (2011). Brand managers' mindful self-management of their professional experience: Consequences for pay, self-efficacy and job performance. *Journal of Brand Management, 18*, 545–569. https://doi.org/10.1057/bm.2010.55
177. Ting, Q. H., Lew, T. Y., Goi, C. L., Sim, A. K. S., & Gim, G. C. W. (2024). Psychological capital and employee engagement as predictors of organisational citizenship behaviour in the industrial revolution 4.0 era: Transfer of training as a mediator. *Current Psychology, 43*(6), 5219–5242. https://doi.org/10.1007/s12144-023-04595-0
178. Kwarteng, S., Frimpong, S. O., Asare, R., & Wiredu, T. J. N. (2024). Effect of employee recognition, employee engagement on their productivity: The role of transformational leadership style at Ghana health service. *Current Psychology, 43*(6), 5502–5513. https://doi.org/10.1007/s12144-023-04708-9
179. Lam, C. K., Walter, F., & Ouyang, K. (2014). Display rule perceptions and job performance in a Chinese retail firm: The moderating role of employees' affect at work. *Asia Pacific Journal of Management, 31*, 575–597. https://doi.org/10.1007/s10490-013-9348-6
180. Zhang, J., Song, L. J., Wang, Y., & Liu, G. (2018). How authentic leadership influences employee proactivity: The sequential mediating effects of psychological empowerment and core self-evaluations and the moderating role of employee political skill. *Frontiers of Business Research in China, 12*(1), 1–21. https://doi.org/10.1186/s11782-018-0026-x
181. Chen, Q., Li, M., & Fan, H. (2023). How does the needs-supplies fit of developmental job experience affect employees' proactive behavior? *Asia Pacific Journal of Management*. https://doi.org/10.1007/s10490-023-09894-5

182. Li, G., & Xie, L. (2023). The effects of job involvement and supervisor developmental feedback on employee creativity: A polynomial regression with response surface analysis. *Current Psychology, 42*(20), 17120–17131. https://doi.org/10.1007/s12144-022-02901-w
183. Qi, H., Jingtao, F., Wenhao, W., & Pervaiz, S. (2023). You are "insisting", or you want to "withdraw"? Research on the negative effect of ethical leadership on leaders themselves. *Current Psychology, 42*(30), 25968–25984. https://doi.org/10.1007/s12144-022-03433-z
184. Karim, J., & Weisz, R. (2011). Emotional intelligence as a moderator of affectivity/emotional labor and emotional labor/psychological distress relationships. *Psychological studies, 56*(4), 348–359. https://doi.org/10.1007/s12646-011-0107-9

Chapter 3
The Role of Emotional Intelligence in Propelling Productivity at Workplace

Introduction by the Author

Exemplification effect on performance is highly negative with a sales executive with low EI, it's vice versa with high EI. Based on the study conducted by Bande and others [86], the sales person's emotional intelligence moderates the negative effects of exemplification. Recent research about emotional intelligence proved that employees with high EQ are more successful at their jobs. Employees can easily perceive emotions of their superiors as they improve their emotional sensitivity. This study proves that exemplification works well when EI of the sales person and the age of the supervisor is high. More than 90% of the top performers of organizations score greater EI values, which proves that social skills are essential for better job performance, satisfaction and reduction in employee turnover. People who have strong emotional intelligence are generally happier and more engaged at work. As a result, they disseminate positive energy to everyone around them, influencing the broader corporate culture. Work environment has a direct impact on employee satisfaction and attrition, emotionally savvy companies are more successful at retaining talent. Emotionally savvy organisations are specifically successful in involving and empowering their staff members, creating purpose cultures, and enabling the development of interpersonal abilities that enable employees to "develop creative ideas on their own." As an outcome, these organisations have much greater client retention and provide significantly superior client experiences than companies that disregard the relevance of emotional intelligence in their work environments.

In the 1990s, psychologist Daniel Goleman is credited with developing the five elements of emotional intelligence at work. (1) Self-awareness; (2) Self-regulation; (3) Motivation; (4) Empathy; and (5) Social skills are all important. The capacity to identify ones own feelings and causes is referred to as self-awareness. Self-awareness may be employed to determine how others perceive you. The capacity to regulate your emotions is referred to as self-regulation. Motivation is a desire to achieve one's own goals and desires. Empathy is a capacity to comprehend and understand the feelings of others. Social skills can be a powerful tool for advancing one's career and leadership abilities.

In 2016, Liu conducted a study to examine the mediating effect of social support to connect EI and job satisfaction. Interpersonal and emotional abilities related EI can benefit an individual's social skills. The Minnesota Satisfaction Questionnaire (MSQ) was the instrument utilised to measure job satisfaction, mediation analysis was used to test the hypothesis that the relationship between emotional intelligence and job satisfaction is mediated by social support. The results proved that emotional intelligence is positively correlated to perceived social support and job satisfaction and further stated that social support mediated the influence of emotional intelligence in job satisfaction. Ohana et. al, conducted a study in 2023 which hypothesised that the employees perception about their firm's corporate social behaviour have a possibility of shaping their work behaviour. The results suggest that the organization displaying low CSR (Corporate Social Responsibility) may cause disengagement for the employees in work.

The relationship between job burnout and work performance has a direct relationship with emotional labour strategies. Emotional display rules has a direct influence on emotional labour strategies by flight attendants. Customer relationship management in service industry require employees to display positive emotions over negative feelings. Emotional display rules cause job stress which creates a disconnection between a flight attendants true emotions and work behaviour. Those employees prefer surface acting to deep acting when pushed abide by emotional display rules. Emotional display rules are mediated by emotional labour strategy, instead of directly impacting burnout and job performance. Burnout has an indirect effect on engagement, close monitoring leads to more burnout. Job demand resources model (JD-R model) helps to reduce employee burnout, engagement and customer service performance.

Work life balance reconceptualises the ability of an individual's responsibilities in all domains of life. Employee perception regarding their job, work environment and supervision has an effect in Work life balance. Work with balance is reconceptualised in this study as effective management and fulfilment of various responsibilities in life through psychological, spiritual, emotional, family and health life. The antecedents of work life balance includes emotional intelligence, resilience, mindful training, flexibility stigma, Person- environment fit and work value ethics. Maintaining a proper work life balances reduces turnover intention. Which in turn improves self-regulation, motivation and social skills towards work environment. In a recent research study conducted by Hammond and others [92], the influence of quality of work life in enhancing productivity in oil and gas industry has been studied. Quality of work life positively impacting job satisfaction will lead to improved productivity and organisational commitment. The study analysed emotional well-being on personal development and job Satisfaction. The other mediating and moderating variables such as social support, personality, leadership styles were provided as variables in order to improve the quality of work life balance on job satisfaction studies. Employees who possess positive emotional health are likely to enjoy the responsibilities assigned by the organisation rather than who have negative emotional well-being. A safe and healthy working environment will in turn positively correlate employee's level of confidence, commitment and efficiency.

Organisations develop efficient and competitive ways to improve organisational climate that supports leadership styles to empower employees in an organisation. Servant leadership can be considered as a virtue, followed by organisations that encourages employee's positive behaviour through direct and indirect effects of self-efficacy and job satisfaction. A study conducted by Isabel and others [93] states that servant leadership can be considered as a direct influence of organisational citizenship behaviour (OCB). Even in situations of high emotional demand and exhaustive workload, employees if they have enough resources, can handle exhaustion positively. Transformational leadership has a positive effect on task performance when employees have a low level of proactive personality.

Another research by Almeida [95] investigates the way in which communication and culture influences corporate reputation and their impact on workers attitude and behaviour like individual performance and organisational commitment. This investigation proves that internal communication have a positive impact on individual performance and increase organisational commitment. This research yet explains culture and communication and its impact on work related outcomes like commitment and individual performance. Employees should identify their weakness before trying to learn and prove their level of emotion intelligence. Going through their life experiences and their problems solved in life will evaluate how much empathetic they can be and handle the similar situations in future. In this way they can improve their emotional intelligence and inspire the employees around them.

Machine Generated Summaries

Disclaimer: The summaries in this chapter were generated from Springer Nature publications using extractive AI auto-summarization: An extraction-based summarizer aims to identify the most important sentences of a text using an algorithm and uses those original sentences to create the auto-summary (unlike generative AI). As the constituted sentences are machine selected, they may not fully reflect the body of the work, so we strongly advise that the original content is read and cited. The auto generated summaries were curated by the editor to meet Springer Nature publication standards. To cite this content, please refer to the original papers.

Machine generated keywords: csr, family, job satisfaction, job, balance, burnout, corporate, satisfaction, responsibility, employee, social support, stakeholder, demand, service employee, supervisor

Are Self-sacrificing Employees Liked by Their Supervisor? [86]

This is a machine-generated summary of:

Bande, Belén; Kimura, Takuma; Fernández-Ferrín, Pilar; Castro-González, Sandra; Goel, Abhishek: Are self-sacrificing employees liked by their supervisor? [86]

Published in: Eurasian Business Review (2023)
Link to original: https://doi.org/https://doi.org/10.1007/s40821-023-00243-6
Copyright of the summarized publication:
The Author(s) 2023
License: OpenAccess CC BY 4.0

This article is licensed under a Creative Commons Attribution 4.0 International License, which permits use, sharing, adaptation, distribution and reproduction in any medium or format, as long as you give appropriate credit to the original author(s) and the source, provide a link to the Creative Commons licence, and indicate if changes were made. The images or other third party material in this article are included in the article's Creative Commons licence, unless indicated otherwise in a credit line to the material. If material is not included in the article's Creative Commons licence and your intended use is not permitted by statutory regulation or exceeds the permitted use, you will need to obtain permission directly from the copyright holder. To view a copy of this licence, visit http://creativecommons.org/licenses/by/4.0/.

If you want to cite the papers, please refer to the original.

For technical reasons we could not place the page where the original quote is coming from.

Abstract-Summary

"This study proposes to expand the exemplification research domain by exploring the emotional and behavioral conditions under which this impression management tactic is effective."

"Data analysis from 206 supervisor–employee dyads reveals that the indirect relationship between exemplification and individual performance through a supervisor's liking is conditional on an employee's emotional intelligence."

"The exemplification effect on performance is sharply negative when a salesperson's emotional intelligence is low, and it becomes insignificant when a salesperson is highly emotionally intelligent."

Introduction

"Studies that have examined the consequences of exemplification at work have arrived at inconsistent results regarding its impact on important work outcomes, revealing that strategic self-sacrificing behaviors can have both negative and positive consequences in terms of organizational outcomes (Bolino [1]; Bolino & others [2, 3]; Harris & others [4]; Liu and others [5]; Wayne & Liden [6])."

"Harris and others [4] found that exemplification was not a significant antecedent of supervisor appraisal of job performance, while Bande and others [7, p. 362] concluded that the effect of impression management behaviors on sales performance appraisal "is not a direct but an indirect one, through the impact of these tactics on the supervisors' liking of the salesperson"."

"The moderating role of a supervisor's age in the effectiveness of a salesperson's use of exemplification tactics is examined."

"This study makes a novel contribution, shedding light on EI's proactive aspects by revealing whether EI enhances the effectiveness of an actor's proactive behavior, such as exemplification."

"This study examines a supervisor's demographic characteristic, i.e., age, as a moderator that affects exemplification effectiveness."

Literature Review

"Based on these arguments, this study hypothesizes that exemplifiers' emotional intelligence improves the influence of exemplifying behaviors on supervisor's liking."

"H2: Salesperson emotional intelligence moderates the indirect effect of exemplification on individual performance through supervisor's liking."

"Due to the positivity effect, older supervisors are more likely to regard subordinates' exemplification as a positive attribute."

"It is therefore expected that exemplifiers with a high EI level will influence their supervisors' emotions more effectively and quickly when a supervisor is older, leading to greater success of the exemplification attempt."

"This study proposes that the role of a salesperson's emotional intelligence in obtaining a favorable performance appraisal using exemplification tactics will depend on a supervisor's age."

"H3: The moderating effect of emotional intelligence on the relationship between exemplification and sales performance appraisal will depend on a supervisor's age."

Methods

"Data were collected by surveying salespeople and their immediate supervisors who worked in multiple firms located in the north-west region of Spain."

"A contact person (sales director/human resources director) in each firm helped to randomly select a sales manager (105 supervisors) and up to three subordinates (210 salespeople)."

"For most of the firms (82%), the ratio was one supervisor to two salespeople."

"All measures used in this study were developed from previously published research, and all scale items used seven-point Likert-type scales (1 = strongly disagree; 7 = strongly agree)."

"The Cronbach's alpha value for the eight-item scale was 0.837 and the composite reliability was 0.893."

"Supervisors' affect toward the salespeople was reported using the three-item scale measure developed by Wayne and Liden [6]."

"Salesperson performance at an individual level was assessed using a nine-item scale developed by Griffin and others [8]."

Results

"The indirect relationship between exemplification and performance appraisal is significant, although negative, and conditional upon a salesperson's EI level."

"When EI is very low (10th percentile), the indirect effect of exemplification on performance is—0.293."

"At high values of EI (above 5.75—75th and 90th percentiles) the indirect effect of exemplification on performance through liking becomes insignificant."

"This effect is an indirect-only mediation because exemplification has no direct effect on salesperson performance appraisal ($\beta = 0.024$; SE $= 0.057$; p $= 0.664$; [−0.088; 0.138])."

"As predicted, the effect of exemplification on performance appraisal through supervisor's liking depends on both the salesperson's EI and on the supervisor's age."

"As the age of a supervisor increases, the buffering effect of EI on the relationship between exemplification and performance appraisal becomes stronger."

Discussion

"This study's findings suggest that the success of an exemplification attempt not only depends on an employee's emotional intelligence, but also on a supervisor's age."

"As predicted, when a supervisor's age increases, the effect of EI on the relationship between exemplification and sales performance appraisal is stronger (more positive)."

"Employees can more easily and accurately perceive their supervisor's emotions as their age increases, enhancing the positive effect of an employee's emotional sensitivity on the exemplification-sales performance relationship."

"In the three-way interaction analysis, the most negative effect between exemplification and performance occurs for low values of EI and high supervisor age."

"This study finds support for the mediating effect of a supervisor's affect toward a subordinate in the relationship between exemplification and performance appraisal, which contributes to explaining the lack of support for a direct relationship found in some previous research (e.g., Brouer and others [9])."

Conclusion

"Our findings suggest that an employee's effective use of IM tactics at work depends on the appropriate perception and interpretation of the target's emotions."

"Our results support the idea that the use of exemplification tactics may have negative consequences for the user when the actor lacks social skill (i.e., EI)."

"The effectiveness of these self-sacrificial behaviors is also a function of the personal characteristics of those at whom these behaviors are directed."

"This study confirms that exemplification is successful when both the EI of the salesperson and the age of the supervisor have high values."

Mediating Effect of Social Support between the Emotional Intelligence and Job Satisfaction of Chinese Employees [87]

This is a machine-generated summary of:
Liu, Dawei: Mediating Effect of Social Support between the Emotional Intelligence and Job Satisfaction of Chinese Employees [87]
Published in: Current Psychology (2016)
Link to original: https://doi.org/https://doi.org/10.1007/s12144-016-9520-5
Copyright of the summarized publication:
Springer Science + Business Media New York 2016
All rights reserved.
If you want to cite the papers, please refer to the original.
For technical reasons we could not place the page where the original quote is coming from.

Abstract-Summary

"This study aims to examine the mediating effect of social support on the relation between emotional intelligence and job satisfaction."

"Results suggest that emotional intelligence and social support are significantly correlated with job satisfaction."

"The results of SEM also indicate that social support partially mediates the effect of emotional intelligence on job satisfaction."

"The final model proves the relationship between emotional intelligence and job satisfaction through social support."

Introduction

"The reasons why employees' EI affect job satisfaction can be summarized as follows: interpersonally, emotional abilities and regulatory processes related to EI can benefit an individual's social relationships, and hence affect work-related emotion and stress (Augusto-Landa & others [10])."

"Minimal research has explored the extent to which social support components of employees mediate the effect of EI on job satisfaction."

"Further studies are still needed to elucidate the trilateral relations among EI, social support, and job satisfaction."

"Testing the concurrent effect of EI and social support on job satisfaction is necessary to formulate an overall hypothesis on their relationships."

"No studies that explore the mediating effect of social support on the relationship between EI and job satisfaction have been conducted."

"With the objective of providing meaningful evidence for external validity, this study aims to examine the effect of EI on job satisfaction through the mediating effect of social support in Chinese organizations."

Method

"The Minnesota Satisfaction Questionnaire (MSQ), developed by Weiss and others, is a 20-item self-report measure of job satisfaction (Hirschfeld [11])."

"To test the hypothesis that the relationship between emotional intelligence and job satisfaction is mediated by social support, we conducted mediation analysis using the two-step procedure of Anderson and Gerbing [12]."

"To confirm the structural relations of the latent structured model, the measurement model included three latent variables (EI, Social Support and Job Satisfaction) was tested to determine the extent of representation by its indicators respectively."

"Mediating effect of social support between emotional intelligence and job satisfaction was tested adopting the Bootstrap estimation procedure in Amos 17.0 (a bootstrap sample of 1200 was specified)."

"For the purpose of controlling the inflated measurement errors from multiple items for the latent variable and improving the reliability and normality of the resulting measures, four item parcels was created for emotional intelligence using the factorial algorithm method (Rogers & Schmitt [13])."

Results

"Results showed that emotional intelligence, perceived social support, and job satisfaction were all positively correlated with each other significantly."

"Those results indicated that emotional intelligence could influence job satisfaction not only directly, but also through the partially mediating effect of perceived social support."

"The effect of EI on job satisfaction through social support accounted for 50.11 %."

"The bootstrap estimation procedure in AMOS 17.0 was used to test the significance of the mediating effect of social support."

"This further indicted social support mediated the effect of emotional intelligence on job satisfaction."

Discussion

"The goal of this study is to test a model that includes social support as a mediator of the relationship between the EI and job satisfaction among Chinese employees."

"Another critical finding is the verification of the mediating effect of perceived social support between EI and job satisfaction."

"Testing the mediating effect proved the evident relationship between EI and job satisfaction through social support, and showed that social support is also an important factor in job satisfaction."

"This study adopted a cross-sectional design, which means that caution should be taken when interpreting the mediation effect of social support in the relationship between EI and job satisfaction."

"This study finds that perceived social support cannot completely mediate the effect of EI on job satisfaction, and thus, other mediating variables could exist in the relationship between EI and job satisfaction."

Why and When can CSR toward Employees Lead to Cyberloafing? The Role of Workplace Boredom and Moral Disengagement [88]

This is a machine-generated summary of:
Ohana, Marc; Murtaza, Ghulam; Haq, Inam ul; Al-Shatti, Esraa; Chi, Zhang: Why and When can CSR toward Employees Lead to Cyberloafing? The Role of Workplace Boredom and Moral Disengagement [88]
Published in: Journal of Business Ethics (2023)
Link to original: https://doi.org/https://doi.org/10.1007/s10551-023-05358-4
Copyright of the summarized publication:
The Author(s), under exclusive licence to Springer Nature B.V. 2023
Copyright comment: Springer Nature or its licensor (e.g. a society or other partner) holds exclusive rights to this article under a publishing agreement with the author(s) or other rightsholder(s); author self-archiving of the accepted manuscript version of this article is solely governed by the terms of such publishing agreement and applicable law.
All rights reserved.

If you want to cite the papers, please refer to the original.
For technical reasons we could not place the page where the original quote is coming from.

Abstract-Summary

"Researchers have recently indicated that employee perceptions of their firm's corporate social responsibility (CSR) may shape their work behaviors."

"We first investigate the mediating role of workplace boredom in explaining the effect of perceived CSR toward employees on cyberloafing behaviors."

"Our research suggests that moral disengagement weakens the effect of internal CSR on workplace boredom, such that for employees high in moral disengagement, the level of internal CSR has a weaker effect on workplace boredom."

Introduction

"We explain that companies displaying low CSR toward their employees may cause disengagement from work and workplace boredom, in turn fostering cyberloafing behaviors as a coping strategy."

"Despite that CSR perceptions may be significantly associated with cyberloafing through workplace boredom, not all individuals who perceive that their organization does not consistently engage in CSR practices experience higher levels of workplace boredom."

"Morally disengaged employees might experience a lower level of workplace boredom in case of poor internal CSR."

"We show how boredom resulting from poor internal CSR practices can increase employees' motivation to engage in cyberloafing."

"In case of poor internal CSR practices, employees with low level of moral disengagement are more likely to develop an unpleasant state that may take the form of workplace boredom."

Theoretical Background and Hypotheses

"We therefore hypothesize that: Workplace boredom mediates the relationship between perceived internal CSR and employee cyberloafing behaviors."

"We then further predict a moderating effect of employee moral disengagement on the negative relationship between the presence of internal CSR practices and workplace boredom."

"We posit that the negative effect of strong internal CSR practices on workplace boredom will be weaker for morally disengaged employees."

"Perceptions of poor internal CSR may thus be less problematic for highly disengaged employees, as they counterbalance the unsupportive work environment with their own immoral actions, such as cheating, loafing, and other unethical behaviors that help them achieve their expectations."

"As the negative effects of CSR toward employees is less important for morally disengaged employees, we expect that perceptions of poor internal CSR will lead to weaker workplace boredom."

Method

"Study 2 is an experimental study based on a between subject vignette procedure where we manipulated CSR toward employees to examine its effect on workplace boredom depending on the level of moral disengagement of participants."

"Each variable was measured only once at one specific point in time (internal CSR and moral disengagement at T1, workplace boredom at T2, and cyberloafing at T3)."

"The measures of internal CSR at time 1 (Cronbach's alpha $= 0.87$), moral disengagement at time 1 (Cronbach's alpha $= 0.90$), workplace boredom at time 2 (Cronbach's alpha $= 0.91$), and cyberloafing at time 3 (Cronbach's alpha $= 0.93$) were the same as in Study 1 and 2."

"The result indicates that moral disengagement can strengthen the negative link between internal CSR and boredom ($\beta = 0.181$; $p = 0.035$), meaning that an increase of one standard deviation in moral disengagement increases the effect of internal CSR on workplace boredom by 0.181."

Discussion

"Our study extends prior research by highlighting the moderating role of moral disengagement in the relationship between CSR as perceived by employee and cyberloafing behaviors."

"Our study provides evidence that for employees high in moral disengagement, the level of internal CSR has a weaker effect on workplace boredom."

"Where employees are characterized by a high level of moral engagement, the effects of poor CSR may be amplified—a proposition opening the door to future research into how the (in)congruence of a company and its employees' moral (dis)engagement might impact upon counterproductive work behavior."

"As we find that workplace boredom plays an important role in transferring the harmful effects of the perceived absence of CSR on employee cyberloafing, organizations are advised to develop policies to reduce boredom, and consequentially cyberloafing behaviors."

"Employees perceiving that their organization implements internal CSR initiatives will lead to a sense of meaning in their work and reduce the feeling of boredom, in turn not engaging in cyberloafing."

Conclusion

"In this paper, we have examined the possible negative effect of the absence of CSR on employee cyberloafing behaviors."

"We find that an absence of perceived CSR may generate negative emotions, such as workplace boredom, and that bored employees are likely to engage in cyberloafing behaviors."

"Moral disengagement weakens the effect of internal CSR on workplace boredom, such that for employees high in moral disengagement, the level of internal CSR has a weaker effect on workplace."

The Effects of Emotional Display Rules on Flight Attendants' Emotional Labor Strategy, Job Burnout and Performance [89]

This is a machine-generated summary of:
Lee, Chongho; An, Myungsook; Noh, Yonghwi: The effects of emotional display rules on flight attendants' emotional labor strategy, job burnout and performance [89]
Published in: Service Business (2014)
Link to original: https://doi.org/https://doi.org/10.1007/s11628-014-0231-4
Copyright of the summarized publication:
Springer-Verlag Berlin Heidelberg 2014
All rights reserved.
If you want to cite the papers, please refer to the original.
For technical reasons we could not place the page where the original quote is coming from.

Abstract-Summary

"This study investigates the effects of emotional display rules of an airline on the emotional labor strategies of flight attendants (i.e., deep acting, surface acting), job burnout, and work performance."

"The results show that the emotional labor strategy performed by flight attendants plays an important role in mediating emotional display rules."

"Emotional display rules did not directly affect job burnout and work performance, but rather influenced the emotional labor strategy used by flight attendants."

"Among emotional labor strategies, deep acting enhanced job performance and reduced burnout, while surface acting improved work performance but increased burnout."

Introduction

"Such social, occupational, and organizational requirements for service employees are considered rules of emotional display (Ashforth and Humphrey 15) and they are especially critical for an airline, a representative service firm that needs to create and maintain a high level of in-flight service quality."

"Emotional display rules play a significant role in customer relationship management in the service industry and function as criteria to help control employees' emotional displays in an effort to promote positive displays over negative ones (Brotheridge & Grandey [14])."

"Considering that in-flight service quality is a critical factor to passenger satisfaction in the airline industry, it is expected that appropriate emotional display rules for flight attendants are necessary to improve the performance of airlines."

"There have been inconsistent views regarding the effect of emotional display rules on the performance of service employees."

"Considering that the airline industry is a representative service industry, this study may provide meaningful insight into other service industries regarding the role of emotional display rules."

Review of Relevant Literature and Hypotheses Development

"Emotional display rules can be used to influence service employee emotions, helping them to achieve an intended job performance (Ashforth & Humphrey [15]; Diefendorff & Richard [16]; Cropanzano & others [17]; Matsumoto & others [18])."

"In a service situation, emotional display rules generally require employees to express more positive emotions and restrain any negative feelings (Schaubroeck & Jones [19]; Brotheridge & Grandey [14]; Glomb & Tews [20])."

"Emotional display rules may cause job stress, triggering discordance between a flight attendant's true emotion and expected behavior (Hochschild [21]; Davidson [22]; Isen [23])."

"Rules of emotional display have the potential to improve job satisfaction of flight attendants (Diefendorff & Richard [16]) through personal efforts to make a positive impression (Grandey [24]; Schaubroeck & Jones [19])."

"It is possible that service employees choose deep acting to reconcile their emotions and regulated emotions because they evaluate their emotion expressions based on emotional display rules whenever they perform emotional labors (Diefendorff & Gosserand [25])."

"Service employees may prefer surface acting to deep acting when pushed to abide by emotional display rules."

"Emotional display rules are positively associated with job performance."

Methodology

"To investigate how emotional display rules, emotional labor strategy, job burnout, and job performance relate to one another, we surveyed flight attendants working at the biggest airline in South Korea."

"The survey questionnaire included the following key variables: emotional display rules, emotional labor strategy, job burnout, and job performance."

"To measure emotional display rules, this study employed four items based on the questionnaire used by Heuven and others [26] to survey flight attendants using the Frankfurt Emotion Work Scales (FEWS) (Zapf & others [27])."

"For job performance, five items from a questionnaire by Goodman and Svyantek [28] were employed."

"Based on a reliability analysis we conducted, the seventh item on the surface acting variable and the fifth item on the job burnout variable were eliminated."

"A confirmatory factor analysis was conducted and as a result, the first item of the deep acting variable was eliminated because the value of SMC was less than 0.40."

Results

"Emotional display rules did not significantly affect surface acting with the value of the path coefficient at 0.149 ($p = 0.059$), while emotional display rules positively influenced deep acting, with the value of the path coefficient 0.344 ($p = 0.000$)."

"Emotional display rules did not significantly affect job burnout (coefficient $= -0.113$, $p = 0.264$) and job performance (coefficient $= 0.110$, $p = 0.125$), which implies that emotional display rules are mediated by an emotional labor strategy instead of directly affecting job burnout and performance."

"While deep acting negatively affected job burnout (coefficient $= -0.218$, $p = 0.042$), it positively influenced job performance (coefficient $= 0.317$, $p = 0.000$)."

"These results show that deep acting may offer flight attendants a sense of achievement by matching their actual emotions to those expected by the airline, thus improving their job performance."

Discussion

"This study is the first to study the relationship between emotional display rules, emotional labor strategy, job burnout, and job performance based on a survey of flight attendants."

"Emotional display rules tended to promote deep acting on the part of flight attendants."

"It should also focus on how flight attendants choose between surface and deep acting when an airline is designing emotional display rules."

"The company could build a supportive service system to induce flight attendants to employ the strategy of deep acting, which reduces job burnout and improves job performance."

"The emotional display rules of an airline may play a significant role in improving organizational performance by promoting a deep acting strategy by flight attendants."

"Although surface acting of flight attendants improves job performance in the short term, it can potentially deteriorate the organization's overall performance by triggering emotional dissonance and exhaustion in flight attendants."

Limitations and Future Research

"It employed a static analysis to investigate the effect of emotional display rules, as flight attendants may frequently change emotional labor strategies to mediate emotional display rules."

"A longitudinal study would provide time-based information to reflect the change in emotional labor strategy by flight attendants."

"It would also be interesting to employ various contingencies to investigate the effects of emotional display rules that might provide diverse insights into how flight attendants react to such rules in terms of organizational culture, job position, emotional intelligence, job characteristics, and different regions of the world."

Service Employee Burnout and Engagement: The Moderating Role of Power Distance Orientation [90]

This is a machine-generated summary of:
Auh, Seigyoung; Menguc, Bulent; Spyropoulou, Stavroula; Wang, Fatima: Service employee burnout and engagement: the moderating role of power distance orientation [90]
Published in: Journal of the Academy of Marketing Science (2015)
Link to original: https://doi.org/https://doi.org/10.1007/s11747-015-0463-4
Copyright of the summarized publication:
Academy of Marketing Science 2015
All rights reserved.
If you want to cite the papers, please refer to the original.
For technical reasons we could not place the page where the original quote is coming from.

Abstract-Summary

"To better understand service employees' job engagement, this study broadens the scope of the job demands-resources (JD-R) model to include power distance orientation (PDO)."

"The inclusion of PDO enriches the JD-R model by providing a key piece of information that has been missing in prior JD-R models: employees' perceptions of the source of job demands (i.e., supervisors) or employees' views of power and hierarchy within the organization."

"Study 1 uses a survey-based field study to show that employees with a high (compared to low) PDO feel more burnout due to supervisors when they are closely monitored by their supervisors."

"Study 1 further supports the finding that employees with high (compared to low) PDO feel less disengagement despite burnout due to supervisors."

Theoretical Background

"The motivational process is explicated by job resources, which are defined as "those physical, psychological, social, or organizational aspects of the job that help to either achieve work goals, reduce job demand and the associated physiological and psychological cost or stimulate personal growth and development" (Bakker & Demerouti [29], p. 312)."

"Personal resources have also been used as moderators to alleviate the strain that job demands exert on employees."

"Despite these efforts, results have been inconsistent and conflicting, with some studies finding that personal resources mitigate the negative effect of job demands (e.g., Pierce & Gardner [30]; Van Yperen & Snijders [31]) and others showing no moderating effect (e.g., Xanthopoulou & others [32])."

"Further, the focus of this study's moderator shifts from personal resources that have been limited to employee characteristics (e.g., Big Five personality traits) to employee attitudes toward the source of the job demand."

Conceptual Model and Hypotheses Development

"We maintain that when employees receive customer service feedback, they feel less burnout despite being closely monitored by supervisors because employees can use the feedback as a motivation to develop, learn, and grow."

"We posit that employees will feel less burnout despite being closely monitored when employees have higher levels of PDO."

"More formally, we propose: H2: Employees will feel less burnout despite being closely monitored by supervisors when employees have high (vs. low) levels of PDO."

"Drawing on the above arguments and in accordance with social exchange theory (Blau [33]) and norms of reciprocity (Rhoades & Eisenberger [34]), we maintain that customer service feedback will be more effective in diminishing burnout for low (vs. high) PDO employees based on the reasoning that low PDO employees expect supervisors to reciprocate in kind through customer service feedback in exchange for work fulfillment."

"Based on the prior arguments, we propose: H4: Customer service feedback will result in less burnout for low (vs. high) PDO employees."

Study 1

"The interaction effect of close monitoring and customer service feedback is related negatively and significantly to burnout ($\gamma = -0.165$, $p < 0.01$)."

"We computed the estimate and confidence interval (CI) for the indirect effects of close monitoring and customer service feedback on engagement through burnout (close monitoring: $\gamma = -0.146$, $p < 0.05$, 95 % bootstrap CI [-0.193, -0.102]; customer service feedback $\gamma = 0.098$, $p < 0.05$, 95 % bootstrap CI [0.066, 0.135])."

"We also tested the direct effects of close monitoring ($\gamma = 0.015$, ns) and customer service feedback ($\gamma = 0.307$, $p < 0.01$) on engagement."

"Although not hypothesized, the direct effects of close monitoring and customer service feedback on burnout were significant and in the expected direction, which supports the fundamental premise of the JD-R model."

Study 2

"When submissiveness was high, close monitoring had a significant indirect effect on burnout through stress ($b = 0.32$; 95 % bias-corrected bootstrap (CI) [0.057, 0.781])."

"When customer service feedback was low, the indirect effect of close monitoring on burnout via stress was positive and significant ($b = 0.34$; 95 % bias-corrected bootstrap (CI) [0.064, 0.807])."

"When customer service feedback was high, the indirect effect of close monitoring on burnout via stress was not significant ($b = 0.16$; 95 % bias-corrected bootstrap (CI) [-0.053, 0.539])."

"Study 2 confirms that stress mediates (1) the interactive effect between close monitoring and submissiveness on burnout but only for respondents in a high submissive work environment and (2) the interactive relationship between close monitoring and customer service feedback on burnout but only for respondents who received low customer service feedback."

Study 3

"We posit that job satisfaction mediates the interactive effect between burnout and PDO on engagement differently because burnout affects job satisfaction to different degrees for low PDO employees compared to high PDO employees (Singh and others 35)."

"We propose that: H5: The interactive effect of burnout and PDO on engagement is mediated via job satisfaction, but only for low PDO employees."

"To further understand the nature of the underlying process behind the interaction between burnout and PDO on engagement, H5 advanced that burnout has an indirect effect on engagement via job satisfaction because satisfaction is negatively affected only when PDO is low."

"When PDO was low, burnout had an indirect and negative effect on engagement via job satisfaction (b $= -0.314$; 95 % bias-corrected bootstrap (CI) [-0.636, -0.131])."

General Discussion

"The different effect of close monitoring on burnout between low and high PDO employees suggests that supervisors need to have a segmented and targeted approach if and when they intend to closely monitor employees."

"Our results underscore the importance of supervisors providing resources such as customer service feedback if they intend to engage in close monitoring because without sufficient resources, stress will increase and lead to greater employee burnout."

"Our research shows that close monitoring leads to more burnout when submissiveness is high and customer service feedback is low as a result of increased stress."

"By manipulating demands and resources, our study shows that close monitoring and customer service feedback lead to burnout and not the other way around."

"We included only one supervisor-related demand (close monitoring) and resource (customer service feedback) along with one moderator (PDO and submissiveness)."

[Section 7]

"We turn to the job demands-resources (JD-R) model, a framework that explains employee wellbeing and productivity based on the demands (e.g., supervisor close monitoring behavior) and resources (e.g., supervisor feedback on ways to improve customer service) employees encounter in their jobs (Bakker & Demerouti [29])."

"This study serves to address two important aspects of the JD-R model that have received scant attention by broadening the scope of the JD-R framework and the burnout and stress literature in the service employee context."

"By capturing PDO as a moderator in the JD-R model, we develop an understanding of the intricate relationships between job demands, resources, and attitudes when employees have different levels of PDO."

"In the sections to follow, we discuss how our study is able to expand extant knowledge on service employee burnout, engagement, and customer service performance through an extension of the JD-R framework."

A Morphological Analyses of the Literature on Employee Work-life Balance [91]

This is a machine-generated summary of:
S, Thilagavathy; S.N, Geetha: A morphological analyses of the literature on employee work-life balance [91]
Published in: Current Psychology (2020)
Link to original: https://doi.org/https://doi.org/10.1007/s12144-020-00968-x
Copyright of the summarized publication:
Springer Science + Business Media, LLC, part of Springer Nature 2020
All rights reserved.
If you want to cite the papers, please refer to the original.
For technical reasons we could not place the page where the original quote is coming from.

Abstract-Summary

"The purpose of this paper is to review the existing literature relating to work-life balance (WLB), develop a morphological analysis (MA) framework and identify research gaps to recommend future research opportunity."

"The MA framework has been constructed on the basis of a review of 201 papers published in 96 journals over a period of three decades from 1991 to 2019."

"Stage I features a five-stage systematic review protocol for recognition and scrutiny of relevant papers for review; Stage 2 exhibits a detailed framework for categorization of the reviewed papers in terms of their fundamental, methodological, chronological and sector-wise orientations."

"Stage 3 exhibits the development of the MA framework based on the themes identified from the reviewed papers and uncover the research gaps."

Theoretical Background

"Several organizations provide a variety of WLB policies that benefit the employees and their family, which, in turn, benefits the organizations at large (Jenkins & Harvey [36])."

"Previous research evidence demonstrated the positive influence of family-supportive organization policy (FSOP) on WLB (Allen [37]; Lapierre & others [38]; Haar & Roche [39]; Wayne & others [40])."

"Employee perception regarding their job, work environment, supervision and organization had significant influence on their WLB (Fontinha & others [41])."

"Even though the organizations offer WLB policies, employee's awareness of its existence has a greater impact on their perception and appreciation of the organization's family-supportiveness (Matthews & others [42])."

"Hammer and others [43] found that WLB interventions provided by organizations had a negative effect, because, employees perceived that the work-family interventions initiated by the organisations were less useful."

"WLB policy utilization and work to non-work self-efficacy were significantly influenced by societal culture."

Methodology

"The research work from 1991 was considered for this review."

"Fundamental classification was done on the basic minutiae of the reviewed journal papers."

"This was followed by a methodological classification based on the research method details given in the papers."

"This classification revealed uncovered and under-covered sectors in WLB research."

"The solution space of a morphological field includes the subset of configurations that satisfy the criteria of internal consistency."

"MA is utilized for identifying the research gaps to facilitate future research."

"The themes recognized and scrutinised through the literature review and the above four classifications were utilized as the dimensions in the MA framework."

"MA technique was applied to the body of knowledge derived from the literature reviewed for the recognition of research gaps (opportunities for future research) in the subject area of WLB."

Results

"In reality, the experiences of the individual with a wider set of personal roles inclusive of real-life experiences while participating in multiple non-work roles beyond family were not taken into consideration while conceptualizing WLB (Hall & others [44])."

"WLB is reconceptualised in this study as the individual's ability to actually fulfil the responsibilities in all the domains of life, namely, work, family, personal and society with ease by utilizing the available resources."

"WLB was reconceptualised in this study in line with the above discussion as "a state of balance that a person could achieve, through effective management and fulfilment of multiple responsibilities at work, at home, and in their community and society, with good physical, psychological, emotional, spiritual, family, and community health, and does so without grief, stress or negative impact, by efficiently utilizing the available resources at work, at home, and in their community and society"."

Morphological Analysis

"Variable 5: WLB policies are the benefits and services provided by the organization to help the employees balance work and life (Jenkins & Harvey [36]; Ferri & others [45])."

"Variable 6: Organizational support includes policies, rules and regulations for administering employees and their various activities which directly or indirectly contribute to the maintenance of the WLB (Haar & Roche [39])."

"Other than demand and resources, there are some factors that have influence on WLB of employees, which, are classified into the following three dimensions."

"Variable 16: WLB Policy utilization is the extent to which the employees utilize the WLB policies for balancing their work and life (Jenkins & Harvey [36]; Jurado-Guerrero & others [46])."

"The factors that were not included in work demand but have significant influence on the WLB of employees are included in this dimension."

"Variable 25: organisational work climate refers to the perception of the employee as grouped under the organization's culture."

Discussion and Conclusion

"And foremost, this paper is the first of its kind to compile the research work on WLB utilizing systematic literature review and morphological analysis."

"Further, this research work has identified the research gaps and provided direction for future research with regard to WLB."

"The geographical distribution revealed that WLB research works were carried out in 36 countries."

"This classification recognised the under-explored geographical areas with regard to WLB research."

"This classification scrutinized the methodology employed in WLB research over the past three decades and revealed that the experimental method was employed in only very few papers."

"Further, classification revealed that only a few WLB papers were published during the period 1991–2000."

"This classification revealed that the influence of certain factors on WLB was only conceptually examined but was not empirically tested."

Theoretical and Practical Implications

"The review of the literature regarding WLB reveals that WLB studies needs greater consistency between the conceptualization of constructs and the operationalization of measures (Chang & others [47])."

"This leaves ample of scope for researchers to retest the WLB theories based on this new conceptualization."

"This showcases the opportunity for the researchers to operationally define and measure WLB in line with the WLB conceptualization developed in this research work."

"Researchers can conduct experimental studies to disclose the influence of emotional intelligence, resilience, mindfulness training, yoga training etc on WLB based on previous empirical research."

"This leaves the scope for the researchers to explore the influence of those demographic factors on WLB in the future."

"The understudied antecedents of WLB were identified through the application of MA and unveiled in the areas for future research."

Future Lines of Research

"Influence of WLB policy utilisation by the employees on WLB can be studied in the light of flexibility stigma, organisational culture, psychological climate, person-environment fit, work value ethics of the employee and societal culture as these variables are proven influencers of WLB policy utilisation."

"The impact of WLB policy backlash on individual outcomes and organizational outcomes under the influence of the variables such as organisational culture, psychological climate, person-environment fit, work value ethics of the employees and societal culture, could be taken up as these variables are also considered as influencers of WLB policy utilisation The impact of the societal factor, culture of the country and societal demand on WLB requires in depth investigation."

"Studies relating to the exploration of the impact of the WLB policies after the implementation of the WLB policies in lights of variables like organisational culture, psychological climate, person-environment fit, work value ethics of the employees and societal culture can be taken up as these variables have a significant effect on WLB policy utilisation."

Limitations

"Like any other research work, this research work also has some limitations."

"One of the major limitations of this study is that only papers in the English language were considered."

"The other limitation is that there is a possible chance of missing a few papers unintentionally which may not be included in this review."

[Section 9]

"The Primary aim of this paper is to systematically review the existing literature relating to work-life balance (WLB) and identify research gaps to enable recommendation of future research possibilities and priorities."

"Although a large body of research have explored the WLB domain in depth, this study is the first to utilize morphological analysis (MA) framework to review WLB literature, thereby enriching the existing research."

"This review was conducted with the following objectives (a) To explore the different concepts of WLB; (b) To identify the various variables that influence WLB; (c) To survey the sectors in which WLB researches were carried out; (d) To identify the unexplored demographic characteristic; (e) To recognize the geographical areas under which the WLB researches were conducted; (f) To develop a MA framework, identify the research gaps in the area of WLB and propose an actionable direction for future research."

How Quality of Work-life Influence Employee Job Satisfaction in a Gas Processing Plant in Ghana [92]

This is a machine-generated summary of:

Hammond, Mavis; Owusu, Nicodemus Osei; Nunoo, Edward Kweku; Boampong, Georgina; Osman, Aminu; Panin, Anthony; Nyametso, Johnie Kodjoe; Essen, Bernice: How quality of work-life influence employee job satisfaction in a gas processing plant in Ghana [92]

Published in: Discover Sustainability (2023)

Link to original: https://doi.org/https://doi.org/10.1007/s43621-023-00127-9

Copyright of the summarized publication:

The Author(s) 2023

License: OpenAccess CC BY 4.0

This article is licensed under a Creative Commons Attribution 4.0 International License, which permits use, sharing, adaptation, distribution and reproduction in any medium or format, as long as you give appropriate credit to the original author(s) and the source, provide a link to the Creative Commons licence, and indicate if changes were made. The images or other third party material in this article are included in the article's Creative Commons licence, unless indicated otherwise in a credit line to the material. If material is not included in the article's Creative Commons licence and your intended use is not permitted by statutory regulation or exceeds the permitted use, you will need to obtain permission directly from the copyright holder. To view a copy of this licence, visit http://creativecommons.org/licenses/by/4.0/.

If you want to cite the papers, please refer to the original.

For technical reasons we could not place the page where the original quote is coming from.

Abstract-Summary

"The influence of quality of work-life on job satisfaction is critical for sustaining high-level skilled workers and enhancing productivity in the oil and gas industry."

"This study examined the influence of quality of work-life on job satisfaction among workers in a gas processing plant."

"The analysis established a positive relationship between employee job satisfaction and the four constructs of quality of work life; safe working environments, Work-life balance, personal development, and emotional well-being at significant levels."

"With the latter construct registering the highest correlation with job satisfaction, the study recommends the management of a functional early guidance support system for workers who may exhibit early symptoms of emotional well-being distress."

Introduction

"Quality of Work-life (QWL) is one important factor accounting for human motivation and improvement in job satisfaction (Saraji & Dargahi, [48])."

"Quality of work-life positively impacting job satisfaction will lead to organisational commitment and increased productivity."

"It is against these gaps in literature that this study is conducted to determine how quality of work-life (QWL) influence job satisfaction among employees in a State-Owned Gas processing plant in Ghana."

"The study assessed the effect of safety working environment on employee job satisfaction, examined the relationship between work-life balance and employee job satisfaction, analysed the effect of personal development and the effect of emotional well-being on employee job satisfaction."

"It is expected to provide relevant information for management to provide conducive working environment where employees can work with minimum stress and make available policies that focus on improving the QWL of employees and job satisfaction."

Contextual Issues

"It outlined further, a conceptual framework to provide direction for assessing the relationships and influence of quality of work-life on job satisfaction in a gas processing plant (Sharma [49])."

"This offer opportunities for managers to design employee motivational quality of work-life schemes to influence job satisfaction."

"To achieve high quality of work-life in a gas processing plant, management must devote time and resources in implementing policies geared towards improving employee job satisfaction and mitigate adverse impacts of poor quality of work-life at the workplace."

"Empirical findings on how determinants of quality of work-life influence job satisfaction among employees have highlighted on safety working environment, work-life balance, personal development and emotional well-being (Agosti & others [50]; Shields & others [51]; Thorsteinson [52])."

"To address these objectives, the following research hypothesis were formulated; H1: Safety working environment positively influence employee job satisfaction, H2: Work life balance positively influence employee job satisfaction, H3: Personal development positively influence employee job satisfaction and; H4: Emotional wellbeing positively influence employee job satisfaction."

Methods and Materials

"To ensure empirical rigour (Friedman [53]), the study examined the influence of quality of work-life on job satisfaction among employees in a gas processing plant using descriptive-analytical research design."

"The instrument depicts background of the respondents including their level of education, age group, and gender and initiated a process where descriptive statistics will be used to analyse the level of agreement of the impact of safety working environment on job satisfaction; the association between work-life balance and job satisfaction; the effect of personal development on job satisfaction; and the influence of emotional well-being on job satisfaction."

"The scope of study was limited to only employees at the gas processing plant focusing on how quality of work-life constructs influence job satisfaction."

"Further studies on possible role of other mediating and moderating constructs such as personality traits, leadership styles, role ambiguity, social support, perceived organisational support and other related factors are laudable to provide new perspectives and contribute to the body of knowledge in the influence of quality of work-life on job satisfaction studies."

Results and Discussion

"Safety working environment is positively related to employee job satisfaction (r = 0.333 p < 0.000), and significant."

"The correlation confirms the first hypothesis (H1) of the study, that working in a safe environment will positively influences employee job satisfaction."

"Correlation between emotional well-being and employee Job satisfaction at significance level 0.00 is also positive indicating that safe working environment has significant positive correlation with employee job satisfaction (r = 0.943 p < 0.000)."

"There is indication quality work-life has strong positive significant outcomes on employee job satisfaction in the gas processing plant."

"Safety working environment positively relates to employee job satisfaction in the gas processing plant with significant influence (t-test = 4.705; p = 0.00)."

"Work-life balance has significant influence on employee job satisfaction among the employees and positively related (Beta = 0.738)."

Conclusion and Recommendations

"The quality of work-life on job satisfaction is critical for safeguarding high level quality employee retention and work productivity in the oil and gas sector."

"It analysed the impact and extent quality of work-life on employee job satisfaction in a gas processing plant in Ghana."

"Employees with positive emotional health and well-being in the workplace are likely to enjoy all work roles assigned them compared to those with negative emotional well-being."

"Workers who are able to effectively manage both their career and personal life are likely to enjoy work roles in the plant."

"The research findings also established positive relationships between safety working environment and employee job satisfaction, an indication that a safe and healthy working environment is likely to increase employee's level of confidence, commitment, efficiency and effectiveness."

"Management must on periodic basis, review the allocation of work duties and job description to ensure employees have achievable workloads."

The Effect of Servant Leadership on Employee Outcomes: Does Endogeneity Matter? [93]

This is a machine-generated summary of:
Isabel, Rosa-Díaz; David, Martín-Ruiz; Gabriel, Cepeda-Carrión: The effect of servant leadership on employee outcomes: does endogeneity matter? [93]

Published in: Quality & Quantity (2021)
Link to original: https://doi.org/https://doi.org/10.1007/s11135-021-01109-7
Copyright of the summarized publication:
The Author(s), under exclusive licence to Springer Nature B.V. part of Springer Nature 2021
All rights reserved.
If you want to cite the papers, please refer to the original.
For technical reasons we could not place the page where the original quote is coming from.

Abstract-Summary

"Servant leadership represents a key element due to its influence on the organization's well-being and proper functioning, both at the individual level (employees) and the global level (team)."

"This research analyzes servant leadership's influence on organizational citizenship behavior (OCB) and how it promotes its efficiency through its two dimensions (OCB towards the employees and OCB towards the organization)."

"The results reveal a significant direct influence of servant leadership on OCB and direct and indirect effects through employee's self-efficacy and job satisfaction."

Introduction

"At the organizational level, healthy organizations develop efficient and competitive ways to work by promoting an organizational climate that supports positive relations and leadership styles to empower employees through autonomy and self-organization (Di Fabio & others [55])."

"Of reasoning, servant leadership can be considered an organizational virtue that encourages positive feelings and behaviors on the part of employees within the organization, and that even leads them to act beyond what is deemed to be mandatory, given their genuine commitment to both the organization and their peers (Organizational Citizenship Behavior, OCB) (Koning & Van Kleef [56])."

"We conduct our research in the context of sports centers–health and sport are top priorities for many people–to analyze the possible influence of the sports center's servant leaders on the behavior, feelings, and attitudes of the employees who work for them."

"This research incorporates the variables employee's self-efficacy and job satisfaction, intending to clarify its role in servant leadership's influence on Organizational Citizenship Behavior (OCB)."

Theoretical Background

"There is evidence that job resources buffer the relationship between job demands and exhaustion; this is, even in situations of high emotional demands and overwhelming workload, if the employee has access to enough resources, they will handle exhaustion positively (Bakker & Demerouti [29])."

"Leaders may influence the working environment of the employee and their well-being and job performance in consequence."

"There is a call to investigate how different leadership styles–including servant leadership–affect employee work engagement and job performance through daily job demands and resources (Bakker & Demerouti [57])."

"Servant leadership has been proposed as an antecedent of several work-related attitudinal results such as employees' commitment and job satisfaction (Coetzer & others [58]; Van Dierendonck & others [59])."

"It states that the attitudes and organizational management of servant leadership can drive employees' self-efficacy, which in turn enhances job satisfaction and OCB behavior in its two dimensions, that is, towards the individuals (OCB_i) and towards the organization (OCB_o)."

Research Method

"The scales used to measure the study variables are presented next (see Appendix), and all of them were operationalized as composites."

"We used the 16-item scale of Lee and Allen [60] to measure OCB."

"This scale provides more detailed information than other general measures of job satisfaction."

"We used the one-dimensional 8-item scale proposed by Chen, Gully, and Eden [61] to measure this variable."

"PLS-SEM permits modeling latent variables based on behavioral research, composite constructs, and different measurement scales."

"The aim of PLS-SEM is, therefore, to investigate the relations between directly non-observable variables (i.e., latent variables), which are, in turn, measured by indicators (i.e., manifest variables), provided by scales (Hair & others [62]; Machitella & others [63]; Signore & others [64])."

"Bootstrapping is a resampling procedure that allows assessing the significance of fit indices, path coefficients, weights, and loadings of each composite's indicators (i.e., latent variable)."

Results

"Endogeneity arises when non-random samples are selected, and in research models where it is not very clear the direction of the relationships between variables and/or some important variables which are not present in the model (Antonakis & others [65])."

"We included instrumental variables (e.g., control variables) in our model, pointing to dependent variables of OCB and the Gaussian copula estimated proposed by Park and Gupta [66] and described by Hult and others [67]."

"The results indicate (p = 0.0002) that none of the constructs have normal-distributed scores, which allows us to analyze endogeneity with Gaussian copulation analysis. (2) Run Gaussian copula analysis adding a copula for each independent variable for each dependent variable."

"Although the Gaussian copula of Servant Leadership is always non-significant, its addition modifies Servant Leadership's parameter from being slightly significant in the models where its copula is not to be significant in the models where its copula is."

"Model 3 is the best to isolate endogeneity, giving values of the least biased relationships for JSAT."

Discussion

"In our illustrative example, servant leadership is characterized by a particular focus on service and care for others, which leads to the development of an ethical work climate (Teng & others [68])."

"Our results highlight the importance of fostering a servant leadership attitude and behavior among the managers of organizations due to its positive effect on employees, which, in turn, tends to develop self-efficiency, autonomy, competence, and motivation, as suggested by the JD-R Theory."

"Servant leadership provides them with greater job satisfaction, an emotional element that also strengthens OCB towards the organization's members and external clients (Di Fabio [55])."

"The present paper provides an illustrative example of how endogeneity can change the interpretation of the results obtained."

"This study presents the results of the first wave of data collection; its cross-sectional nature limits our ability to analyze the long-term effects of leadership over the employees."

Is Transformational Leadership Always Good for Employee Task Performance? Examining Curvilinear and Moderated Relationships [94]

This is a machine-generated summary of:

Chen, Yashuo; Ning, Ranran; Yang, Tong; Feng, Shangjun; Yang, Chunjiang: Is transformational leadership always good for employee task performance? Examining curvilinear and moderated relationships [94]

Published in: Frontiers of Business Research in China (2018)

Link to original: https://doi.org/https://doi.org/10.1186/s11782-018-0044-8
Copyright of the summarized publication:
The Author(s). 2018
License: OpenAccess CC BY 4.0

This article is distributed under the terms of the Creative Commons Attribution 4.0 International License (http://creativecommons.org/licenses/by/4.0/), which permits unrestricted use, distribution, and reproduction in any medium, provided you give appropriate credit to the original author(s) and the source, provide a link to the Creative Commons license, and indicate if changes were made.

If you want to cite the papers, please refer to the original.

For technical reasons we could not place the page where the original quote is coming from.

Abstract-Summary

"The paradoxical perspective indicates that conflicting positive and negative effects of transformational leadership can coexist, which provides possibility and rationality for thorough consideration of employees' task performance influenced by transformational leaders."

"Integrating the principle of diminishing marginal utility and the "Too-Much-of-a-Good-Thing (TMGT)" effect, this research explores an inverted U-shaped relationship between transformational leadership and employee task performance."

"Applying social cognitive theory, we assume an employee's proactive personality moderates the curvilinear influence of transformational leadership on employees' task performance."

"Results from a study of data from 209 supervisor-subordinate relationships from China showed that the inverted U-shaped relationship between transformational leadership and employees' task performance was moderated by employees' proactive personality."

Introduction

"Based on the consideration of both advantages and disadvantages coexisting in inspired leadership (Keeley [69]), we posit that there may be a potential curvilinear pattern in the relationship between transformational leadership and desirable outcomes in the workplace, including the nature of employee task performance."

"Considering this important yet unaddressed issue of the effects of transformational leadership on employee task performance, in this research we empirically examine the potential nonlinear relation (inverted U-shape) in the aforementioned relationship."

"We explicitly investigate how subordinates' proactive personality moderates the curvilinear influence of transformational leadership on employee task performance."

"In our model we simultaneously include transformational leadership as the antecedent of task performance and employees' proactive personality as moderator in the influence of transformational leadership on task performance which fills the research gap on leadership that has been heavily leader-focused but with little attention paid to followers as a differentiated group."

Literature Review and Hypotheses Development

"Transformational leadership, when it is in middle and low degrees, has a greater positive effect on task performance when employees possess a low level of proactive personality."

"Excessive transformational leadership has a less negative effect on task performance when employees hold a high level of proactive personality."

"When leaders begin to perform transformational leadership such as providing personal attention based on needs, provision of resources to overcome problems and encouragement of performance (Stone & others [70]), employees with a low proactive personality would possess advantageous resources and support in finishing work tasks."

"We hypothesize as follows: Hypothesis 2: Employee proactive personality positively moderates the relationship between transformational leadership and employee task performance."

"Transformational leadership has a greater positive impact on task performance when employees have a low level of proactive personality."

Study 1

"We prepared two detailed operations manuals, including steps and screenshots in order to make participants aware of how to complete the questionnaires online."

"The completed questionnaires were collected by the researchers via WeChat, a widely used instant communication tool in China, in order to alleviate participants' potential concern about the exposure of their answers."

"Employees opened the questionnaires designated for subordinates to start the answering process."

"During Part 1, the measure of transformational leadership, proactive personality and demographic information was completed by subordinates; we received 308 questionnaires which could be used in subsequent analysis."

"During Part 2 (3 months later), the measures of employees' task performance was completed by immediate supervisors."

"After deleting the questionnaires with unmatched leader-employee pairs and incomplete answers, 209 supervisor-subordinate dyads were used in the present study, yielding a 59.7% response rate."

Analysis and Results

"Before hypotheses testing, we first conducted CFA (Mplus) procedures to verify the distinctiveness of the three variables included in the present research: transformational leadership, proactive personality and task performance."

"We tested the possibility of non-linearity (H1) in the relationship between transformational leadership and task performance as follows:where $TL^2_i = TL_i \times TL_i$, supporting the inverted U-shaped relationship between transformational leadership and task performance must satisfy the following conditions: β_0 and $\beta_1 > 0$; $\beta_2 < 0$."

"We tested our second hypothesis for the role of proactive personality in moderating the relationship between transformational leadership and employee task performance."

"We followed hierarchical regression analysis using SPSS software, and the independent variables (transformational leadership) and proactive personality variables were all mean-center for testing the interaction effects to reduce potential multicollinearity problems (Aiken & West [71])."

"Hypothesis 2 predicts that a proactive personality moderates the curvilinear relationship between transformational leadership and task performance."

Study 2

"Study 2 was conducted to test all of our hypotheses again, to replicate the findings of Study 1 in a bank context, and corroborate our results across studies (Mathison [72]; Webb & others [73])."

"We hope our findings provide more confidence in the interpretation of these results and their robustness."

Methodology

"In Study 2, 168 employees with only one immediate supervisor, working in the Bank of China, Qinhuangdao Branch, were recruited."

"Fifty-five immediate supervisors of those employees also participated in the survey."

"In the first wave, we collected demographic information, transformational leadership and a measure of proactive personality from employees."

"In the second wave, which began 2 weeks following the end of the first wave, we collected demographic information and employees' task performance from supervisors."

"Each employee received a unique pairing code that we allocated when they finished the questionnaires, and their immediate supervisors were notified of the pairing code of each employee."

"Similar to Study 1, we controlled for employees' age, gender, organizational tenure, and level of education."

"The measure of organizational tenure was the number of months a participant had been in the current organization and career, and age was evaluated in years."

Analysis and Results

"The result of Harman's single factor test shows that no single factor emerges and no single factor accounts for > 50% of the variance of all the relevant items."

"Transformational leadership is positively related to task performance."

"Cronbach's alpha coefficients of transformational leadership, proactive personality and task performance are 0.937, 0.819 and 0.969 respectively, which signifies that all of them have good reliability."

"There is a curvilinear relationship between transformational leadership and employee task performance."

"We tested the moderating influence of employees' proactive personality on the relationship between transformational leadership and task performance."

Discussion

"By adopting a paradox perspective, TMGT effect, and the principle of diminishing marginal utility, the study explains that the influence of transformational leadership on employee task performance is more complex than the simple linear relationship conventionally assumed in previous studies."

"Based on social cognitive theory, our study finds that proactive personality positively moderates the curvilinear relationship between transformational leadership and task performance."

"The level of individual proactive personality needs to be considered as an important influential factor in predicting transformational leadership effectiveness and productivity; however, research which directly examines the interactional effects between transformational leadership and proactive personality on employees' performance outcomes is scare (Wang & others [74])."

"Our study directly examines the effects of interaction between transformational leadership and proactive personality on employee task performance."

"This study only explores whether proactive personality moderates the relationship between transformational leadership and employee task performance."

[Section 9]

"Enron, the seventh largest company in the US at its peak, suffered the fate of its final demise the subsequent year."

"Although "Enron is too complex a story to avail of one single explanation (e.g., an extremely prevalent excessive transformational leadership within the organizational life) for its rise and fall," the undeniable fact is that there were "compelling vision and totalistic vision(s)," "charismatic and extremely powerful" leaders and "higher levels of compliance from followers" on the eve of bankruptcy, which provides some beneficial inspiration to consider the dark side of transformational leadership. —"

The Antecedents of Corporate Reputation and Image and Their Impacts on Employee Commitment and Performance: The Moderating Role of CSR [95]

This is a machine-generated summary of:
 Almeida, Maria da Graça Marques Casimiro; Coelho, Arnaldo Fernandes Matos: The Antecedents of Corporate Reputation and Image and Their Impacts on Employee Commitment and Performance: The Moderating Role of CSR [95]
 Published in: Corporate Reputation Review (2018)
 Link to original: https://doi.org/https://doi.org/10.1057/s41299-018-0053-8
 Copyright of the summarized publication:
 Springer Nature Limited & Reputation Institute 2018
 All rights reserved.
 If you want to cite the papers, please refer to the original.
 For technical reasons we could not place the page where the original quote is coming from.

Abstract-Summary

"The aim of this investigation is to identify how culture and communication may influence corporate reputation (CR) and corporate image and their impact on workers' attitudes and behaviour, like organizational commitment and individual performance."

"The moderating role of the perceptions of corporate social responsibility (CSR) is also analysed."

"They show, as well, how corporate reputation impacts on commitment which contributes to improving individual performance."

"Perception of CSR practices may increase the way CR is perceived and boost the bonds between employees and their organization."

"These results may raise the interest in deepening investigation in this field, showing how CSR practices create a new context to investigate these relationships."

"This investigation shows how organizations involved in responsible attitudes and practices are challenged to find the right balance between making a profit and serving the community."

"CR, commitment and productivity may be strengthened when companies develop a bigger engagement with socially responsible practices."

Introduction

"An increased reputation may reinforce the links between employees and the organization, thereby improving the corporate image and increasing the commitment and performance (Bauman & Skitka [75]), which may be boosted in a work environment rich in social practices."

"CR plays an important role in the way employees relate with the organization, and therefore it (a) promotes personal fulfilment; (b) increases identification with the organization; (c) helps the organization meet their objectives; and (d) boosts the sense of responsibility and the way they interact with the outside world."

"Management can achieve significant advances in corporate strategic objectives using the synergetic interaction between employees and CR (Cravens & Oliver [76]), knowing that CR may be a critical link between employees and management."

"The objectives of this study are to understand the antecedents of the CR and its impacts on organizational commitment and individual performance from the perspective of employees, and the moderating role of perceived CSR practices in these relationships."

Research Background and Hypotheses Development

"Corporate culture is an agent of absolute importance to build the reputation of an organization, impacting on the different outcomes such as employee morale, safety, quality of products and services, customer satisfaction, profitability and performance (Gümüs & Öksüz [77])."

"The corporate image is defined as the total sum of its reputation, the way it organizes and operates its activities and conducts its business, the attitudes of their employees and even the way they respond to clients and associates (Powell [78])."

"CSR practices may influence and boost a positive organizational image that enhances employees' pride and willingness to be associated with such a reputable organization (Turker [79])."

"A culture that values and promotes the maintenance of corporate reputation will affect the employee's perception of the company's image (Cravens & Oliver [76], p. 297)."

Method

"In order to test the proposed investigation model and the research hypotheses, data collection was based on a structured questionnaire."

"The scale is composed of eleven items like "I trust in the data on products and services"."

"A second-order model was used for the latent construct individual performance (Johns & Miraglia [80]) Items like "Attends functions that are not required but that help the company image" and "All things considered this manager performs his/her job the way I like to see it performed"."

"According to Podsakoff and others [81], the common method variance (CMV) tests will help identify the existence of variables that can cause measurement errors and systematic bias in the estimation of the relationships between constructs."

"The emergence of this problem may arise when the information about the independent and dependent variables comes from the same respondent; the same scale format is used throughout the questionnaire; and different constructs are measured at the same time and using the same instrument."

Finding and Discussion

"The relationship between CR and image is statistically significant (SRW = 0.620: P < 0.05), therefore supporting H5."

"Workers perceiving a higher CSR activity (SRW = 0.341: P < 0.05) tend to give more importance to social practices and less to image (Lee [82]; Kim & others [83]; Farooq & others [84]), while the lack of socially engaged practices lives these impacts to image, giving support to the idea that CSR may moderate this relationship."

"The relationship between CR and individual performance is not statistically significant (SRW = 0.036: P > 0.05), thus not supporting H8."

"Commitment has a positive impact on individual performance (SRW = 0.267: P < 0.05), thus supporting H9."

"More than the specific and direct impacts CSR may have, this investigation shows that socially engaged practices may boost the relationships between culture, communication and CR and their outcomes like commitment and individual performance."

Contributions

"This investigation shows how CR, based on internal communication and culture, may impact on individual performance, particularly increasing organizational commitment."

"This investigation brings additional contributions explaining the chain of effects starting on the CR formation, explained by culture and communication, and ending exploring its impacts on image- and on work-related outcomes, like commitment and individual performance."

"We introduced the moderating role of CSR showing how it may influence the internal relationships between CR-, image- and the work-related outcomes, which may be an important topic for further investigation, according to Odriozola and others [85]."

"A stronger perception of CSR practices may increase the way CR is perceived and boost the bonds between employees and their organization, therefore increasing individual performance."

"A CSR environment may increase the impacts of the HRM measures, therefore reinforcing the impacts on work-related outcomes like commitment and individual performance."

Limitations and Future Investigation

"This research is based on a sample of workers from a union of cooperatives from the dairy industry."

"The measures used, especially the CR scale, is usually used for other stakeholders like consumers and shareholders, but also for employees, when it comes to comparing the results among different stakeholders."

"It could be extended and applied to other stakeholders like customers and shareholders, to compare results as well, as comparing these results with cooperatives from other regions and cultures would help to understand the impacts of different cultures on the way CR acts."

"Measures adopted may not fit equally among different stakeholders, especially workers."

"The development of a multidimensional scale that can collect CR evaluation from different stakeholders, with good psychometric properties, would be a good task to be performed to ensure some comparability of results."

Concluding Remarks

"This research highlights the importance of intangible assets such as reputation management."

"Corporate reputation has received growing attention in recent decades, while research from the employee perspective is relatively limited."

"Employees, as one of the most important internal stakeholders' group, are currently drawing attention from both researchers and practitioners."

"The results of this study reveal opportunities for managers to use these findings as a contribution to increase the competitiveness of their companies throughout a better use of human resources management, based on CR and CSR."

"It is expected that the results of this research can help companies of the cooperative sector to change and adapt their management practices and traditional principles and to achieve greater convergence with the challenges that organizations will face in this twenty-first century."

Bibliography

1. Bolino, M. C. (1999). Citizenship and impression management: Good soldiers or good actors? *Academy of Management Review, 24*(1), 82–98.
2. Bolino, M. C., Varela, J. A., Bande, B., & Turnley, W. H. (2006). The impact of impression-management tactics on supervisor ratings of organizational citizenship behavior. *Journal of Organizational Behavior, 27*(3), 281–297.
3. Bolino, M. C., Kacmar, K. M., Turnley, W. H., & Gilstrap, J. B. (2008). A multi-level review of impression management motives and behaviors. *Journal of Management, 34*(6), 1080–1109.
4. Harris, K. J., Kacmar, K. M., Zivnuska, S., & Shaw, J. D. (2007). The impact of political skill on impression management effectiveness. *Journal of Applied Psychology, 92*(1), 278–285.
5. Liu, Y., Loi, R., & Lam, L. W. (2013). Exemplification and supervisor-rated performance: The moderating role of ethical leadership. *International Journal of Selection and Assessment, 21*(2), 145–154.
6. Wayne, S. J., & Liden, R. C. (1995). Effects of impression management on performance ratings: A longitudinal study. *Academy of Management Journal, 38*(1), 232–260.
7. Bande, B., Fernández-Ferrín, P., Otero-Neira, C., & Varela, J. (2017). Impression management tactics and performance ratings: A moderated-mediation framework. *Journal of Business-to-Business Marketing, 24*(1), 19–34.
8. Griffin, M. A., Neal, A., & Parker, S. K. (2007). A new model of work role performance: Positive behavior in uncertain and interdependent contexts. *Academy of Management Journal, 50*(2), 327–347.
9. Brouer, R. L., Badaway, R. L., Gallagher, V. C., & Haber, J. A. (2015). Political skill dimensionality and impression management choice and effective use. *Journal of Business and Psychology, 30*(2), 217–233.
10. Augusto-Landa, J. M., Pulido-Martos, M., & Lopez-Zafra, E. (2011). Does perceived emotional intelligence and optimism/pessimism predict psychological well-being? *Journal of Happiness Studies, 12*(3), 463–474.
11. Hirschfeld, R. R. (2000). Does revising the intrinsic and extrinsic subscales of the Minnesota satisfaction questionnaire short form make a difference? *Educational and Psychological Measurement, 60*(2), 255–270.
12. Anderson, J. C., & Gerbing, D. W. (1988). Structural equation modeling in practice: A review and recommended two-step approach. *Psychological Bulletin, 103*, 411.
13. Rogers, W. M., & Schmitt, N. (2004). Parameter recovery and model fit using multidimensional composites: A comparison of four empirical parceling algorithms. *Multivariate Behavioral Research, 39*(3), 379–412.
14. Brotheridge, C. M., & Grandey, A. A. (2002). Emotional labor and burnout: Comparing two perspectives of "people work." *Journal of Vocational Behavior, 60*(1), 17–39.
15. Ashforth, B., & Humphrey, R. H. (1993). Emotional labor in service role: The influence of identity. *Academy of Management Review, 18*, 88–115.
16. Diefendorff, J. M., & Richard, E. M. (2003). Antecedents and consequences of emotional display rule perceptions. *Journal of Applied Psychology, 88*(2), 284–294.
17. Cropanzano, R., Weiss, H. M., & Elias, S. M. (2004). The impact of display rules and emotional labor on psychological well-being at work. In P. L. Perrew & D. C. Ganster (Eds.), *Research in occupational stress and well being* (pp. 45–89). Elsevier.
18. Matsumoto, D., Yoo, S. H., Hirayama, S., & Petrova, G. (2005). Validation of an individual-level measure of display rules: The display rule assessment inventory (DRAI). *Emotion, 5*(1), 23–40.

19. Schaubroeck, J., & Jones, J. R. (2000). Antecedents of workplace emotional labor dimensions and moderators of their effects on physical symptoms. *Journal of Organizational Behavior, 21*(2), 163–183.
20. Glomb, T. M., & Tews, M. J. (2004). Emotional labor: A conceptualization and scale development. *Journal of Vocational Behavior, 64*(1), 1–23.
21. Hochschild, A. R. (1983). *The managed heart: Commercialization of human feeling*. University of California Press.
22. Davidson, R. J. (1998). Affective style and affective disorders: Perspectives from affective neuroscience. *Cognition and Emotion, 12*, 307–330.
23. Isen, A. M. (1999). Positive affect. In T. Dalgleish and M. Power (Eds.), *The handbook of cognition and emotion*. Wiley.
24. Grandey, A. A. (2003). When 'the show must go on'. Surface acting and deep acting as determinants of emotional exhaustion and peer-rated service delivery. *Academy of Management Journal, 46*(1), 86–96.
25. Diefendorff, J. M., & Gosserand, R. H. (2003). Understanding the emotional labor process: A control theory perspective. *Journal of Organizational Behavior, 24*(8), 945–959.
26. Heuven, E., Bakker, A. B., & Schaufeli, W. B. (2006). The role of self-efficacy in performing emotion work. *Journal of Vocational Behavior, 69*(2), 222–235.
27. Zapf, D., Vogt, C., Seifert, C., Mertini, H., & Isic, A. (1999). Emotion work as a source of stress: The concept and development of an instrument. *European Journal of Work and Organizational Psychology, 8*(3), 371–340.
28. Goodman, S. A., & Svyantek, D. J. (1999). Personorganization fit and contextual performance: Do shared values matter? *Journal of Vocational Behavior, 55*, 254–275.
29. Bakker, A. B., & Demerouti, E. (2007). The job demands-resources model: State of the art. *Journal of Managerial Psychology*. https://doi.org/10.1108/02683940710733115
30. Pierce, J. L., & Gardner, D. G. (2004). Self-esteem within work and organizational context: A review of the organization-based self-esteem literature. *Journal of Management, 30*(5), 591–622.
31. Van Yperen, N. W., & Snijders, T. A. B. (2000). A multilevel analysis of the demands-control model: Is stress at work determined by factors at the group level or the individual level? *Journal of Occupational Health Psychology, 5*(1), 182–190.
32. Xanthopoulou, D., Bakker, A. B., Demerouti, E., & Schaufeli, W. B. (2007). The role of personal resources in the job demands-resources model. *International Journal of Stress Management, 14*(2), 121–141.
33. Blau, P. (1964). *Exchange and power in social life* (1st ed.). Wiley.
34. Rhoades, L., & Eisenberger, R. (2002). Perceived organizational support: A review of the literature. *Journal of Applied Psychology, 87*(4), 698–714.
35. Singh, J., Goolsby, J., & Rhoads, G. (1994). Behavioral and psychological consequences of boundary spanning burnout for customer service representatives. *Journal of Marketing Research, 31*(31), 558–569.
36. Jenkins, K., & Harvey, S. B. (2019). Australian experiences. *Mental Health in the Workplace* (pp. 49–66). Springer.
37. Allen, T. D. (2001). Family-supportive work environments: The role of Organisational perceptions. *Journal of Vocational Behaviour, 58*(3), 414–435. https://doi.org/10.1006/jvbe.2000.1774
38. Lapierre, L., Spector, P., Allen, T., Poelmans, S., Cooper, C., O'Driscoll, M., Sanchez, J., Brough, P., & Kinnunen, U. (2008). Family-supportive organization perceptions, multiple dimensions of work-family conflict, and employee satisfaction: Test of model across five samples. *Journal of Vocational Behaviour, 73*(1), 92–106. https://doi.org/10.1016/j.jvb.2008.02.001
39. Haar, J. M., & Roche, M. (2010). Family-supportive organization perceptions and employee outcomes: The mediating effects of life satisfaction. *The International Journal of Human Resource Management, 21*(7), 999–1014. https://doi.org/10.1080/09585191003783462

40. Wayne, J., Randel, A., & Stevens, J. (2006). The role of identity and work family support in WFE and work-related consequences. *Journal of Vocational Behaviour, 69*(3), 445–461. https://doi.org/10.1016/j.jvb.2006.07.002
41. Fontinha, R., Easton, S., & Van Laar, D. (2019). Overtime and quality of working life in academics and nonacademics: The role of perceived work-life balance. *International Journal of Stress Management, 26*(2), 173. https://doi.org/10.1037/str0000067
42. Matthews, R. A., Mills, M. J., Trout, R. C., & English, L. (2014). Family-supportive supervisor behaviors, work engagement, and subjective well-being: A contextually dependent mediated process. *Journal of Occupational Health Psychology, 19*(2), 168–181. https://doi.org/10.1037/a0036012
43. Hammer, L. B., Kossek, E. E., Anger, W. K., Bodner, T., & Zimmerman, K. L. (2011). Clarifying work–family intervention processes: The roles of work–family conflict and family-supportive supervisor behaviors. *Journal of Applied Psychology, 96*(1), 134–150.
44. Hall, D. T., Kossek, E. E., Briscoe, J. P., Pichler, S., & Lee, M. D. (2013). Nonwork orientations relative to career: A multidimensional measure. *Journal of Vocational Behavior, 83*(3), 539–550. https://doi.org/10.1016/j.jvb.2013.07.005
45. Ferri, L. M., Pedrini, M., & Riva, E. (2018). The impact of different supports on work-family conflict. *Employee Relations, 40*(5), 903–920. https://doi.org/10.1108/ER-09-2017-0211
46. Jurado-Guerrero, T., Monferrer, J. M., Botía-Morillas, C., & Abril, F. (2018). Formal and informal workplace support for new fathers in Spain. In *Fathers, childcare and work: Cultures, practices and policies* (pp. 131–153). Emerald Publishing Limited.
47. Chang, A., McDonald, P., & Burton, P. (2010). Methodological choices in work-life balance research 1987 to 2006: A critical review. *The International Journal of Human Resource Management, 21*(13), 2381–2413. https://doi.org/10.1080/09585192.2010.516592
48. Saraji, G. N., & Dargahi, H. (2006). Study of quality of work-life. *Iranian Journal of Public Health, 35*(4), 8–14.
49. Sharma, D. K. (2016). Quality of work life & its key dimensions: A cross-sectional analysis of private, public sector and foreign banks in India. *Amity Journal of Management, 4*(1), 28–39.
50. Agosti, M. T., Andersson, I., Ejlertsson, G., et al. (2015). Shift work to balance everyday life—A salutogenic nursing perspective in home help service in Sweden. *BMC Nursing, 14*, 2. https://doi.org/10.1186/s12912-014-0054-6
51. Shields, L., Pratt, J., & Hunter, J. (2006). Family centred care: A review of qualitative studies. *Journal of Clinical Nursing, 15*(1), 1317–1323. https://doi.org/10.1111/j.1365-2702.2006.01433.x
52. Thorsteinson, T. J. (2003). Job attitudes of part-time vs full-time workers: A meta-analytic review. *Journal of Occupational and Organizational Psychology, 76*(2), 151–177.
53. Friedman, M. (1953). *The methodology of positive economics.* University of Chicago Press.
54. Sarstedt, M., Ringle, C. M., Cheah, J. H., Ting, H., Moisescu, O. I., & Radomir, L. (2019). Structural model robustness checks in PLS-SEM. *Tourism Economics.* https://doi.org/10.1177/1354816618823921
55. Di Fabio, A. (2017). Positive Healthy Organizations: Promoting well-being, meaningfulness, and sustainability in organizations. *Frontiers in Psychology, 8*, 1938.
56. Koning, L. F., & Van Kleef, G. A. (2015). How leaders' emotional displays shape followers' organizational citizenship behavior. *The Leadership Quarterly, 26*(4), 489–501.
57. Bakker, A. B., & Demerouti, E. (2017). Job demands-resources theory: Taking stock and looking forward. *Journal of Occupational Health Psychology, 22*(3), 273–285. https://doi.org/10.1037/ocp0000056
58. Coetzer, M. F., Bussin, M., & Geldenhuys, M. (2017). The functions of servant leadership. *Administrative Sciences.* https://doi.org/10.3390/admsci7010005
59. Van Dierendonck, D., Stam, D., Boersma, P., De Windt, N., & Alkema, J. (2014). Same difference? Exploring the differential mechanisms linking servant leadership and transformational leadership to follower outcomes. *The Leadership Quarterly, 25*, 544–562.
60. Lee, K., & Allen, N. J. (2002). Organizational citizenship behavior and workplace deviance: The role of affect and cognitions. *Journal of Applied Psychology, 87*(1), 131–142.

Bibliography

61. Chen, G., Gully, S. M., & Eden, D. (2001). Validation of a new general self-efficacy scale. *Organizational Res. Methods, 4*(1), 62–83.
62. Hair, J. F., Jr., Hult, G. T. M., Ringle, C. M., Sarstedt, M., Castillo Apraiz, J., Cepeda Carrión, G. A., Roldán, J. L. (2019). Manual de Partial Least Squares Structural Equation Modeling (PLS-SEM) (Segunda Edición); OmniaScience, Sage Publications. ISBN: 978-84-947996-2-4.
63. Macchitella, L., Marinelli, C. V., Signore, F., Ciavolino, E., & Angelelli, P. (2020). Sleepiness, neuropsychological skills, and scholastic learning in children. *Brain Sciences, 10*(8), 529.
64. Signore, F., Catalano, A., De Carlo, E., Madaro, A., & Ingusci, E. (2019). The role of employability in students during academic experience: A preliminary study through PLS-PM technique. *Electronic Journal of Applied Statistical Analysis, 12*(4), 720–747.
65. Antonakis, J., Bendahan, S., Jacquart, P., & Lalive, R. (2010). On making causal claims: A review and recommendations. *The Leadership Quarterly, 21*(6), 1086–1120. https://doi.org/10.1016/j.leaqua.2010.10.010
66. Park, S., & Gupta, S. (2012). Handling endogenous regressors by joint estimation using copulas. *Marketing Sci., 31*(4), 567–586.
67. Hult, G. T. M., Hair, J. F., Proksch, D., Sarstedt, M., Pinkwart, A., & Ringle, C. M. (2018). Addressing endogeneity in international marketing applications of partial least squares structural equation modeling. *Journal of International Marketing, 26*(3), 1–21. https://doi.org/10.1509/jim.17.0151
68. Teng, C.-C., Lu, A. C. C., Huang, Z.-Y., & Fang, C.-H. (2020). Ethical work climate, organizational identification, leader-member-exchange (LMX) and organizational citizenship behavior (OCB): A study of three-star hotels in Taiwan. *International Journal of Contemporary Hospitality Management, 32*(1), 212–229. https://doi.org/10.1108/IJCHM-07-2018-0563
69. Keeley, M. (1995). The trouble with transformational leadership: Toward a federalist ethic for organizations. *Business Ethics Quarterly, 5*(1), 67–96.
70. Stone, A. G., Russell, R. F., & Patterson, K. (2004). Transformational versus servant leadership: A difference in leader focus. *Leadership & Organization Development Journal, 25*(4), 349–361.
71. Aiken, L. S., & West, S. G. (1994). Multiple regression: Testing and interpreting interactions. *Evaluation Practice, 45*(1), 119–120.
72. Mathison, S. (1988). Why triangulate? *Educational Researcher, 17*(2), 13–17.
73. Webb, E. J., Campbell, D. T., Schwartz, R. D., & Sechrest, L. (1966). *Unobtrusive measures: Nonreactive research in the social sciences* (Vol. 111). Rand McNally.
74. Wang, G., Oh, I.-S., Courtright, S. H., & Colbert, A. E. (2011). Transformational leadership and performance across criteria and levels: A meta-analytic review of 25 years of research. *Group & Organization Management, 36*(2), 223–270.
75. Bauman, C. W., & Skitka, L. J. (2012). Corporate social responsibility as a source of employee satisfaction. *Research in Organizational Behavior, 32*, 63–86.
76. Cravens, K. S., & Oliver, E. G. (2006). Employees: The key link to corporate reputation management. *Business Horizons, 49*(4), 293–302.
77. Gümüş, M., & Öksüz, B. (2009). Key role within reputation process: Corporate social responsibility communication. *Journal of Yasar University., 4*(14), 2129–2150.
78. Powell, S. M. (2011). The nexus between ethical corporate marketing, ethical corporate identity and corporate social responsibility: An internal organisational perspective. *European Journal of Marketing, 45*(9/10), 1365–1379.
79. Turker, D. (2009). How corporate social responsibility influences organizational commitment. *Journal of Business Ethics, 89*(2), 189–204.
80. Johns, G., & Miraglia, M. (2015). The reliability, validity, and accuracy of self-reported absenteeism from work: A meta-analysis. *Journal of Occupational Health Psychology, 20*(N.1), 1–14.
81. Podsakoff, P. M., MacKenzie, S. B., Lee, J. Y., & Podsakoff, N. P. (2003). Common method biases in behavioral research: A critical review of the literature and recommended remedies. *Journal of Applied Psychology, 88*(5), 879–903.

82. Lee, M. D. P. (2008). A review of the theories of corporate social responsibility: Its evolutionary path and the road ahead. *International Journal of Management Reviews, 10*(1), 53–73.
83. Kim, H., Lee, M., Lee, H., & Kim, N. (2010). Corporate social responsibility and employee–company identification. *Journal of Business Ethics, 95*(4), 557–569.
84. Farooq, M., Farooq, O., & Jasimuddin, S. M. (2014). Employees response to corporate social responsibility: Exploring the role of employees' collectivist orientation. *European Management Journal, 32*(6), 916–927.
85. Odriozola, M. D., Martín, A., & Luna, L. (2015). The relationship between labour social responsibility practices and reputation. *International Journal of Manpower, 36*(2), 236–251.
86. Bande, B., Kimura, T., Fernández-Ferrín, P., Castro-González, S., Goel, A. (2023). Are self-sacrificing employees liked by their supervisor? *Eurasian Business Review, 14*(1), 257–284. https://doi.org/10.1007/s40821-023-00243-6
87. Liu, D. (2016). Mediating effect of social support between the emotional intelligence and job satisfaction of Chinese employees. *Current Psychology, 37*, 366–372. https://doi.org/10.1007/s12144-016-9520-5
88. Ohana, M., Murtaza, G., Haq, I. U., Al-Shatti, E., Chi, Z. (2023). Why and when can CSR toward employees lead to Cyberloafing? The role of workplace boredom and moral disengagement. *Journal of Business Ethics, 189*(1), 133–148. https://doi.org/10.1007/s10551-023-05358-4
89. Lee, C., An, M., Noh, Y. (2014). The effects of emotional display rules on flight attendants' emotional labor strategy, job burnout and performance. *Service Business, 9*, 409–425. https://doi.org/10.1007/s11628-014-0231-4
90. Auh, S., Menguc, B., Spyropoulou, S., Wang, F. (2015). Service employee burnout and engagement: The moderating role of power distance orientation. *Journal of the Academy of Marketing Science, 44*, 726–745. https://doi.org/10.1007/s11747-015-0463-4
91. Thilagavathy, S., & Geetha, S. N. (2020). A morphological analyses of the literature on employee work-life balance. *Current Psychology*, 1–26. https://doi.org/10.1007/s12144-020-00968-x
92. Hammond, M., Owusu, N. O., Nunoo, E. K., Boampong, G., Osman, A., Panin, A., Nyametso, J. K., Essen, B. (2023). How quality of work-life influence employee job satisfaction in a gas processing plant in Ghana. *Discover Sustainability, 4*(1), 10. https://doi.org/10.1007/s43621-023-00127-9
93. Isabel, R.-D., David, M.-R., Gabriel, C.-C. (2021). The effect of servant leadership on employee outcomes: Does endogeneity matter? *Quality & Quantity, 57*(suppl 4), 637–655. https://doi.org/10.1007/s11135-021-01109-7
94. Chen, Y., Ning, R., Yang, T., Feng, S., Yang, C. (2018). Is transformational leadership always good for employee task performance? Examining curvilinear and moderated relationships. *Frontiers of Business Research in China, 12*, 1–28. https://doi.org/10.1186/s11782-018-0044-8
95. Almeida, M. D. G. M. C., & Coelho, A. F. M. (2018). The antecedents of corporate reputation and image and their impacts on employee commitment and performance: The moderating role of CSR. *Corporate Reputation Review, 22*, 10–25. https://doi.org/10.1057/s41299-018-0053-8

Chapter 4
Stress and Emotional Intelligence

Introduction by the Author

It is essential to have emotional self-management, not only for employees, but also for entrepreneurs. The trait emotional self -management moderates the relationship between the size of the firm and the amount of benefits enjoyed by the employees. The study conducted by Elmadag [53] extends the research about job stress in service provision by validating the influence of alleviating job stress and associated service quality. Multiple service industry assesses the influence of employee's satisfaction related to job stress and work affect. The research extends and exploits the types of rewards that influence of CCE attitudes that affect customer service experience. The results proved that job stress decreases commitment to the organization and customer orientation. A study undergone by Wei and others [55] states that influence of store's employees emotional intelligence have an impact on repurchase intention of customers.

The trait emotional intelligence of online store employees was analysed by Wei and others [55] and find out that emotional intelligence has a positive impact on psychological empowerment, in turn it has a positive impact on service recovery quality and repurchase intention. Situational experiment is used to explore the employee's emotional intelligence and psychological empowerment with mediating effect with service recovery quality. A study conducted by Lee [57] clarifies the inconsistent relationship between job satisfaction and emotional labour and incorporates emotional intelligence as a mediator in public service employees, South Korea. The study revealed that job satisfaction and deep acting is positively related and emotional self-regulation is partially mediated in public service employees, South Korea. In the absence of emotional self-regulation, employees may often show negative emotion. Based on the study the employees with high emotional intelligence use deep acting more than surface acting. In order to increase job satisfaction, the employees should be promoted to assert their rights as emotional labour workers. Recent studies have highlighted emotional intelligence as a mediator in emotional

© The Author(s), under exclusive license to Springer Nature Singapore Pte Ltd. 2024
R. Mekhala (ed.), *Emotional Intelligence Matters*,
https://doi.org/10.1007/978-981-99-7727-7_4

labour construct resulting in job satisfaction. The relationship between spiritual leadership and employee followership behaviour is examined and results indicates that leaders' intrinsic motivation is recognised when spiritual qualities and sense of belongingness is valued, Cui and others [58].

Emotional intelligence is related to the ability to deal well with stress. People have a number of challenges when it comes to (a) identifying and achieving their goals and demands, (b) fostering interpersonal and personal balance, and (c) increasing their engagement with their environment. It is vital to keep an individual's private characteristics and external circumstances in sync. It is created and maintained by stimulating a person's capacity to use stress coping strategies in order to achieve equilibrium between themselves and their external surroundings. Emotionally intelligent children, according to research, are healthier, happier, and more versatile, and these attributes enhance desirable academic results. Lower emotional intelligence abilities are typified by an increase in criminal activity and teen suicide, episodes of sadness, anxiety, a high aggressiveness, social troubles, dropping out of school, and a lack of spiritual interest. Knowing a person's proficiency, which includes self-awareness, self-control, and motivation, is essential since it governs how an individual performs his routine.

The stress originated from cultural shock on emotional labour, job satisfaction and turnover intention among foreign employees was investigated by Lai and others [51]. Since emotional labour and job satisfaction predicts turnover intention, foreign employee's satisfaction mediates the relationship between cultural shock and turnover intention. The conceptual model was developed to investigate the above variables where perceived managerial support is high, when the relationship between cultural shock and job satisfaction becomes weaker. The practise of meditation, sports, outstanding dietary habits, calmness, comedy, and entertaining pursuits are all excellent stress-reduction metrics. Techniques of dealing with stress varied based on components such as personality traits, state of mind throughout exposure to the unpleasant circumstance, and a person's view of the situation.

In 1994, Cohen outlines the following methods of stress management.

- Rational thinking refers to an individual's capacity to think clearly regarding the causes and origins of stress.
- Individualised imagining: a willingness to consider potential futures and the ramifications of the current circumstance.
- The promotion of positive feelings during conflict.

The study of the relationship between psychological capacity and personal health and well-being has generated a lot of interest. Enhanced emotional intelligence skills contributes to increased interactions with health specialists, which induces an individual's tendency to seek help and follow advice. An emotional-centered coping strategy regulates emotions by proactively altering the metaphorical significance of stressful situations without affecting the distressing experience itself. A skilled coping strategy aids in the creation of a healthy psychological response in extremely challenging circumstances, which is the foundation of excellent physical and mental health.

The parts of EI are useful in forecasting how people may react under tough situations. A survey of 575 graduates from two Chinese institutions indicated a substantial relationship between emotional intelligence and active stress reduction measures. In addition, the research findings revealed that self-management has an instant and good impact on stress management measures. The study looked at the relationship between emotional intelligence and the ability to handle stressful situations in 219 nursing students at Konyang University in Korea. The ability to solve difficulties and get social assistance were found to be positively related to emotional intelligence capacity. Furthermore, it was revealed that effective management and emotional effectiveness aided students in developing useful stress-coping mechanisms. Similarly, Vein explored the relationship between interpersonal skills and ways to cope with stress in students at Nigeria's University of Delta, and the findings revealed a positive relationship between emotional intelligence and stress handling methods. The study also discovered that people with stronger intellectual abilities were better equipped to deal with stress.

Machine Generated Summaries

Disclaimer: The summaries in this chapter were generated from Springer Nature publications using extractive AI auto-summarization: An extraction-based summarizer aims to identify the most important sentences of a text using an algorithm and uses those original sentences to create the auto-summary (unlike generative AI). As the constituted sentences are machine selected, they may not fully reflect the body of the work, so we strongly advise that the original content is read and cited. The auto generated summaries were curated by the editor to meet Springer Nature publication standards. To cite this content, please refer to the original papers.

Machine generated keywords: service, employee, customer, labor, leadership, emotional labor, service employee, culture, job, behavior, intrinsic, expectation, job satisfaction, online, brand

The Effects of Culture Shock on Foreign Employees in the Service Industry [51]

This is a machine-generated summary of:
Lai, Hung-Sheng; Hu, Hsin-Hui; Chen, Zhang-Yu-Jing: The effects of culture shock on foreign employees in the service industry [51]
Published in: Service Business (2020)
Link to original: https://doi.org/https://doi.org/10.1007/s11628-020-00420-x
Copyright of the summarized publication:
Springer-Verlag GmbH Germany, part of Springer Nature 2020

All rights reserved.
If you want to cite the papers, please refer to the original.
For technical reasons we could not place the page where the original quote is coming from.

Abstract-Summary

"This study explores the effects of culture shock on emotional labor, job satisfaction, and the turnover intentions of service employees."

"It further examines the moderating role of perceived managerial support on the relationships between culture shock, emotional labor, and job satisfaction."

"Results suggest that culture shock has positive impacts emotional labor but negative impacts on job satisfaction."

"The relationship between culture shock and foreign employee turnover intentions is mediated by emotional labor and job satisfaction."

Introduction

"Non-resident employees are playing an important role in service organizations, which necessitates competent cross-cultural management."

"To improve work outcomes of foreign employees, service firms have seriously to face culture shock issues because of its influence on job satisfaction.""

"Managers in service firms should understand the key issues of culture shock by foreign employees during their employment."

"To address those research gaps, this study explored the effects of culture shock on emotional labor, job satisfaction, and turnover intention among foreign employees."

"The moderating role of perceived managerial support on the relationships between culture shock, emotional labor, and job satisfaction was also examined."

"Research that investigates the effects of culture shock should therefore help elucidate a more comprehensive understanding and increase the ability of foreign employees to successfully adapt to life in their new cultural environment."

Theoretical Framework and Hypotheses

"Review, we then developed a conceptual model to investigate the effects of culture shock on emotional labor, job satisfaction, and turnover intention among foreign employees."

"Emotional labor and job satisfaction may serve not only as an antecedent to turnover intention, but as a medium between culture shock and foreign employees' turnover intentions."

"These support the conclusion that emotional labor and job satisfaction contribute to employees' turnover intentions."

"Since emotional labor and job satisfaction predict turnover intentions, it is reasonable to suggest that employees' turnover intention will be exacerbated by culture shock perceived by service employees."

"Foreign employees' job satisfaction mediates the relationship between culture shock and turnover intentions."

"When perceived managerial support is high, the relationship between culture shock and job satisfaction in foreign employees is weaker than when perceived managerial support is low."

Methodology

"In 2016, the number of non-resident employees working in hotels, restaurants and similar reached 49,990, while the total number of full-time employees in these industries was around 57,300 (Government of Macao Special Administrative Region Statistics and Census Service [1])."

"The research participants were foreign employees working in the 36 hotels currently operating in Macao."

"In accordance with the research framework and literature review, the questionnaire consisted of six sections: a culture shock measurement; an emotional labor scale; a perceived managerial support scale; a job satisfaction scale; a turnover intention scale; and demographic information."

"Emotional Labor in this research was measured using the items related to surface acting and deep acting from Brotheridge and Lee's [2] Emotional Labor Scale."

"The perceived managerial support scale has four items and was adopted from the study of Foley and others [3]."

Results

"Structural equation model analysis was conducted including an overall goodness of fit test, and path analysis was conducted to simultaneously examine the relationships between culture shock, emotional labor, job satisfaction, and turnover intention."

"Contrary to expectations, the moderating effect for perceived managerial support on the relationship between culture shock and emotional labor was not supported ($z = -0.05$, $p =$ n.s.)."

"The multi-group moderation test reveals that perceived managerial support negatively moderated the impact of the relationship between culture shock and job satisfaction ($z = 1.94$, $p < 0.05$; for the group with low levels of perceived managerial support, $\beta = -0.82$; for the group with high levels of perceived managerial support, $\beta = -0.53$)."

Conclusions and Implications

"Previous study delineated the relationships among perceived managerial support, emotional labor, job satisfaction, and turnover intention, but not a cultural shock."

"Some previous studies have provided support for the direct effect of emotional labor and job satisfaction on turnover intentions, the results further implied that emotional labor and job satisfaction are mediators of the effects of culture shock on foreign employees' turnover intentions."

"With limited empirical support, the researchers have demonstrated that culture shock is an antecedent of higher emotional labor and lower levels of job satisfaction, which is in turn associated with foreign employees' turnover intentions."

"That perceived managerial support changes the nature of the relationship between culture shock in foreign employees and job satisfaction."

"How to solve the employees' culture shock is one of the most issues to improve foreign employees' job satisfaction and to reduce emotional labor and turnover intention."

The Impact of Emotional Self-management on Benefit Offerings and Employment Growth: An Analysis of the Fastest Growing Businesses in the United States [52]

This is a machine-generated summary of:

Yoon, Jeewhan; May, Kevin; Kang, Jae H.; Solomon, George T.: The impact of emotional self-management on benefit offerings and employment growth: an analysis of the fastest growing businesses in the United States [52]

Published in: International Entrepreneurship and Management Journal (2018)
Link to original: https://doi.org/https://doi.org/10.1007/s11365-018-0542-3
Copyright of the summarized publication:
Springer Science + Business Media, LLC, part of Springer Nature 2018
All rights reserved.
If you want to cite the papers, please refer to the original.
For technical reasons we could not place the page where the original quote is coming from.

Abstract-Summary

"Using Entrepreneur Magazine's list of "Hot 500" fast-growth firms, we surveyed the founders of these firms on their emotional self-management and combined these self-reported responses with objective firm-level data on employment and benefit offerings, gathered using Entrepreneur Magazine's in-house experts, Princeton Review."

"Based on a review of the literature, we hypothesized that entrepreneurs' emotional self-management moderates the relationship between the size of the firm and the total number of benefits offered to employees."

"Results showed that the total number of benefits offered to employees was positively related to employment growth as a short-term outcome."

Introduction

"This study aimed to investigate whether entrepreneurs' emotional self-management has a moderating role in the relationship between firm size and number of benefits offered to employees and thus employment growth."

"There are limited studies linking entrepreneurs' emotional aspects to firm HR policy, so the two main objectives of the current study were to propose and test (1) the moderating role of entrepreneurs' emotional self-management in the relationship between the size of the entrepreneurial firm and benefit offerings and (2) a conceptual relationship between benefits offered to employees and a firm's growth in employment."

"This study examined the moderating role of entrepreneurs' emotional self-management in the relationship between firm size and the total number of benefits offered."

"We were able to show support for a moderated mediation effect (Preacher & others [4]) in which the effect of firm size on employment growth through number of benefits was conditional on entrepreneurs' level of emotional self-management."

Theory and Hypotheses Development

"We predicted that entrepreneurs' emotional self-management plays an important moderating role in the relationship between the size of the firm and the number of benefits offered to employees."

"To arrive at this model, we initially discuss the direct relationship between the size of the firm and the number of benefits offered to employees, and then we discuss the moderating role of entrepreneurs' emotional self-management in this relationship."

"We therefore offer the following hypothesis that the relationship between the size of the firm and the total number of benefits will be less positive when entrepreneurs' emotional self-management is high."

"H1: Entrepreneurs' emotional self-management negatively moderates the relationship between the size of the firm and the total number of benefits offered to employees."

"H3: The indirect relationship between the size of the firm and employment growth through total number of benefits offered to employees is moderated by an entrepreneur's emotional self-management."

Methods

"Entrepreneur Magazine calculated a ranking for each firm based on a combination of factors, including the percent employment growth via performance data gathered from publicly available records."

"Each survey response was paired with benefit offerings and employment growth data supplied by Entrepreneur Magazine to create a master dataset."

"The study relied on objective information on firms' employment data and number of benefits offered to employees, as well as founders' emotional self-management assessment."

"Combining these two datasets allowed us to determine whether entrepreneurs with high emotional self-management reduced the number of benefit offerings to their employees compared with entrepreneurs with lower emotional self-management."

"To reduce the threat of multicollinearity, we summed the actual number of employees for the year in which the survey data were collected to generate a variable labeled 'size of firm.'"

Results

"Hypothesis 1 predicted an interaction effect between firm size and entrepreneurs' emotional self-management to influence the number of benefits."

"As predicted, the relationship between firm size and number of benefits was more positive when entrepreneurs' emotional self-management was low than when it was high."

"To test this hypothesis, we regressed the dependent variable on the number of benefits while controlling for the predictor variables and the interaction term between firm size and entrepreneurs' emotional self-management."

"Using Preacher and others's [4] macro (discussed earlier), we probed the conditional indirect effect of firm size on employment growth at different levels of entrepreneurs' emotional self-management (Hypothesis 3)."

"Hypothesis 3 predicted that this effect would be more strongly positive at low levels of entrepreneurs' emotional self-management."

Discussion

"We examined the moderating role of entrepreneurs' emotional self-management in the indirect relationship between the size of the firm and employment growth through the total number of benefits offered."

"The results showed that entrepreneurs' emotional self-management moderates the relationship between firm size and the total number of benefits offered, which in turn positively relates to employment growth."

"Entrepreneurs with high levels of emotional self-management tend to find balance between the needs of employees for benefits and the financial burden of firms in offering them."

"The first contribution is our finding of an interaction effect between the level of entrepreneurs' emotional self-management and firm size on the number of benefits being offered."

"This study helps further the understanding of entrepreneurs' emotional self-management in influencing firm decisions such as the number of benefits offered."

Conclusion

"This study examined the moderating role of entrepreneurs' emotional self-management in the relationship between firm size and the total number of benefits offered."

"Findings showed that entrepreneurs' emotional self-management moderated the relationship between firm size and number of benefits offered to employees and thus employment growth."

"We were able to show support for a moderated mediation effect (Preacher & others [4]), in which the effect of firm size on employment growth through number of benefits was conditional on entrepreneurs' level of emotional self-management."

"Many firms face constrained resources and struggle to attract, hire, and retain employees, it would be prudent for founders to cultivate a high level of emotional self-management, as it affects the growth of the entrepreneurial venture."

Alleviating Job Stress to Improve Service Employee Work Affect: The Influence of Rewarding [53]

This is a machine-generated summary of:

Elmadağ, Ayşe Banu; Ellinger, Alexander E.: Alleviating job stress to improve service employee work affect: the influence of rewarding [53]

Published in: Service Business (2017)

Link to original: https://doi.org/https://doi.org/10.1007/s11628-017-0340-y

Copyright of the summarized publication:
Springer-Verlag Berlin Heidelberg 2017
All rights reserved.

If you want to cite the papers, please refer to the original.

For technical reasons we could not place the page where the original quote is coming from.

Abstract-Summary

"Drawing on equity theory, this research examines the influences of alternative rewarding approaches on CCE job stress and work-related attitudes, by assessing the effects of intrinsic (social recognition) and extrinsic (monetary) rewarding on CCE job stress, commitment to the organization, and customer orientation."

"Results of a survey of 220 CCEs from multiple service organizations indicate that social recognition reduces CCE job stress but that, contrary to expectations, monetary rewarding increases it."

Introduction

"The current research draws on equity theory to assess the relative influence of alternative types of rewarding on CCE job stress and work affect."

"Researchers therefore contend that job stress must be effectively mitigated to improve service worker attitudes that influence the quality of service provision (Singh [5]; Taris [6])."

"A frequently employed managerial intervention that undoubtedly affects employee job stress and work affect is rewarding."

"This research examines the influence of rewarding in potentially stressful service provision contexts where CCEs' boundary spanning roles require them to interact with supervisors and co-workers as well as customers."

"Based on survey data from a sample of CCEs from multiple service industries, we propose and test a conceptual framework that assesses the influences of alternative types of rewarding on CCE job stress, commitment to the organization and customer orientation."

Background

"CCEs are the firm in the minds of its customers because customer evaluations of organizations are largely based on their impressions of service employees (Hau & others [7]; Berry [8]; Wentzel [9])."

"Although personal attention has an important role as a reinforcing managerial intervention employed in organizations (Simons [10]), the influence of intrinsic rewarding on customer-facing employee job stress has been relatively ignored."

"Research tends to associate extrinsic rewarding with decreased levels of job stress because, in addition to providing an indication of the individual's value to the organization, material remuneration influences the type of lifestyle that an individual can lead."

"Commitment to the organization and customer orientation are desirable work-related attitudes for frontline service employees that interact with customers."

"The linkages between commitment to the organization, customer orientation, and superior service provision are well established in the services marketing literature."

Conceptual Framework and Study Hypotheses

"Based on the same theoretical foundations and on the general belief that rewarding promotes favorable work-related outcomes, extrinsic rewarding also enables firms to strike a balance between inputs and outputs by materially rewarding employees for their efforts."

"We also anticipate that employee satisfaction with remuneration and other work-related incentives and opportunities is negatively associated with job stress: Extrinsic rewarding decreases job stress."

"We therefore propose that intrinsic rewarding encourages employees, to reciprocate by exhibiting higher levels of desirable work-related affect: Intrinsic rewards increase employee (a) commitment to the organization and (b) customer orientation."

"Based on the same theoretical rationale and the general belief that rewarding promotes favorable work-related outcomes, we also anticipate that: Extrinsic rewards increase employee (a) commitment to the organization and (b) customer orientation."

"We therefore expect that: Job stress decreases employee (a) commitment to the organization and (b) customer orientation."

Method

"The 3-item intrinsic rewards satisfaction scale includes items like 'I am satisfied with the way I am treated by the people I work with.'"

"The 3-item extrinsic rewards satisfaction scale includes items like 'I am satisfied with the fringe benefits I receive.'"

"In the confirmatory factor analysis (CFA), we included all items for Extrinsic Rewards Satisfaction, Intrinsic Rewards Satisfaction, Job Stress, Commitment to the Organization, and Customer Orientation."

"In conjunction with the reliability assessment, we also examined the factor loadings and t values, and assessed the variance extracted (Anderson & Gerbing [11])."

"Following the procedure suggested by Fornell and Larcker [12], discriminant validity was assessed by comparing the variance extracted for each construct to the square of each off-diagonal value within the phi matrix for that construct."

"The square root of average variance extracted for both Extrinsic Rewards Satisfaction and Commitment to the Organization exceeded this value."

Analyses and Results

"Consistent with expectations, the study findings indicate that intrinsic rewards negatively influence job stress ($\beta = -.43$, $t = 3.96$)."

"H2 is not supported since the findings reveal that extrinsic rewards significantly increase job stress ($\beta = .44$, $t = 3.93$)."

"To our expectations, the results also fail to identify any significant effects between intrinsic rewarding and either commitment to the organization or customer orientation."

"As anticipated, the study findings provide support for H4a and H4b by confirming that extrinsic rewards favorably influence both commitment to the organization ($\beta = .82$, t = 10.45) and customer orientation ($\beta = .40$, t = 2.60)."

"The influence of job stress on customer orientation was negative and significant, providing support for H5b."

"The study findings provide support for the direct influence of extrinsic rewards on customer orientation ($\beta = .40$, t = 2.60)."

Discussion

"Our findings extend current knowledge about job stress in service provision contexts by examining the influence of rewarding as a means of alleviating job stress and improving CCE work-related affect that is associated with superior service quality."

"Drawing on the perceptions of a sample of CCEs from multiple service industries appears to be particularly appropriate for assessing the influences of employees' satisfaction with their firms' rewarding on their job stress and work-related affect."

"We do not propose that our findings suggest that firms can improve CCE work-related affect and associated service levels by ramping up job stress in conjunction with extrinsic rewarding."

"Our research findings extend current knowledge about frontline service provider job stress and offer guidance for how organizations can appropriately exploit different types of rewarding to favorably influence the CCE attitudes that so profoundly affect customers' service experiences."

To Drink or Not to Drink; That is the Question! Antecedents and Consequences of Employee Business Drinking [54]

This is a machine-generated summary of:
 Shao, Meng; Gu, Jibao; Wu, Jianlin: To drink or not to drink; that is the question! Antecedents and consequences of employee business drinking [54]
 Published in: Asia Pacific Journal of Management (2020)
 Link to original: https://doi.org/https://doi.org/10.1007/s10490-020-09731-z
 Copyright of the summarized publication:
 Springer Science + Business Media, LLC, part of Springer Nature 2020
 All rights reserved.
 If you want to cite the papers, please refer to the original.
 For technical reasons we could not place the page where the original quote is coming from.

Abstract-Summary

"This study focuses on employee business drinking (EBD), defined as employee drinking with clients for business matters."

"Based on role theory, the antecedents and consequences of EBD are examined using three-wave data obtained from 183 full-time Chinese employees."

"The results show that the leader business drinking norms and coworker business drinking norms have positive effects on EBD."

"Employees with high performance drinking motives and high alcohol tolerance are more likely to participate in EBD."

Literature Review and Hypotheses

"An employee who perceives high levels of leader or coworker business drinking norms is more likely to regard drinking with clients as an encouraged behavior during business events."

"Employees with high performance drinking motives hold the implicit expectation that drinking behaviors would result in positive work-related outcomes, such as improvement in tasks, goal accomplishment, and the building of better business relationships (Liu & others [13])."

"Employees with a higher alcohol tolerance might be able to perform more appropriate business drinking behaviors, such as taking care of the clients and livening the atmosphere."

"Compared with an employee with a lower tolerance, an employee with a higher alcohol tolerance shows higher capability of drinking with the clients, perceives lower self-behavioral cost and has more opportunities to be invited by his or her clients, leader, or coworkers to participate in business drinking events."

Method

"A five-item veteran peers' alcohol-use norms scale adapted from Liu and others [13] was adjusted for this variable by changing "my team" to "my leader"."

"Sample items included "My leader often drinks alcohol with the clients" and "Drinking alcohol together is an important part of the interactions between my leader and the clients.""

"Sample items included, "My coworker often drinks alcohol with the clients" and "Drinking alcohol together is an important part of the interactions between my coworker and the clients.""

"A four-item client alcohol-use norms scale adapted from Liu and others [13] was adjusted for this variable by changing "our client" to "my clients"."

"Sample items included "My clients often drink alcohol during business meetings" and "For my clients, drinking alcohol is an important way to strengthen business relationships.""

Results

"The distinctiveness of the eight variables (leader business drinking norms, coworker business drinking norms, client business drinking norms, performance drinking motives, alcohol tolerance, LMX, TMX, and client ties) was examined by contrasting an 8-factor model against one 7-factor model, one 6-factor model, one 5-factor model, one 4-factor model, and one 1-factor model."

"The hypotheses were tested using multiple regression models."

"Eight models were estimated to test the hypotheses."

"Hypotheses 6, 7, and 8 predicted that EBD was positively related to LMX, TMX, and client ties."

Discussion

"Based on role theory, this study aims to specify the business context of employee alcohol use and identify the antecedents and consequences of EBD."

"The first major contribution of this study is extending prior research on employee alcohol use to the context of business drinking."

"We specified the business context of employee alcohol use, which allows the research to focus on understanding the phenomenon of "employee drinking during business events" and investigating the antecedents and consequences of EBD."

"In terms of self-perspective, this study shows that employees' performance drinking motives and alcohol tolerance are positively related to EBD."

"Empirical evidence for the positive effect of EBD on LMX, TMX, and client ties is also provided in this study, which is the first to empirically test the positive work-related consequences of employee alcohol use."

[Section 5]

"The leader, the coworker, and the client fill roles that are complementary to the employee, so we propose that their business drinking norms set an employee's behavioral expectations for complementary roles."

"We posit performance drinking motives as role preferences and alcohol tolerance as role abilities, which together form an employee's self-behavioral expectations in shaping EBD."

"The leader, coworker, and client serve in complementary roles to the employee and are most likely to participate in business drinking events together, three related patterns of relationships are identified for further exploration: leader-member exchange (LMX), team-member exchange (TMX), and client ties."

"This study makes three important contributions to the literature on employee alcohol use and role theory."

"This study extended the research on employee alcohol use to business drinking context."

"By focusing on employee drinking behaviors during business events, this study extends the literature on employee alcohol use."

Research on the Influence Mechanism of Emotional Intelligence and Psychological Empowerment on Customers' Repurchase Intention Under the Situation of Online Shopping Service Recovery [55]

This is a machine-generated summary of:
Wei, Jiahua; Zhu, Sai; Hou, Zhiping; Dong, Hualong; Li, Jun: Research on the influence mechanism of emotional intelligence and psychological empowerment on customers' repurchase intention under the situation of online shopping service recovery [55]
Published in: Current Psychology (2022)
Link to original: https://doi.org/https://doi.org/10.1007/s12144-022-02841-5
Copyright of the summarized publication:
The Author(s), under exclusive licence to Springer Science + Business Media, LLC, part of Springer Nature 2022
All rights reserved.
If you want to cite the papers, please refer to the original.
For technical reasons we could not place the page where the original quote is coming from.

Abstract-Summary

"Based on the online shopping service recovery scenario, this study discusses the impact of online store employees' emotional intelligence and psychological empowerment on customers' repurchase intention."

"Through empirical analysis, this study obtains the following results: The emotional intelligence and psychological empowerment of online store employees have a positive impact on the service recovery quality, the service recovery quality has a positive impact on customers' repurchase intention, and the emotional intelligence and psychological empowerment of online store employees have an indirect impact on customers' repurchase intention through the mediating effect t of service recovery quality, Online store reputation plays a positive moderating effect in the relationship between service recovery quality and customers' repurchase intention."

"This study expands the applicable scenarios of emotional intelligence and psychological empowerment, will provide strategic reference for online stores to carry out effective service recovery, and promote the healthy development of online shopping industry."

Introduction

"In the online shopping service recovery scenario, will the emotional intelligence and psychological empowerment of online store employees directly affect the service recovery quality?"

"In order to solve the practical problems that cannot be explained by the current research, this study will use the situational experiment method to explore the impact of online store employees' emotional intelligence and psychological empowerment on service recovery quality, as well as the impact of service recovery quality on customer repurchase, and analyze the mediating effect of service recovery quality, It also examines the moderating effect of online store reputation in the impact of service recovery quality on customers' repurchase intention."

"This study will help to deepen the current online shopping and service recovery theory, expand the applicable scenarios of emotional intelligence and psychological empowerment, provide strategic reference for online stores to carry out effective service recovery, improve customers' repurchase intention, and promote the healthy development of online shopping industry."

Theoretical Basis and Research Hypothesis

"The following research hypotheses are proposed: H1: Emotional intelligence of online store employees will have a positive impact on service recovery quality."

"H4: Service recovery quality plays a mediating effect in the relationship between emotional intelligence of online store employee and customers' repurchase intention."

"H5: Service recovery quality plays a mediating effect in the relationship between psychological empowerment of online store employees and customers' repurchase intention."

"The following research hypotheses are proposed: H6: Online store reputation plays a positive moderating effect in the impact of service recovery quality on customers' repurchase intention."

"In the current study, some scholars have constructed relevant research models on the relationship between variables such as emotional intelligence, psychological empowerment, service recovery quality, customer satisfaction and customers' repurchase intention, which provides a theoretical reference for this study."

Research Design

"The customer questionnaire includes three variables: Service recovery quality, online store reputation and customer repurchase intention, which are used to investigate the samples playing customers in the scenario experiment."

"The subjects who played the online store employees filled in the employee questionnaire, including emotional intelligence and psychological empowerment, a total of two variables, while the subjects who played the online store customers filled in the customer questionnaire, including service recovery quality, customer repurchase intention and online store reputation, a total of three variables."

"In each experiment, the subjects were randomly assigned to 8 experimental scenarios, with 8 people in each scenario, of which 4 played the role of online store employees and 4 played the role of online store customers."

"The subjects put themselves in the selected scenario in combination with the description materials of the scenario and their own service recovery experience, play the selected roles (online store employees or online store customers)."

Data Analysis

"The results show that the service recovery quality has a significant positive impact on customers' repurchase intention ($\beta = 0.577$, $P < 0.05$), so the study hypothesis H3 passed the test."

"From the multi-level regression results, it is found that the interaction coefficient between consumer forgiveness and online store reputation is positive and statistically significant($\beta = 0.324$, $P < 0.05$), indicating that online store reputation plays a positive moderating effect in the relationship between service recovery quality and customers' repurchase intention, and the research hypothesis H6 is supported."

"The simple slope test results of this study show that when the online store reputation is low, the service recovery quality has a weak positive impact on customers' repurchase intention($\beta = 0.209$, $P < 0.05$), and when the online store has a high reputation, the service recovery quality has a strong positive impact on customers' repurchase intention($\beta = 0.743$, $P < 0.01$)."

Conclusion and Discussion

"This study takes online shopping service recovery as the research situation, carries out empirical research through the method of situational experiment, and analyzes the impact of online store employees' emotional intelligence and psychological empowerment on customers' repurchase intention."

"The above research conclusions show that the impact of online store employees' emotional intelligence and psychological empowerment on customers' repurchase intention needs to be realized through the intermediary variables of service recovery quality."

"This study explored the relationship between emotional intelligence and psychological empowerment on service recovery quality and customers' repurchase intention under the situation of online shopping service recovery, and tested the regulatory effect of online store reputation, but did not involve the research on customers' perceived fairness and emotional contagion."

An Empirical Study on the Impact of Employee Voice and Silence on Destructive Leadership and Organizational Culture [56]

This is a machine-generated summary of:
Joseph, Shaji; Shetty, Naithika: An empirical study on the impact of employee voice and silence on destructive leadership and organizational culture [56]
Published in: Asian Journal of Business Ethics (2022)
Link to original: https://doi.org/https://doi.org/10.1007/s13520-022-00155-0
Copyright of the summarized publication:
The Author(s), under exclusive licence to Springer Nature B.V. 2022

Copyright comment: Springer Nature or its licensor holds exclusive rights to this article under a publishing agreement with the author(s) or other rightsholder(s); author self-archiving of the accepted manuscript version of this article is solely governed by the terms of such publishing agreement and applicable law.

All rights reserved.
If you want to cite the papers, please refer to the original.
For technical reasons we could not place the page where the original quote is coming from.

Abstract-Summary

"This paper is an outcome of the business ethics course conducted during the third semester of the MBA course and aims to examine how a subordinate employee's response, either by raising a concern or being quiet to repeated misbehavior of the leader, impacts an organization."

"The analysis shows that silence and voice in an organization have an impact on the organization's culture."

"The implications of this study show that leaders violate the integrity of the organization by vandalizing the organization's objectives, outcomes, assets, and well-being of the co-employees."

"Previous studies have not focused on the mediating role of organizational culture on employee voice or silence."

Introduction

"The behavior of the leader and the organizational culture impacts the employee."

"Between all this, organizational culture plays a vital role in employee silence, voice, and destructive behavior."

"This paper will focus on providing insight into how a healthy organizational culture impacts employee silence or voice and mediating destructive leadership's role in creating this culture that suppresses employee voice."

"This paper aims to provide a conceptual contribution to finding which organizational culture leads to destructive leaders and how it impacts employee behavior."

"The authors felt the need to study destructive leadership because (1) as there is sizable research already undertaken on the positive impact of leadership on creating a culture of voice and (2) a felt experience of the role of the leaders in suppressing employee voice while working in the IT companies."

Literature Review

"This section explains destructive leadership, characteristics, types of destructive leadership, employee behavior concerning employee voice, employee silence, and organization culture."

"Toxic leadership behaviors are a series of dysfunctional conduct that a leader demonstrates to fulfill his needs and personal motive and to gain an advantage by compromising the trust of the people, team, and organization (Schmidt [15])."

"Students in this paper explored the issue of employee silence and employee voice that lead to increased corruption in business organizations."

"Prosocial silence (social): In an organization, suppressing the voice to benefit the positive employee relationship between each other and within the team gives rise to prosocial silence."

"The personality of the leader, the follower, or the culture and values of the organization may also influence silence (Schilling & Kluge [16])."

"In an organization where subordinates hang back to share their opinion, information, or ideas only because of their leader, their behavior has created an environment of non-cooperation (Morrison [17]; Cullinane & Donaghey [18])."

Research Methodology

"The data was collected using a five-point Likert scale questionnaire."

"The data was collected using a survey among mid-scale IT companies based in Pune, India, with an employee strength of 250–300."

"The researchers collected the data through emails and LinkedIn contacts."

"The research was conducted during the Covid-19-induced lockdown and depended on an online survey to collect the data."

Data Analysis and Findings

"For destructive leadership and organizational culture, the alpha value is 0.7."

"Composite reliability for the measurement model should be greater than 0.6; the measurement model silence, destructive leadership, and organizational culture have the required internal consistency between the indicator variables."

"The direct effect of silence on organizational culture is −0.04 with a significance of 0.684; since the p-value is more than 0.05, the direct effect is insignificant."

"The indirect effect of silence on organizational culture through destructive leadership is −0.399 with a significant p-value."

"The total effect is −0.439 with a significant p-value."

"Mediation analysis between voice, destructive leadership, and organizational culture shows a direct effect of 0.083 with 0.54 significance."

"The indirect effect is 0.306 with a value of 0.023, and the total effect is 0.389 with 0.011 significance."

Discussion and Implication

"The current study focused on the impact of destructive leadership and the organizational culture on employee silence and voice in the organization."

"Hypothesis H4 states that destructive leadership is a mediator between employee silence and organizational culture."

"Mediation analysis has proven that the impact of employee silence on organizational culture is not significant, but with destructive leadership as a mediator, the impact is significant."

"Hypothesis H5 states that destructive leadership is a mediator between employee voice and organizational culture."

"Mediation analysis has proven that the impact of employee voice on organizational culture is not significant, but with destructive leadership as a mediator, the impact is significant."

"In a generative organization, the employee voice on destructive leadership positively impacts the organization's culture as it helps the organization meet its vision and employee satisfaction."

"Employee voice brings a positive effect on organizations that have destructive leadership."

Conclusion

"The research studied the impact of employee voice and silence on destructive leadership and the relationship between organizational culture."

"The study's results revealed that employee silence and voice impact destructive leadership and how destructive leadership plays an important role in mediating between organizational culture and employee voice—silence."

"The study results advocate the addition of many possible variables that may moderate or mediate between destructive leadership, voice, silence, and organizational culture."

"Establishing the causality between the destructive personality and the silence or voice relationship is difficult."

"There is a need for future researchers to find a relationship by using behavioral experiments or panel studies."

"Scope, researchers could consider a leader's perspective, for example, a leader's trust in subordinates as an important catalyst in the destructive personality – silence, voice relationship."

Relationship Between Emotional Labor and Job Satisfaction: Testing Mediating Role of Emotional Intelligence on South Korean Public Service Employees [57]

This is a machine-generated summary of:
Lee, Hyun Jung: Relationship between Emotional Labor and Job Satisfaction: Testing Mediating Role of Emotional Intelligence on South Korean Public Service Employees [57]
Published in: Public Organization Review (2020)
Link to original: https://doi.org/https://doi.org/10.1007/s11115-020-00490-5
Copyright of the summarized publication:
Springer Science + Business Media, LLC, part of Springer Nature 2020
All rights reserved.
If you want to cite the papers, please refer to the original.
For technical reasons we could not place the page where the original quote is coming from.

Abstract-Summary

"Prior studies on the consequences of the dimensions of emotional labor (surface acting and deep acting) have revealed the mixed findings, especially relations with job satisfaction in the public service."

"To clarify inconsistent results of the relationship between emotional labor and job satisfaction, this study incorporates emotional intelligence as the mediator in a sample of public service employees in South Korea."

"The findings revealed that only deep acting and job satisfaction was significantly and positively related and only emotional-self regulation was partially mediated among the dimensions of emotional intelligence between deep acting and job satisfaction."

Literature Review

"Like department store clerks or call center representatives who respond to customers in a pleasant manner, public service employees also perform emotional labor."

"Surface acting and deep acting are two emotive strategies used to display appropriate emotions to fit organizational norms, called display rules, to which service employees must comply when interacting with customers (Hochschild [19]; Grandey [20]; Ashforth & Humphrey [21])."

"The intention of deep acting is to make one's emotional display appear authentic (Allen & others [22]) so that customers who receive services feel satisfied and return."

"Without the emotional self-regulation skill, service workers often show negative emotion (e.g., irritation, fear, anxiety, sadness) to customers."

"Emotional intelligence is an individual ability, it may assist an individual when performing work that involves emotional labor, just as the ability to recognize one's own emotions may help employees know when they need to alter their emotional expressions (O'Boyle & others [23])."

Emotional Intelligence as a Mediator between Emotional Labor and Job Satisfaction

"In order to confirm existing studies, the author examines the mediating role of each dimension of emotional intelligence (emotional self-awareness, emotional other-awareness, and emotional self-regulation) to see how each affects the relationship between emotional labor (surface acting and deep acting) and job satisfaction."

"Hypothesis 3a: Emotional self-awareness mediates the relationship between surface acting and job satisfaction."

"Hypothesis 3b: Emotional other awareness mediates the relationship between surface acting and job satisfaction."

"Hypothesis 3c: Emotional self-regulation mediates the relationship between surface acting and job satisfaction."

"Through this understanding, highly emotionally intelligent people attempt to use deep acting more than surface acting to provide better service, which likely generates pride in work and job satisfaction (Opengart [24]; Cheung & others [25])."

"Hypothesis 4a: Emotional self- awareness mediates the relationship between deep acting and job satisfaction."

"Hypothesis 4b: Emotional other awareness mediates the relationship between deep acting and job satisfaction."

"Hypothesis 4c: Emotional self-regulation mediates the relationship between deep acting and job satisfaction."

Research Design

"Among the three dimensions of emotional intelligence, only emotional self-regulation significantly but partially mediated between deep acting and job satisfaction (.048; SE = .025; 90% CI (.003, .104))."

"Most studies in the sample of public service employees in Western culture countries have found that surface acting is negatively associated with job satisfaction due to emotional dissonance (Bhave & Glomb [26])."

"This finding implies that South Korean public service employees may have other elements, other than self-emotional regulation skill, that also make them job satisfaction."

"Some of the examples can be a social status as being a public servant, having a life-time tenure position, and/or regular working hours etc However, in terms of emotive skills, self-emotional regulation is the most effective way for South Korean public service employees to develop and sustain emotional labor jobs successfully."

"Emotional self-awareness and emotional other-awareness did not mediate the relationship between emotional labor and job satisfaction in South Korean public service employees."

Conclusion

"Based on an assumption that those who perform emotional labor are more highly satisfied with their jobs when they possess higher levels of emotional intelligence skills, this study examined how each emotional intelligence skills mediate emotional labor and job satisfaction in a sample of South Korean public service employees."

"These techniques are useful tools for public service employees how to regulate their own emotions when engaging deep acting."

"To promote South Korean public service employees to engage more deep acting, government should help public service employees assert their rights according to 'emotional laborer protection law'."

"And to increase public service employees' job satisfaction, public organizations in South Korea should actively promote public service employees to assert their rights as same as emotional labor workers in the private services."

Limitations

"As a first attempt to examine those relationships in South Korean public service workers, this study possesses a number of limitations."

"The participants of this study are from a limited sample- public service employees who work in administrative service; thus, the same theoretical framework involved in administrative services may show different results in other samples."

"Studies on the mediating role of emotional intelligence are not common within the public administration arena."

"To yield supported evidence of a causal relationship, future studies should use various samples with different methodologies."

166   4 Stress and Emotional Intelligence

[Section 6]

"To understand the mechanisms that undergird this shift, a number of recent studies have focused on employee emotions, emotional labor, and emotional intelligence of public service workers (see, Guy & Lee [27]; Lee [28, 29]; Potipiroon & others [30]; Yang & others [31]; Mastracci & Adams [32]; Sloan [33]; Hsieh & others [34])."

"To promote positive outcomes in public service, especially in job satisfaction—as it has generally been used as a positive variable, although existing findings have been fairly inconsistent—this study investigates the relationship between emotional labor and job satisfaction, taking into account the mediating role of emotional intelligence."

"There have been few studies that have examined the strength of the mediating relationship of emotional intelligence on emotional labor and job satisfaction in the public services."

"In order to provide a better understanding of how emotional intelligence can function as a mediator in the proposed model, the author offers a more thorough investigation into the effect of each emotional labor construct on job satisfaction, with each dimension of emotional intelligence playing a mediating role by targeting frontline public service employees who are employed in administrative services in South Korea."

How Spiritual Leadership Leads to Employee Followership Behavior: The Role of Relational Identification and Spiritual Intelligence [58]

This is a machine-generated summary of:

Cui, Zunkang; Ji, Xiaotong; Liu, Pingqing; Li, Ruiyan: How spiritual leadership leads to employee followership behavior: the role of relational identification and spiritual intelligence [58]

Published in: Current Psychology (2023)

Link to original: https://doi.org/https://doi.org/10.1007/s12144-023-04772-1

Copyright of the summarized publication:

The Author(s), under exclusive licence to Springer Science + Business Media, LLC, part of Springer Nature 2023

Copyright comment: Springer Nature or its licensor (e.g. a society or other partner) holds exclusive rights to this article under a publishing agreement with the author(s) or other rightsholder(s); author self-archiving of the accepted manuscript version of this article is solely governed by the terms of such publishing agreement and applicable law.

All rights reserved.

If you want to cite the papers, please refer to the original.

For technical reasons we could not place the page where the original quote is coming from.

Abstract-Summary

"Based on self-determination theory and using a questionnaire method, this research investigated the relationship between spiritual leadership and employee followership behavior, and explored the roles of relational identification and spiritual intelligence in this relationship."

"The findings suggested that spiritual leadership had a positive relationship with employee followership behavior, and that relational identification played a mediating role in this positive relationship."

"The positive relationship between spiritual leadership and relational identification was more significant when employees' spiritual intelligence was high than when it was low."

"The indirect effect of spiritual leadership on employee followership behavior through relational identification relied on employees' spiritual intelligence, such that the indirect effect was stronger when employees' spiritual intelligence was high than when it was low."

Introduction

"Only when leaders value their employees' sense of meaning and intrinsic motivation, and when recognize employees' spiritual qualities and values, will employees feel be appreciated and have a sense of belonging, and thus be willing to obey leaders, learn from them, and demonstrate proactive followership behavior (e.g., Shamir [35]; Shamir & others [36]; van Knippenberg & others [37])."

"Self-determination theory may be applicable to the analysis of the relationship between spiritual leadership and employees' followership behavior."

"Spiritual leadership, as an external situational factor, may influence employees' followership behavior."

"It can therefore be hypothesized that employees' relational identification with their leaders may play a mediating role between spiritual leadership and employee followership behavior."

"Based on self-determination theory, this research aims to extend existing research on employees' followership behavior and spiritual leadership in the following aspects."

Literature Review and Hypotheses

"Spiritual leadership meets the needs of employees for competence, autonomy, and relatedness, stimulates their motivation for self-realization (Deci & Ryan [38]), and thus triggers employees' followership behaviors."

"Based on self-concept-based theory (Shamir & others [36]), spiritual leadership can provide employees with autonomous and supportive relationship situations, which is conducive to improving employees' sense of work self-worth and prosocial motivation, thus encouraging their relationship identification with leaders."

"We infer that spiritual leadership, as a supportive and altruistic organizational scenario, encourages employees to exhibit more followership behavior by increasing their level of relational identification with the leader."

"Relational identification mediates the relationship between spiritual leadership and employee followership behavior."

"Spiritual intelligence moderates the indirect effect of spiritual leadership on employee followership behavior through relational identification, such that the indirect effect is stronger when spiritual intelligence is high than when it is low."

Method

"In order to ensure the validity of the data and improve the external validity of the study, this study adopts a multi-source, paired questionnaire survey method to reduce and avoid the problem of common method bias as much as possible."

"The findings of Podsakoff and others [39] suggested that the research about leaders and employees using the paired method to collect data is more conducive to avoiding homology bias and improving accuracy and objectivity."

"The questionnaires were designed for the survey from the leadership level and the employee level respectively, so as to reduce and avoid the common method deviation as much as possible and ensure the validity of the data."

"The members of the research group designed two kinds of questionnaires in advance: the employee version and the leadership version, and numbered and paired the questionnaires."

Results

"We conducted a confirmatory factor analysis using Mplus version 7.0 to test the discrimination between spiritual leadership, spiritual intelligence, relational identification and followership behavior."

"This study followed the steps for testing mediation effects (Baron & Kenny [40]), using the hierarchical regression method to test the mediating role of relational identification."

"When spiritual leadership and relational identification were simultaneously included in the regression model of followership behavior (Model 7), relational identification was positively associated with followership behavior ($\beta = 0.50$, $p < 0.001$), whereas the effect of spiritual leadership on followership behavior was significantly lower ($\beta = 0.11$, $p < 0.05$) compared to Model 6."

"The results showed that the indirect effect of spiritual leadership on followership behavior was within the 95% confidence interval [0.06, 0.24], which did not contain 0, indicating that the mediating effect of relational identification between spiritual leadership and followership behavior existed."

Discussion

"Our research extended the literature on the positive effects of leaders' behaviors on employee outcomes by identifying relational identification as a key to open "the black box" between spiritual leadership and employees' followership behavior."

"Based on self-determination theory, our research has found that spiritual leadership can bring about relational identification by providing employees with an autonomous and supportive environment that meets their basic psychological needs, which in turn enhanced employees' followership behavior, providing a new theoretical perspective."

"To better respond to whether, how and when spiritual leadership influences employees' followership behavior, our research further investigated an integrative model that the extent to which relational identification transmits the effect of spiritual leadership on employees' followership behavior relied on spiritual intelligence."

"Future research can investigate the incremental effect and differential performance of spiritual leadership affecting employees' positive followership behavior compared with other leadership types."

Conclusion

"Based on self-determination theory, we provided a complete picture of how and when spiritual leadership enhanced employees' followership behavior."

"Spiritual leadership enhanced employee followership behavior by influencing their relational identification."

"Spiritual intelligence moderated the indirect effect of spiritual leadership on followership behavior via relational identification, such that the indirect effect was stronger when spiritual intelligence was high than when it was low."

It Takes a Village: Examining How and When Brand-specific Transformational Leadership Affects Employees in Internal Brand Management [59]

This is a machine-generated summary of:
  Xiong, Lina: It takes a village: examining how and when brand-specific transformational leadership affects employees in internal brand management [59]
  Published in: Journal of Brand Management (2023)
  Link to original: https://doi.org/https://doi.org/10.1057/s41262-022-00308-3
  Copyright of the summarized publication:
  The Author(s), under exclusive licence to Springer Nature Limited 2023
  Copyright comment: Springer Nature or its licensor (e.g. a society or other partner) holds exclusive rights to this article under a publishing agreement with the author(s)

or other rightsholder(s); author self-archiving of the accepted manuscript version of this article is solely governed by the terms of such publishing agreement and applicable law.

All rights reserved.

If you want to cite the papers, please refer to the original.

For technical reasons we could not place the page where the original quote is coming from.

Abstract-Summary

"This study demonstrates the positive role of brand-specific transformational leadership in promoting employees' highly engaged brand building behavior (investment-of-self) and their resistance to outside competing job offers."

"Drawing upon cognitive dissonance theory, this study shows that the impact of brand-specific transformational leadership is mediated by employees' sense of brand community internally, as well as moderated by perceived brand promise accuracy."

"These results supported the essential role of achieving employees' cognitive consonance in brand communication both internally and externally."

"These results are supported by 203 US hospitality employee responses from multiple data collections purposefully designed with temporal and cognitive distance."

Introduction

"IBM focuses on aligning employees' attitudes and behavior with specific brand values so that they are able to deliver the promised brand experience to customers."

"Hospitality employees from different departments are expected to create consistent and coherent brand experiences that are aligned with an organization's promoted brand to meet customer expectations (Xiong & King [43])."

"When seeking to deliver such brand-aligned experiences, researchers have argued for the importance of leadership when ensuring employees are motivated and proficient at creating and adapting their own set of knowledge and skills, as well as curating an internal community in delivering the brand promise to customers (Barros-Arrieta & García-Cali [44]; Buil & others [45])."

"In previous internal branding studies, TFL is also shown to contribute to employees' brand-supporting behavior, both in-role (e.g., standard job responsibilities) and extra-role (e.g., helping coworkers) (Buil & others [45]; Uen & others [46])."

Literature Review

"As brand-specific TFL further emphasizes employees' internalization of brand values through empowering, modeling, and coaching (Morhart & others [47]), employees are more likely to draw upon not just the organization-provided brand information, but also their own experiences and intuition to create brand-consistent experiences for customers."

"Given these recommended research directions and drawing on recent research advancement in internal branding, this study focuses on brand-specific TFL's role in affecting employees' investment-of-self in brand building and competitive resistance to employment opportunities in other organizations."

"Building upon transformational leadership research and internal branding literature, this study proposes that brand-specific TFL's impact on employees' investment-of-self into brand building and their competitive resistance to outside offers is mediated by employees' sense of an internal brand community and moderated by perceived brand promise accuracy."

Method

"Considering survey insights are self-reported, in order to aid objectivity of responses and limit respondents' perceived saliency among questions in the same survey, special attention was paid to the introduction of temporal and cognitive distance among closely related construct questions (MacKenzie & Podsakoff [48]; Podsakoff & others [39])."

"The antecedent variables and outcome variables were deliberately separated in two rounds of surveys to the same individual respondent."

"After a four-week period (Crossley & others [49]), a second round of data collection was conducted by sending questions regarding antecedent variables to the 457 respondents who provided completed responses in the first round."

"Each full response contains the responses to questions in both surveys from the same individual respondent."

"This four-week lag that separated data collections of antecedent variables and outcome variables can reduce the potential for common method bias, as respondents are less likely to be influenced by the saliency among questions if they are placed in different surveys (Crossley & others [49]; MacKenzie & Podsakoff [48])."

Data Analyses

"With respect to the hypothesized moderating role of perceived brand promise accuracy (H6) between brand-specific TFL and employee sense of brand community, the procedures recommended by Aiken and others [50] in testing interaction effects were followed."

"The interaction term (brand-specific TFL × perceived brand promise accuracy), brand-specific TFL and perceived brand promise accuracy were then included in the structural model as three antecedent variables linking to employee sense of brand community."

"It is shown that at a high level of perceived brand promise accuracy (i.e., the value is one standard deviation above the mean), brand-specific TFL has a strong and positive impact on employee sense of brand community ($\beta = 0.429$, $p < 0.05$)."

"When perceived brand promise accuracy is at a low level (i.e., the value is one standard deviation below the mean), the impact of brand-specific TFL on employee sense of brand community becomes insignificant ($\beta = 0.186$, $p = 0.157$)."

Discussion and Theoretical Implications

"The findings also demonstrated brand-specific TFL effects through employee sense of an internal brand community and is moderated by perceived brand promise accuracy based on cognitive dissonance theory."

"This study further provides a cognitive dissonance perspective to explain how brand-specific TFL affects employees' investment-of-self and competitive resistance through employee sense of brand community."

"Along with the cognitive dissonance arguments in supporting the role of an internal brand community, this study further shows that brand-specific TFL's effect on employees is stronger when employees perceive the brand promise to be accurate, reducing potential cognitive dissonance between internal and external brand communication."

"This study adds to the understanding of employee sense of brand community by showing the significant antecedent role of brand-specific TFL."

"This study built upon this notion and incorporated employee investment-of-self from psychological ownership studies (e.g., Brown & others [41]; Pierce & others [42]) as a highly relevant outcome of internal branding, which is propelled by brand-specific TFL and employee sense of community."

Practical Implications

"Consistent with Buil and others [45] and Morhart and others [47], it is believed that brand-specific TFL is a desired leadership style for hospitality organizations that seek to build and sustain a successful brand through employees' brand-aligned performance."

"In Morhart and others [47], managers are likely to achieve better outcomes in internal branding when they promote a unified brand vision, live the brand values, coach employees to develop their interpretation of brand-aligned performance, and provide individualized support to employees."

"The ability to foster a supportive internal brand community, enhance employees' willingness to stay with the organization in a competitive labor market, and promote employees' self-devotion to brand building are suggested as effective measures to evaluate brand-specific transformational leaders' effectiveness."

"Given the strong mediation effect of employee sense of brand community, it is suggested that hospitality organizations pay special attention to the informal internal community in the organization as it may alter the effects of brand-specific TFL."

Limitations and Future Research

"Considering the self-reported nature of this study, future studies are encouraged to collect data from multiple sources including manager reviews, employee insights, and/or customer evaluations on different constructs."

"As in many studies that examine social environments (e.g., a brand community) with ongoing exchanges among members, it would be beneficial to obtain longitudinal data to capture the continuous reciprocation among employees to gain more insights on the full dynamics the effects of brand-specific TFL."

"The data in this study were collected from a broad selection of US-based hospitality employees, however, the cultural characteristics of US organizations can be very different from those in other countries."

"Future studies are encouraged to establish a nomological network of other typical internal branding outcomes (e.g., employee work engagement and brand identification) under brand-specific transformational leadership."

Bibliography

1. Government of Macao Special Administrative Region Statistics and Census Service (DSEC). (2017). Employed population by industry. https://www.dsec.gov.mo/PredefinedReport.aspx?lang=en-USReportID=10
2. Brotheridge, C. M., & Lee, R. T. (2003). Development and validation of the emotional labour scale. *Journal of Occupational and Organizational Psychology, 76*(3), 365–379.
3. Foley, S., Hang-Yue, N., & Lui, S. (2005). The effects of work stressors, perceived organizational support, and gender on work-family conflict in Hong Kong. *Asia Pacific Journal of Management, 22*(3), 237–256.
4. Preacher, K. J., Rucker, D. D., & Hayes, A. F. (2007). Addressing moderated mediation hypotheses: Theory, methods, and prescriptions. *Multivariate Behavioral Research, 42*, 185–227.
5. Singh, J. (2000). Performance productivity and quality of front line employees in service organizations. *Journal of Marketing, 64*, 15–34.
6. Taris, T. W. (2006). Is there a relationship between burnout and objective performance? A critical review of 16 studies. *Work and Stress, 20*(4), 316–334.
7. Hau, L. N., Anh, P. N. T., & Thuy, P. N. (2016). The effects of interaction behaviors of service frontliners on customer participation in the value co-creation: A study of health care service. *Service Business.* https://doi.org/10.1007/s11628-016-0307-4
8. Berry, L. L. (1995). Relationship marketing of services-growing interest, emerging perspectives. *Journal of the Academy of Marketing Science, 23*(4), 236–245.
9. Wentzel, D. (2009). The effect of employee behavior on brand personality impressions and brand attitudes. *Journal of the Academy of Marketing Science, 37*(3), 359–374.

10. Simons, R. (1991). Strategic orientation and top management attention to control systems. *Strategic Management Journal, 12*(1), 49–62.
11. Anderson, J. C., & Gerbing, D. W. (1988). Structural equation modeling in practice: A review and recommended two-step approach. *Psychological Bulletin, 103*, 411.
12. Fornell, C., & Larcker, D. F. (1981). Evaluating structural equation models with unobservable variables and measurement error. *Journal of Marketing Research, 19*, 39–50.
13. Liu, S., Wang, M., Bamberger, P., Shi, J., & Bacharach, S. B. (2015). The dark side of socialization: A longitudinal investigation of newcomer alcohol use. *Academy of Management Journal, 58*(2), 334–355.
14. Oyerinde, O. F. (2020). Leadership style, work environment, organizational silence and institutional effectiveness of polytechnic libraries, South-West Nigeria. *The International Information and Library Review, 52*(2), 79–94.
15. Schmidt, G. B. (2014). Virtual leadership: An important leadership context. *Industrial and Organizational Psychology.* https://doi.org/10.1111/iops.12129
16. Schilling, J., & Kluge, A. (2009). Barriers to organizational learning: An integration of theory and research. *International Journal of Management Reviews.* https://doi.org/10.1111/j.1468-2370.2008.00242.x
17. Morrison, J. L. (2014). Daft, Richard L. The leadership experience (6th ed.). *Journal of Education for Business.*
18. Cullinane, N., & Donaghey, J. (2020). *Employee silence.* Edward Elgar Publishing.
19. Hochschild, A. H. (1983). *The managed heart: Commercialization of human feeling.* University of California Press.
20. Grandey, A. A. (2000). Emotional regulation in the workplace: A new way to conceptualize emotional labor. *Journal of Occupational Health Psychology, 5*(1), 95–110.
21. Ashforth, B. E., & Humphrey, A. R. H. (1993). Emotional labor in service roles: The influence of identity. *The Academy of Management Review, 18*(1), 88–115.
22. Allen, J. A., Pugh, S. D., Grandey, A. A., & Groth, M. (2010). Following display rules in good or bad faith? Customer orientation as a moderator of the display rule-emotional labor relationship. *Human Performance, 23*(2), 101–115.
23. O'Boyle, E., Humphrey, R. H., Pollack, J. M., & Story, P. H. (2011). Emotional intelligence and job performance: A meta-analysis. *Journal of Organizational Behavior, 32*(5), 788–818.
24. Opengart, R. (2005). Emotional intelligence and emotion work: Examining constructs from an interdisciplinary framework. *Human Resource Development Review, 4*(1), 49–62.
25. Cheung, F., Tang, C., & Tang, S. (2011). Psychological capital as a moderator between emotional labor, burnout, and job satisfaction among school teachers in China. *International Journal of Stress Management, 18*(4), 348–371.
26. Bhave, D. P., & Glomb, T. M. (2016). The role of occupational emotional labor requirements on the surface acting-job satisfaction relationship. *Journal of Management, 42*(3), 722–741.
27. Guy, M. E., & Lee, H. J. (2015). How emotional intelligence mediates emotional labor in public service jobs. *Review of Public Personnel Administration, 35*(3), 261–277.
28. Lee, H. J. (2018). How emotional intelligence relates to job satisfaction and burnout in public service jobs. *International Review of Administrative Sciences, 84*(4), 729–745.
29. Lee, H. J. (2018). Relation between display rules and emotive behavior strategies and its outcomes among south Korean public service employees. *Public Performance & Management Review, 41*(4), 723–744.
30. Potipiroon, W., Srisuthisa-ard, A., & Faerman, S. (2019). Public service motivation and customer service behavior: Testing the mediating role of emotional labour and the moderating role of gender. *Public Management Review, 21*(5), 650–668.
31. Yang, S. B., Guy, M. E., Azhar, A., Hsieh, C. W., Lee, H. J., Lu, X., & Mastracci, S. (2018). Comparing apples and manzanas: Instrument development for cross-national analysis of emotional labour in public service jobs. *International Journal of Work Organisation and Emotion, 9*(3), 264–282.
32. Mastracci, S. H., & Adams, I. (2019). Is emotional labor easier in collectivist or individualist cultures? An East-West comparison. *Public Personnel Management, 48*(3), 325–344.

33. Sloan, M. M. (2014). The consequences of emotional labor for public sector workers and the mitigating role of self-efficacy. *American Review of Public Administration, 44*(3), 274–290.
34. Hsieh, C. W., Hsieh, J. Y., & Huang, I. Y. F. (2016). Self-efficacy as a mediator and moderator between emotional labor and job satisfaction: A case study of public service employees in Taiwan. *Public Performance & Management Review, 40*(1), 71–96.
35. Shamir, B. (1991). Meaning, self and motivation in organizations. *Organization Studies, 12*(3), 405–424. https://doi.org/10.1177/017084069101200304
36. Shamir, B., House, R. J., & Arthur, M. B. (1993). The motivational effects of charismatic leadership: A self-concept based theory. *Organization Science, 4*(4), 577–594.
37. van Knippenberg, D., van Knippenberg, B., De Cremer, D., & Hogg, M. A. (2004). Leadership, self, and identity: A review and research agenda. *Leadership Quarterly, 15*(6), 825–856. https://doi.org/10.1016/j.leaqua.2004.09.002
38. Deci, E. L., & Ryan, R. M. (2000). The "what" and "why" of goal pursuits: Human needs and the self-determination of behavior. *Psychological Inquiry, 11*(4), 227–268.
39. Podsakoff, P. M., Mackenzie, S. B., Lee, J. Y., & Podsakoff, N. P. (2003). Common method biases in behavioral research: A critical review of the literature and recommended remedies. *Journal of Applied Psychology, 88*(5), 879–903.
40. Baron, R. M., & Kenny, D. A. (1986). The moderator–mediator variable distinction in social psychological research: Conceptual, strategic, and statistical considerations. *Journal of Personality and Social Psychology, 51*(6), 1173–1182.
41. Brown, G., Pierce, J. L., & Crossley, C. (2014). Toward an understanding of the development of ownership feelings. *Journal of Organizational Behavior, 35*(3), 318–338.
42. Pierce, J. L., Kostova, T., & Dirks, K. T. (2001). Toward a theory of psychological ownership in organizations. *Academy of Management Review, 26*(2), 298–310.
43. Xiong, L., & King, C. (2020). Exploring how employee sense of brand community affects their attitudes and behavior. *Journal of Hospitality and Tourism Research, 44*(4), 567–596.
44. Barros-Arrieta, D., & García-Cali, E. (2021). Internal branding: Conceptualization from a literature review and opportunities for future research. *Journal of Brand Management, 28*(2), 133–151.
45. Buil, I., Martínez, E., & Matute, J. (2019). Transformational leadership and employee performance: The role of identification, engagement and proactive personality. *International Journal of Hospitality Management, 77*, 64–75.
46. Uen, J. F., Wu, T., Teng, H. C., & Liu, Y. S. (2012). Transformational leadership and branding behavior in Taiwanese hotels. *International Journal of Contemporary Hospitality Management., 24*(1), 26–43.
47. Morhart, F. M., Herzog, W., & Tomczak, T. (2009). Brand-specific leadership: Turning employees into brand champions. *Journal of Marketing, 73*, 122–142.
48. MacKenzie, S. B., & Podsakoff, P. M. (2012). Common method bias in marketing: Causes, mechanisms, and procedural remedies. *Journal of Retailing, 88*(4), 542–555. https://doi.org/10.1016/j.jretai.2012.08.001
49. Crossley, C. D., Bennett, R. J., Jex, S. M., & Burnfield, J. L. (2007). Development of a global measure of job embeddedness and integration into a traditional model of voluntary turnover. *Journal of Applied Psychology, 92*(4), 1031–1042.
50. Aiken, L. S., West, S. G., & Reno, R. R. (1991). *Multiple regression: Testing and interpreting interactions*. Sage.
51. Lai, H. S., Hu, H. H., & Chen, Z. Y. J. (2020). The effects of culture shock on foreign employees in the service industry. *Service Business, 14*(3), 361–385. https://doi.org/10.1007/s11628-020-00420-x
52. Yoon, J., May, K., Kang, J. H., & Solomon, G. T. (2018). The impact of emotional self-management on benefit offerings and employment growth: an analysis of the fastest growing businesses in the United States. *International Entrepreneurship and Management Journal, 15*, 175–195. https://doi.org/10.1007/s11365-018-0542-3
53. Elmadağ, A. B., & Ellinger, A. E. (2017). Alleviating job stress to improve service employee work affect: The influence of rewarding. *Service Business, 12*, 121–141. https://doi.org/10.1007/s11628-017-0340-y

54. Shao, M., Gu, J., & Wu, J. (2020). To drink or not to drink; that is the question! Antecedents and consequences of employee business drinking. *Asia Pacific Journal of Management, 39*(1), 343–363. https://doi.org/10.1007/s10490-020-09731-z
55. Wei, J., Zhu, S., Hou, Z., Dong, H., & Li, J. (2022). Research on the influence mechanism of emotional intelligence and psychological empowerment on customers' repurchase intention under the situation of online shopping service recovery. *Current Psychology, 42*(21), 17595–17611. https://doi.org/10.1007/s12144-022-02841-5
56. Joseph, S., & Shetty, N. (2022). An empirical study on the impact of employee voice and silence on destructive leadership and organizational culture. *Asian Journal of Business Ethics, 11*(suppl 1), 85–101. https://doi.org/10.1007/s13520-022-00155-0
57. Lee, H. J. (2020). Relationship between emotional labor and job satisfaction: Testing mediating role of emotional intelligence on South Korean Public Service Employees. *Public Organization Review, 21*(2), 337–353. https://doi.org/10.1007/s11115-020-00490-5
58. Cui, Z., Ji, X., Liu, P., & Li, R. (2023). How spiritual leadership leads to employee followership behavior: the role of relational identification and spiritual intelligence. *Current Psychology, 43*(6), 5729–5741. https://doi.org/10.1007/s12144-023-04772-1
59. Xiong, L. (2023). It takes a village: examining how and when brand-specific transformational leadership affects employees in internal brand management. *Journal of Brand Management, 30*(4), 333. https://doi.org/10.1057/s41262-022-00308-3

Chapter 5
Emotional Intelligence and Leadership

Introduction by the Author

WLEIS (Wong & Law Emotional Intelligence Scale) and the Leader Efficacy Questionnaire (LEQ) were used as instruments for comparing emotional intelligence and leader's self-efficacy perception, Harper (2015). The study revealed that women possess higher levels of emotional intelligence, leader self-efficacy, leader self-regulation and self- emotional appraisal. The results suggested that gender may be a gauge for predicting higher levels of emotional intelligence and the individual levels of skill assessment and skill development can be done using the single instrument, which is an outcome of the study to measure emotional intelligence and leader's self-efficacy. The psychological constructs, skills and abilities constitute a positive correlation between emotional intelligence and leader's self-efficacy. The research study done among 230 employees which was divided as 56 groups used SEM and linear modelling proves that emotional stability is positively related with emergent leadership, Wu, [142].

Leaders establish the tone for the organisation. If they lacks mental capacity, it could have far-reaching effects, resulting in reduced staff engagement and a greater turnover rate. Leaders must understand how their feelings and behaviours affect those around them in order to be effective. A more effective leader connects with and collaborates with other people in a more effective way. A research study conducted by Dorfmann [107] states that there is a positive relationship between leader's perceptions with the utilisation of their emotional intelligence and leader's self-efficacy in the work environment. The emergent leader's emotional stability becomes salient when group task is high. The emotional disorder threshold increases with increase in group level relationship, (Liden [108]). The capacity to quickly recover from chaotic and negative emotions resulting from conflict on group level relationship should implement the perception of group members as group leaders. The employee's perception to relationship and task conflict within the group has a positive correlation with emotional stability and perceived capacity to develop as a leader.

A recent research by Boyar (2022) the leaders are able to organize, interpret and evaluate the information to perform an assigned task in order to produce the result in behavioural change. Each scenario needs the leader to work on their cognitive and social data to be processed in choosing leadership style. Those leaders who are demonstrating high emotional intelligence can adapt to situational demands. The process may take longer and complete information to bring out accurate conclusions. The results proved that emotional intelligence abilities when combined with inductive reasoning can forecast potential leader adaptability and moderates the relationship between inductive reasoning and leader adaptability. Forty narrative interviews of various countries facing crisis for a period of 18 months revealed that communicating in an open way to their employees may help in crisis situation. Lin and others in 2021 investigated the way in which how value based leadership theory influence team- performance. Emotional regulation has a positive and direct impact on the kind of leadership adopted in an organization. The research aims at investigating influence of abusive supervision and the significant relationship between transformational leadership and work behaviour and employee well-being. The results reveal that ethical leadership indirectly promotes young firm's ambidexterity.

Emotional intelligence is seen as a critical skill for successful managers in spotting and resolving problems among their team members. Therefore, behavioural intellect is an important component of many different forms of leadership. Interestingly, emotional intelligence is a good factor for determining a leadership style's success. According to experts, emotional intelligence is an excellent criterion for determining the efficiency of a leadership style. Experts feel that a leader's IQ, technical capabilities, and interpersonal abilities are meaningless if he or she lacks emotional intelligence. The increasing significance of emotional intelligence in leadership has compelled many leaders to learn and incorporate it into their method of leadership in order to foster creativity, job satisfaction, and a healthy working environment in their organisation. If any leader lacks emotional intelligence, then his/her intelligence quotient (IQ), technical capabilities, and interpersonal abilities are irrelevant. The increasing significance of emotional intelligence in leadership has compelled many leaders to learn and incorporate it into their approach to management in order to foster creativity, job satisfaction, and a healthy working environment in their organisation.

A critical analysis on Elon Musk leadership style in Tesla employs a structured observation technique and servant leadership trait in order to add practical values in his leadership trait.

Machine Generated Summaries

Disclaimer: The summaries in this chapter were generated from Springer Nature publications using extractive AI auto-summarization: An extraction-based summarizer aims to identify the most important sentences of a text using an algorithm and uses those original sentences to create the auto-summary (unlike generative AI). As the constituted sentences are machine selected, they may not fully reflect the body of the work, so we strongly advise that the original content is read and cited. The auto generated summaries were curated by the editor to meet Springer Nature publication standards. To cite this content, please refer to the original papers.

Machine generated keywords: leadership, transformational, transformational leadership, leader, follower, ethical, subordinate, bass, style, education, organizational, crisis, team, emotional, change.

Correctional Executives' Leadership Self-Efficacy and Their Perceptions of Emotional Intelligence [189]

This is a machine-generated summary of:
Harper, Donta S.: Correctional Executives' Leadership Self-Efficacy and Their Perceptions of Emotional Intelligence [189]
Published in: American Journal of Criminal Justice (2015)
Link to original: https://doi.org/10.1007/s12103-015-9319-1
Copyright of the summarized publication:
The Author(s) 2015
License: OpenAccess CC BY 4.0
This article is distributed under the terms of the Creative Commons Attribution 4.0 International License (http://creativecommons.org/licenses/by/4.0/), which permits unrestricted use, distribution, and reproduction in any medium, provided you give appropriate credit to the original author(s) and the source, provide a link to the Creative Commons license, and indicate if changes were made.

If you want to cite the papers, please refer to the original.

For technical reasons we could not place the page where the original quote is coming from.

Abstract-Summary

"This quantitative study involved examining a leadership model of the relationship between emotional intelligence and leader self-efficacy perceptions among correctional executives and senior-level leaders."

"Participants were asked to complete the WLEIS (Wong & Law Emotional Intelligence Scale) and the Leader Efficacy Questionnaire (LEQ)."

"The study findings yielded a statistically significant difference among leaders' perceptions of their utilization of emotional intelligence and leader self-efficacy in the work environment."

"The study findings further suggest that gender is predictive across the instrumentation models for this study, with women exhibiting higher levels of emotional intelligence, self-emotional appraisal, use of emotion, leader self-efficacy, and leader self-regulation efficacy."

Research Design

"The sample represented correctional executives and senior-level leaders from across the US."

"Correctional executives and senior-level leaders were targeted through professional associations for executives and through direct communication surveys sent to the agency email addresses that were found and to the worldwide web names whose position title was either correctional executive or correctional senior-level leader."

"A survey instrument was sent via email by the SurveyMonkey® link to study participants consisting of executives and senior-level leaders, professional associations, listserv, and professional and trade organizations for corrections."

"Participants consisted of 47 executives (42 %) and 65 senior-level leaders (58 %)."

"Authors indicate the LEQ has been validated across seven diverse sample groups and has shown to predict outcomes related to leader performance, enhanced motivation to lead others, and highly effective leadership style, such as transformational leadership (Hannah & Avolio [1])."

Results

"The WLEIS SEA, UOE, and ROE dimensions and the LEQ LME component do not correlate among variables SEA $r = .187$, $p = .058$, UOE $r = .155$, $p = .115$ and ROE $r = .185$, $p = .058$."

"All other dimensions of the WLEIS and LEQ indicate significant correlation and therefore further support hypothesis 1, a positive relationship among emotional intelligence and leader self-efficacy."

"There were significant differences between males and females among the dimensions of emotional intelligence."

"There was also a significant difference between males and females on the LEQ subcomponent LRSE."

"These findings support hypothesis 2, retaining the alternative hypothesis that there is predictability of a positive relationship with corrections leaders' sense of use of leader (SEA) self-emotional appraisal, (UOE) use of emotion, and (LRSE) leader self-regulation efficacy was predictable at the significant level $p < .025$."

Discussion

"These findings suggesting that gender might be a gauge for predicting higher levels of emotional intelligence are similar to the study findings of Siegling and others [2] for trait emotional intelligence or self-efficacy among leaders and non-leaders."

"The study findings indicate that developing emotional intelligence and self-efficacy should constitute a significant part of this competency model to train correctional executives and senior-level leaders."

"Further research could also lead to development of a single instrument for measuring emotional intelligence and leader self-efficacy at the organizational and individual levels to assess skills and abilities for skill development."

"Although this study certainly has value for the corrections industry, assumptions that emotional intelligence and self-efficacy correlate to strong leadership in other industries might not prove true due to the uniqueness of the corrections industry."

"Despite these limitations, the study findings do provide a step in the right direction towards understanding the impacts of emotional intelligence and self-efficacy on the leadership of correctional executives and senior-level leaders."

[Section 4]

"Leaders in the corrections industry have not adequately relied on scientific literature that explores two important concepts that impact correctional leadership: self-efficacy and emotional intelligence."

"The following hypotheses are proposed: H1 – There is an overall positive relationship between correctional executives' sense of leader self-efficacy and their emotional intelligence perceptions."

"H2 – There is predictability of a positive relationship in correctional executives' sense of leader self-efficacy and emotional intelligence subscales based on their perceptions."

"Although Ramchunder and Martins [3] studied policemen in South Africa and Sarkhosh and Rezaee [4] studied teachers, there is an absence of research investigating the link between emotional intelligence and leader self-efficacy for correctional leaders in the United States."

"Research investigating emotional intelligence and leader self-efficacy would be relevant in the corrections industry for several reasons."

"The psychological constructs, skills, and abilities that positively contribute to organizational performance were examined by correlating emotional intelligence and leader self-efficacy through surveying correctional leaders' perceptions of their own emotional intelligence and leader self-efficacy."

A Multi-level Study of Emergent Group Leadership: Effects of Emotional Stability and Group Conflict [190]

This is a machine-generated summary of:
Li, Yan; Chun, Hui; Ashkanasy, Neal M.; Ahlstrom, David: A multi-level study of emergent group leadership: Effects of emotional stability and group conflict [190]
Published in: Asia Pacific Journal of Management (2012)
Link to original: https://doi.org/https://doi.org/10.1007/s10490-012-9298-4
Copyright of the summarized publication:
Springer Science+Business Media, LLC 2012
All rights reserved.
If you want to cite the papers, please refer to the original.
For technical reasons we could not place the page where the original quote is coming from.

Abstract-Summary

"Based on data from 230 employees in 56 work groups in eight Chinese firms, and analyzed using structural equation and hierarchical linear modeling, the results support the idea that emotional stability is positively related with emergent leadership, but negatively with group task and relationship conflict."

"We also found that group task and relationship conflict moderated associations between emotional stability and emergent leadership, although the moderating effect of relationship conflict was marginal."

"From a practical perspective, our findings suggest that mangers can expect leadership in conflicted groups to emerge from more emotionally stable group members."

Theory and Hypotheses

"We propose that organizational member perceptions of their own suitability to emerge as a leader is determined in part by the individual's emotional stability and the moderating effect of group task and relationship conflict."

"The emotional stability of emergent leaders (disorder threshold and emotional resilience) should tend to become more salient when group relational or task conflict is high."

"We hypothesize: The strength of the positive relationship between group members' self-perceptions of emergent leadership and emotional disorder threshold (H1a) increases with increasing group-level relationship (H3a) and task conflict (H3b)."

"Similar to our arguments pertaining to emotional disorder threshold, ability to recover quickly from negative and chaotic emotions resulting from group-level relationship or task conflict should facilitate group members' perceptions of their own emergence as group leaders."

"Thus: The strength of the relationship between group members' self-perceptions of emergent leadership and their emotional resilience (H1b) increases with increasing group-level relationship (H4a) and task conflict (H4b)."

Methods

"Participants in this study comprised employees of eight firms located in a large Chinese metropolitan area."

"We conducted the study with the full cooperation of each participating firm's management, who provided a register of employees and work-groups; and the informed consent of all participants."

"If a group's size was less than five, all members were invited to participate."

"Each participant also rated the group's task and relationship conflict."

"The six items corresponded with specific negative emotions, for example, 'Do you recover quickly from feeling upset?'"

"We used the intra-group conflict scale (ICS) developed by Jehn ([5]; see also Pearson, Ensley, & Amason [6]) to measure group relationship and task conflict."

"The relationship conflict scale comprised of four items, for example, 'There is much emotional conflict among members in my work unit.'"

"The task conflict scale included four items, for example, 'How many disagreements over different ideas were there?'"

Results

"The next stage of our analysis was to check for significant between-group differences in relationship and task conflict."

"We employed hierarchical linear modeling (HLM) to estimate the between-group differences of group task and relationship conflict."

"These results support the idea that group members achieved consistent perception on their group-level task and relationship conflict."

"The HLM analysis also facilitated the test of Hypotheses 3 and 4, that the relationship between emergent leadership and emotional stability would be stronger for higher conflict groups."

"The Level 2 (group-level) variables are the aggregated members' perceptions of relationship and task conflict within their work units."

"With the exception of H3a (disorder threshold and relationship conflict), the results of the HLM analysis supported our predictions that the positive relationship between emotional stability and members' perception of their capacity to lead the group is stronger in the presence of group-level conflict."

Discussion

"Group members' self-perceptions that they can take a leadership role are seen to emerge as a consequence of emotional stability."

"The relationship between emotional stability and members' perceived capacity to emerge as a leader is, moreover, subject to members' perceptions of relationship and task conflict within the group."

"While we expected to find that members would be less likely to see themselves emerging as leaders in low conflict groups, we also expected to find that the emotional stability–emergent leadership relationship would be stronger in high conflict groups than in low conflict groups."

"The contribution of this finding from a practical perspective is that mangers can expect leadership in conflicted groups to emerge from more emotionally stable members with a balanced view (cf. Dunbar & Ahlstrom [7])."

Conclusion

"These results support our theorizing about the nexus of emotional stability, self-perceptions of emergent leadership capability, and group-level conflict."

"We confirmed that group members' perceptions for emergent leadership are associated with emotional stability, both in terms of emotional disorder threshold (Li & others [8]) and emotional resilience (an individual's ability to recover quickly from emotional distress, see Tugade & Fredrickson [9])."

"We also found that, while members tend to see themselves as less likely to emerge as leaders in situations where group relationship and task conflict is present, the positive relationship between emotional stability and perceptions of emergent leadership becomes stronger in situations of heightened group-level conflict."

"This study demonstrates that leadership emergence is determined, at least in part, from an interaction of group members' individual-level emotional stability and members' perceptions of group conflict."

[Section 6]

"We assess how emergent leadership is determined by group conflict and members' emotional stability."

"The challenge with much of the research to date in organizational group leadership is that leaders are assumed to have been appointed via organizational authority, rather than having emerged from the group itself."

"Therefore, we seek to understand how the individual-level emotional traits of emotional stability might influence leader emergence under varying conditions of group relationship and task conflict."

"We begin by developing our hypotheses and state clearly the new structure of emotional stability, its self-organization theoretical foundation, its functions on emergent leadership based on group evolution theory at the individual level, and its contingent associations with variation in higher-level group contexts: group task and relationship conflict."

An Adaptive Leadership Approach: The Impact of Reasoning and Emotional Intelligence (EI) Abilities on Leader Adaptability [191]

This is a machine-generated summary of:
 Boyar, Scott L.; Savage, Grant T.; Williams, Eric S.: An Adaptive Leadership Approach: The Impact of Reasoning and Emotional Intelligence (EI) Abilities on Leader Adaptability [191]
 Published in: Employee Responsibilities and Rights Journal (2022)
 Link to original: https://doi.org/https://doi.org/10.1007/s10672-022-09428-z
 Copyright of the summarized publication:
 The Author(s), under exclusive licence to Springer Science+Business Media, LLC, part of Springer Nature 2022
 Copyright comment: Springer Nature or its licensor (e.g. a society or other partner) holds exclusive rights to this article under a publishing agreement with the author(s) or other rightsholder(s); author self-archiving of the accepted manuscript version of this article is solely governed by the terms of such publishing agreement and applicable law.
 All rights reserved.
 If you want to cite the papers, please refer to the original.
 For technical reasons we could not place the page where the original quote is coming from.

Abstract-Summary

"We incorporate adaptive and situational leadership theories along with trait process models to examine two types of reasoning abilities, inductive and deductive along with the direct and moderating effect of EI on potential leader adaptability."

"Using a three wave panel design, we found that inductive reasoning and EI predicted adaptive leadership; we further showed that EI moderated the inductive-adaptive leadership relationship where higher levels of EI and inductive reasoning abilities predicted potential leader adaptability."

Theoretical Framework

"Within the adaptive leadership framework, leaders interpret, organize, and process information about others' abilities to complete a specific task in order to effect behavioral change."

"Each situation requires leaders to process cognitive (e.g., reasoning abilities) and social information in choosing the appropriate leadership style."

"The ability to use and manage emotions should lead to more adaptive behaviors by improving the social-emotional information processing by more effectively appraising the situation and interacting with others to identify the appropriate leader behaviors to affect desired outcomes."

"Leaders demonstrating high levels of deductive reasoning along with high EI will also adapt to situational demands, but because the information processing may take longer and require more complete information to draw accurate conclusions (i.e., choosing the perfect leadership style), the overall effect will be significant, yet weaker than inductive."

Sample and Procedure

"Using OLS regression we assessed over time the direct effect of two types of reasoning abilities, inductive and deductive, and ability-based emotional intelligence on potential leader adaptability."

"We employed Model 1 in Hayes's [10] PROCESS Macro to test these interactions and assess the conditional effect ($\Theta_{X \rightarrow Y}$) of reasoning and EI on potential leader adaptability."

"We further probed the interaction using the Johnson and Neyman [11] technique to identify the point in the distribution of values of EI where it became significant in influencing the conditional of effect ($\Theta_{X \rightarrow Y}$) of inductive reasoning ability on potential leader adaptability."

"Sample, when EI scores reached 99.33 (and higher) they became a significant moderator creating a region of significance that accounted for 64.16% of the scores above the zero in the 95% confidence interval for the conditional effect ($\Theta_{X \rightarrow Y}$) of inductive reasoning ability on potential leader adaptability."

Discussion

"While leaders likely have a preferred leadership approach, being flexible and adaptive to situational demands is critical for success (Zaccaro & others [12]), and we demonstrate that both inductive reasoning and emotional intelligence abilities are significant predictors of potential leader adaptability."

"The mechanisms for processing information to make decisions is also important, and we demonstrated that inductive reasoning predicts adaptive leadership for potential leaders and was influenced by EI abilities."

"Our study shows that the greater the inductive ability along with moderate to high levels of EI may result in greater leader flexibility to more accurately choose a leadership approach given the situation and follower needs, which is consistent with Zaccaro & others's [12] initial claim."

"We show that inductive reasoning and emotional intelligence abilities predict potential leader adaptability, and that EI moderates the relationship between inductive reasoning and leader adaptability."

[Section 4]

"We hope to address this shortcoming in the literature by examining the relationship between specific components of cognitive and social abilities and potential leader adaptability for a sample of potential leaders."

"We suggest that emotional intelligence (EI) is an important social ability that will likewise predict potential leader adaptability."

"Capturing EI, which is one's ability to process and organize emotion-related information, should lead to better decisions for potential leaders (Zaccaro & Torres [13])."

"The purpose of this study is to better understand how cognitive and social abilities influence leader behaviors within an adaptive leadership framework."

Recovering Troubled IT Projects: The Roles of Transformational Leadership and Project Complexity [192]

This is a machine-generated summary of:
Lei, Hui; Fang, Xiang; Rajkumar, T. M.; Holsapple, Clyde: Recovering Troubled IT Projects: The Roles of Transformational Leadership and Project Complexity [192]
Published in: Information Systems Frontiers (2020)
Link to original: https://doi.org/https://doi.org/10.1007/s10796-020-10068-7
Copyright of the summarized publication:
Springer Science+Business Media, LLC, part of Springer Nature 2020
All rights reserved.
If you want to cite the papers, please refer to the original.
For technical reasons we could not place the page where the original quote is coming from.

Abstract-Summary

"Understanding how leadership and project complexity affect a recovery process could enable organizations to do a better job in recovering troubled projects."

"The recovery process and project complexity have not been integrated into the relationship between leadership and project recovery."

"Change leadership, leadership effectiveness, and project complexity are empirically determined to be positively associated with the recovery process based on quantitative data collected from 166 IT project team members."

"The recovery process significantly affects product success and process success of troubled projects."

"The findings imply that organizations should focus more on leadership effectiveness to improve recovery processes."

Introduction

"Such troubled projects often require significant management oversight and leadership supervision to recover and be successful."

"We could not find any empirical studies that focused on the recovery process within IT troubled projects or its impact on project success."

"Project complexity-related risk is unpredictable, investigating how complexity alters the relationship between leadership effectiveness and the recovery process may reveal new perspectives about troubled project recovery."

"How does the recovery process affect leadership's impact on project success?"

"This research combines the notion of recovery processes from crisis management literature with the practice of transformational leadership in troubled project environments."

"A better understanding of how project complexity affects the relationship between leadership effectiveness and the process of recovery in troubled projects will lead to a better understanding of mechanisms that impact project success."

Background/Theory Development

"We posit that, in a troubled project context, transformational leadership affects project outcomes via change leadership, leadership effectiveness, and recovery processes."

"An effective leader can influence the team members to challenge their assumptions, come up with new ways of working, improve the credibility of the project team, and control the operational resources in order to impact the recovery processes and help lead the project out of trouble."

"Given the above discussion and the effects change leadership has on the primary processes for recovery: operational containment, credibility protection restoration, and organizational learning, we expect: H3: Change leadership is positively related to troubled project recovery processes."

"Given the above discussion, we expect that: H4: Leadership effectiveness is positively related to troubled project recovery process."

"This shifting of focus away from transformational leadership moderates leadership effectiveness (Ayman & others [14]) and, along with project complexity, makes operational containment harder and influences process recovery."

Methodology

"Seven constructs, namely transformational leadership, change leadership, leadership effectiveness, recovery process, complexity and size, product success, and process success, are introduced in our research model."

"For the recovery process construct, we use the ten remedial tasks Iacovou and Dexter (Iacovou & Dexter [15]) propose for troubled projects."

"Participants in the study were asked to rate how well each task was completed by the leader in the project recovery process."

"We first conducted an exploratory factor analysis on the transformational leadership items and confirmed that the items loaded on the six factors: articulating a vision, providing a role model, communicating high performance expectations, providing individualized support, fostering the acceptance of group goals, and providing intellectual stimulation (Podsakoff & others [16])."

"Except for the moderation effect of project complexity on the relationship between leadership effectiveness and recovery process, the results indicate that all the other hypotheses held."

Discussion and Implications of Analysis Results

"Organizations with troubled IT projects should focus more on improving transformational leadership via articulating a vision that focuses on the recovery and projects' goals, providing a role model for team members, and communicating high performance expectations to team members."

"Project team members may need to select and utilize the appropriate remedies within the recovery process."

"Project team members have a better chance to recover troubled projects and satisfy the three objectives of effective recovery—enabling organizations to contain potential operational impact, protecting against credibility threats, and adapting based on the learning."

"The significant positive relationship between complexity and the recovery process may imply that reducing complexity could potentially hurt a recovery process, as organizational learning may go down while project complexity decreases."

"While practitioners could argue that reduced complexity may enhance operational containment and, therefore, help a recovery process, it is possible that the impact of reduced organizational learning could offset the impact of improved operational containment due to decreased project complexity."

Conclusions

"Our study followed Iacovou and Dexter [15] crisis management approach, which includes organizational learning within the construct of the recovery process, and further considered the relationship of the recovery process with transformational leadership and project success."

"This study found that transformational leadership ultimately affects both the process success and the product success of troubled IT projects via change leadership, leadership effectiveness, and the recovery process."

"Future studies could focus on breaking down recovery process into three sub-dimensions (operational containment, credibility protection, and organizational learning), and identifying how each dimension might be improved by leadership effectiveness and change leadership at different levels of complexity."

"Such studies may lead to a better understanding of how to adjust change leadership, leadership effectiveness, and complexity collectively, rather than individually, to best support each of the dimensions of the recovery process of a troubled project."

Leading in the Paradoxical World of Crises: How Leaders Navigate Through Crises [193]

This is a machine-generated summary of:

Förster, Charlotte; Paparella, Caroline; Duchek, Stephanie; Güttel, Wolfgang H.: Leading in the Paradoxical World of Crises: How Leaders Navigate Through Crises [193]

Published in: Schmalenbach Journal of Business Research (2022)

Link to original: https://doi.org/https://doi.org/10.1007/s41471-022-00147-7

Copyright of the summarized publication:
The Author(s) 2022

License: OpenAccess CC BY 4.0

This article is licensed under a Creative Commons Attribution 4.0 International License, which permits use, sharing, adaptation, distribution and reproduction in any medium or format, as long as you give appropriate credit to the original author(s) and the source, provide a link to the Creative Commons licence, and indicate if changes were made. The images or other third party material in this article are included in the article's Creative Commons licence, unless indicated otherwise in a credit line to the material. If material is not included in the article's Creative Commons licence and your intended use is not permitted by statutory regulation or exceeds the permitted use, you will need to obtain permission directly from the copyright holder. To view a copy of this licence, visit http://creativecommons.org/licenses/by/4.0/.

If you want to cite the papers, please refer to the original.

For technical reasons we could not place the page where the original quote is coming from.

Abstract-Summary

"Using an inductive analysis of 32 interviews on crisis leadership, we show that in the case of an acute crisis, leaders apply different paradoxical behaviors to cope effectively with the situation and navigate their organizations through these events."

"Our study contributes to existing literature by, first, showing that the distinctiveness of crises results from the fact that leaders are confronted with paradoxes that they can otherwise smoothly separate in terms of time or organization, second, revealing that the leader's paradoxical behaviors as a respond are derived from their mindset to consciously recognize the contradictory demands of the crisis, and third, from their action in terms of a compressed situational leadership."

"By identifying six pairs of paradoxical behaviors, we demonstrate how leaders effectively deal with the unsolvable contradictions that arise from the crisis, and thus contribute to the organizations' ability to cope with crises."

Introduction

"Even though we know that leaders have a crucial role in an organizational crisis (e.g., Pearson & Clair [17]; Weick [18]) and individual resources are vital to developing organizational resilience (Lengnick-Hall & others [19]; Riolli & Savicki [20]; Horne & Orr [21]; Mallak [22]; McCann & Selsky [23]; Shin & others [24]), researchers have yet to examine the relationship of leaders and organizational resilience in greater detail (e.g., Williams & others [25])."

"Through the inductive analysis of 32 in-depth interviews and by focusing on the leaders' role in a major organizational crisis, we show that deriving from both the leader's mindset to consciously recognize the contradictory demands of the crisis and the leader's action in terms of a compressed situational leadership, leaders apply different paradoxical behaviors to cope effectively with the situation and navigate their organizations through crisis."

"We contribute to the literature on organizational resilience by elucidating the role of the leader in existence-threatening organizational crisis."

"With a specific focus on the 'cognitive and behavior attributes that facilitate resilience' (Williams & others [25], p. 752), we argue that leaders' paradoxical behaviors help leaders to navigate through crisis, and thus foster organizational resilience."

Theoretical Background

"resilience as the ability to use crises for advancing organizational processes and developing new capabilities (e.g., Lengnick-Hall & others [19]), and [3]."

"To develop organizational resilience, individual resources are particularly important (Lengnick-Hall & others [19]; Riolli & Savicki [20]; Horne & Orr [21]; Mallak

[22]; McCann & Selsky [23]; Shin & others [24]), especially with a view toward the upper echelon of the organization (Carmeli & others [26])."

"Previous research in this context has recognized the leaders' influence on their employees' resilience (e.g., Avey & others [27]; Gooty & others [28]; Walumbwa & others [29]; Harland & others [30]; Rego & others [31])."

"On a theoretical level, Samba and others [32] as well as Norman and others [33] each developed a model depicting the potential influence of the leader on organizational resilience."

"Norman and others [33] theoretically explained how the leaders' state of hope influences not only their own but also their followers' resiliency, which leads to organizational resilience affecting the long-term success."

"Referring to the crucial role leadership plays in the context of organizational resilience (Samba & others [32]; Norman & others [33]; Sutcliffe & others [34]; Williams & others [25]), our study aims to examin how leaders handle existence-threatening organizational crises, and therefore navigate their organizations through these events."

Methodology

"Due to the particularity of the crisis situation and the limited previous research on the leaders' role in the pursuit of a resilient organizational response to crises (e.g., Williams & others [25]), we considered a qualitative research approach to be appropriate for our study, especially since our aim is to reveal new concepts instead of confirming old ones (Wickert & De Bakker [35])."

"Data collection included 40 narrative interviews with leaders of various organizations facing severe crises over a period of 18 months."

"Owing to our study restrictions, we only selected those interviews in which the leaders classified the experienced crisis as major and existence-threatening for the organization."

"To the heterogeneity in terms of company sizes and business sectors, all of our interviewed leaders were key persons responsible for the handling and coordination of the respective organizational crisis."

"When we interviewed a leader from an organization (a global leader in the market for sustainable botanic cellulose fibers) who encountered grievous problems by facing a radical drop in the worldwide cotton price of 40%, we aligned our questions with this crisis to better understand how the leaders in charge encompassed the challenge they faced and how they handled the crisis effectively."

Findings

"That only works if this topic of trust is already at a very good level in the company." (I30, founder/manager, constructing software and recruitment, 2008 financial crisis) Although creating trust was an important behavior mentioned by our leaders, they also stressed that communicating openly with their employees was essential for prevailing in a critical situation."

"Some leaders also reported long-term cooperation with competitors or other firms of the value chain that turned out to be crucial to the company's survival. '[It is important] to build a relationship with competitors, where you are not seen as a competitor but as a market participant (...) who has his core competencies in these areas but is also ready, if it is not his core competency, to pass service to the best possible company.' (I6, controller, technology, 2008 financial crisis) In addition, the interviewees also worked with consultants to obtain an outside perspective to improve their decision-making."

Discussion

"We therefore explain our contributions that, first, the leader's perception of paradoxical demands in crisis is crucial, second, that the leaders' mindset of conscious recognition is an important response and, third, the action of compressed situational leadership contributes to organizational resilience might help organization to build organizational resilience during crisis."

"In order to shed light on the role of the leader in existence-threatening organizational crisis, we demonstrate that paradoxes are not only important when it comes to organizational change (e.g., Carmine & others [36]; Jay [37]; Luscher & Lewis [38]; Smith & Tracey [39]) but also when organizational crises emerge (Giustiniano & others [40])."

"There are typically more operational than strategic issues, which tempts leaders even more to engage at the operational level, which considerably impacts decision-making during crisis (Boin & others [41])."

"They are also able to create an organizational atmosphere consisting of trust and cohesion which is important in building organizational resilience during crisis (Gittell & others [42]; Mafabi & others [43])."

Conclusion, Implications, and Limitations

"Defining organizational resilience more broadly as the organizations' ability to handle crisis and grow through it (e.g., Gilly & others [44]; Williams & others [25]), we identified the leaders' mindset of conscious recognition and their action of compressed situational leadership as crucial to the leaders' ability to align their behaviors to the paradoxical demands of the crisis."

"Since 'each type of crisis is unique' including 'different threats and challenges' for both the organization as well as the leaders (Wu & others [45, p. 17]; James & others [46]), future studies could deepen our initial insights by examining leaders' crisis behavior in specific types of crises and with different organizational cultures."

"Our study provides first insight into how leaders can effectively deal with paradoxes arising in crisis situations and how this behavior might help them foster organizational resilience."

Impact of Abusive Supervision on Intention to Leave: A Moderated Mediation Model of Organizational-Based Self Esteem and Emotional Exhaustion [194]

This is a machine-generated summary of:
 Ahmad, Ifzal; Begum, Khalida: Impact of abusive supervision on intention to leave: a moderated mediation model of organizational-based self esteem and emotional exhaustion [194]
 Published in: Asian Business & Management (2020)
 Link to original: https://doi.org/https://doi.org/10.1057/s41291-020-00116-0
 Copyright of the summarized publication:
Springer Nature Limited 2020
All rights reserved.
If you want to cite the papers, please refer to the original.
For technical reasons we could not place the page where the original quote is coming from.

Abstract-Summary

"This study was aimed to offer and test a novel model explaining how abusive supervision enhances employees' intention to leave in a high-power distance society of Pakistan."

"Drawing from the unfolding model of voluntary turnover as an overarching theory, we proposed that emotional exhaustion will strengthen the relationship between abusive supervision and intention to leave, and organizational-based self esteem (OBSE) will mitigate this relationship."

"Results showed that abusive supervision has both direct and indirect impact on intention to leave such that emotional exhaustion strengthens this relationship."

Introduction

"Researchers in the past have studied the impact of abusive supervision on intention to leave, limited studies are available to explore such mechanisms which can mitigate/reduce its impacts (Peltokorpi [47]; Pradhan & Jena [48])."

"Few if any studies have attempted to explore the moderated mediating role between abusive supervision and intention to leave, predominantly, those moderators which can mitigate its negative impacts on intention to leave (Peltokorpi [47]; Pradhan & Jena [48])."

"We explore the moderated mediating model of abusive supervision and employees' intention to leave, such that employees' emotional exhaustion serves as mediator and organizational-based self esteem (OBSE) as a moderator."

"Tepper & others [49] in their recent review stressed on exploring the incremental predictive power/the underlying mechanism through which abusive supervision leads to employees' intention to leave."

"Although, past studies have explored the direct impact of abusive supervision on emotional exhaustion (Peltokorpi [47]; Wu & Hu [50]), it is believed that emotional exhaustion can also be a key mediator between abusive supervision and intention to leave (Tepper [51])."

Theoretical Framework and Hypotheses Development

"Pakistan's banking industry is facing a challenge of high employee turnover, and among the many reasons for this turnover, are substandard working conditions, lack of developmental opportunities, and supervisor's abusive behavior (Saeed & others [52])."

"We believe while facing abusive behavior from supervisors, employees in developing countries where power distance orientation is high, will delay resignation, and in that dissatisfied or demoralized state, will start searching alternatives as explained in the unfolding model paths 3 and 5."

"Our argument for the moderating role of OBSE between Abusive supervision and employees' emotional exhaustion is based on the behavioral plasticity concept of Brockner [53]."

"When faced with abusive supervision (a negative cue), employees with low OBSE may not cope with this negative cue compared to employees with high OBSE, resulting in more psychological distress (i.e., emotional exhaustion), and withdrawal behavior in the form of increased intention to leave as per the path 3 and 5 of the unfolding model."

Methods

"A total of 500 questionnaires comprising of scales for measuring abusive supervision and OBSE along with questions pertaining to demographics of the respondents were distributed."

"After 2 weeks, the author visited again to collect part 1 of the questionnaire and distribute part 2 comprising scales to measure emotional exhaustion and intention to leave at stage 2."

"Abusive supervision was measured by using the 15 items' scale developed by Tepper [51]."

"OBSE was measured by using the 10 items' scale of Pierce and others [54]."

"A sample item from the scale is 'I count around here.'"

"A sample item from this scale is 'I wondered if anything is worthwhile.'"

"Intention to leave was measured by using the 4 items' scale of Kelloway and others [55]."

"A sample item from this scale includes 'I am thinking about leaving this organization'."

Results

"The results suggest that abusive supervision has no significant correlation with OBSE ($r = 0.02$, $p > 0.05$), and has significant correlation with intention to leave ($r = 0.47$, $p < 0.01$), and emotional exhaustion ($r = 0.42$, $p < 0.01$)."

"We specifically performed CFA on our four-factor model comprising abusive supervision, OBSE, emotional exhaustion and intention to leave."

"We loaded items of two latent variables, i.e., abusive supervision and OBSE on one factor, and the other two i.e., emotional exhaustion and intention to leave, on another factor (model 2), and checked its model-fit values."

"For the results of direct impact of AS on intention to leave, and the mediating role of emotional exhaustion, model 4 of PROCESS macro was employed."

"The moderating effect of OBSE is confirmed in the mediated relationship of abusive supervision on intention to leave with emotional exhaustion as mediator."

Discussion

"This study was aimed to investigate the impact of abusive supervision on employees' intention to leave through moderated mediation model where OBSE was used as a moderator and emotional exhaustion was used as mediator."

"This result is consistent with the previous studies (Saleem & others [56]) which argue that consistent pressure and abusive behavior from the supervisors push individuals towards negative reactions such as intention to leave the organization."

"This study responds to the recent review of abusive supervision by Tepper and others [49], who stressed on exploring the mediating mechanisms through which abusive supervision leads to enhancing intention to leave."

"Past studies have found that employees in low power distance societies may abruptly quit the job in the face of abusive supervision (Lee & others [57]); however, this is not the case in high-power distance society such as Pakistan."

Conclusion

"This study provides a novel insight in explaining the relationship between abusive supervision and employees' intention to leave."

"Several theoretical and practical implications have been noted from this study."

"Several future directions for furthering literature on abusive supervision have also been offered."

Transformational Leadership, Innovative Work Behavior, and Employee Well-Being [195]

This is a machine-generated summary of:
Sharifirad, Mohammad Sadegh: Transformational leadership, innovative work behavior, and employee well-being [195]
Published in: Global Business Perspectives (2013)
Link to original: https://doi.org/https://doi.org/10.1007/s40196-013-0019-2
Copyright of the summarized publication:
International Network of Business and Management 2013
All rights reserved.
If you want to cite the papers, please refer to the original.
For technical reasons we could not place the page where the original quote is coming from.

Abstract-Summary

"Different studies have shown that transformational leadership, which is categorized as a positive leadership, can increase employee's well-being and innovation."

"This research investigates the mediating roles of leader's active empathetic listening and psychological safety through a survey data collected from 583 postgraduate management students in three top universities in Iran working either full-time or part-time."

"Results of the analyses revealed that leader's active empathetic listening and psychological safety fully mediated the influence of TL on innovative work behavior, and partially mediated the influence of TL on employee well-being."

"It investigates the mediating roles of leader's active empathetic listening and psychological safety as two interpersonal factors on innovative work behavior and employee well-being."

"Findings of the study make contributions to the body of research in a number of related disciplines, such as transformational leadership, employee well-being, and innovative work behavior."

Introduction

"Confirming positive leadership thesis, researchers have established associations between TL, innovative work behavior and employee well-being based on research done in Western societies (e.g., Gong & others [58]; Arnold & others [59]; Densten [60]; Sivanathan & others [61]; Seltzer & others [62])."

"This study aims to bridge the above-mentioned gap in this knowledge by exploring the relationship between transformational leadership, employee well-being and innovative work behavior in three Iranian societies."

"We intend to examine the roles of leaders active empathetic listening and perceived psychological safety by the follower as two links between transformational leadership and two constructs of employees' innovative work behavior and well-being."

"Aligned with this point, we use active empathetic listening and psychological safety to reflect the quality of relationships and organizational climate, respectively, and posit them as mediators between transformational leadership and two outcomes for the followers: innovative work behavior and well-being."

Theory and Hypotheses

"In [63], Reuvers and his colleagues after doing research in four Australian hospitals revealed a positive and significant relationship between transformational leadership and innovative work behavior."

"As evidenced through the previously reviewed studies, this study conforms to the theorized relationship that transformational leadership positively influences followers' innovative work behavior (Hater & Bass [64]; Bass & Avolio [65])."

"Transformational leadership is positively related to innovative work behavior."

"Leader's active empathetic listening is positively related to innovative work behavior."

"Perceived psychological safety is positively related to innovative work behavior."

"Taking Hypothesis 5 and Hypotheses 6a and 6b together, and based on the earlier studies showing that a work environment that emphasizes positive work relationships is a central source of positive states and experiences such as satisfaction, enrichment, development, and growth (Dutton [66]; Dutton & Heaphy [67]; Quinn & Dutton [68]) we therefore hypothesize that: Perceived psychological safety is a mediator between TL and employee well-being."

Method

"In order to insure that the questionnaire was not lengthy, selected items from job satisfaction, perceived work stress, and stress symptoms were used."

"The scale had the following four subscales (26 items total) and sample items: morale building (e.g., 'My immediate supervisor shares happiness and woe with his/

her subordinates'); inspirational motivation (e.g., 'My immediate supervisor explains to his/her subordinates the long-term meaning of their work'); individualized consideration (e.g., 'My immediate supervisor would like to help his/her subordinates with their problems in life and family'); charisma (e.g., 'My immediate supervisor is good at and never hesitates to take actions when dealing with tough problems')."

"Response options for items used a 5-point scale, ranging from 1 (strongly disagree) to 5 (strongly agree)."

"To measure perceived work stress, we selected two items from prior studies (Siu & others [69, 70]) to measure perceived work stress."

Results

"The fit indices revealed measurement equivalence given that both the constrained model (χ^2 [251] = 635.33, CFI = 0.93, TLI = 0.92, RMSEA = 0.07) and the unconstrained model (χ^2 [239] = 609.57, CFI = 0.92, TLI = 0.91, RMSEA = 0.07) were acceptable, with an insignificant change in Chi square ($\Delta\chi$ (12) = 25.76, P > 0.05)."

"After evaluating the fit indices of the model (χ^2[131] = 480.01, CFI = 0.93, TLI = 0.92, RMSEA = 0.07), which showed a good fit, we figured out that the path from TL to innovative work behavior was not significant."

"We tested model 3 based on Model 2 by deleting the direct path from TL to innovative work behavior (χ^2 [132] = 479.46, CFI = 0.93, TLI = 0.92, RMSEA = 0.07)."

Discussion

"The purpose of the study was to examine the relationship between transformational leadership and two constructs of innovative work behavior and employee well-being in Iranian societies through the mediating roles of active empathetic listening and psychological safety."

"Leader's active empathetic listening and perceived psychological safety fully mediated the relationship between transformational leadership and innovative work behavior."

"Our results have confirmed the significant relationship between TL and outcomes in Iranian societies and extended the literature by illustrating the importance of leader's active empathetic listening and psychological safety in the processes from TL to employee well-being and innovative work behavior."

"It extends the literature of listening by addressing it as the mediating role between transformational leadership and two constructs of employee well-being and innovative work behavior."

"This research can add active empathetic listening as a partial mediator between transformational leadership and psychological safety and highlights the impact of leader's active empathetic listening as an antecedent of psychological safety."

Conclusion

"In spite of these limitations, the study here helps to understand two mechanisms (i.e., leader's active empathetic listening and psychological safety) through which transformational leaders may enhance employee well-being and promote creative work behavior."

"These findings highlight the fact that researchers and managers need to consider how transformational leaders and the interpersonal work context can foster employee well-being and innovative work behavior."

"Thinking about listening as a simple but effective tool can cause the unearthing of employees' internal feelings and needs; therefore, a transformational leader can capitalize upon employees' ideas and show himself as a coach and supporter at workplace."

Ethical Leadership and Ambidexterity in Young Firms: Examining the CEO-TMT Interface [196]

This is a machine-generated summary of:
Ling, Yan; Hammond, Michelle; Wei, Li-Qun: Ethical leadership and ambidexterity in young firms: examining the CEO-TMT Interface [196]
Published in: International Entrepreneurship and Management Journal (2020)
Link to original: https://doi.org/https://doi.org/10.1007/s11365-020-00695-6
Copyright of the summarized publication:
Springer Science+Business Media, LLC, part of Springer Nature 2020
All rights reserved.
If you want to cite the papers, please refer to the original.
For technical reasons we could not place the page where the original quote is coming from.

Abstract-Summary

"To enrich the knowledge of the value of ethical leadership in a more entrepreneurial setting, we focus on technology-based young firms and theorize through the lens of CEO-TMT interface whether and how founder-CEOs' ethical leadership influences young firms' ambidexterity."

"We argue that founder-CEOs' ethical leadership can enhance young firms' ambidexterity in an indirect way, through promoting top management team (TMT) members' advice-seeking behavior and team satisfaction."

Introduction

"Consistent with others who have found the relationship between top leadership behavior and firm-level outcomes to be indirect through TMT-level characteristics (e.g., Hmieleski, Cole, & Baron [71]; Ling & others [72]), we would not expect a direct relationship between founder-CEOs' ethical leadership and young firms' ambidexterity."

"Although our findings from China, a country characterized by Eastern culture and the institutional change from central planning to market competition (Wei & Ling [73]), may not be equally applicable everywhere, this study contributes to the entrepreneurship literature by taking the lead in attending to founder-CEOs' ethical leadership, linking it to young firms' outcomes, and identifying the mechanism underlying the linkage."

"We hope not only to advance the knowledge of ethical leadership's influences on firm-level outcomes in a more entrepreneurial setting but also to propose a venue through which technology-based young firms may be better able to attain ambidexterity—founder-CEOs' ethical leadership."

Theoretical Background and Hypotheses Development

"We propose that founder-CEOs' ethical leadership is likely to influence TMT members' shared behavior in the form of advice-seeking behavior and shared attitude in the form of team satisfaction."

"Applying these considerations to TMTs in young firms, we expect that founder-CEOs' ethical leadership should promote satisfaction shared among TMT members, especially given that their founder status and the firm's simple structure grant them additional discretion and opportunities to demonstrate their virtuous interpersonal behaviors and thus affect team members' perception of the team."

"By integrating the prior hypotheses of the direct effects among constructs, we propose that shared advice-seeking behaviors and team satisfaction among TMT members would mediate the relationship between founder-CEOs' ethical leadership and young firms' ambidexterity."

"TMTs' advice-seeking behavior will mediate the indirect association between founder-CEOs' ethical leadership and young firms' ambidexterity."

Method

"Confirmatory factor analyses (CFA) with various model structures were compared to the four-factor measurement model, which included ethical leadership, advice-seeking behavior, team satisfaction, and ambidexterity."

"We also checked bivariate correlations by only using one team member's (who did not assess ambidexterity) measure of founder-CEO's ethical leadership, excluding founder-CEO from the assessments of advice-seeking behaviors and team satisfaction, and only using the measure of ambidexterity from the founder-CEO."

"The measures were significantly correlated with the assessments based on the full sample (ethical leadership correlation = .94; advice-seeking correlation = .93; team satisfaction correlation = .89; and ambidexterity correlation = .92)."

"We first identified whether the firm is a family firm (self-reported by the founder-CEO) as an instrumental variable, which predicts our independent variable (i.e., CEO's ethical leadership) but does not predict our mediators (i.e., advice-seeking behavior and team satisfaction)."

Discussion

"Integrating social learning theory underlying ethical leadership literature (Bandura [74]) with the CEO-TMT interface noted in upper echelons literature (Klotz & others [75]), we hypothesized that founder-CEOs' ethical leadership indirectly promotes young firms' ambidexterity through affecting TMT members' collective behavior (advice-seeking behavior) and attitude (team satisfaction)."

"Extending this line of research, future research may examine, for example, whether founder-CEOs' ethical leadership affects TMT characteristics (e.g., TMT members' collective goals for the firm) which, in turn, influences young firms' ability to successfully complete an initial public offering."

"Our results demonstrate that the ethical leadership of founder-CEOs affects TMT members' shared behaviors and attitudes, which, in turn, affect young firms' ambidexterity."

"Although this choice originated from our wish to provide a more direct examination of ethical leaders' influence on the outcome of technology-based young firms, future research may direct attention to other firm-level phenomena to further the understanding of the consequences of ethical leadership of founder-CEOs."

Conclusion

"A conceptual model that alludes to the importance of founder-CEOs' ethical leadership in shaping TMTs' behaviors and attitudes, which, in turn, facilitate the firm's achievement of ambidexterity."

"Our results support our theorizing about the process."

"In so doing, we enrich the relevant literature by applying ethical leadership to a more entrepreneurial setting."

"We demonstrate the potential in applying the CEO-TMT interface perspective to better understand the mechanisms underlying the influence of this important leadership style in young firms."

Learning Value-Based Leadership in Teams: The Moderation of Emotional Regulation [197]

This is a machine-generated summary of:
Lin, Chieh-Peng; Jhang, Chi; Wang, Yu-Min: Learning value-based leadership in teams: the moderation of emotional regulation [197]
Published in: Review of Managerial Science (2021)
Link to original: https://doi.org/https://doi.org/10.1007/s11846-021-00483-8
Copyright of the summarized publication:
The Author(s), under exclusive licence to Springer-Verlag GmbH Germany, part of Springer Nature 2021
All rights reserved.
If you want to cite the papers, please refer to the original.
For technical reasons we could not place the page where the original quote is coming from.

Abstract-Summary

"Drawing upon value-based leadership theory, this research proposes a model to elaborate how value-based leadership can be learned by leaders to influence team performance."

"Team performance is indirectly influenced by benevolent leadership and moral leadership via two mediators that consist of learning goal orientation and interactional justice."

"Emotional regulation hypothetically moderates the effects of benevolent leadership and moral leadership on the mediators."

Introduction

"How learning goal orientation and interactional justice are simultaneously motivated by value-based leadership to influence team performance has not been explored yet, leading to the first research gap that this study aims to fill."

"It links value-based leadership to learning goal orientation and interactional justice so as to explain team performance in a single model setting, which has not yet been evaluated."

"Without a simultaneous evaluation of learning goal orientation and interactional justice as dual mediators, our understanding about the influence of value-based leadership on team performance will be highly limited, and managerial initiatives directed at developing effective leadership and improving team performance will turn out to be unjustifiable based on blind faith."

"This study contributes to the theoretical knowledge of value-based leadership by developing an inclusive model with the addition of learning goal orientation and interactional justice based on the social exchange theory."

Research Model and Hypotheses

"Team performance is indirectly influenced by benevolent leadership and moral leadership via two mediators that include interactional justice and learning goal orientation."

"Learning goal orientation mediates the positive relationship between benevolent leadership and team performance."

"Learning goal orientation mediates the positive relationship between moral leadership and team performance."

"Interactional justice mediates the positive relationship between benevolent leadership and team performance."

"Interactional justice mediates the positive relationship between moral leadership and team performance."

"Benevolent leadership enhances learning goal orientation and interactional justice more strongly among teams with higher emotional regulation than those with lower emotional regulation."

"The positive effects of moral leadership on learning goal orientation and interactional justice are likely weakened among teams with poor emotional regulation, leading to the next hypotheses."

Methods

"Team members measured five variables: team performance, learning goal orientation, interactional justice, benevolent leadership, and moral leadership."

"The moderator measured by team leaders is considered team-level data, because they are the key people who can easily observe and evaluate the overall emotional regulation from a collective viewpoint due to their daily contacts with each member individually in the same team."

"In Model 3 this study found the significant effects of interactional justice and learning goal orientation on team performance with the coefficients of 0.53 ($p < 0.01$) and 0.30 ($p < 0.01$) respectively."

"The results revealed that the learning goal orientation and interactional justice in Model 3 remained significant in Model 4, whereas the effects of benevolent leadership and moral leadership on team performance were not significant."

Discussion

"The positive effect of moral leadership on learning goal orientation in this study is consistent with (but theoretically distinct from) the previous argument based on the social learning theory (Moss & others [76])."

"Team workers with stronger emotional regulation may have sufficient resources to precisely follow moral leadership and to enhance their valued motives such as interactional justice and learning goal orientation, consequently achieving great team performance."

"Complementing what has been learned about value-based leadership in the literature, this study illustrates that when levels of emotional regulation are low, leaders should provide supportive resources (e.g., mindfulness training, emotional therapy) as the first priority so that their value-based leadership can effectively work."

"Due to its theoretical foundation based on the social exchange theory and value-based leadership theory, this study does not address cultural or political variables (e.g., uncertainty avoidance, masculinity, politics, opportunism) to clarify team performance."

The Impact of Emotional Leadership on Chinese Subordinates' Work Engagement: Role of Intrinsic Motivation and Traditionality [198]

This is a machine-generated summary of:

Wan, Jin; Zhou, Wenjun; Qin, Mingyue; Zhou, Haiming; Li, Pingping: The impact of emotional leadership on Chinese subordinates' work engagement: role of intrinsic motivation and traditionality [198]

Published in: BMC Psychology (2022)

Link to original: https://doi.org/https://doi.org/10.1186/s40359-022-01022-0

Copyright of the summarized publication:

The Author(s) 2022

License: OpenAccess CC BY+CC0 4.0

This article is licensed under a Creative Commons Attribution 4.0 International License, which permits use, sharing, adaptation, distribution and reproduction in any medium or format, as long as you give appropriate credit to the original author(s) and the source, provide a link to the Creative Commons licence, and indicate if changes were made. The images or other third party material in this article are included in the article's Creative Commons licence, unless indicated otherwise in a credit line to the material. If material is not included in the article's Creative Commons licence and your intended use is not permitted by statutory regulation or exceeds the permitted use, you will need to obtain permission directly from the copyright holder. To view a copy of this licence, visit http://creativecommons.org/licenses/by/4.0/. The Creative

Commons Public Domain Dedication waiver (http://creativecommons.org/public domain/zero/1.0/) applies to the data made available in this article, unless otherwise stated in a credit line to the data.

If you want to cite the papers, please refer to the original.

For technical reasons we could not place the page where the original quote is coming from.

Abstract-Summary

"Based on self-determination theory, this study examined the impact of emotional leadership on subordinates' work engagement, as well as the mediating role of subordinates' intrinsic motivation and the moderating role of traditionality."

"A questionnaire survey was conducted, in which 347 Chinese enterprise employees were asked to rate their own experiences with emotional leadership, work engagement and intrinsic motivation."

"Emotional leadership has a significant direct positive effect on subordinates' work engagement and positively influences subordinates' work engagement through the mediation of subordinates' intrinsic motivation."

"The effect of emotional leadership on intrinsic motivation is stronger for those with high traditionality than for those with low traditionality."

"Emotional leadership can improve subordinates' work engagement by stimulating their intrinsic motivation."

"Managers need to be able to effectively regulate and manage subordinates' emotions to stimulate their intrinsic motivation and to differentiate the management of subordinates with different levels of traditionality to improve subordinates' work engagement."

Introduction

"Few studies have examined the influence of emotional leadership on subordinates' work behavior."

"Previous studies have rarely directly tested the relationship between emotional leadership and subordinates' work engagement."

"Previous research has discussed the impact of leadership on subordinates' work attitudes and behaviors from the affective perspective [77, 78], while it also affects subordinates through motivational pathways [79] by meeting their needs for autonomy, competence, and relationships [80–84], resulting in work engagement, which has rarely been investigated in the field of emotional leadership."

"Traditionality, as an individual characteristic with a typical Chinese cultural imprint and reflecting differences in individual values, has a significant impact on employees' behaviors [85] and may be an important moderator in the process of leadership influencing subordinates' work engagement."

"Based on self-determination theory, this study investigated the influence of emotional leadership on subordinates' work engagement and examined the role of intrinsic motivation and traditionality to enrich emotional leadership effectiveness research and provide a reference for enhancing subordinates' work engagement."

Literature Review and Hypotheses

"Leaders with high emotional leadership usually provide subordinates with adequate altruistic care and resource support, allow them to organize their own work schedules, and boost their confidence in completing difficult tasks by boosting morale, which will enhance their subordinates' sense of job autonomy and competence [82, 83]; on the other hand, leaders with high emotional leadership often engage in positive emotional interactions and open communication with subordinates, which is conducive to building a harmonious relationship between supervisors and subordinate [84], which can meet the relationship needs of subordinates."

"Emotional leadership is effective in meeting subordinates' autonomy, competence and relationship needs, which in turn stimulate the intrinsic motivation of subordinates."

"This study proposes Hypothesis 2: Emotional leadership motivates subordinates' intrinsic motivation, which in turn increases their work engagement."

"Subordinates' intrinsic motivation plays a mediating role between leaders' emotional leadership and subordinates' work engagement."

"This study proposes Hypothesis 3: Traditionality positively moderates the relationship between emotional leadership and subordinates' intrinsic motivation."

"The positive effect of emotional leadership on intrinsic motivation is stronger for subordinates with high traditionality."

Study 1: Experimental Study

"Within the two groups, participants were randomly divided into high and low emotional leadership subgroups and then read the high and low emotional leadership materials, respectively."

"After reading the materials, all participants rated the leaders in the material they had read using a five-point emotional leadership scale (for a detailed description of the scale, see the Measures section)."

"Reliability analysis was used to test the reliability of the scales, while correlation analysis and hierarchical regression analysis were used to test the hypothesis to investigate the relationship between the independent variable emotional leadership, the mediating variable intrinsic motivation, the moderating variable traditionality and the outcome variable work engagement."

"To test the positive impact of emotional leadership on intrinsic motivation and the moderating role of traditionality, ANOVA was used to compare the intrinsic motivation of different groups."

Results

"In M3, the positive effect of emotional leadership on work engagement was significant ($\beta = 0.78$, $p < 0.001$); thus, Hypothesis 1 was supported."

"In M1, the positive effect of emotional leadership on intrinsic motivation was significant ($\beta = 0.90$, $p < 0.001$)."

"In M4, the positive effect of intrinsic motivation level on work engagement was significant ($\beta = 0.76$, $p < 0.001$), and the β coefficient of emotional leadership on work engagement decreased from 0.78 to 0.10 and was no longer significant."

"In M2, the interaction term between emotional leadership and traditionality had a significant positive effect on intrinsic motivation ($\beta = 0.09$, $p < 0.05$); thus, Hypothesis 3 was supported."

Study 2: Questionnaire Study

"Correlation analysis and hierarchical regression analysis were used to test the hypothesis to investigate the relationship between the independent variable emotional leadership, the mediating variable intrinsic motivation, the moderating variable traditionality and the outcome variable work engagement."

"In M6, the positive effect of employees' intrinsic motivation on work engagement was significant ($\beta = 0.70$, $p < 0.01$), but the β coefficient of emotional leadership on employee work engagement decreased from 0.38 to 0.19, indicating that employee's intrinsic motivation partially mediates the relationship between emotional leadership and work engagement; thus, Hypothesis 2 was supported."

"In M3, the interaction term between emotional leadership and employee traditionality had a significant positive effect on intrinsic motivation ($\beta = 0.15$, $p < 0.01$) after considering the control variables."

Discussion

"When addressing Hypothesis 2, we found that subordinates' intrinsic motivation plays a mediating role between leaders' emotional leadership and subordinates' work engagement, which helps to enrich the understanding of the mechanisms by which emotional leadership affects employee engagement by introducing intrinsic motivation as a 'bridge' between them."

"Based on self-determination theory, this study found that emotional leadership promotes subordinates' work engagement not only by enhancing their positive emotions but also by stimulating their intrinsic motivation to work by satisfying their needs for autonomy, competence and relationships."

"This study confirms the moderating role of traditionality in the relationship between emotional leadership and subordinates' intrinsic motivation, which validates the influence of different cultural values on subordinates' motivation and contributes to the contextualization of management theory."

"This study explored the impact of emotional leadership on subordinates' work engagement from self-determination theory; more mechanisms of emotional leadership can be explored from the perspective of other theories in the future."

Conclusions

"Based on self-determination theory, this study not only revealed the impact of emotional leadership on subordinates' work engagement, extending the research on the leadership antecedents of subordinates' work engagement and supporting the insight that leadership emotions are an important factor in employee engagement but also took intrinsic motivation as a bridge connecting them and clarifying the motivation path of emotional leadership on work engagement."

"This study found that intrinsic motivation only partially mediated the effect of emotional leadership on work engagement, and other pathways of emotional leadership's impact on work engagement could be explored in the future."

"It introduced traditionality as a boundary condition and found that emotional leadership has different effects on intrinsic motivation for subordinates with different personalities, echoing the call that individual differences in characteristics should be taken into account when discussing subordinates' processing of emotional information about leadership."

Impact of Self-leadership on Employee Voice Behavior: A Moderated Mediating Model [199]

This is a machine-generated summary of:

Liu, Qin; Zhou, Hao: Impact of self-leadership on employee voice behavior: a moderated mediating model [199]

Published in: Current Psychology (2023)

Link to original: https://doi.org/https://doi.org/10.1007/s12144-023-04407-5

Copyright of the summarized publication:

The Author(s), under exclusive licence to Springer Science+Business Media, LLC, part of Springer Nature 2023

Copyright comment: Springer Nature or its licensor (e.g. a society or other partner) holds exclusive rights to this article under a publishing agreement with the author(s) or other rightsholder(s); author self-archiving of the accepted manuscript version of this article is solely governed by the terms of such publishing agreement and applicable law.

All rights reserved.

If you want to cite the papers, please refer to the original.

For technical reasons we could not place the page where the original quote is coming from.

Abstract-Summary

"This study explores this field and enriches the research on extra-role outcomes of self-leadership."

"Based on self-determination theory, this research verifies the mechanism of self-leadership on employee voice, with thriving at work as a mediator and job characteristics (expressed as the motivating potential score) as a moderator."

"Using a three-wave survey of 405 nurses, the results of confirmatory factor analyses show that the data fit of the hypothetical five-factor measurement model is acceptable and we find that (1) self-leadership is positively associated with thriving at work, (2) thriving at work is positively associated with promotive and prohibitive voice, (3) thriving at work mediates the relationship of self-leadership on voice behavior, and (4) job characteristics moderate the relationship between self-leadership and thriving at work, such that this relationship is stronger for employees with a poor job characteristic."

Introduction

"According to self-determination theory (SDT), this study holds that thriving at work, meaning that 'individuals feel vitality and learning at work' (Spreitzer & others [86]), conveys the effect of self-leadership on voice."

"This study will further demonstrate whether the effect of personal characteristics (i.e., self-leadership) on thriving at work is differs with different job characteristics."

"This paper will examine how job characteristics, as a moderator, influence the effect of self-leadership on thriving at work."

"This research will explore the underlying process of self-leadership on employee voice, with thriving at work as the mediator and job characteristic (i.e., MPS) as the moderator."

"The following are the contributions of this study: first, self-leadership positively affects voice behavior via thriving at work, which enriches the study of self-leadership in terms of extra-role behavior."

Literature Review and Hypotheses

"When the job characteristic is poor, self-leadership has a stronger effect on intrinsic motivation, i.e., thriving at work."

"We hypothesize the following: Hypothesis 4: Job characteristics (MPS) will moderate the relationship between self-leadership and thriving at work, such that this relationship is stronger for employees with a poor job characteristic (low MPS)."

"We have elaborated the mechanism of self-leadership on voice behavior, in which thriving at work acts as a mediator and the job characteristic (i.e., MPS) plays a moderating role."

"We have the following hypothesis: Hypothesis 5: The job characteristic (MPS) moderates the mediating relationship between self-leadership and promotive voice (Hypothesis 5a)/prohibitive voice (Hypothesis 5b) via thriving at work, such that this mediating effect is stronger for employees with a poor job characteristic (low MPS)."

Methods

"We conducted three surveys at 2-week intervals and collected the following information of participants: the first round for self-leadership, proactive personality, MPS, and demographics (gender, age, tenure, marriage, education, professional title, and department); the second round for thriving at work; and the third round for promotive and prohibitive voice."

"It is calculated using the five indicators via the following formula: The items of the scale were from the Job Diagnostic Survey that measured the job characteristic model (Hackman & Oldham [87, 88])."

"We measured thriving at work using Porath and others's [89] 10-item scale."

"We measured voice using Liang and others's [90] 10-item scale."

"Similar to other literature on voice (Li & others [91]) and taking into account possible response bias, we selected gender, age, organizational tenure, marriage, education, professional title, and department as control variables."

Results

"Hypothesis 3: proposed that thriving at work plays a mediating role between self-leadership and employee voice."

"The mediating effect of thriving at work between self-leadership and prohibitive voice is significant (indirect effect = 0.105, 95% CI [0.034, 0.215]), again supporting Hypothesis 3b."

"Hypothesis 5 provides that the job characteristic (expressed as MPS) moderates the mediation effect of thriving at work between self-leadership and voice behavior."

"For prohibitive voice, the mediating role of thriving at work is significant (indirect effect = 0.089, 95% CI [0.012, 0.203]) when the MPS is low (M − 1 SD) and is not significant (indirect effect = 0.015, 95% CI [−0.106, 0.111]) when the MPS is high (M + 1 SD)."

"Although there is no relevant hypothesis, we empirically analyzed the role of the two dimensions of thriving (learning and vitality) in the self-leadership- promotive/prohibitive voice relationship, using Hayes's [92] PROCESS macro."

Discussion

"Self-leadership positively affects employee voice via thriving at work, which advances the study on self-leadership in terms of the extra-role behavior."

"This study found that self-leadership, as a new antecedent, promotes employees to thrive at work."

"Strong self-leadership provides employees with sufficient nutriments to satisfy the three basic needs and promotes intrinsic motivation, which further promotes employees to pursue higher-order needs and increase extra-role behaviors, such as voice behavior (Lim & others [93]; Gagne & Deci [94])."

"This research found that the job characteristic (expressed as MPS) is a boundary condition that fluctuates the effect of self-leadership on thriving at work and voice behavior."

"The current study demonstrated that self-leadership positively affects promotive and prohibitive voice behaviors through thriving at work."

"To self-leadership, organizations can also promote thriving at work in other ways to promote voice behavior."

"The results showed that the effects of self-leadership and job characteristics on thriving at work and voice behavior are interchangeable."

Conclusion

"To explore the relationship between self-leadership and extra-role behavior, we investigated its relationship with voice behavior from the perspective of the SDT."

"We found that thriving at work mediated the effect of self-leadership on employee voice, and the job characteristic (expressed as MPS) moderated the relationship between self-leadership and thriving at work."

"The stronger the self-leadership, the better the vitality and learning state, and the more the employees' voice behavior will be stimulated."

"Future research could continue to demonstrate the effects of self-leadership on other extra-role behaviors such as organization citizenship behavior to individual or organization."

Longitudinal Effects of Job Insecurity on Employee Outcomes: The Moderating Role of Emotional Intelligence and the Leader-member Exchange [200]

This is a machine-generated summary of:

Cheng, Ting; Huang, Guo-hua; Lee, Cynthia; Ren, Xiaopeng: Longitudinal effects of job insecurity on employee outcomes: The moderating role of emotional intelligence and the leader-member exchange [200]

Published in: Asia Pacific Journal of Management (2010)
Link to original: https://doi.org/https://doi.org/10.1007/s10490-010-9227-3
Copyright of the summarized publication:
Springer Science+Business Media, LLC 2010
All rights reserved.
If you want to cite the papers, please refer to the original.
For technical reasons we could not place the page where the original quote is coming from.

Abstract-Summary

"The longitudinal study reported herein examines the buffering effects of individual and social resources (emotional intelligence and the leader-member exchange relationship) on the relationships between job insecurity and employee reactions (somatic complaints and organizational commitment) and the relationships between employee reactions over time."

Emotional Intelligence and Leader-Member Exchange as Moderators

"It was argued that all four components of emotional intelligence contribute to the complex relationship between job insecurity and employee reactions and help to buffer employees' negative emotional reactions, including decreased affective commitment and increased job-related tension."

"We thus put forward the following hypotheses: Emotional intelligence moderates the effects of job insecurity on immediate employee outcomes (somatic complaints and organizational commitment)."

"The effect of job insecurity on somatic complaints (H1a) and affective organizational commitment (H1b) is weaker for individuals with high levels of emotional intelligence."

"Emotional intelligence moderates the effects of job insecurity, somatic complaints, and organizational commitment at Time 1 (T1) on subsequent employee outcomes (somatic complaints and organizational commitment) at Time 2 (T2)."

Method

"We conducted a one-way ANOVA of employment on the job insecurity scales of the three hospitals, and found no significant differences."

"At the time of data collection, the hospitals under study were over-staffed with regard to nurses."

"At the time of the initial survey (i.e., T1), Hospital 1 had 105 nurses, and we obtained completed responses from 83 of them, resulting in a 79 percent response rate."

"Job insecurity and the emotional intelligence scale were measured at T1."

"Job insecurity was measured using the scale developed by Ashford, Lee, and Bobko [95], which has been validated in a Chinese sample (Lee, Bobko, Ashford, Chen, & Ren [96]; Lee, Bobko, & Chen [97]) and has demonstrated its generalizability in several other cultural contexts (e.g., Kinnunen & others [98]; Rosenblatt & Ruvio [99])."

"The WLEIS is a 16-item self-report measure that was developed and validated among Chinese respondents (Wong, Law, & Wong [100]; Wong, Wong, & Law [101])."

"Organizational commitment was measured by Mowday, Steers, and Porter's [102] nine-item scale using a seven-point format that ranged from strongly agree [7] to strongly disagree [1]."

Results

"Our hypotheses, we conducted confirmatory factor analysis (CFA) with LISREL 8.5 (Jöreskog & Sörbom [103]) to examine the validity of our measurement model for emotional intelligence, LMX, and the outcome variables of somatic complaints and organizational commitment at both T1 and T2."

"The results of the moderated regression show that, consistent with Hypotheses 2b, emotional intelligence moderated the longitudinal effect of T1 somatic complaints on T2 somatic complaints ($\beta = -.25$, $p < .05$), and consistent with Hypotheses 3e, LMX moderated the effect of T1 somatic complaints on T2 organizational commitment ($\beta = .32$, $p < .01$)."

"Models 3 and 4 show that the interaction terms as a block explain the additional variances of the T2 outcomes over and beyond the main effects of job insecurity, the moderators, and the T1 outcome variables ($\Delta R^2 = .06$, $p < .10$ for somatic complaints; $\Delta R^2 = .12$, $p < .01$ for organizational commitment)."

Discussion

"The purpose of this study was to investigate the moderating effects of employees' individual resource (emotional intelligence) and social resource (LMX) in the context of job insecurity."

"We examined whether emotional intelligence could attenuate the immediate and long-term negative impacts of job insecurity on employee outcomes (organizational commitment and somatic well-being), and the effects of employee reactions at T1 on subsequent outcomes at T2."

"This study contributes to the job stress and coping literature by examining the buffering effects of emotional intelligence and LMX on employees' reactions to perceptions of job insecurity."

"The moderating effect of LMX found in this study is also consistent with previous evidence demonstrating that, in the context of job insecurity, work-based social support can buffer the negative outcomes of such insecurity (Lim [104, 105])."

"Our data show that emotional intelligence does not moderate the relationship among job insecurity, somatic complaints, and organizational commitment which is inconsistent with our propositions."

[Section 5]

"Like other work stressors, job insecurity is hypothesized to be related to adverse consequences for both individuals (such as psychological and somatic complaints) and organizations (such as organizational commitment and job satisfaction) (Sverke, Chaison, & Sjöberg [106])."

"Considering both short- and long-term detrimental effects of job insecurity, it is important to understand whether these moderators might have sustainable buffering effects in the stressor-strain relationship and whether the potential buffers could attenuate the effects of prior strain on subsequent strain."

"The primary objective of this study is to explore the effects of two buffering variables—one individual resource variable (i.e., the emotional intelligence of the employee) and one social resource variable (i.e., leader-member exchange (LMX) between the employee and his or her immediate supervisor)—on the relationship between job insecurity and employee outcomes, including individual somatic complaint and organizational commitment."

Does Transformational Leadership Facilitate Technological Innovation? The Moderating Roles of Innovative Culture and Incentive Compensation [201]

This is a machine-generated summary of:

Chen, Mavis Yi-Ching; Lin, Carol Yeh-Yun; Lin, Hsing-Er; McDonough, Edward F.: Does transformational leadership facilitate technological innovation? The moderating roles of innovative culture and incentive compensation [201]

Published in: Asia Pacific Journal of Management (2012)

Link to original: https://doi.org/https://doi.org/10.1007/s10490-012-9285-9

Copyright of the summarized publication:

Springer Science+Business Media, LLC 2012

All rights reserved.

If you want to cite the papers, please refer to the original.

For technical reasons we could not place the page where the original quote is coming from.

Abstract-Summary

"The present research investigates the relationships between SBU-level transformational leadership and technological innovation, as well as the moderating effects of innovative culture and incentive compensation."

"The results indicate that transformational leadership behaviors promote technological innovation at the SBU level."

"Financial-incentive adoption neutralizes the relationship between transformational leadership and technological innovation."

Theory and Hypotheses

"A system of financial incentives is more appropriate for transactional leaders' efforts rather than transformational leaders to foster innovation because transactional leadership based on contingent rewards involves the clear delineation of expectations and goals on the part of a leader, as well as what followers can expect in the way of rewards if they cooperate (Avolio & others [109]; Waldman & Bass [110]).Thus, we propose that financial rewards will neutralize the relationship between transformational leadership behaviors and technological innovation outcomes."

"Transformational leaders effectively use non-financial incentives including support, providing feedback, recognition and development to better motivate employees and increase their innovative performance (Iles [111]; Nelson [112])."

"We propose: Non-financial incentives in compensation systems enhance the effect of transformational leadership on technological innovation at the SBU level, such that the effect of transformational leadership on technological innovation will be stronger when the level of non-financial incentives is higher."

Methodology

"Our research sample targeted Taiwanese SBUs regarding the relationships among transformational leadership, innovative culture, incentive compensation, and technological innovation."

"In each SBU, the senior manager was asked to answer the degree of the technological innovation adoption, and employees were asked to answer the questions concerning transformational leadership behaviors attributable to the senior managers, the organizational culture orientation, and the incentive compensation for innovation."

"To aggregate individual SBU employees' survey responses to SBU level, we first calculated inter-rater agreement following the formula developed by James, Demaree, and Wolf [113] for transformational leadership, innovative culture, and incentive-compensation scales."

"The ICC(1) values for transformational leadership, innovative culture, and incentive compensation were .56, .47, and .35, respectively."

"The ICC(2) values for transformational leadership, innovative culture, and incentive compensation were .99, .98, and .99, respectively."

Results

"The results show that the proposed positive relationship between transformational leadership behaviors and technological innovation (Hypothesis 1) was supported ($\beta = .153, p < .05$)."

"The results indicate that innovative culture both was positively associated with technological innovation ($\beta = .729, p < .001$) and significantly weakened the positive effect that transformational leadership had on technological innovation ($\beta = -.273, p < .05$)."

"Hypotheses 4 and 5 concern the moderating effect of financial and non-financial incentives on the relationship between transformational leadership and technological innovation."

"As predicted, the interaction effect between transformational leadership and financial incentives was negatively related to technological innovation ($\beta = -.139, p < .05$)."

"Although we posited that non-financial incentives would enhance the relationship between transformational leadership and technological innovation, the results show that the coefficient is positive but not significant ($\beta = .113$, n.s.)."

Discussion and Conclusions

"We investigated the effects of transformational leadership on technological innovation at the SBU level, as well as the moderating effects of innovative culture and incentive compensation."

"As for the moderating role of innovative culture, this study examined both the enhancing and substituting effects of innovative culture, thus providing a more comprehensive picture of how transformational leaders impact technological innovation."

"Contrary to prior research (e.g., Howell & Avolio [114]; Jung & others [115]), our findings lend support to the idea that strong innovative culture at the SBU level may substitute for transformational leadership behaviors."

"Our results suggest that the adoption of financial incentives neutralized the relationship between transformational leadership and technological innovation with a negative moderating effect."

"As an extension to our innovative culture, future research can examine models comparing moderating or mediating effect of various cultural dimensions between transformational leadership and technological innovation in Asia."

[Section 5]

"This study fills these voids by investigating the influence of transformational leadership on technological innovation at the SBU level."

"Leadership behaviors exist within the context of organizations, therefore it is crucial to clarify how situational moderators amplify or limit the effectiveness of transformational leadership in facilitating innovation (Damanpour [116]; Elenkov & others [117]; Gumusluoglu & Ilsev [118]; Howell & Avolio [114]; Jung & others [119]; Jung & others [115]; Pawar & Eastman [120]; Xenikou & Simosi [121])."

"This study examines the moderating effects of innovative culture and incentive compensation on the transformational leadership–technological innovation relationship."

"It is appealing to examine the effect of innovation culture and incentive systems on the transformational leadership–technological innovation relationship for shedding some light on Taiwan and other economies that aspire to excel in technology innovation."

"By examining the moderating effect of innovative culture on the transformational leadership–technological innovation relationship at the SBU level, we provide a more nuanced understanding of the role of transformational leadership and the role of innovative culture."

The Role of Transformational Leadership and Institutional Entrepreneurship in Organizational Change in Indian Public Organizations [202]

This is a machine-generated summary of:

Rao-Nicholson, Rekha; Mohyuddin, Syed: The role of transformational leadership and institutional entrepreneurship in organizational change in Indian public organizations [202]

Published in: Asian Business & Management (2023)

Link to original: https://doi.org/htttps://doi.org/10.1057/s41291-023-00218-5

Copyright of the summarized publication:

Springer Nature Limited 2023

Copyright comment: Springer Nature or its licensor (e.g. a society or other partner) holds exclusive rights to this article under a publishing agreement with the author(s) or other rightsholder(s); author self-archiving of the accepted manuscript version of this article is solely governed by the terms of such publishing agreement and applicable law.

All rights reserved.

If you want to cite the papers, please refer to the original.

For technical reasons we could not place the page where the original quote is coming from.

Machine Generated Summaries

Abstract-Summary

"Drawing on theories of transformational leadership and institutional entrepreneurship, this study explores the causal drivers that transformed a public organization involved in the construction of the Delhi Metro."

"It explores the under-examined antecedents that drive organizational change, seeking to understand the links between leadership and entrepreneurship and significant reforms in the operation of a public organization."

"The findings of the study affirm that transformational leadership and entrepreneurship can drive successful outcomes in a major public infrastructure organization."

Introduction

"The literature has continued to examine the impact of institutional entrepreneurship and transformation leadership on organizational change separately."

"There are studies in the education sector which consider both institutional entrepreneurship and transformational leadership (Ma & others [122]; Raby & others [123]), but these two factors are not widely examined in the context of public organizations."

"We explore the links between transformational leadership and institutional entrepreneurship and the potential for change in a particular Indian public organization."

"Our work makes two key contributions: first, we contribute to the literature on how transformational leadership and institutional entrepreneurship can operate together to drive change in public organizations."

"By combining these two strands, often treated separately in the literature, we show that transformational leadership has the potential to nurture institutional entrepreneurship, within public organizations."

"We contribute to the literature by providing evidence that the influence of transformational leadership and institutional entrepreneurship extends beyond routine changes in public organizations."

Literature Review

"Those studies observed that transformational leadership is the leadership style most suitable for organizational change as these kinds of leaders support employees to engage better with changes in their work environment (Bass [124])."

"It could, therefore, be beneficial to link the two ideas of transformational leadership and institutional entrepreneurship and examine how both factors operate in tandem to influence organizational change in public organizations."

"Work, there is still limited insight into how transformational leadership manifests and influences organizational changes in public organizations in India."

"Some studies have shown that institutional entrepreneurship developed collectively, when several network actors (organizations or individuals) collaborate, is more likely to generate institutional change in the field than when change is initiated by a sole actor (Wijen & Ansari [125])."

Methods

"We selected the DMRC as the public organization for the purpose of this study and collected data on the corporation and the Delhi Metro construction project."

"This study focused on various stakeholders, including the focal public organization and other key partners involved in the project: the DMRC, external contractors, and financiers."

"The second stage of the study consisted of data collection via interviews."

"The third stage of data collection involved a dual approach of further archival data collection to verify the emerging themes from our data analysis and conducting observational visits to the construction sites and Delhi Metro stations."

"The researchers involved in this project began the coding process of our data after our interviews, and many categories resulted as we individually categorized everything broadly at this stage."

"After this initial analysis, researchers independently triangulated coding based on the information from interviews and secondary sources and extant literature."

Findings

"The public organization, in this case, Indian Railways, was primarily responsible for the development of MRTS, had to understand the changing needs of urban transport infrastructure development and effectively generate and increase its own capability for project management."

"Dr. E. Sreedharan, Managing Director, Delhi Metro, was appointed to the post following an illustrious career with the Indian Railways."

"The top management team, especially, the managing director, was vocally focused on the welfare of the employees of the DMRC as well as the many contractors working on this project."

"The UKAS auditor Andrew Marlow highlighted the organizational innovation undertaken by DMRC, speaking on IBN-Live in 2007: The fact that DMRC included occupational health and safety in an integrated management system is particularly laudable… DMRC's efforts on water harvesting and energy saving are a model for other big organization to follow."

Discussion

"Our paper provides a useful contribution by articulating the role that transformational leadership and institutional entrepreneurship can play in a developing country public organization."

"In line with the existing studies on public organizations in the developing county context, this study provides support for the role that institutional entrepreneurship plays in organizational change."

"As observed in a previous study (Brodnik & Brown [126]), the influence of transformational leadership and institutional entrepreneurship extends beyond routine changes in public organizations."

"This case study provides practicing managers with an insight into the changes in an incumbent public organization in the context of an emerging economy."

"Our study shows that transformational leadership and institutional entrepreneurship can drive successful outcomes in a large public infrastructure organization, the empirical methodology does not support the identification of the moderation or mediating effects of these factors."

Conclusion

"This study looks at a dynamically changing public organization and the role of transformational leadership and institutional entrepreneurship in initiating and driving these changes."

"The research highlights that the role of transformational leadership and institutional leadership was critical to achievement of the timely completion of the construction of the Delhi Metro construction project."

"This can serve as an example for other organizational stakeholders and can help the public organization sector to achieve a new reputation for energy and innovation."

How Can Managers, Acting as Brokers, Be Ambidextrous? The Effect of Trust Brokerage on Managers' Ambidexterity [203]

This is a machine-generated summary of:

Lv, Hongjiang; Zhao, Xinghua; Cao, Man; Ding, Jingjing: How can managers, acting as brokers, be ambidextrous? The effect of trust brokerage on managers' ambidexterity [203]

Published in: Asian Business & Management (2022)
Link to original: https://doi.org/10.1057/s41291-022-00189-z
Copyright of the summarized publication:
Springer Nature Limited 2022

All rights reserved.
If you want to cite the papers, please refer to the original.
For technical reasons we could not place the page where the original quote is coming from.

Abstract-Summary

"To address this gap, this study examines a specific content of brokerage-trust brokerage, and investigates how and when managers with trust brokerage can affect their exploitation, exploration, and ambidexterity."

"Managers' managerial self-efficacy partially mediates the relationship between managers' trust brokerage and managers' exploitation/ambidexterity."

"Managers' managerial self-efficacy fully mediates the relationship between managers' trust brokerage and managers' exploration."

Introduction

"By promoting instrumental exchanges and emotional exchanges simultaneously, managers with trust brokerages (i.e., 'coordinators') may function better and provide a nuanced understanding of subsequent influence process and important outcomes in the social network literature."

"Although previous studies have examined the critical role of network features in explaining managers' ambidexterity (Mom & others [127]; Rogan & Mors [128]), they have focused primarily on the overall network structure, such as network heterogeneity (Cabeza-Pullés & others [129]), overlooking the effects of specific brokerage such as trust brokerage."

"Our study identified managerial self-efficacy as a pivotal psychological mechanism underlying the relationship between managers' trust brokerage and their ambidexterity, which extends the current literature on social networks and managers' ambidexterity."

"Our focus on the moderating role of managers' trust network density, which is an important whole-network feature, adds to studies concerning brokerage and its moderators."

"We suggest that managers' ambidexterity results from the network structure and network content of trust brokerage, which echoes Brass's [130] call to investigate individuals' roles by integrating social network and psychological perspectives."

Theory and Hypotheses

"Combining hypotheses 2 and 3, we further assert that managers' trust brokerage affects managers' ambidexterity, exploration, and exploitation through managerial self-efficacy."

"We put forward the following hypothesis: Managerial self-efficacy mediates the relationship between managers' trust brokerage and managers' exploitation (H4a), exploration (H4b) and ambidexterity (H4c)."

"We suggest that managers' trust network density moderates the indirect effect of managers' trust brokerage on managers' exploitation, exploration and ambidexterity through managerial self-efficacy."

"According to social cognitive theory (Bandura [131]), managers' trust network density can act as a social context that helps trust brokers receive emotional support and recognition from others, and ultimately leading to managers' managerial self-efficacy and subsequent managers' exploitation, exploration and ambidexterity."

"Managers' trust network density moderates the indirect effect of managers' trust brokerage on managers' exploitation (H6a), exploration (H6b) and ambidexterity (H6c) through managerial self-efficacy."

Method

"To ensure that our sample has the typical characteristics of distributed work or telecommuting and innovation, we selected the award-winning teams of a management innovation achievements review organized by the China Enterprise Federation and the Industrial and Information Technology Committee in 5 years."

"At Time 1107 managers and 333 employees provided the whole trust network data, HR managers reported team size."

"We used the betweenness centrality of the trust network to measure the manager's trust brokerage, as each manager's betweenness centrality in his or her team was calculated as the proportion of times an individual occupied a position between two other actors who were unconnected (Freeman [132])."

"Managers and team members reported the overall trust network by using the trust network scale developed by Mishra [133]."

"Based on each team's trust network matrix, the manager's betweenness centrality of the trust network was calculated using UCINET 6.0 (Borgatti & others [134])."

Results

"Managerial self-efficacy was also significantly and positively correlated with managers' ambidexterity, exploration, and exploitation (r ranging from 0.28 to 0.39)."

"The relationship between managers' trust brokerage and managerial self-efficacy was also significant ($\beta = 0.01$, $p < 0.01$)."

"The results showed that managerial self-efficacy mediates the relationship between managers' trust brokerage and managers' exploitation, exploration, and ambidexterity."

"The relationships between managers' trust brokerage and managers' exploitation and ambidexterity were partly mediated by managerial self-efficacy."

"The results showed that the indirect effect of managers' trust brokerage on managers' exploitation (B = 0.01; 95% CI [0.00, 0.01]), managers' exploration (B = 0.01; 95% CI = [0.00, 0.01]) and managers' ambidexterity (B = 0.06; 95% CI [0.01, 0.12]) was significant, which further supported Hypothesis 4a, Hypothesis 4b, and Hypothesis 4c."

Discussion

"Managers' managerial self-efficacy partially mediates the relationship between managers' trust brokerage and their exploitation/ambidexterity, while fully mediating the relationship between managers' trust brokerage and managers' exploration."

"Our findings revealed that managers' managerial self-efficacy can act as a pivotal mechanism underlying the relationship between managers' trust brokerage and managers' ambidexterity."

"Drawing on social cognitive theory, we found that managerial self-efficacy is an important mediator between managers' trust brokerage and their ambidexterity."

"We also found that managers' managerial self-efficacy plays a full mediating role in the impact of managers' trust brokerage on their exploration."

"Managers' managerial self-efficacy plays a partial mediating role in the impact of managers' trust brokerage on their exploitation, which means that there are other mechanisms in this relationship."

"By illustrating the differential process through which managers' trust brokerage boosts their exploration, exploitation and ambidexterity, our research provides a more comprehensive understanding of the influence process of individual ambidexterity."

Limitations and Future Research

"How to cater to role segmentation is of great significance for managers engaging in exploration and exploitation (Tempelaar & Rosenkranz [135])."

"We suggest that future research can also be advanced by exploring how managers' specific roles affect their exploration, exploitation, and ambidexterity."

"Our results showed that managerial self-efficacy partly mediated the relationship between managers' trust brokerage and exploitation as well as ambidexterity."

"Future research could consider other mediators in this relationship, such as knowledge or information flows."

Conclusion

"Drawing on social cognitive theory and social network theory, we examine how managers' trust brokerage influences their ambidexterity."

"By investigating the specific content of brokerage-trust brokerage, rather than the structure of brokerage, our study demonstrates that trust brokerage facilitates both instrumental exchange and emotional exchange, which boost managers' managerial self-efficacy and subsequent ambidexterity."

"Managers' trust network density strengthens the effect of trust brokerage on managerial self-efficacy."

"Our results provide novel insights into the current literature by integrating brokerage with ambidexterity."

A Critical Analysis of Elon Musk's Leadership in Tesla Motors [204]

This is a machine-generated summary of:
Khan, Md. Rahat: A critical analysis of Elon Musk's leadership in Tesla motors [204]
Published in: Journal of Global Entrepreneurship Research (2021)
Link to original: https://doi.org/10.1007/s40497-021-00284-z
Copyright of the summarized publication:
The Author(s), under exclusive licence to Faculty of Entrepreneurship, University of Tehran 2021
All rights reserved.
If you want to cite the papers, please refer to the original.
For technical reasons we could not place the page where the original quote is coming from.

Abstract-Summary

"This present study applies qualitative research method to evaluate the entrepreneurial roles and leadership styles of Elon Musk in Tesla motors."

"The study places its focus on the general review of Elon Musk's leadership and attempts to match the leadership traits with some traditional leadership approaches widely recognized in leadership theory."

"The study employs a structured observation technique assimilating numerous secondary sources with a view to analyzing Musk's leadership traits in Tesla motor."

"The study offers some recommends for Elon Musk to follow, such as the champion/corporate intrapreneur and the servant leadership approaches so that they add practical values in his leading trait."

Introduction

"Leadership is a challenge not only to lead an organization but also to lead the environment as the business environment is changing dynamically."

"The current study is narrowly focusing on the leadership traits of Elon Musk in Tesla motors."

"The basic aim of the study is to find out to what extent the patterns of leadership tactics match with Musk's leadership in Tesla motors."

"This particular study will try to observe Elon Musk's leadership practices in Tesla motors and try to unearth which sorts of leadership attributes exist in Mask's leadership."

"The following part of the study will discuss some leadership attributes under the shape of literature review."

"The study will evaluate and narrate about Elon Musk and his Tesla motors."

"The study will analyze the leadership style based on Elon Musk's leadership."

Review of Literature

"The participative leadership behavior shows that the leader has the confidence in, and contiguity and admiration for the subordinates and this type of leadership behavior fosters high amount of trust towards the leader (Dirks & Ferrin [136, p. 614])."

"A multicultural leader is able to apply multicultural leadership by assessing the value of various cultures."

"Pedagogical leadership demands extraordinary keenness and aptitude based on the secret attitudes of the leader."

"On the other hand, Pedagogical leadership is the art of employees' learning, and the execution is cleared by each leader's own learning perception (Lahtinen [137])."

"The spotlight of servant leadership is on the others instead of on one's own and on understanding the task of the leader as a servant (Greenleaf [138])."

Methodology

"He said, 'It breaks my heart when someone is injured...I've asked that every injury be reported directly to me, without exception...I would like to meet with each injured individual so I can understand, from them, exactly what we need to do to make it better...Then I will go down to the production line and perform the same task that they perform...[Managers at Tesla] lead from the front line, not from some safe and comfortable ivory tower' The statement reflects Musk's concern for employees as per the management grid (Blake & Mouton [139])."

"If Musk liked your idea, he wouldn't hesitate to put it into action" During the interview, participating employees were asked about Musk's leadership skills regarding how he could properly utilize his employees to become a better manpower in Tesla Inc. Most of the participants said, No one is better than him to properly utilize employees in organization."

"An engineer who worked in Tesla as a production engineer has shared her opinion about the high level standard in Musk's leadership."

Result and Discussion

"The CEO and co-founder of Tesla, Elon Musk has been admired globally for both of his leadership and entrepreneurial skills."

"The recent leadership and role of Musk in Tesla have considerably made concern to investors and stakeholders."

"The above turmoil was blamed by the stakeholders just for Musk's exhausted physical health along with 120 h of work per week and he stayed three/four days in factory without departing outside (Steward & others [140])."

"Few recommendations should obviously be made about Elon Musk and his leadership."

"Musk should distribute some of his work-load for his physical as well as mental health."

"Musk needs to work on his human skill (Katz [141]) as well."

"Personality in talking, in decision-making, in behavior is always evaluated by people who are surrounded by true influential characteristics like Elon Musk."

"Musk also needs to work on his public speeches approach as well."

Conclusion

"This particular research basically tries to understand the certain leadership characteristics of Elon Musk in Tesla motors."

"In analysis, the study has tried to match those leadership characteristics in comparison to leadership practices which are implemented by Elon Musk in his Tesla motors."

"The findings and discussion show that Elon Musk has incorporated the participative or distributive leadership, pedagogical leadership style, creative leadership, change leadership, and intelligence leadership; however, he has some shortcomings in servant leadership style."

"The study has tried to assess the leadership traits of Elon Musk in Tesla, yet many things can be done in future works."

"A structured questionnaire can be made based on this current research to survey Tesla's employees who undergoes through the direct leadership of Elon."

"Some other organizations or leaders can take some lessons from this research as well as Elon's leadership characteristics to improve the quality of leadership practice in their respective organizations."

Cultural Congruence or Compensation? A Meta-Analytic Test of Transformational and Transactional Leadership Effects Across Cultures [205]

This is a machine-generated summary of:
Rockstuhl, Thomas; Wu, Dongyuan; Dulebohn, James H.; Liao, Chenwei; Hoch, Julia E.: Cultural congruence or compensation? A meta-analytic test of transformational and transactional leadership effects across cultures [205]
Published in: Journal of International Business Studies (2022).
Link to original: https://doi.org/https://doi.org/10.1057/s41267-022-00559-x
Copyright of the summarized publication:
Academy of International Business 2022
Copyright comment: Springer Nature or its licensor holds exclusive rights to this article under a publishing agreement with the author(s) or other rightsholder(s); author self-archiving of the accepted manuscript version of this article is solely governed by the terms of such publishing agreement and applicable law.
All rights reserved.
If you want to cite the papers, please refer to the original.
For technical reasons we could not place the page where the original quote is coming from.

Abstract-Summary

"Prior research is equivocal about whether leadership is more effective when it matches typical cultural practices (the cultural congruence argument) or compensates for 'ineffective' cultural practices (the cultural compensation argument)."

"A meta-analysis of 460 field samples of transformational leadership (N = 124,646) and 139 field samples of transactional leadership (N = 38,327) across 53 cultures revealed three key results: First, both transformational and transactional leadership universally relate positively to follower performance outcomes."

"The positive effects of transformational leadership on convergent performance outcomes are more pronounced in cultures characterized by norms of vertical differentiation (including high power distance) and harmony (including collectivism), consistent with the cultural congruence perspective."

"The positive effects of transactional leadership on divergent performance outcomes are more pronounced in cultures characterized by norms of low performance-focus (including low uncertainty avoidance), consistent with the cultural compensation perspective."

Machine Generated Summaries

Literature Review and Hypothesis Development

"The cultural congruence and cultural compensation perspectives suggest that a matching between cultural norms and leadership behavior strengthens (vs. weakens) relationships of transformational and transactional leadership with follower performance outcomes."

"Combining our arguments and these empirical findings on the alignment of transformational and transactional leadership with the general cultural congruence proposition, we propose: The positive relationship of transformational leadership with outcomes is stronger in countries with lower rather than higher performance-focus norms."

"We theorize that vertical differentiation cultures align with transactional leadership because such norms encourage and reward more command-and-control or autocratic leader behaviors that give greater power to those in higher positions and expect loyalty from followers (Dorfman & others [143])."

"Based on the cultural congruence proposition, which holds that alignment between leadership behaviors and cultural norms strengthens leadership effects, we thus propose: The positive relationship of transformational leadership with outcomes is stronger in countries with lower rather than higher vertical differentiation norms."

Method

"In our meta-analysis, we included transformational and transactional leadership studies that considered leadership at the individual, team, and organizational levels in relation to particular outcomes such as individual, team, and organization performance, respectively."

"We only included studies that reported behavioral outcomes of transformational and transactional leadership and included sample size along with correlations between leadership and outcomes."

"Two raters independently coded each study in terms of sample size, effect size, reliability and standard deviation of transformational leadership and its correlates, country of study, type of transformational and transactional leadership measure used, and other control variables."

"Following the three-level variance known meta-analysis approach, we treated the study effect sizes (relationships of transformational or transactional leadership with outcomes) as random effects at level 1 (the within-study level), with study characteristics modeled as random effects at level 2 (the between-study level), and included culture characteristics as random effects at level 3 (the country/region level)."

Results

"Based on the cultural congruence perspective, Hypothesis 1 predicted that performance-focus would weaken relationships of transformational leadership with outcomes (H1a) but strengthen relationships of transactional leadership with outcomes (H1b)."

"Hypothesis 2 predicted the opposite pattern for performance-focus effects on relationships of transformational (H2a) and transactional (H2b) leadership with outcomes based on the cultural compensation perspective."

"Based on the cultural congruence perspective, Hypothesis 3 predicted that vertical differentiation would weaken relationships of transformational leadership with outcomes (H3a) but strengthen relationships of transactional leadership with outcomes (H3b)."

"Hypothesis 4 predicted the opposite pattern for the effects of vertical differentiation on relationships of transformational (H4a) and transactional (H4b) leadership with outcomes based on the cultural compensation perspective."

"Hypothesis 6 predicted the opposite pattern for harmony effects on relationships of transformational (H6a) and transactional (H6b) leadership with outcomes based on the cultural compensation perspective."

Discussion

"To shed light on how culture influences leadership, we systematically examined the effect of cultural norm differences on relationships of transformational and transactional leadership with a common set of behavioral outcomes."

"We observed cultural compensation effects, such that descriptive norms associated with performance-focus weakened transactional leadership effects, for divergent outcomes (i.e., creativity or innovation) only."

"Integrating and extending the parts touched by previous cross-cultural meta-analyses (Crede & others [144]; Jackson & others [145]; Watts & others [146]), we systematically considered the influence of three higher-order factors of descriptive cultural norms (i.e., performance-focus, vertical differentiation, and harmony) on relationships of transformational and transactional leadership with convergent versus divergent behavioral outcomes."

"We found that cultural compensation effects occurred for transactional leadership, cultural differences in norms of performance-focus, and divergent outcomes."

"We encourage future research to continue to examine the effects of transformational and transactional leadership, especially on divergent performance outcomes, across a wide range of cultures."

Conclusion

"Results based on 460 and 139 independent samples (N = 124,646 and N = 38,327) from 53 cultures provide not only the most comprehensive benchmark of cultural effects on leadership effects to date, but also set the conceptual foundations for a culturally sensitive transformational and transactional leadership theory."

Machine Generated Summaries 231

"We show that (1) both transformational and transactional leadership universally relate positively to follower performance outcomes; (2) the positive effects of transformational leadership on convergent (i.e., proficiency-based) performance outcomes are more pronounced in countries with norms of high vertical differentiation and harmony, consistent with the cultural congruence perspective; and (3) the positive effects of transactional leadership on divergent (i.e., innovation-based) performance outcomes are more pronounced in countries with norms of low performance-focus, consistent with the cultural compensation perspective."

"We hope our theoretical clarification of culture as a boundary condition to leadership effects and our results will provide a springboard for future cross-cultural research on the efficacy of transformational and transactional leadership."

Notes

"1 Bass [147] originally named this dimension charisma."

"As recounted by Antonakis [148], because charisma may connote idolization of the leader, later publications renamed this dimension as idealized influence (i.e., connoting idealization)."

"Research further distinguished components of idealized influence that are behavioral versus attributional (Avolio, Bass, & Jung [149])."

[Section 7]

"Various reviews of this burgeoning literature suggest that cultural differences influence the effectiveness of leadership behaviors across national cultures (e.g., Dorfman [150]; Stackhouse & others [151]; Taras, Kirkman, & Steel [152])."

"Three competing theoretical perspectives have emerged to explain cultural influences on the effectiveness of leadership behaviors (House, Wright, & Aditya [153])."

"Crede and others [144] and Watts and others [146] both studied cultural influences on transformational leadership, but differed in the scope of cultural dimensions and types of outcomes considered."

"We systematically examine the influence of cultural norms on relationships of transformational and transactional leadership with a common set of behavioral outcomes."

"Such a comprehensive meta-analysis is critical to offer a more complete picture of the relative merits of the cultural congruence, cultural compensation, and near universality arguments for the full transformational and transactional leadership framework."

"Understanding when the cultural congruence versus compensation perspective is more pronounced is critical to advance more nuanced theorizing about the role of national culture in leadership effectiveness."

The Relationship Between Ethical Leadership and Unethical Pro-Organizational Behavior: Linear or Curvilinear Effects? [206]

This is a machine-generated summary of:
   Miao, Q.; Newman, A.; Yu, J.; Xu, L.: The Relationship Between Ethical Leadership and Unethical Pro-Organizational Behavior: Linear or Curvilinear Effects? [206]
   Published in: Journal of Business Ethics (2012)
   Link to original: https://doi.org/https://doi.org/10.1007/s10551-012-1504-2
   Copyright of the summarized publication:
   Springer Science+Business Media Dordrecht 2012
   All rights reserved.
   If you want to cite the papers, please refer to the original.
   For technical reasons we could not place the page where the original quote is coming from.

Abstract-Summary

"We examine the nature of the relationship between ethical leadership and unethical pro-organizational behavior (UPB), defined as unethical behavior conducted by employees with the aim of benefiting their organization, and whether the strength of the relationship differs between subordinates experiencing high and low identification with supervisor."

"Further, we find that the strength of this inverted u-curve relationship differs between subordinates with high and low identification with supervisor."

"To say, the inverted u-shaped relationship between ethical leadership and UPB was stronger when subordinates experienced high levels of identification with supervisor."

Introduction

"Subordinates working under low levels of ethical leadership will be less willing to engage risky behaviors such as UPB, given the low quality of social exchange relationship with their supervisor, and those working under high levels of ethical leadership will be provided with a clearer message that unethical behavior, even when it is pro-organizational in nature like UPB, will not be accepted through social modeling by the leader."

"Only at high levels of ethical leadership will the social learning effects of ethical leadership on subordinates outweigh the effects that high-quality social exchange relationships may have in engendering positive behavior towards the organization, when it is unethical in nature."

"The study also contributes to the literature by investigating whether the strength of the relationship between ethical leadership and UPB differs between subordinates with high and low levels of identification with supervisor."

Literature Review

"Of all, ethical leaders conduct behaviors that are 'normatively appropriate' in the eyes of followers, and thus build up credit as ethical role models."

"Ethical leaders set clear ethical standards and regulate the ethical behavior of followers through reward and punishment."

"The moral person dimension involves the exhibition of certain traits such as honesty, integrity and trustworthiness, certain behaviors such as doing the right thing, being considerate and approachable to followers, and certain decision-making styles that reflect the leader's ethical principles."

"Brown and Treviño [154] argue that the moral manager dimension implies an important transactional aspect of ethical leadership: the use of a reward and discipline system to regulate ethical and unethical behaviors."

"Social learning theory (Bandura [155, 156]) provides a theoretical basis to explain how ethical leaders affect the behavior of followers."

Unethical Pro-Organizational Behavior

"Unethical pro-organizational behavior (UPB) refers to 'actions that are intended to promote the effective functioning of the organization or its members, and violate core societal values, mores, laws, or standards of proper conduct' (Umphress & Bingham [157, p. 622])."

"UPB is unethical, i.e. it is behavior that violates widely held standards of ethical behavior as measured by values, laws or social norms, and not group or organizational norms."

"Umphress and others [158] argue that UPB cannot be completely separated from other self-centered unethical behaviors because behaviors benefiting the organization may also benefit the individual themselves."

"Unethical behaviors of only self-serving purposes are not classified as UPB."

"Umphress and others [158] argue that organizational identification and positive reciprocity beliefs might influence the propensity of an individual to conduct unethical behaviour in favour of the organization."

The Relationship Between Ethical Leadership and UPB

"Given the findings of these studies, we propose an inverted u-shaped (curvilinear) relationship between the ethical leadership behavior of the supervisor and the tendency of subordinates to engage in UPB."

"We argue that subordinates experiencing moderate levels of ethical leadership will engage in greater UPB than those guided by low levels of ethical leadership because they typically have a higher quality of social exchange relationship with their supervisors, and stronger identification with the organization (Brown & Treviño [154]; Walumbwa & others [159])."

"Only at high levels of ethical leadership will the social learning effects of ethical leadership on subordinates' ethical conduct outweigh the effects that high quality social exchange relationships may have in engendering positive behavior towards the organization such as UPB."

"We develop the following hypothesis: There will be an inverted u-shaped (curvilinear) relationship between the ethical leadership behavior of the supervisor and subordinate UPB."

The Moderating Effects of Identification with Supervisor

"Consistent with this definition, we examine whether the strength of the u-shaped (curvilinear) relationship between ethical leadership and UPB differs between subordinates with high and low levels of identification with supervisor."

"We argue that the proposed curvilinear relationship between ethical leadership and UPB will be stronger for subordinates with high levels of identification with supervisor than those with low levels, as identification with supervisor leads subordinates to exhibit greater sensitivity to the expectations of their supervisor, internalize the goals and values of the supervisor as their own, and work harder in the interests of their supervisor and the organization (van Knippenberg [160]; Aron [161]; van Knippenberg & others [162]; Sluss & Ashforth [163, 164])."

"It might be expected that subordinates experiencing high levels of identification with their supervisor will be more likely to engage in UPB when they are guided by moderate levels of ethical leadership, given that in line with their supervisor's thinking, they will typically consider the interests of the organization to be more important than addressing ethical issues."

Methodology

"Survey invitations were distributed electronically to 1,000 alumni from the database by e-mail, with the assurance that their responses would be treated confidentially."

"The time lag between each wave of the survey was intended to reduce the likelihood of common method variance and mitigate respondent fatigue."

"At Time 1 participants were required to rate the ethical leadership of their immediate supervisor, the ethical environment in their organization and provide demographic information."

"At Time 3 participants who had responded at Time 2 assessed the extent to which they engaged in UPB."

"362 participants completed the first wave of the survey, followed by 252 and 239 in the second and third waves respectively."
"This amounted to a final response rate of 24 percent."
"We compared the responses between partial respondents and full respondents to waves one and two of the survey."

Measures

"Ethical leadership was measured using the 10-item ELS scale developed by Brown and others [165]."
"Respondents were asked to rate the ethical leadership of their immediate supervisor using a five-point Likert scale (where 1 = strongly disagree and 5 = strongly agree)."
"Unethical pro-organizational behavior (UPB) was measured using a 6-item self-report scale adapted from Umphress and others [158]."
"Respondents required to rate the extent to which they engaged in UPB using a five-point Likert scale (where 1 = strongly disagree and 5 = strongly agree)."
"Respondents were asked to rate the extent to which they identified with their immediate supervisor using a five-point Likert scale (where 1 = strongly disagree and 5 = strongly agree)."
"The ethical environment of the organizational was also controlled for using a 14-item scale developed by Treviño and others [166] as it has been shown to influence the unethical behavior of employees."

Analysis and Results

"In Model 3, the non-linear effects of ethical leadership on UPB were examined through entering a quadratic term (ethical leadership × ethical leadership) into the regression."
"In Models 4 and 5, in order to better understand the influence of identification with supervisor on the relationship between ethical leadership and UPB, the sample was split into two groups; individuals with low-to-moderate levels of identification with supervisor and those with moderate-to-high levels of identification with supervisor."
"In line with Hypothesis 2, we found that the inverted u-shaped relationship between ethical leadership and UPB was stronger for the group with high identification with supervisor."
"As can been seen in the figure, at low levels of ethical leadership the positive impact of ethical leadership on UPB is stronger for those with high identification with supervisor than those with low identification with supervisor."
"At high levels of ethical leadership, the negative effect of ethical leadership on UPB is also stronger for those with high identification with supervisor."

Discussion

"Consistent with our hypotheses, we found an inverted u-shaped relationship between ethical leadership and UPB, and that the relationship was stronger for subordinates who experienced high levels of identification with supervisor."

"Our findings can be put down to the reciprocation effect of a positive social exchange relationship between the supervisor and the subordinate at moderate levels of ethical leadership."

"Supervisors exhibiting moderate levels of ethical leadership will typically fail to prioritize addressing ethical values over the pursuit of other organizational interests, and thus deliver unclear and inconsistent messages to subordinates as to the importance of acting in an ethical manner."

"In these ways, supervisors who exercise high levels of ethical leadership should therefore reduce UPB amongst their subordinates."

"Since supervisors with moderate levels of ethical leadership enjoy positive social relationships with subordinates and prioritize meeting organizational goals over addressing ethical issues, subordinates working under supervisors of this kind are most likely to conduct UPBs."

Managerial Implications

"Our study acknowledges that ethical leadership may be utilized by organizations as a way of reducing their employees' UPB, and finds a curvilinear relationship between ethical leadership and UPB."

"Only when implemented strictly and consistently is ethical leadership able to raise the ethical awareness of subordinates, regulate their unethical conduct, and reduce the likelihood of UPB."

"In order to reduce subordinate UPB, managers need to establish clear standards to evaluate and punish unethical behaviours, even when conducted in favour of the organization."

"In order to reduce UPB in their organizations, top-level managers should refine their organizational values and integrate ethics into the core values of the organization."

"Our finding that identification with supervisor impacts on the relationship between ethical leadership and UPB implies that the moral virtues of the supervisor play an important role in regulating subordinates unethical conduct."

Limitations and Suggestions for Future Research

"We believe that due to the sensitive nature of the questionnaire, contacting the participants directly rather than through their organization enabled us to reduce the potential for social desirability effects, given there was no possibility of negative consequences from respondents' employing organizations."

"Research, multiple respondents might be used to measure subordinates' UPB."

"More work needs to be done to ascertain the generalizability of our research findings outside the narrow context in which our study was conducted."

"Future research may also seek to ascertain the role played by co-workers in influencing the UPB of employees in the workplace."

"More work could be done to examine the extent to which training and developing the moral virtues of supervisors as well as employees as suggested by Mele [167, 168], has a positive impact in terms of reducing UPB."

Conclusion

"This study provided the first empirical examination of the impact of ethical leadership on the UPB of subordinates using a sample drawn from the Chinese public sector."

"Unlike previous studies which found a linear relationship between ethical leadership and unethical behaviour, we identified an inverted u-shaped relationship between ethical leadership and UPB."

"We found that this relationship was only significant when identification with supervisor was at a moderate-to-high level."

"These findings indicate the inherent difficulties faced by organizations in reducing UPB given its pro-organizational nature."

The Effect of Organizational Citizenship Behavior and Leadership Effectiveness on Public Sectors Organizational Performance: Study in the Department of Education, Youth and Sports in Maluku Province, Indonesia [207]

This is a machine-generated summary of:

Notanubun, Zainuddin: The Effect of Organizational Citizenship Behavior and Leadership Effectiveness on Public Sectors Organizational Performance: Study in the Department of Education, Youth and Sports in Maluku Province, Indonesia [207]
Published in: Public Organization Review (2020)
Link to original: https://doi.org/https://doi.org/10.1007/s11115-020-00475-4
Copyright of the summarized publication:
Springer Science+Business Media, LLC, part of Springer Nature 2020
All rights reserved.
If you want to cite the papers, please refer to the original.
For technical reasons we could not place the page where the original quote is coming from.

Abstract-Summary

"Results of the study showed that in simultaneous organizational citizenship behavior and leadership effectiveness give effect to the strongest towards the achievement of organizational performance."

Introduction

"The Department of Education, Youth and Sports in Maluku Province is one of the main public sector organizations to improve the quality of human resources, especially for the people of Maluku."

"Although the role of information technology influences work effectiveness, it does not reduce the effect of employee attitudes, employee work behavior and emotional intelligence on individual performance and organizational performance (Rayner & others [169]; Fatima & others [170]; Aksoy & others [171])."

"OCBs are important for employees of the Department of Education, Youth and Sports in Maluku Province because the individual behavioral characteristics require additional personnel to take action that exceeds the role description determined by the organization (Yoon [172])."

"Various conditions in the composition of human resources in the Maluku Provincial Office of Education, Youth and Sports and their impact on the work environment, work behavior, characteristics and work motives of each employee in an organization with organizational performance, must be balanced by effective leadership."

Literature Review and Hypothesis

"OCBs consists of five dimensions (Organ [173]; Yoon [172]), namely: (1) Altruism is a reflection of mutual assistance between employees without coercion on tasks related to organizational activities. (2) Conscientiousness is a reflection of the performance of prerequisites that exceed the minimum standard. (3) Civic virtue is a reflection of voluntary participation and support for organizational functions both professionally and socially. (4) Sportsmanship is a reflection of behavior that provides tolerance for less than ideal conditions without complaining. (5) Courtesy is a reflection of behavior that can alleviate problems related to work faced by other employees."

"The essence of LE is the ability of leaders to influence subordinates in achieving organizational goals."

"Armstrong [174] explains that the essence of organizational performance is a shared process between leaders, individuals and groups that are managed."

"Performance can also be measured through organizational behavior, results and effectiveness."

Methods

"Instruments in this study are questionnaire and test."

"Before the data collection, instrument was put into a trial in order to test the validity and reliability, so that it can pass the qualification to be used as a means of measuring variable in the collection of research data."

"Each item of the questionnaire was tested on 30 civil servants of the Department of Education, Youth and Sports."

"All statement items are tested to determine reliability using Cronbach's alpha general formula to meet reliability requirements (Hinton [175])."

"After the instrument meets the requirements of validity and reliability, the instrument is distributed to the respondents."

Results and Discussion

"Of the analysis in the research model diagram shows that the OCBs with OP variables have a correlation with moderate relationship strength (0.671), but between dimensions of OCBs with OP variables are generally in the category of low relationship strengths on altruism dimensions (0.364), conscientiousness (0.429) and civic virtue (0.391), while the courtesy and sportsmanship dimensions are in the medium category (0.582 and 0.508)."

"Of hypothesis testing showed that OCBs shown to affect OP at the Department of Education, Youth and Sports and partially correlated to the category of the strength of the relationship was medium ($R = 0.671$)."

"Hypothesis test results LE against OP showed that LE shown to affect OP at the Department of Education, Youth and Sports and partially correlated to the category of the strength of a strong relationship."

Conclusion

"The performance of the Department of Education, Youth and Sports in Maluku Province as a public sector organization in the achievement of OP is strongly influenced by LE."

"OCBs lack of functioning as a driving force for performance in order to maximize the achievement of OP is due to a lack of quality resources and skills because the majority of employee education qualifications are still low and the lack of rewards and incentives as a form of appreciation for employee performance at the Department of Education, Youth and Sports."

"These seven factors have become the main key to the success of the public sector OP in the Department of Education, Youth and Sports in Maluku Province, Indonesia."

Machiavellianism and Task-Orientated Leadership: Moderating Effect of Job Autonomy [208]

This is a machine-generated summary of:
Rehman, Usama; Shahnawaz, Mohammad Ghazi: Machiavellianism and task-orientated leadership: moderating effect of job autonomy [208]
Published in: Leadership, Education, Personality: An Interdisciplinary Journal (2021)
Link to original: https://doi.org/https://doi.org/10.1365/s42681-021-00024-7
Copyright of the summarized publication:
The Author(s) 2021
License: OpenAccess CC BY (German language version) 4.0
Dieser Artikel wird unter der Creative Commons Namensnennung 4.0 International Lizenz veröffentlicht, welche die Nutzung, Vervielfältigung, Bearbeitung, Verbreitung und Wiedergabe in jeglichem Medium und Format erlaubt, sofern Sie den/die ursprünglichen Autor(en) und die Quelle ordnungsgemäß nennen, einen Link zur Creative Commons Lizenz beifügen und angeben, ob Änderungen vorgenommen wurden. Die in diesem Artikel enthaltenen Bilder und sonstiges Drittmaterial unterliegen ebenfalls der genannten Creative Commons Lizenz, sofern sich aus der Abbildungslegende nichts anderes ergibt. Sofern das betreffende Material nicht unter der genannten Creative Commons Lizenz steht und die betreffende Handlung nicht nach gesetzlichen Vorschriften erlaubt ist, ist für die oben aufgeführten Weiterverwendungen des Materials die Einwilligung des jeweiligen Rechteinhabers einzuholen. Weitere Details zur Lizenz entnehmen Sie bitte der Lizenzinformation auf http://creativecommons.org/licenses/by/4.0/deed.de.
If you want to cite the papers, please refer to the original.
For technical reasons we could not place the page where the original quote is coming from.

Abstract-Summary

"Despite the negative connotation of Machiavellianism, Machs are found in all kinds of organization and at almost all levels."
"The present study explored the relationship between Machiavellianism and Task-Oriented Leadership."
"Machiavellian Personality scale (MPS), Task oriented Leadership style questionnaire, and Work autonomy scale were used to collect data."
"Results revealed a significant positive relationship between Machiavellianism and Task-oriented leadership."
"the relationship between the two constructs was moderated by high and average level of job autonomy."

Introduction

"Machs preferred leadership roles than low Machiavellians (Gies [176])."

"Machiavellian leaders can also be flexible and adapt as per the situation and yet would follow task orientation style to reach their goal (Dahling & others [177])."

"Machiavellianism and task orientation were found to be significant predictors of team's effectiveness (Jones & White [178])."

"It seems that the task orientation is the core of Machiavellian managers."

"H1: Machiavellianism would be positively associated with task-oriented leadership."

"Machiavellians would also need favorable context to manifest itself in behaviors including task-oriented style/behavior."

"It was hypothesized that job autonomy would be the contextual factor that would lead Machs to manifest task-oriented style."

"In the context of the present study, we proposed that job autonomy would moderate the relationship between machiavellianism and task-oriented leadership."

"H2: The relationship between Machiavellianism and Task-oriented leadership would be moderated by Job autonomy."

Method

"Following convenience sampling approximately 250 managers of multiple private organizations were approached, out of which 180 managers gave their written consent and participated in the current study."

"All the participants were briefed about the nature of the study."

"The data comprised of 52 females and 128 males."

"The inferences were drawn from the data of 168 managers, out of which 122 were males, and 46 were female managers."

Measures

"The scale has 16 items and assesses four dimensions: Amorality, Distrust, Desire for Control, and Desire for status."

"Some of the sample items are 'I would cheat if there was a low chance of getting caught,' 'I like to give the orders in interpersonal situations,' 'Status is a good sign of success in life.'"

"9-item work autonomy scale from Breaugh's Instrument [179] was used to assess job autonomy."

"Some of the sample items are 'I am free to choose the methods to use in carrying out my work,' 'I am able to choose the way to go about my job (the procedures to utilize),' 'I have control over the scheduling of my work.'"

"Some of the sample items are 'I take special care that works gets top priority,' 'I maintain high standard of performance,' 'I see that my subordinates work to their capacity.'"

Results

"The results showed that only 18% of the variance was explained by a single factor, which indicated that the data was free from common method bias."

"For job autonomy, the mean was found to be 33.1 with 5.6 standard deviations, indicating high job autonomy."

"The correlation coefficient ($r = 0.15$, $p < .05$) shows a significant positive correlation between Machiavellianism and Job autonomy."

"The relationship between Machiavellianism and task-oriented leadership was found be positive and significant ($r = 0.22$, $p < .01$)."

"The correlation coefficient ($r = 0.45$, $p < .01$) also shows that there exists a significant positive relationship between Job autonomy and Task-oriented Leadership."

"Job Autonomy was found to be strongest predictor of task-oriented behavior ($b = 0.44$, $p < .01$), followed by Machiavellianism ($b = 0.11$, $p = < .05$)."

Discussion

"A significant positive relationship was found between Machiavellianism and task-oriented leadership."

"A manager high on Machiavellianism would focus on task completion as they are not people-oriented (Dahling & others [177])."

"As the sample of the present study comprised of lower and middle-level managers (the average experience being 4.2 years), their task was to manage and supervise the work of subordinates, hence task-oriented leadership seems more relevant than other forms of leadership."

"It can safely concluded that Machs manifest task-oriented leadership especially at lower and middle level of organizations."

"It was also found that job autonomy moderated the relation between Machiavellianism and task-oriented leadership."

"The results provide evidence that Machs would manifest task-oriented leadership directly as well as when relevant situational factors such as sufficient amount of job autonomy is given to get the assigned work done."

Conclusion and Limitations

"The present research examined the relationship between Machiavellianism and task-oriented leadership directly as well as in interaction with job autonomy."

"The results showed that Machiavellians would manifest task-oriented leadership especially when job autonomy is high or average."

"The results of the present study provides further evidence that Machs are not pathological all the time and they can be functional under appropriate situations (e.g., job autonomy)."

"Some of them had only 3 subordinates, while few had 15."

Transformational Leadership and Follower Task Performance: The Role of Susceptibility to Positive Emotions and Follower Positive Emotions [209]

This is a machine-generated summary of:

Liang, Shin-Guang; Steve Chi, Shu-Cheng: Transformational Leadership and Follower Task Performance: The Role of Susceptibility to Positive Emotions and Follower Positive Emotions [209]

Published in: Journal of Business and Psychology (2012)

Link to original: https://doi.org/https://doi.org/10.1007/s10869-012-9261-x

Copyright of the summarized publication:

Springer Science+Business Media, LLC 2012

All rights reserved.

If you want to cite the papers, please refer to the original.

For technical reasons we could not place the page where the original quote is coming from.

Abstract-Summary

"We apply susceptibility to positive emotions (STPE) as the moderator and follower positive emotions (PE) as the mediator in the relationship between follower perceptions of TFL and follower task performance (TP)."

"The HLM results confirmed that follower perceptions of TFL were positively related to follower PE."

"Further, individual differences in STPE moderated the relationship between follower perceptions of TFL and follower PE."

"Follower PE mediated the moderated relationship among TFL, STPE, and follower TP."

"This study advances understanding of when, how, and why TFL can enhance follower TP."

"The findings also address the complex role of STPE and follower PE in the relationship between follower perceptions of TFL and follower TP."

"This study enhances understanding of how TFL functions by accounting for followers' STPE."

Theory and Hypotheses

"According to the emotional contagion perspective, we suggest that transformational leaders express PE and behaviors, which are perceived by and transferred to followers, resulting in the experience of PE by followers."

"Followers with higher levels of STPE generally should respond more easily to their transformational leaders' emotions and behaviors because they are likely to pay closer attention to leadership behaviors, to read leaders' positive emotional and nonverbal expressions, and ultimately to experience stronger PE when aroused."

"Johnson [180] found that followers' susceptibility to emotional contagion moderated the positive relationship between leaders' PE and followers' PE in the workplace."

"Followers with higher levels of STPE may respond more strongly and positively to transformational leaders' emotions and behaviors by experiencing stronger PE and subsequently exhibiting better TP."

Methods

"Since, in our study, multiple subordinates rated the same supervisor within their unit, we examined whether TFL could be conceptualized and aggregated into the unit-level."

"We were interested in understanding how individual followers respond to their transformational leaders' emotions and behaviors, and we did not want to examine the effects of a shared or a unit-level analysis of TFL on individual follower PE and TP."

"We obtained the subordinates' responses of demographic variables such as gender, age, educational level, and work-unit tenure to control for potential confounding effects on follower TP (Kamdar & Van Dyne [181])."

"Our hypotheses, to confirm the existence of group membership or rater effects in our data, we ran null models with no predictors at the individual level and the unit-level, taking follower PE or follower TP as the dependent variables."

Results

"The results showed that TFL was positively related to follower PE ($r = .39, p < .01$) and to follower TP ($r = .41, p < .01$)."

"Follower PE and TP were positively correlated ($r = .58, p < .01$)."

"We conducted a series of confirmatory factor analyses to see whether measures of TFL, STPE, follower PE, and follower TP captured distinctive theoretical constructs."

"Prior to testing our hypotheses, on the basis of Hofmann's [182] suggestions, we first examined the extent to which group membership or a supervisor's rating effect exists in both the mediating variable (i.e., follower PE) and the outcome variable (i.e., follower TP).The results of null models in HLM confirmed that there was significant between-unit variance in follower PE: $\chi^2 = 131.84$, df $= 41$, $p < .001$."

Discussion

"We also theorized and found that individual differences in STPE moderated the relationship between follower perceptions of TFL and PE."

"This study extends past research by suggesting the mediating mechanism of follower PE in the moderated relationships among TFL, STPE, and follower TP."

"To tackle the possibility of reverse causality directly, we conducted a multilevel mediation test and found that follower PE mediated the relationship between the unit-level TFL and TP at the individual level."

"It is possible that leaders' emotional expressions might explain the proposed relationship between TFL and follower PE; we cannot unequivocally conclude that the effect of TFL on follower PE occurred through the process of emotional contagion."

"Since our data showed that STPE enhanced the relationship between TFL and follower PE, such results lent support to the possibility that emotional contagion was occurring."

[Section 5]

"We contend that the TP of followers could result from a joint effect of perceptions of leadership and personality traits (i.e., susceptibility of PE) by enhancing followers' emotional experiences."

"Based on the process of emotional contagion, we propose that the link between follower perceptions of TFL and follower PE may be contingent on individual differences in susceptibility to positive emotions (STPE)."

"We seek to understand the extent to which individual differences in STPE influence the relationship between follower perceptions of TFL and follower PE at work."

"Previous research on TFL has focused primarily on the effect of leadership behaviors without attending to followers' individuality, both in terms of personality traits and differential perceptions of TFL."

"We attempt to integrate the TFL and emotion research by examining the mediating role of follower PE in explaining the effects of the interaction between follower perceptions of TFL and STPE on TP."

Heightening Citizenship Behaviours of Academicians Through Transformational Leadership: Evidence Based Interventions [210]

This is a machine-generated summary of:
Majeed, Nauman; Jamshed, Samia: Heightening citizenship behaviours of academicians through transformational leadership: Evidence based interventions [210]
Published in: Quality & Quantity (2021)
Link to original: https://doi.org/https://doi.org/10.1007/s11135-021-01146-2
Copyright of the summarized publication:
The Author(s), under exclusive licence to Springer Nature B.V. 2021
All rights reserved.
If you want to cite the papers, please refer to the original.
For technical reasons we could not place the page where the original quote is coming from.

Abstract-Summary

"Such behavior can be stimulated through a leadership style that has received rare attention."

"This study proposed an integrated research model that explores how transformational leadership influences citizenship behaviors through rarely used dimensions Organizational Citizenship Behaviour Organization and Organizational Citizenship Behaviour Individual by addressing the mediating role of workplace spirituality and emotional intelligence."

"We integrated two theoretical models of social exchange and transformational leadership to describe the underlying linkages."

"The findings of this study provide empirical evidence and encouraging justifications for the substantial influence of workplace spirituality and emotional intelligence on the relationship between transformational leadership and citizenship behaviours."

Introduction

"In the unique, dynamic, and intensive setting in which institutions work, Organizational Citizenship Behaviour (OCB) a discretionary behavior, not formally perceived or compensated, is viewed as an exceptionally valuable contribution to the successful running and effective functioning of an organization."

"An in-depth understanding of how transformational leadership style is related to seldom utilize Organizational Citizenship Behaviour Organization (OCBO) & Organizational Citizenship Behaviour Individual (OCBI) behaviors is missing in observational research."

"Organizations are lacking in the spirituality of employees and in providing a meaningful work environment to their human resources that results in high turnover intentions and inadequate organizational performance."

"This study aims to assess whether workplace spirituality has an intervening influence on the relationship between transformational leadership and OCB."

"This research attempts to examine the association between transformational leadership and OCB of academicians working in higher educational institutions of Pakistan."

Research Model and Hypotheses Development

"The research model is developed based on five constructs: (1) Transformational leadership, (2) Workplace spirituality, (3) Emotional Intelligence, (4) Organizational Citizenship Behaviour—Organization (OCBO), and (5) Organizational Citizenship Behaviour—Individual (OCBI)."

"The relationship between transformational leadership and Organizational Citizenship Behaviour (OCBO) is mediated by workplace spirituality."

"The relationship between transformational leadership and Organizational Citizenship Behaviour (OCBI) is mediated by workplace spirituality."

"Leaders' emotional intelligence, Organizational Citizenship Behaviour (OCB), and leadership style, all these acts as a central role in the success of the organization."

"The following hypothesis will examine the relationship between transformational leadership, emotional intelligence and Organizational Citizenship Behaviours (OCBO and OCBI)."

"Transformational leadership is positively associated with Emotional Intelligence."

"The relationship between transformational leadership and Organizational Citizenship Behaviour (OCBO) is mediated by emotional intelligence."

"The relationship between transformational leadership and Organizational Citizenship Behaviour (OCBI) is mediated by emotional intelligence."

Research Methodology

"The questionnaire utilized for this research study consisted of 68 items and contained five sections."

"The scale comprised of 20 items related to behavioral aspects of transformational leadership."

"OCB behaviors were measured in the third section through a scale developed by Lee and Allen [185]."

"Lee and Allen [185] constructed a scale designed to operationalize OCBI and OCBO.OCBO and OCBI were assessed utilizing the scale comprised of 16 items."

"This study utilized McKee and others [186] 16 item scale comprised of three dimensions that were developed for assessing workplace spirituality."

"The unit of analysis is individual (academicians), as this study aimed at the collection of data from academicians who are employed permanently in public sector universities of Pakistan."

"Through ordering of questions and careful selection of items from well-developed scales, measurement error was addressed along with significant consideration being given to the validity and reliability of the instrument."

Data Analysis

"Numerous evaluations were conducted on the structural model by evaluating the path coefficients, coefficients of determination (R^2), mediation analysis, effect size (f^2), and examining the goodness of fit of the model (GoF)."

"The dominant types of research in business and social sciences recently are utilizing multi-group analysis with higher-order constructs for which PLS-Path Modelling can be of significant value (Ciavolino & others [187])."

"In the PLS path model, a situation in which a mediating variable to some extent absorbs the effect of an exogenous on an endogenous construct represents mediation (Hair & others [188])."

"In the PLS path model, a situation in which a mediating variable to some extent absorbs the effect of an exogenous on an endogenous construct represents mediation (Hair & others [188])."

"Utilizing the path coefficients when the mediator is included in the model, the significance of the indirect effect and associated T-values are checked."

Discussion

"The result of this study showed that there was a positive and significant relationship between employees' spirituality in the workplace and Organizational Citizenship Behaviour (OCBO and OCBI) of the teachers working in public sector universities of Pakistan."

"The findings of this study support the argument of Shekari (2014) which reveals that workplace spirituality is positively associated with OCB backing the concept that a higher level of workplace spirituality will prompt better execution in the performance of citizenship behaviors."

"The findings of this study relationship between workplace spirituality and organizational citizenship behavior are confirmed by the argument of prior studies (Afsar & others [183]; Majeed & others [184])."

"Consistent with these studies, the findings of this study support the argument that there is a significant positive relationship between transformational leadership and emotional intelligence."

"This study finding has shown emotional intelligence as a mediator between transformational leadership and OCBO, however, emotional intelligence does not mediate the relationship between TL and OCBI."

Future Research Directions

"Future research utilizing a longitudinal approach should be considered for deeper insight more profound knowledge of the subject, and a more clear decision about the causal impact of every variable."

"To accomplish the objectives of the research quota sampling technique is employed."

"A random sampling technique to increase the generalizability of the finding of the research is recommended for future research."

"This research has broadened learning and has played a valuable role in extending knowledge through which transformational leadership expands a person's OCB."

Implications for Theory and Practice

"Leaders should recognize that to enhance the OCB of employees and promote workplace spirituality to a higher level, demonstration of transformational leadership style and emotional intelligence is essential."

"The integrated research model offers a theoretical lens to understand how transformational leadership can increase the citizenship behaviors of the faculty members of higher education institutions."

"In literature, a little consideration is shown towards modeling workplace spirituality and emotional intelligence as mediators of the relationship between transformational leadership and OCB behaviors."

"University managers ought to understand that to nurture OCBO and OCBI to the increased level, display of leadership style, walk the talk approach, efforts in making the workplace a spiritual workplace and emotional intelligence is crucial."

Conclusion

"The findings of this study provide empirical evidence for the significant influence of workplace spirituality and emotional intelligence on the relationship between transformational leadership and OCB."

"The study findings approve the influence of workplace spirituality and emotional intelligence on the relationship between transformational leadership and OCB."

"This research has broadened learning and has played a valuable role in extending knowledge through which transformational leadership expands a person's OCB."

"The study concludes by synthesizing theories of social exchange and transformational leadership and that transformational leadership, workplace spirituality, and emotional intelligence maximizes the organizational citizenship behaviors of academicians in higher education institutions."

Bibliography

1. Hannah, S. T., & Avolio, B. J. (2013). *Leader efficacy questionnaire.* Mind Garden.
2. Siegling, A. B., Nielsen, C., & Petrides, K. V. (2014). Trait emotional intelligence and leadership in a European multinational company. *Personality and Individual Differences, 65*(2014), 65–68.
3. Ramchunder, Y. & Martins, N. (2014). The role of self-efficacy, emotional intelligence and leadership style as attributes of leadership effectiveness. *SA Journal of Industrial Psychology/ SA Tydsrif vir Bedryfsielkunde, 40*(1), Art., #1100, 11 pages. https://doi.org/10.4101/sajipp.v40i1100
4. Sarkhosh, M., & Rezaee, A. A. (2014). *How does university teachers' emotional intelligence relate to self-efficacy beliefs?* University of Tehran.
5. Jehn, K. A. (1997). A qualitative analysis of conflict types and dimensions in organizational groups. *Administrative Science Quarterly, 42*, 530–557.
6. Pearson, A., Ensley, M. D., & Amason, A. C. (2002). An assessment and refinement of Jehn's intragroup conflict scale. *International Journal of Conflict Management, 13*(2), 110–126.
7. Dunbar, R., & Ahlstrom, D. (1995). Seeking the institutional balance of power: Avoiding the power of a balanced view. *Academy of Management Review, 20*(1), 171–192.
8. Li, Y., Ashkanasy, N. M., & Ahlstrom, D. (2010). Complexity theory and affect structure: A dynamic approach to modeling emotional changes in organizations. In W. J. Zerbe, C. E. J. Härtel, & N. M. Ashkanasy (Eds.). *Research on emotion in organizations* (vol. 6, pp. 139–165). Emerald Group.
9. Tugade, M. M., & Fredrickson, B. L. (2004). Emotions: Positive emotions and health. In N. Anderson (Ed.), *Encyclopedia of health and behavior* (pp. 306–310). Sage.
10. Hayes, A. F. (2018). *Introduction to mediation, moderation, and conditional process analysis: A regression-based approach* (2nd ed.). Guilford Press.
11. Johnson, P. O., & Neyman, J. (1936). Tests of certain linear hypotheses and their application to some educational problems. *Statistical Research Memoirs, 1*, 57–93.
12. Zaccaro, S. J., Gilbert, J. A., Thor, K. H., & Mumford, M. D. (1991). Leadership and social intelligence: Linking social perspectiveness and behavioral flexibility to leader effectiveness. *The Leadership Quarterly, 2*(4), 317–342.
13. Zaccaro, S. J., & Torres, E. M. (2020). Leader social acuity. In M. D. Mumford, & C. A. Higgs (Eds.), *Leader Thinking skills: Capacities for contemporary leadership.* Routledge.
14. Ayman, R., Chemers, M. M., & Fiedler, F. (1995). The contingency model of leadership effectiveness: Its levels of analysis. *The Leadership Quarterly, 6*(2), 147–167.
15. Iacovou, C. L., & Dexter, A. S. (2004). Turning around runaway information technology projects. *California Management Review, 46*(4), 68–88.
16. Podsakoff, P. M., MacKenzie, S. B., & Bommer, W. H. (1996). Transformational leader behaviors and substitutes for leadership as determinants of employee satisfaction, commitment, trust, and organizational citizenship behaviors. *Journal of Management, 22*(2), 259–298. https://doi.org/10.1016/S0149-2063(96)90049-5
17. Pearson, C. M., & Clair, J. A. (1998). Reframing crisis management. *Academy of Management Review, 23*(1), 59–76. https://doi.org/10.2307/259099
18. Weick, K. E. (1993). The collapse of sensemaking in organizations: The Mann Gulch disaster. *Administrative Science Quarterly, 38*(4), 628–652. https://doi.org/10.2307/2393339
19. Lengnick-Hall, C. A., Beck, T. E., & Lengnick-Hall, M. L. (2011). Developing a capacity for organizational resilience through strategic human resource management. *Human Resource Management Review, 21*(3), 243–255. https://doi.org/10.1016/j.hrmr.2010.07.001
20. Riolli, L., & Savicki, V. (2003). Information system organizational resilience. *Omega, 31*(3), 227–233. https://doi.org/10.1016/S0305-0483(03)00023-9
21. Horne, J. F., III., & Orr, J. E. (1998). Assessing behaviors that create resilient organizations. *Employment Relations Today, 24*(4), 29–39.
22. Mallak, L. A. (1998). Measuring resilience in health care provider organizations. *Health Manpower Management, 24*(4), 148–152. https://doi.org/10.1108/09552069810215755

23. McCann, J. E., & Selsky, J. W. (2012). *Mastering turbulence: The essential capabilities of agile and resilient individuals, teams, and organizations* (1st ed.). Jossey-Bass.
24. Shin, J., Taylor, S. M., & Seo, M.-G. (2012). Resources for change: The relationships of organizational inducements and psychological resilience to employees' attitudes and behaviors toward organizational change. *Academy of Management Journal, 55*(3), 727–748. https://doi.org/10.5465/amj.2010.0325
25. Williams, T. A., Gruber, D. A., Sutcliffe, K. M., Shepherd, D. A., & Zaho, E. Y. (2017). Organizational response to adversity: Fusing crisis leadership and resilience research streams. *Academy of Management Annals, 11*(2), 733–769. https://doi.org/10.5465/annals.2015.0134
26. Carmeli, A., Friedman, Y., & Tishler, A. (2013). Cultivating a resilient top leadership team: The importance of relational connections and strategic decision comprehensiveness. *Safety Science, 51*(1), 148–159. https://doi.org/10.1016/j.ssci.2012.06.002
27. Avey, J. B., Avolio, B. J., & Luthans, F. (2011). Experimentally analyzing the impact of leader positivity on follower positivity and performance. *The Leadership Quarterly, 22*(2), 282–294. https://doi.org/10.1016/j.leaqua.2011.02.004
28. Gooty, J., Gavin, M. B., Johnson, P., & Lance Frazier, M. (2009). In the eyes of the beholder: Transformational leadership, positive psychological capital, and performance. *Journal of Leadership & Organizational Studies, 15*(4), 353–367. https://doi.org/10.1177/1548051809332021
29. Walumbwa, F. O., Peterson, S. J., Avolio, B. J., & Hartnell, C. A. (2010). An investigation of the relationships among leader and follower psychological capital, service climate, and job performance. *Personnel Psychology, 63*(4), 937–963. https://doi.org/10.1111/j.1744-6570.2010.01193.x
30. Harland, L., Harrison, W., Jones, J. R., & Reiter-Palmon, R. (2005). Leadership behaviors and subordinate resilience. *Journal of Leadership & Organizational Studies, 11*(2), 2–14. https://doi.org/10.1177/107179190501100202
31. Rego, A., Sousa, F., Marques, C., & Cunha, M. P. E. (2012). Authentic leadership promoting employees' psychological capital and creativity. *Journal of Business Research, 65*(3), 429–437.
32. Samba, C., Vera Dusya, T., Dejun, K., & Maldonado, T. (2017). Organizational resilience and positive leadership: An integrative framework. *Academy of Management Proceedings, 2017*(1), 11903. https://doi.org/10.5465/AMBPP.2017.11903abstract
33. Norman, S., Luthans, B., & Luthans, K. (2005). The proposed contagion effect of hopeful leaders on the resiliency of employees and organizations. *Journal of Leadership & Organizational Studies, 12*(2), 56–64. https://doi.org/10.1177/107179190501200205
34. Sutcliffe, K. M., Paine, L., & Pronovost, P. J. (2017). Re-examining high reliability: Actively organising for safety. *BMJ Quality & Safety, 26*(3), 248–251. https://doi.org/10.1136/bmjqs-2015-004698
35. Wickert, C., & de Bakker, F. G. A. (2018). Pitching for social change: Toward a relational approach to selling and buying social issues. *Academy of Management Discoveries, 4*(1), 50–73. https://doi.org/10.5465/amd.2015.0009
36. Carmine, S., Andriopoulos, C., Gotsi, M., Härtel, C. E. J., Krzeminska, A., Mafico, N., Pradies, C., Raza, H., Raza-Ullah, T., Schrage, S., Sharma, G., Slawinski, N., Stadtler, L., Tunarosa, A., Winther-Hansen, C., & Keller, J. (2021). A paradox approach to organizational tensions during the pandemic crisis. *Journal of leadership inquiry, 30*(2), 138–153. https://doi.org/10.1177/1056492620986863
37. Jay, J. (2013). Navigating paradox as a mechanism of change and innovation in hybrid organizations. *Academy of Management Journal, 56*(1), 137–159. https://doi.org/10.5465/amj.2010.0772
38. Luscher, L. S., & Lewis, M. W. (2008). Organizational change and managerial sensemaking: Working through paradox. *Academy of Management Journal, 51*(2), 221–240. https://doi.org/10.5465/amj.2008.31767217
39. Smith, W. K., & Tracey, P. (2016). Institutional complexity and paradox theory: Complementarities of competing demands. *Strategic Organization, 14*(4), 455–466. https://doi.org/10.1177/1476127016638565

40. Giustiniano, L., Cunha, M. P., Simpson, A. V., & Rego, A. (2020). Resilient leadership as paradox work: Notes from COVID-19. *Management and Organization Review, 16*(5), 971–975. https://doi.org/10.1017/mor.2020.57
41. Boin, A., Kuipers, S., & Overdijk, W. (2013). Leadership in times of crisis: A framework for assessment. *International Review of Public Administration, 18*(1), 79–91. https://doi.org/10.1080/12294659.2013.10805241
42. Gittell, J. H., Cameron, K., Lim, S., & Rivas, V. (2006). Relationships, layoffs, and organizational resilience: Airline industry responses to September 11. *The Journal of Applied Behavioral Science, 42*(3), 300–329. https://doi.org/10.1177/0021886306286466
43. Mafabi, S., Munene, J. C., & Ahiauzu, A. (2015). Creative climate and organisational resilience: The mediating role of innovation. *International Journal of Organizational Analysis, 23*(4), 564–587. https://doi.org/10.1108/IJOA-07-2012-0596
44. Gilly, J.-P., Kechidi, M., & Talbot, D. (2014). Resilience of organisations and territories: The role of pivot firms. *European Management Journal, 32*(4), 596–602. https://doi.org/10.1016/j.emj.2013.09.004
45. Wu, L. L., Bo, S., Newman, A., & Schwarz, G. (2021). Crisis leadership: A review and future research agenda. *The Leadership Quarterly, 32*(6), 1–22. https://doi.org/10.1016/j.leaqua.2021.101518
46. James, E. H., Wooten, L. P., & Dushek, K. (2011). Crisis management: Informing a new leadership research agenda. *Academy of Management Annals, 5*(1), 455–493. https://doi.org/10.5465/19416520.2011.589594
47. Peltokorpi, V. (2018). Abusive supervision and emotional exhaustion: The moderating role of power distance orientation and the mediating role of interaction avoidance. *Asia Pacific Journal of Human Resources*. https://doi.org/10.1111/1744-7941.12188
48. Pradhan, S., & Jena, L. K. (2017). Effect of abusive supervision on employee's intention to quit and the neutralizing role of meaningful work in Indian IT organizations. *International Journal of Organizational Analysis, 25*(5), 825–838.
49. Tepper, B. J., Simon, L., & Park, H. M. (2017). Abusive supervision. *Annual Review of Organizational Psychology and Organizational Behavior, 4*, 123–152.
50. Wu, T. Y., & Hu, C. (2009). Abusive supervision and employee emotional exhaustion: Dispositional antecedents and boundaries. *Group & Organization Management, 34*(2), 143–169.
51. Tepper, B. J. (2000). Consequences of abusive supervision. *Academy of Management Journal, 43*, 178–190.
52. Saeed, I., Waseem, M., Sikander, S., & Rizwan, M. (2014). The relationship of turnover intention with job satisfaction, job performance, leader member exchange, emotional intelligence and organizational commitment. *International Journal of Learning and Development, 4*(2), 242–256.
53. Brockner, J. (1988). *Self-esteem at work: Research, theory, and practice*. Lexington Books.
54. Pierce, J. L., Gardner, D. G., Cummings, L. L., & Dunham, R. B. (1989). Organization-based self-esteem: Construct definition, measurement, and validation. *Academy of Management Journal, 32*(3), 622–648.
55. Kelloway, E. K., Gottlieb, B. H., & Barham, L. (1999). The source, nature, and direction of work and family conflict: A longitudinal investigation. *Journal of Occupational Health Psychology, 4*(4), 337–346.
56. Saleem, S., Yusaf, S., Sarwar, N., Raziq, M. M., & Malik, O. F. (2018). Linking abusive supervision to psychological distress and turnover intentions among police personnel: The moderating role of continuance commitment. *Journal of Interpersonal Violence*. https://doi.org/10.1177/0886260518791592
57. Lee, T. W., Mitchell, T. R., Wise, L., & Fireman, S. (1996). An unfolding model of voluntary employee turnover. *Academy of Management Journal, 39*, 5–36.
58. Gong, Y., Huang, J., & Farh, J. (2009). Employee learning orientation, transformational leadership, and employee creativity: The mediating role of employee creative self-efficacy. *Academy of Management Journal, 52*(4), 765–778.

59. Arnold, K. A., Turner, N., Barling, J., Kelloway, E. K., & McKee, M. C. (2007). Transformational leadership and psychological well-being: The mediating role of meaningful work. *Journal of Occupational Health Psychology, 12*(3), 193–203.
60. Densten, I. L. (2005). The relationship between visioning behaviors of leaders and follower burnout. *British Journal of Management, 16*(2), 105–118.
61. Sivanathan, N., Arnold, K. A., Turner, N., & Barling, J. (2004). Leading well: Transformational leadership and well-being. In A. Linley & S. Joseph (Eds.), *Positive psychology in practice* (pp. 241–255). Wiley.
62. Seltzer, J., Numerof, R. E., & Bass, B. M. (1989). Transformational leadership: Is it a source of more or less burnout or stress? *Journal of Health and Human Resources Administration, 12*, 174–185.
63. Reuvers, M., van Engen, M. L., Vinkenburg, C. J., & Wilson-Evered, E. (2008). Transformational leadership and innovative work behavior: Exploring the relevance of gender differences. *Creativity and Innovation Management, 17*, 227–244.
64. Hater, J., & Bass, B. M. (1988). Superiors' evaluations and subordinates' perceptions of transformational and transactional leadership. *Journal of Applied Psychology, 73*, 695–702.
65. Bass, B. M., & Avolio, B. J. (1990). *Transformational leadership development: Manual for the Multifactor Leadership Questionnaire*. Consulting Psychologist Press.
66. Dutton, J. E. (2003). *Energize your workplace: How to build and sustain high-quality connections at work*. Jossey-Bass Publishers.
67. Dutton, J. E., & Heaphy, E. D. (2003). The power of high-quality relationships at work. In K. S. Cameron, J. E. Dutton, & R. E. Quinn (Eds.), *Positive organizational scholarship* (pp. 263–278). Berrett-Koehler Publishers.
68. Quinn, R. W., & Dutton, J. E. (2005). Coordination as energy-in-conversation. *Academy of Management Review, 30*, 36–57.
69. Siu, O. L., Spector, P. E., & Cooper, C. L. (2006). A three-phase study to develop and validate a Chinese coping strategies scale in Greater China. *Personality and Individual Differences, 41*(3), 537–548.
70. Siu, O. L., Lu, C. Q., & Spector, P. E. (2007). Employees' well-being in Greater China: The direct and moderating effects of general self-efficacy. *Applied Psychology: An International Review, 56*(2), 288–301.
71. Hmieleski, K. M., Cole, M. S., & Baron, R. A. (2012). Shared authentic leadership and new venture performance. *Journal of Management, 38*(5), 1476–1499.
72. Ling, Y., Simsek, Z., Lubatkin, M. H., & Veiga, J. F. (2008). Transformational leadership's role in promoting corporate entrepreneurship: Examining the CEO-TMT interface. *Academy of Management Journal, 51*(3), 557–576.
73. Wei, L., & Ling, Y. (2015). CEO characteristics and corporate entrepreneurship in transition economies: Evidence from China. *Journal of Business Research, 68*, 1157–1165.
74. Bandura, A. (1986). *Social foundations of thought and action*. Prentice-Hall.
75. Klotz, A. C., Hmieleski, K. M., Bradley, B. H., & Busenitz, L. W. (2014). New venture teams: A review of the literature and roadmap for future research. *Journal of Management, 40*(1), 226–255.
76. Moss SE, Song M, Hannah ST, Wang Z, Sumanth JJ (2019) The duty to improve oneself: How duty orientation mediates the relationship between ethical leadership and followers' feedback-seeking and feedback-avoiding behavior. *Journal of Business Ethics*, 1–17
77. Qin, P., & Liu, Y. (2019). The empirical research of the influence of leadership positive emotion on counterproductive work behavior. *Psychology, 10*(6), 877–902. https://doi.org/10.4236/psych.2019.106057
78. Park, I. J., Shim, S. H., Hai, S., et al. (2021). Cool down emotion, don't be fickle! The role of paradoxical leadership in the relationship between emotional stability and creativity. *International Journal of Human Resource Management*. https://doi.org/10.1080/09585192.2021.1891115
79. Al-Sada, M., Al-Esmael, B., & Faisal, M. N. (2017). Influence of organizational culture and leadership style on employee satisfaction, commitment and motivation in the educational

sector in Qatar. *EuroMed Journal of Business, 12*(2), 163–188. https://doi.org/10.1108/EMJB-02-2016-0003
80. Deci, E. L., & Ryan, R. M. (1985). The general causality orientations scale: Self-determination in personality. *Journal of Research in Personality, 19*(2), 109–134. https://doi.org/10.1016/0092-6566(85)90023-6
81. Putra, E. D., Cho, S., & Liu, J. (2017). Extrinsic and intrinsic motivation on work engagement in the hospitality industry: Test of motivation crowding theory. *Tourism and Hospitality Research, 17*(2), 228–241. https://doi.org/10.1177/1467358415613393
82. Kaplan, S., Cortina, J., Ruark, G., et al. (2014). The role of organizational leaders in employee emotion management: A theoretical model. *The Leadership Quarterly, 25*(3), 563–580. https://doi.org/10.1016/j.leaqua.2013.11.015
83. Martela, F., Gómez, M., Unanue, W., et al. (2021). What makes work meaningful? Longitudinal evidence for the importance of autonomy and beneficence for meaningful work. *Journal of Vocational Behavior, 131*, 103631–103645. https://doi.org/10.1016/j.jvb.2021.103631
84. Toegel, G., Kilduff, M., & Anand, N. (2013). Emotion helping by managers: An emergent understanding of discrepant role expectations and outcomes. *Academy of Management Journal, 56*(2), 334–357. https://doi.org/10.5465/amj.2010.0512
85. Farh, J. L., Earley, P. C., & Lin, S. C. (1997). Impetus for action: A cultural analysis of justice and organizational citizenship behavior in Chinese society. *Administrative Science Quarterly, 42*(3), 421–444.
86. Spreitzer, G., Porath, C. L., & Gibson, C. B. (2012). Toward human sustainability: How to enable more thriving at work. *Organizational Dynamics, 41*(2), 155–162. https://doi.org/10.1016/j.orgdyn.2012.01.009
87. Hackman, J. R., & Oldham, G. R. (1974). The job diagnostic survey: An instrument for the diagnosis of jobs and the evaluation of job redesign projects. Technical Report No. 4. Department of Administrative Sciences, Yale University.
88. Hackman, J. R., & Oldham, G. R. (1975). Development of job diagnostic survey. *Journal of Applied Psychology, 60*(2), 159–170. https://doi.org/10.1037/h0076546
89. Porath, C., Spreitzer, G., Gibson, C., & Garnett, F. G. (2012). Thriving at work: Toward its measurement, construct validation, and theoretical refinement. *Journal of Organizational Behavior, 33*(2), 250–275. https://doi.org/10.1002/job.756
90. Liang, J., Farh, C. I. C., & Farh, J. L. (2012). Psychological antecedents of promotive and prohibitive voice: A two-wave examination. *Academy of Management Journal, 55*(1), 71–92.
91. Li, C. W., Liang, J., & Farh, J. L. (2020). Speaking up when water is murky: An uncertainty-based model linking perceived organizational politics to employee voice. *Journal of Management, 46*(3), 443–469. https://doi.org/10.1177/0149206318798025
92. Hayes, A. F. (2013). *Introduction to mediation, moderation, and conditional process analysis: a regression-based approach*. Guilford Publications.
93. Lim, H. W., Li, N., Fang, D. P., & Wu, C. L. (2018). Impact of safety climate on types of safety motivation and performance: Multigroup invariance analysis. *Journal of Management in Engineering, 34*(3), 04018002. https://doi.org/10.1061/(asce)me.1943-5479.0000595
94. Gagné, M., & Deci, E. (2005). Self determination theory and work motivation. *Journal of Organizational Behavior, 26*(4), 331–362.
95. Ashford, S. J., Lee, C., & Bobko, P. (1989). Content, causes, and consequences of job insecurity: A theory-based measure and substantive test. *Academy of Management Journal, 4*, 803–829.
96. Lee, C., Bobko, P., Ashford, S., Chen, Z. X., & Ren, X. (2008). Cross-cultural development of an abridged job insecurity measure. *Journal of Organizational Behavior, 29*, 373–390.
97. Lee, C., Bobko, P., & Chen, Z. X. (2006). Investigation of the multidimensional model of job insecurity in two countries. *Applied Psychology: An International Review, 55*, 167–195.
98. Kinnunen, U., Mauno, S., Nätti, J., & Happonen, M. (2000). Organizational antecedents and outcomes of job insecurity: A longitudinal study in three organizations in Finland. *Journal of Organizational Behavior, 21*, 443–459.

99. Rosenblatt, Z., & Ruvio, A. (1996). A test of a multidimensional model of job insecurity: The case of Israeli teachers. *Journal of Organizational Behavior, 17*, 587–605.
100. Wong, C. S., Law, K. S., & Wong, P. M. (2004). Development and validation of a forced choice emotional intelligence for Chinese respondents in Hong Kong. *Asia Pacific Journal of Management, 21*(4), 535–559.
101. Wong, C. S., Wong, P. M., & Law, K. S. (2007). Evidence on the practical utility of Wong's emotional intelligence scale in Hong Kong and Mainland China. *Asia Pacific Journal of Management, 24*(1), 43–60.
102. Mowday, R. T., Steers, R. M., & Porter, L. W. (1979). The measurement of organizational commitment. *Journal of Vocational Behavior, 14*(2), 224–247. https://doi.org/10.1016/0001-8791(79)90072-1
103. Jöreskog, K., & Sörbom, D. (2001). *LISREL 8.5.* Scientific Software International.
104. Lim, V. K. G. (1996). Job insecurity and its outcomes: Moderating effects of work-based and nonwork-based social support. *Human Relations, 2*, 171–194.
105. Lim, V. K. G. (1997). Moderating effects of work-based support on the relationship between job insecurity and its consequences. *Work and Stress, 11*, 251–266.
106. Sverke, M., Chaison, G. N., & Sjöberg, A. (2004). Do union mergers affect the members? Short- and long-term effects on attitudes and behavior. *Economic and Industrial Democracy, 25*, 103–124.
107. Dorfman, P. W., & Howell, J. P. (1988). Dimensions of national culture and effective leadership patterns: Hofstede revisited. In E. G. McGoun (Ed.), *Advances in international comparative management, 3* (pp. 127–149). JAI Press.
108. Liden, R. C. (2012). Leadership research in Asia: A brief assessment and suggestions for the future. *Asia Pacific Journal of Management.* https://doi.org/10.1007/s10490-011-9276-2
109. Avolio, B. J., Bass, B. M., & Jung, D. I. (1999). Re-examining the components of transformational and transactional leadership using the multifactor leadership. *Journal of Occupational & Organizational Psychology, 72*(4), 441–462.
110. Waldman, D. A., & Bass, B. M. (1991). Transformational leadership at different phases of the innovation process. *Journal of High Technology Management Research, 2*, 169–180.
111. Iles, P. (2001). Leadership and leadership development: Time for a new direction? *British Journal of Administrative Management, 27*, 22–23.
112. Nelson, B. (2001). *Please don't just do what I tell you, do what needs to be done: Every employee's guide to making work more rewarding.* Hyperion.
113. James, L. R., Demaree, R. G., & Wolf, G. (1984). Estimating within-group interrater reliability with and without response bias. *Journal of Applied Psychology, 69*(1), 85–98.
114. Howell, J. M., & Avolio, B. J. (1993). Transformational leadership, transactional leadership, locus of control, and support for innovation: Key predictors of consolidated-business-unit performance. *Journal of Applied Psychology, 78*(6), 891–902.
115. Jung, D., Wu, A., & Chow, C. (2008). Towards understanding the direct and indirect effects of CEO's transformational leadership on firm innovation. *Leadership Quarterly, 19*, 582–594.
116. Damanpour, F. (1991). Organizational innovation: A meta-analysis of effects of determinants and moderators. *Academy of Management Journal, 34*(3), 555–590.
117. Elenkov, D., Judge, W., & Wright, P. (2005). Strategic leadership and executive innovation influence: An international multi-cluster comparative study. *Strategic Management Journal, 26*, 665–682.
118. Gumusluoglu, L., & Ilsev, A. (2009). Transformational leadership and organizational innovation: The roles of internal and external support for innovation. *Journal of Product Innovation Management, 26*, 264–277.
119. Jung, D., Chow, C., & Wu, A. (2003). The role of transformational leadership in enhancing organizational innovation: Hypotheses and some preliminary findings. *Leadership Quarterly, 14*, 525–544.
120. Pawar, B. S., & Eastman, K. K. (1997). The nature and implications of contextual influences on transformational leadership: A conceptual examination. *Academy of Management Review, 22*, 80–109.

121. Xenikou, A., & Simosi, M. (2006). Organizational culture and transformational leadership as predictor of business unit performance. *Journal of Managerial Psychology, 21*(6), 566–579.
122. Ma, H., Lang, C., Liu, Y., & Gao, Y. (2020). Constructing a hierarchical framework for assessing the application of big data technology in entrepreneurship education. *Frontiers in Psychology, 11*, 551389.
123. Raby, R. L., Fischer, H., & Cruz, N. I. (2023). Community college international leaders' sensemaking: Entrepreneurial leadership skills and behavior. *Community College Review, 51*(1), 52–74.
124. Bass, B. M. (1999). Two decades of research and development in transformational leadership. *European Journal of Work & Organizational Psychology, 8*(1), 9–32.
125. Wijen, F., & Ansari, S. (2007). Overcoming inaction through collective institutional entrepreneurship: Insights from regime theory. *Organization Studies, 28*(7), 1079–1100.
126. Brodnik, C., & Brown, R. (2018). Strategies for developing transformative capacity in urban water management sectors: The case of Melbourne, Australia. *Technological Forecasting and Social Change, 137*, 147–159.
127. Mom, T. J. M., van den Bosch, F. A. J., & Volberda, H. W. (2009). Understanding variation in managers' ambidexterity: Investigating direct and interaction effects of formal structural and personal coordination mechanisms. *Organization Science, 20*(4), 812–828.
128. Rogan, M., & Mors, M. L. (2014). A network perspective on individual-level ambidexterity in organizations. *Organization Science, 25*(6), 1860–1877.
129. Cabeza-Pullés, D., Fernández-Pérez, V., & Roldán-Bravo, M. I. (2020). Internal networking and innovation ambidexterity: The mediating role of knowledge management processes in university research. *European Management Journal, 38*(3), 450–461.
130. Brass, D. J. (2022). New developments in social network analysis. *Annual Review of Organizational Psychology and Organizational Behavior, 9*, 225–246.
131. Bandura, A. (1986). *Social foundations of thought & action: A social cognitive theory*. Prentice Hall.
132. Freeman, L. C. (1979). Centrality in social networks conceptual clarification. *Social Networks, 1*(3), 215–239.
133. Mishra, A. K. (1996). Organizational responses to crisis: The centrality of trust. In K. M. Roderick & T. Thomas (Eds.), *Trust in organizations* (pp. 261–281). Sage.
134. Borgatti, S. P., Everett, M. G., & Freeman, L. C. (2002). *UCINET for windows: Software for social network analysis*.
135. Tempelaar, M. P., & Rosenkranz, N. A. (2019). Switching hats: The effect of role transition on individual ambidexterity. *Journal of Management, 45*(4), 1517–1539.
136. Dirks, K. T., & Ferrin, D. L. (2002). Trust in leadership: Meta-analytic findings and implications for research and practice. *Journal of Applied Psychology, 87*(4), 611–628.
137. Lahtinen, J. (2017). What is pedagogical leadership? http://learningscoop.fi/what-is-pedagogical-leadership/
138. Greenleaf, R. K. (1977). *Servant leadership: A journey into the nature of legitimate power and greatness*. Paulist Press.
139. Blake, R. R., & Mouton, J. S. (1964). *The new managerial grid: Strategic new insights into a proven system for increasing organization productivity and individual effectiveness, plus a revealing examination of how your managerial style can affect your mental and physical health*. Gulf Publishing.
140. Steward, J. B. (2018). A question for Tesla's board: What was Elon Musk's mental state? https://www.nytimes.com/2018/08/15/business/elon-musk-tesla-board.html
141. Katz, R. L. (2009). *Skills of an effective administrator*. Harvard Business Review Press.
142. Wu, J. B., Tsui, A. S., & Kinicki, A. J. (2010). Consequences of differentiated leadership in groups. *Academy of Management Journal, 53*(1), 90–106.
143. Dorfman, P., Javidan, M., Hanges, P., Dastmalchian, A., & House, R. (2012). GLOBE: A twenty-year journey into the intriguing world of culture and leadership. *Journal of World Business, 47*(4), 504–518.

144. Crede, M., Jong, J., & Harms, P. (2019). The generalizability of transformational leadership across cultures: A meta-analysis. *Journal of Managerial Psychology, 34*(3), 139–155.
145. Jackson, T. A., Meyer, J. P., & Wang, X. H. (2013). Leadership, commitment, and culture: A meta-analysis. *Journal of Leadership & Organizational Studies, 20*(1), 84–106.
146. Watts, L. L., Steele, L. M., & Den Hartog, D. N. (2020). Uncertainty avoidance moderates the relationship between transformational leadership and innovation: A meta-analysis. *Journal of International Business Studies, 51*(1), 138–145.
147. Bass, B. M. (1985). *Leadership and performance beyond expectations*. Free Press.
148. Antonakis, J. (2012). Transformational and charismatic leadership. In D. V. Day & J. Antonakis (Eds.), *The nature of leadership* (2nd ed., pp. 256–288). Sage Publications.
149. Avolio, B. J., Bass, B. M., & Jung, D. I. (1995). *MLQ Multifactor leadership questionnaire: Technical report*. Mindgarden.
150. Dorfman, P. W. (1996). International and cross-cultural leadership research. In B. J. Punnett & O. Shenkar (Eds.), *Handbook for international management research* (pp. 267–349). University of Michigan Press.
151. Stackhouse, M., Kirkman, B., Steel, P., & Taras, V. (2018). National culture and leadership. In N. Anderson, D. S. Ones, H. K. Sinangil, & C. Viswesveran (Eds.), *Handbook of industrial, work & organizational psychology* (vol. 3, 2nd ed., pp. 206–236). Sage.
152. Taras, V., Kirkman, B. L., & Steel, P. (2010). Examining the impact of culture's consequences: A three-decade, multilevel, meta-analytic review of Hofstede's cultural value dimensions. *Journal of Applied Psychology, 95*, 405–439.
153. House, R. J., Wright, N. S., & Aditya, R. N. (1997). Cross-cultural research on organizational leadership: A critical analysis and a proposed theory. In P. C. Earley & M. Erez (Eds.), *New perspectives on international industrial/organizational psychology* (pp. 535–625). The New Lexington Press/Jossey-Bass Publishers.
154. Brown, M. E., & Trevino, L. K. (2006). Ethical leadership: A review and future directions. *Leadership Quarterly, 17*(6), 595–616.
155. Bandura, A. (1977). *Social learning theory*. Prentice-Hall.
156. Bandura, A. (1986). *Social foundations of thought and action: A social cognitive theory*. Prentice-Hall.
157. Umphress, E. E., & Bingham, J. B. (2011). When employees do bad things for good reasons: Examining unethical pro-organizational behaviors. *Organization Science, 22*, 621–640.
158. Umphress, E. E., Bingham, J. B., & Mitchell, M. S. (2010). Unethical behavior in the name of the company: The moderating effect of organizational identification and positive reciprocity beliefs influencing unethical pro-organizational behavior. *Journal of Applied Psychology, 95*, 769–780.
159. Walumbwa, F. O., Mayer, D. M., Wang, P., Wang, H., Workman, K., & Christensen, A. (2011). Linking ethical leadership to employee performance: The roles of leader-member exchange, self-efficacy, and organizational identification. *Organizational Behavior and Human Decision Processes, 115*(2), 204–213.
160. van Knippenberg, D. (2000). Work motivation and performance: A social identity perspective. *Applied Psychology: An International Review, 49*, 357–371.
161. Aron, A. (2003). Self and close relationships. In M. R. Leary & J. P. Tagney (Eds.), *Handbook of self and identity*. The Guilford Press.
162. van Knippenberg, D., van Knippenberg, B., De Cremer, D., & Hogg, M. A. (2004). Leadership, self, and identity: A review and research agenda. *Leadership Quarterly, 15*(6), 825–856. https://doi.org/10.1016/j.leaqua.2004.09.002
163. Sluss, D. M., & Ashforth, B. E. (2007). Relational identity and identification: Defining ourselves through work relationships. *Academy of Management Review, 32*, 9–32.
164. Sluss, D. M., & Ashforth, B. E. (2008). How relational and organizational identification converge: Processes and conditions. *Organization Science, 19*, 807–823.
165. Brown, M. E., Treviño, L. K., & Harrison, D. A. (2005). Ethical leadership: A social learning perspective for construct development and testing. *Organizational Behavior and Human Decision Processes, 97*(2), 117–213.

166. Treviño, L. K., Butterfield, K. D., & McCabe, D. M. (1998). The ethical context in organizations: Influences on employee attitudes and behaviors. *Business Ethics Quarterly, 8*, 447–476.
167. Mele, D. (2005). Ethical education in accounting: Integrating rules, values and virtues. *Journal of Business Ethics, 57*, 97–109.
168. Mele, D. (2009). *Business ethics in action, seeking human excellence in organizations*. Palgrave Macmillan.
169. Rayner, J., Lawton, A., & Williams, H. M. (2012). Organizational citizenship behavior and the public service ethos: Whither the organization? *Journal of Business Ethics, 106*(2), 117–130.
170. Fatima, M., Shafique, M., Qadeer, F., & Ahmad, R. (2015). HR practices and employee performance relationship in higher education: Mediating role of job embeddedness, perceived organizational support and trust. *Pakistan Journal of Statistics and Operation Research, 11*(3), 421–439.
171. Aksoy, Y., Ayranci, E., & Gozukara, E. (2016). A research on the relationship between knowledge sharing and employee performance: The moderating role of unethical behaviors in organizational level. *European Scientific Journal, 12*(4), 335–352.
172. Yoon, C. (2009). The effects of organizational citizenship behaviors on ERP system success. *Computers in Human Behavior, 25*(2), 421–428.
173. Organ, D. W. (1988). *Organizational citizenship behavior: The good soldier syndrome*. Lexington Books.
174. Armstrong, M. (1994). *Performance management*. Kogan Page Limited.
175. Hinton, P. R. (2004). *Statistics explained* (2nd ed.). Routledge.
176. Geis, F. L. (1968). Machiavellianism in a semireal world. In *Proceedings of the 76th Annual Convention of the American Psychological Association, 3*, 407–408.
177. Dahling, J. J., Kuyumcu, D., & Librizzi, E. H. (2012). Machiavellianism, unethical behavior, and well-being in organizational life. In R. A. Giacalone & M. D. Promislo (Ed.), *Handbook of unethical work behavior: Implications for individual well-being* (1st ed., pp. 183–194). Taylor & Francis. https://doi.org/10.4324/9781315703848
178. Jones, R. E., & White, C. S. (1983). Relationships between machiavellianism, task orientation and team effectiveness. *Psychological Reports, 53*(3), 859–866. https://doi.org/10.2466/pr0.1983.53.3.859
179. Breaugh, J. A. (1999). Further investigation of the work autonomy scales: Two studies. *Journal of Business and Psychology, 13*, 357–373. https://doi.org/10.1023/A:1022926416628
180. Johnson, S. K. (2008). I second that emotion: Effects of emotional contagion and affect at work on leader and follower outcomes. *The Leadership Quarterly, 19*, 1–19.
181. Kamdar, D., & Van Dyne, L. (2007). The joint effects of personality and workplace social exchange relationships in predicting task performance and citizenship performance. *Journal of Applied Psychology, 92*, 1286–1298.
182. Hofmann, D. A. (1997). An overview of the logic and rational of hierarchical linear models. *Journal of Management, 23*, 723–744.
183. Afsar, B., Badir, Y., & Kiani, U. S. (2016). Linking spiritual leadership and employee pro-environmental behavior: The influence of workplace spirituality, intrinsic motivation, and environmental passion. *Journal of Environmental Psychology, 45*, 79–88.
184. Majeed, N., Jamshed, S., Nazri, M., & Mustamil, N. M. (2019). Walk the talk: Bringing spirituality to workplace through transformational leadership and emotional intelligence in higher education institutions. *Jurnal Pengurusan, 56*, 169–182.
185. Lee, K., & Allen, N. J. (2002). Organizational citizenship behavior and workplace deviance: The role of affect and cognitions. *Journal of Applied Psychology, 87*(1), 131–142.
186. McKee, M. C., Driscoll, C., Kelloway, E. K., & Kelley, E. (2011). Exploring linkages among transformational leadership, workplace spirituality and well-being in health care workers. *Journal of Management, Spirituality & Religion, 8*(3), 233–255.
187. Ciavolino, E., Salvatore, S., Mossi, P., & Lagetto, G. (2019). High-order PLS path model for multi-group analysis: The prosumership service quality model. *Quality & Quantity, 53*(5), 2371–2384.

188. Hair, J. F., Jr., Hult, G. T. M., Ringle, C., & Sarstedt, M. (2016). *A primer on partial least squares structural equation modeling (PLS-SEM)*. Sage Publications.
189. Harper, D. S. (2015). Correctional executives' leadership self-efficacy and their perceptions of emotional intelligence. *American Journal of Criminal Justice*. https://doi.org/10.1007/s12103-015-9319-1
190. Li, Y., Chun, H., Ashkanasy, N. M., & Ahlstrom, D. (2012). A multi-level study of emergent group leadership: Effects of emotional stability and group conflict. *Asia Pacific Journal of Management*. https://doi.org/10.1007/s10490-012-9298-4
191. Boyar, S. L., Savage, G. T., & Williams, E. S. (2021). An adaptive leadership approach: The impact of reasoning and emotional intelligence (EI) abilities on leader adaptability. *Employee Responsibilities and Rights Journal*. https://doi.org/10.1007/s10672-022-09428-z
192. Lei, H., Fang, X., Rajkumar, T. M., & Holsapple, C. (2020). Recovering troubled IT projects: The roles of transformational leadership and project complexity. *Information Systems Frontiers*. https://doi.org/10.1007/s10796-020-10068-7
193. Förster, C., Paparella, C., Duchek, S., Güttel, W. H. (2022). Leading in the paradoxical world of crises: How leaders navigate through crises. *Schmalenbach Journal of Business Research*. https://doi.org/10.1007/s41471-022-00147-7
194. Ahmad, I., & Begum, K. (2020). Impact of abusive supervision on intention to leave: A moderated mediation model of organizational-based self esteem and emotional exhaustion. *Asian Business & Management*. https://doi.org/10.1057/s41291-020-00116-0
195. Sharifirad, M. S. (2013). Transformational leadership, innovative work behavior, and employee well-being. *Global Business Perspectives*. https://doi.org/10.1007/s40196-013-0019-2
196. Ling, Y., Hammond, M., & Wei, L.-Q. (2020). Ethical leadership and ambidexterity in young firms: Examining the CEO-TMT interface. *International Entrepreneurship and Management Journal*. https://doi.org/10.1007/s11365-020-00695-6
197. Lin, C.-P., Jhang, C., Wang, Y.-M. (2021). Learning value-based leadership in teams: The moderation of emotional regulation. *Review of Managerial Science*. https://doi.org/10.1007/s11846-021-00483-8
198. Wan, J., Zhou, W., Qin, M., Zhou, H., & Li, P. (2023). The impact of emotional leadership on Chinese subordinates' work engagement: Role of intrinsic motivation and traditionality. *BMC Psychology*. https://doi.org/10.1186/s40359-022-01022-0
199. Liu, Q., & Zhou, H. (2020). Impact of self-leadership on employee voice behavior: A moderated mediating model. *Current Psychology*. https://doi.org/10.1007/s12144-023-04407-5
200. Cheng, T., Huang, G.-H., Lee, C., & Ren, X. (2010). Longitudinal effects of job insecurity on employee outcomes: The moderating role of emotional intelligence and the leader-member exchange. *Asia Pacific Journal of Management*. https://doi.org/10.1007/s10490-010-9227-3
201. Chen, M. Y.-C., Lin, C. Y.-Y., Lin, H.-E., & McDonough, E. F. (2012). Does transformational leadership facilitate technological innovation? The moderating roles of innovative culture and incentive compensation. *Asia Pacific Journal of Management*. https://doi.org/10.1007/s10490-012-9285-9
202. Rao-Nicholson, R., & Mohyuddin, S. (2023). The role of transformational leadership and institutional entrepreneurship in organizational change in Indian public organizations. *Asian Business & Management*. https://doi.org/10.1057/s41291-023-00218-5
203. Lv, H., Zhao, X., Cao, M., & Ding, J. (2022). How can managers, acting as brokers, be ambidextrous? The effect of trust brokerage on managers' ambidexterity. *Asian Business & Management*. https://doi.org/10.1057/s41291-022-00189-z
204. Khan, M. R. (2021). A critical analysis of Elon Musk's leadership in Tesla motors. *Journal of Global Entrepreneurship Research*. https://doi.org/10.1007/s40497-021-00284-z
205. Rockstuhl, T., Wu, D., Dulebohn, J. H., Liao, C., & Hoch, J. E. (2021). Cultural congruence or compensation? A meta-analytic test of transformational and transactional leadership effects across cultures. *Journal of International Business Studies*. https://doi.org/10.1057/s41267-022-00559-x

206. Miao, Q., Newman, A., Yu, J., & Xu, L. (2012). The relationship between ethical leadership and unethical pro-organizational behavior: Linear or curvilinear effects? *Journal of Business Ethics*. https://doi.org/10.1007/s10551-012-1504-2
207. Notanubun, Z. (2020). The effect of organizational citizenship behavior and leadership effectiveness on public sectors organizational performance: Study in the Department of Education, Youth and Sports in Maluku Province, Indonesia. *Public Organization Review*. https://doi.org/10.1007/s11115-020-00475-4
208. Rehman, U., Shahnawaz, M. G. (2021). Machiavellianism and task-orientated leadership: Moderating effect of job autonomy. *Leadership, Education, Personality: An Interdisciplinary Journal*. https://doi.org/10.1365/s42681-021-00024-7
209. Liang, S.-G., & Steve Chi, S.-C. (2012). Transformational leadership and follower task performance: The role of susceptibility to positive emotions and follower positive emotions. *Journal of Business and Psychology*. https://doi.org/10.1007/s10869-012-9261-x
210. Majeed, N., & Jamshed, S. (2021). Heightening citizenship behaviours of academicians through transformational leadership: Evidence based interventions. *Quality & Quantity*. https://doi.org/10.1007/s11135-021-01146-2

Chapter 6
Emotional Intelligence in Human Resource Management

Introduction by the Author

Emotional intelligence affects every element of human existence, allowing people to perform with self-assurance, resilience, drive, and empathy. HR executives rely on emotional intelligence (EI) to lead, manage, and cooperate with people, while executives, in particular, and use EI to promote engagement, motivation, continuation, and productivity. Employees may develop healthy connections, grow and progress, collaborate and communicate effectively, and achieve goals when they have high EI. Raina (2022) investigated impact of compassionate empathetic behaviour on employee well-being. The research revolves around three stages of empathic concerns; cognitive, emotional and compassionate concerns. The third view compassionate or emotional concerns contain both affective and cognitive components. The main focus of the study is to evaluate the empathic concerns of leaders towards well-being of employees from the perspective of Self Determination Theory (SDT). This study unravels the pandemic situation and is indicating that a higher degree of empathy was required as safety and security.

The role of innovative work behaviour and employee mindfulness is learned as a mediator in leadership style by Khan and others (2022). The combination of mindfulness and innovative work behaviour are a killer combination to bring out productivity of employees. Variables discussed in this study include employee mindfulness, innovative work behaviour and inclusive leadership with the interactive effect of personality traits. This study proves that employee mindfulness can be improved by inclusive leadership style. Pengg (2022) investigated through social identity theory, the impact of servant leadership through employee resilience. Choi (2023) examined the mediating role of employee well-being between relationship conflict and counterproductive work-behaviour based on emotional intelligence. Emotionally intelligent employees experience lower affective well- being following relationship conflict which leads to Counter Work Behaviour (CWB), Richardson [1].

© The Author(s), under exclusive license to Springer Nature Singapore Pte Ltd. 2024
R. Mekhala (ed.), *Emotional Intelligence Matters*,
https://doi.org/10.1007/978-981-99-7727-7_6

Human resources may organise training sessions to assist leaders in exercising listening actively, solving issues, resolving disputes, self-respect, and resilience. Giving team leaders and managers these abilities allows them to turn difficult and possibly stressful situations into chances for growth. Providing a space for health activities like art, physical activity, and music can assist employees in tuning into their true potential. Developing a workforce of good workers and leaders who value their own and others' worth adds to workplace optimism, Mishra [4]. EQ creates the framework for employees to thrive and form strong interpersonal ties, allowing companies to foster a more purposeful and pleasant workplace. The indirect effect of relationship conflict is positive, when EI is high. When the roles of negative emotions mediate the link between the stressors and counter productive work behaviour, emotionally intelligent employees experience lower affective well- being.

Human Resources Managers should have high emotional intelligence in order to be effective in their roles. We can pretend to enjoy our profession for the rest of our life, yet we are all human, and it is difficult to work for eight hours in a day without feeling any emotions. Every day, employees and HR managers will experience a wide spectrum of emotions. To effectively manage human resources in an organisation, a HR manager must be skilled at managing the feelings of the employees. Human Resources Manager will be present throughout an employee's career life cycle, from recruitment to on boarding to resignation or termination. A HR Manager must handle all emotionally charged events in an employee's professional and personal lives, because important events in their lives can disrupt work and damage organisational productivity, Al Omar [31]. As a consequence, everyone in the workforce must develop strong emotional intelligence skills. It's better to build practises with leaders or managers in the organisation to make them beneficial, who positively affect others. HR can also share teamwork practices by teaching employees how to comprehend and interpret the emotions of others, Petrides [51].

Machine Generated Summaries

Disclaimer: The summaries in this chapter were generated from Springer Nature publications using extractive AI auto-summarization: An extraction-based summarizer aims to identify the most important sentences of a text using an algorithm and uses those original sentences to create the auto-summary (unlike generative AI). As the constituted sentences are machine selected, they may not fully reflect the body of the work, so we strongly advise that the original content is read and cited. The auto generated summaries were curated by the editor to meet Springer Nature publication standards. To cite this content, please refer to the original papers.

Machine generated keywords: wellbeing, covid, wellbee, engagement, health, risk, behaviour, lose, pandemic, mental health, mental, project, survey, failure, employee wellbee.

Investigating the Serial Psychological Processes of Workplace COVID-19 Infection Risk and Employees' Performance [58]

This is a machine-generated summary of:
 Chuang, Ya-Ting; Chiang, Hua-Ling; Lin, An-Pan: Investigating the serial psychological processes of workplace COVID-19 infection risk and employees' performance [58]
 Published in: Current Psychology (2023)
 Link to original: https://doi.org/10.1007/s12144-023-04583-4
 Copyright of the summarized publication:
 The Author(s), under exclusive licence to Springer Science+Business Media, LLC, part of Springer Nature 2023
 Copyright comment: Springer Nature or its licensor (e.g. a society or other partner) holds exclusive rights to this article under a publishing agreement with the author(s) or other rightsholder(s); author self-archiving of the accepted manuscript version of this article is solely governed by the terms of such publishing agreement and applicable law.
 All rights reserved.
 If you want to cite the papers, please refer to the original.
 For technical reasons we could not place the page where the original quote is coming from.

Abstract-Summary

"Drawing on concepts from conservation of resources theory, this study examines the effects of perceived workplace COVID-19 infection risk on employees' in-role (i.e., task), extra-role (i.e., OCBs: organizational citizenship behaviors), and creative performance via three mediators, namely, uncertainty, self-control, and psychological capital (i.e., PsyCap), and the moderation of leaders' safety commitment."

"The Bayesian multilevel results reveal that COVID-19 infection risk (Time 1) is negatively associated with creativity (Time 3) as well as supervisor-rated task performance and OCBs (Time 3) via PsyCap."

"The relationship between COVID-19 infection risk and creativity is mediated by the serial psychological processes of uncertainty (Time 2), self-control (Time 2), and PsyCap (Time 3)."

"Conditional indirect results show that the effect of uncertainty on PsyCap via self-control is significant for supervisors with high-level safety commitment, and the effect of self-control on creative performance via PsyCap is significant for supervisors with both high- and low-level safety commitment."

Introduction

"Drawing on conservation of resources theory (COR; Hobfoll [2]; Hobfoll & others [3]), we are interested in the psychological loss process associated with the risk of COVID-19 infection and the ways in which such an inner process influences employees' work-related performance."

"This study suggests that uncertainty, self-control, and psychological capital (PsyCap) can be mediators of the impact of COVID-19 infection risk on job performance, and these three mediators play different roles in the psychological resource loss chain."

"Investigating the relationships among those variables can unveil the inner mechanism underlying the influence of workplace COVID-19 infection risk on employees' work-related performance and explicate how this crisis impacts psychological resource loss and job outcomes."

"We analyze ways of intervening in the psychological mechanism underlying the impact of workplace COVID-19 infection risk on employee performance and extend this investigation to encompass leaders' safety commitments."

Theoretical Development

"We propose that the risk of workplace COVID-19 infection causes fluctuations in employees' psychological resources, namely uncertainty, self-control, and PsyCap, thereby impacting their task performance, OCBs, and creativity; the reasons for these impacts are described below."

"In line with the above reasoning concerning these three potential mediators, i.e., uncertainty, self-control, and PsyCap, which have been suggested to influence the relationship between COVID-19 infection risk in the workplace and work-related performance, we propose the following hypotheses: Workplace COVID-19 infection risk is positively associated with (a) uncertainty and negatively associated with (b) self-control and (c) PsyCap."

"According to the review presented above, uncertainty, self-control ability, and PsyCap are associated with the relationship between workplace COVID-19 infection risk and work-related performance, and these three potential mediators are related to one another."

"Workplace COVID-19 infection risk is negatively associated with work-related performance, i.e., (a) task performance, (b) OCBs, and (c) creativity, via the chain of uncertainty, self-control, and PsyCap."

Method

"The second-wave survey was distributed one week after the first survey (Time 2) and measured employees' self-rated uncertainty and self-control."

Machine Generated Summaries

"The final-wave survey was administered one week after the second survey (Time 3) and measured employee PsyCap and self-rated creative performance as well as supervisor-rated job performance and OCBs of employees."

"Participants were required to respond to the statement 'During the epidemic alert period, please estimate the extent to which you were aware of the risk of COVID-19 infection in the workplace' on a 9-point Likert scale, with responses ranging from 1 (extremely low) to 9 (extremely high)."

"Supervisors were asked about their management of team workplace safety issues during the period of the COVID-19 epidemic alert on a 5-point Likert scale, with responses ranging from 0 (not at all) to 4 (to a large extent)."

Results

"The results indicate that the mediating effects support the relationship between COVID-19 infection risk and creative performance via the mediation of PsyCap (indirect effect=-0.024, 95% CI = [-0.044, − 0.007]), and the serial mediating effect of uncertainty, self-control, and PsyCap (indirect effect=-0.002, 95% CI = [-0.005, − 0.001]) is supported; the CI excluded zero."

"The results indicate that the conditional indirect effect for uncertainty via self-control on PsyCap (indirect effect = − 0.173, 95% CI= [-0.297, − 0.068]) is significant for supervisors with higher levels of safety commitment but not for supervisors with lower levels of safety commitment (indirect effect=-0.024, 95% CI= [-0.067, 0.098])."

Discussion

"This study draws on COR theory to reveal how workplace COVID-19 infection risk diminishes employees' job performance and focuses on three mediators, i.e., uncertainty, self-control, and PsyCap, to explicate the process of psychological resource loss; supervisors' safety commitment is used as a cross-level moderator to illustrate the assurance actions taken by leaders, as resource investment behaviors can buffer the resource loss chain from crises pertaining to work-related performance."

"Uncertainty does not mediate the relationship between COVID-19 infection risk and work-related performance directly but does influence the individual's self-control ability; self-control is not directly affected by COVID-19 infection risk, and it does not influence work-related performance, but it does play a role in the relationship between uncertainty and PsyCap; in addition, leaders' safety commitment can mitigate not only the impact of uncertainty on self-control (Hypothesis 9a) but also the impact of self-control on PsyCap (Hypothesis 9b), especially in the self-reported creative performance condition."

Conclusions

"Although many countries have gradually moved toward coexistence with the virus, the risk of reinfection and sequelae of infection continue to pose challenges."

"Those risks of illness continue to impact employees' psychological states and cause uncertainty, loss of self-control ability, and depletion of PsyCap."

"These impacts can consequentially damage the effectiveness of the organization by reducing employees' work-related performance."

"Leaders should take responsibility for ensuring the workplace safety of their employees and decrease the potential psychological resource losses of employees to maintain organizational competitive advantage."

Does Perfectionism Influence Individual Financial Risk Tolerance and Financial Well-Being? Evidence From an Online Survey Data From the US [59]

This is a machine-generated summary of:

Wang, Di; McGroarty, Frank: Does perfectionism influence individual financial risk tolerance and financial well-being? Evidence from an online survey data from the US [59]

Published in: SN Business & Economics (2022)

Link to original: https://doi.org/10.1007/s43546-022-00339-7

Copyright of the summarized publication:

The Author(s) 2022

License: OpenAccess CC BY 4.0

This article is licensed under a Creative Commons Attribution 4.0 International License, which permits use, sharing, adaptation, distribution and reproduction in any medium or format, as long as you give appropriate credit to the original author(s) and the source, provide a link to the Creative Commons licence, and indicate if changes were made. The images or other third party material in this article are included in the article's Creative Commons licence, unless indicated otherwise in a credit line to the material. If material is not included in the article's Creative Commons licence and your intended use is not permitted by statutory regulation or exceeds the permitted use, you will need to obtain permission directly from the copyright holder. To view a copy of this licence, visit http://creativecommons.org/licenses/by/4.0/.

If you want to cite the papers, please refer to the original.

For technical reasons we could not place the page where the original quote is coming from.

Abstract-Summary

"Perfectionism influences various aspects of our lives, such as academic study, music, athletics, and work."

"Perfectionism has two essential facets: striving and evaluative concerns."

"This study aims to investigate whether perfectionism influence tolerance for financial risk, wealth accumulation and gambling behavior."

"Perfectionistic striving is positively associated with financial risk tolerance, but perfectionistic concerns have no impact on financial risk tolerance."

"Perfectionistic striving (concerns) positively (negatively) predicts liquid wealth mediated by investment knowledge."

"This study contributes to theory by documenting that perfectionism can influence financial satisfaction or well-being."

Introduction

"Although the effects of perfectionism on multiple domains of life (e.g., academic study, music, athletics, work) have been widely studied (Sotardi & Dubien [5]; Spagnoli & others [6, 7]), there is a lack of evidence to support the contention that perfectionism influences individual decision-making on investments or personal financial well-being."

"Little is known regarding whether and how perfectionism influences individual risk tolerance and wealth accumulation."

"It appears worthwhile to investigate the potential effects of perfectionism on financial risk tolerance and wealth accumulation."

"The first objective is to examine whether perfectionism is associated with financial risk tolerance and, if so, how."

"Financial risk tolerance increases with the extent of perfectionistic striving, whereas evaluative concerns are not directly associated with financial risk tolerance."

"It reinforces the view that perfectionism has both active and negative aspects that contribute to positive or adverse consequences, respectively, for instance, increased and decreased wealth accumulation, or increased and reduced risk tolerance."

Literature Review

"We hypothesize as follows: Perfectionistic striving is positively associated with financial risk tolerance."

"We anticipate the following: Perfectionistic concerns are negatively associated with financial risk tolerance."

"Perfectionistic striving is positively associated with self-efficacy and aspiration level (Stoeber & others [8]), whereas self-efficacy is positively related to mental effort and achievement (Schunk [9])."

"We hypothesize that individuals with high personal standards (high striving) may tend to spend more money on gambling if they have been participating in gambling because they can offset the financial risk by the prospect of obtaining more money from gambling."

"We also hypothesize that individuals with intensive concerns about mistakes or doubts regarding outcomes (high evaluative concerns) are more likely to spend less money on gambling if they have been participating in gambling because they may prefer to optimize the consequences of their financial decisions and to dodge mistakes and subsequently avoid negative feedback (Brand & Altstötter-Gleich [10])."

Data Description

"We used a web survey after sending email invitations to potential respondents."

"We used a sampling service purchased from an online panel vendor, Qualtrics, whose panel team supports survey construction by providing an assistant to develop complicated electronic questionnaires, distribute the survey to an established panel group and record the results."

"The Qualtrics panel teams distributed our survey to reliable and targeted groups in the panel with an email invitation."

"To diminish self-selection bias, Qualtrics sends potential respondents one email invitation containing the internet link to the survey and basic information (Afthanorhan & others [11]; Al Halbusi & others [12, 13]), such as the research purpose of the survey, how much time the survey will take and the incentives being offered."

"We include the perfectionism measures, financial risk tolerance, investment knowledge, and demographic variables in the statistical model."

Methods

"We apply OLS and quantile regressions as well as ordered logistic model successively to examine whether there is a significant relationship between perfectionism and financial risk tolerance in the entire sample."

"The second objective of this paper is to examine whether investment knowledge mediates the effect of perfectionism on liquid wealth."

"Complementary mediation refers to when an indirect effect (a × b) and a direct effect (c′) both exist and have the same sign."

"Competitive mediation refers to when an indirect effect (a × b) and a direct effect (c′) both exist but have opposite signs."

"Indirect-only mediation (full mediation) refers to the existence of an indirect effect (a × b) but without a direct effect (c′)."

"If we detect a mediation effect, we proceed to the bootstrap test, as proposed by Preacher and Hayes [14, 15], to verify the significance of the indirect effect (a × b)."

Results

"The results of the bootstrap test suggest that investment knowledge mediates the link between striving and liquid wealth (indirect effect = a*b = 0.208*1.035 = 0.216, SE = 0.057, CI = from 0.119 to 0.343)."

"OLS regression was conducted to investigate the mediation effect of investment knowledge on the relationship between evaluative concerns (average) and the accumulation of liquid wealth."

"The results of the bootstrap test suggest that investment knowledge mediates the link between evaluative concerns and liquid assets (indirect effect = a*b = − 0.108*1.035 = − 0.112, SE = 0.057, CI = from − 0.231 to − 0.004)."

"The indirect effect (− 0.112) between evaluative concerns and liquid assets via investment knowledge is negative and significant, which supports H2b."

Discussion

"Our results support H1a, which states that, among the general population, perfectionistic striving is positively associated with financial risk tolerance."

"Weller and Thulin [16] do not investigate the effect of the positive aspect of perfectionism on individual risk attitudes; we fill this gap by demonstrating that perfectionistic striving drives financial risk tolerance."

"It appears that the positive association between perfectionistic striving and financial risk tolerance may be due to the aim of achieving financial well-being, which is a key determinant of general life happiness (Kruger [17])."

"Perfectionistic concerns are supposed to be negatively associated with financial risk tolerance because such concerns are related to mistakes (Stoeber & others [8])."

"The second finding is that striving (evaluative concerns) is associated with increased (decreased) investment knowledge, which is then associated with increased (decreased) liquid wealth."

Conclusion

"Our main finding is that perfectionistic striving is positively associated with the level of financial risk tolerance, whereas our results do not indicate that evaluative concerns are directly associated with financial risk tolerance."

"Striving (evaluative concerns) is associated with increased (decreased) investment knowledge, which is in turn associated with increased (decreased) liquid wealth."

"These empirical results provide evidence that can help to achieve research objectives which are investigating the relationship between perfectionism, financial risk tolerance, wealth accumulation, and gambling expenditure."

"In reporting these relationships, this preliminary study has several important implications for theoretical and empirical research in behavioral finance."

"With respect to the study's empirical implications, perfectionistic concerns do not necessarily lead to negative outcomes."

"The paper does not explain why striving motivates an increase in risk tolerance whereas evaluative concerns do not."

How Do Job Insecurity and Perceived Well-Being Affect Expatriate Employees' Willingness to Share or Hide Knowledge? [60]

This is a machine-generated summary of:
  Ali, Murad; Ali, Imran; Albort-Morant, Gema; Leal-Rodríguez, Antonio Luis: How do job insecurity and perceived well-being affect expatriate employees' willingness to share or hide knowledge? [60]
  Published in: International Entrepreneurship and Management Journal (2020)
  Link to original: https://doi.org/10.1007/s11365-020-00638-1
  Copyright of the summarized publication:
  Springer Science+Business Media, LLC, part of Springer Nature 2020
  All rights reserved.
  If you want to cite the papers, please refer to the original.
  For technical reasons we could not place the page where the original quote is coming from.

Abstract-Summary

"It is important to understand how this job insecurity might affect expatriate employees' perceptions of well-being and knowledge management behaviors."

"This study examines the influence of job insecurity on employees' perceptions of well-being and knowledge sharing or knowledge hiding strategies."

"The data for this study were collected from 265 expatriate employees working at different organizations in Saudi Arabia."

"The study shows the significant influence of job insecurity and employees' perceptions of work engagement and knowledge sharing."

"No significant association was observed between job insecurity and knowledge hiding."

"Work engagement has a significant association with knowledge sharing and burnout."

"Burnout is significantly associated with knowledge hiding behaviors by expatriate employees."

Introduction

"Few studies have examined expatriate employees' perceptions of well-being and these employees' intentions to share or hide knowledge in contexts of job insecurity."

"Examining how the negative outcomes of job insecurity can be minimized to yield better knowledge outcomes among expatriate employees is crucial."

"This paper sheds light on this issue by answering the following research questions: How do expatriate employees behave in terms of knowledge sharing and knowledge hiding in contexts of job insecurity?"

"Scant research has examined the effect of employees' perceptions of well-being on intentions to share or hide knowledge in contexts of job insecurity."

"This paper examines the direct influence of job insecurity on expatriate employees' knowledge sharing and knowledge hiding behaviors."

"This study shows whether expatriate employees are willing to share their knowledge depending on their perceived well-being at work."

Theoretical Background and Hypotheses

"We propose the following hypothesis: H1: Job insecurity is negatively related to expatriate employees' work engagement."

"In situations of job insecurity, where employees have predominantly negative perceptions and negative energy in relation to their organizations, employees tend not to share their knowledge."

"We therefore propose the following hypothesis: H3: Job insecurity is negatively related to expatriate employees' knowledge sharing behaviors."

"Based on these arguments, we propose the following hypothesis: H4: Job insecurity is positively related to expatriate employees' knowledge hiding behavior."

"We therefore propose the following hypothesis: H6: Work engagement is positively related to employees' knowledge sharing behaviors."

"The conceptual model shows negative links between job insecurity and work engagement and between job insecurity and knowledge sharing; in contrast, positive associations are shown between job insecurity and burnout and between job insecurity and knowledge hiding behaviors."

Method

"The use of PLS-SEM in this study is suitable for five reasons. (1) This study focused on predicting and explaining the variance in key target constructs (e.g., knowledge sharing and knowledge hiding). (2) The research model had a complex structure in terms of the type of hypothetical relationships and level of multidimensionality (first- and second-order constructs). (3) The relationships between the main constructs of the study were believed to be in the early stages of theory development and thus provided an opportunity for new phenomena to be explored. (4) Latent variable scores were used in the subsequent analysis of predictive relevance, particularly in the implementation of the two-stage approach for modeling the multidimensionality of work engagement and burnout. (5) This study benefited from the advantages of PLS-SEM in terms of less rigorous requirements of restrictive assumptions, which enabled us to create and estimate the model without imposing additional limiting constraints (Hair & others [18])."

Results

"The evaluation of the measurement model focused on the psychometric properties of reliability, validity, and dimensionality for each construct."

"These properties were assessed prior to undertaking hypothesis testing via exploratory factor analysis (EFA) by evaluating the reliability, average variance extracted (AVE), square root of the AVE, and inter-construct correlations."

"Work engagement was modeled as a composite reflective construct (Mode A) made up of two first-order reflective dimensions: work engagement and organizational engagement."

"For PLS-SEM models, a Q^2 value of more than 0 in the cross-validated redundancy report indicates predictive relevance."

"We followed Henseler and others's [19] approach and used the standardized root mean square residual (SRMR) as an index for model validation."

"The model estimation with PLS-SEM in this study reveals an SRMR value of 0.07, which confirms the overall fit of the PLS-SEM path model (Henseler & others [19]; Hair & others [18])."

Discussion and Conclusions

"The study assesses the direct influence of job insecurity on expatriate employees' knowledge sharing and knowledge hiding behaviors."

"When expatriate employees fear they will lose their jobs, they increase their engagement at work and share more knowledge."

"They reveal the prominent role of work engagement promotion and burnout prevention in driving knowledge sharing behaviors by expatriate employees."

"Our study sheds light on whether expatriate employees are willing to share or hide knowledge based on their perceived workplace well-being in contexts of job insecurity due to government localization policies."

"Comparative analysis between local employees' and expatriate employees' perceptions of job insecurity, work engagement, burnout, knowledge sharing, and hiding behaviors might provide interesting findings in the future."

"Other constructs could also be used to explain why expatriate employees are willing to engage at work and share knowledge despite facing a high level of job insecurity."

Moving Crisis to Opportunities: A Corporate Perspective on the Impact of Compassionate Empathic Behaviour on the Well-Being of Employees [61]

This is a machine-generated summary of:
Raina, Reeta: Moving Crisis to Opportunities: A Corporate Perspective on the Impact of Compassionate Empathic Behaviour on the Well-Being of Employees [61]

Published in: International Journal of Global Business and Competitiveness (2022)
Link to original: https://doi.org/10.1007/s42943-021-00040-w
Copyright of the summarized publication:
Global Institute of Flexible Systems Management 2021
All rights reserved.
If you want to cite the papers, please refer to the original.
For technical reasons we could not place the page where the original quote is coming from.

Abstract-Summary

"The present study aims at investigating how did the leadership use prosocial empathic skills during this pandemic to manage the mental well-being of their respective employees, so that they are motivated and engaged for meaningful performance."

"The major themes that emerged from the structured interviews of the apex leadership were (1) compassionate empathic behaviour impacts the employee motivation and performance; (2) open, honest and timely vertical communication promotes trust and bonding; (3) support for employee autonomy impacts their well-being; (4) encouraging competence and self-efficacy in employees; (5) promoting positive and healthy relationships by displaying compassionate empathy positively impacts mental health and thereby employee performance during crisis."

"Right from providing unified Communication platform, to displaying empathic leadership, the apex leadership unanimously believes that people are their best assets and if managed well in the crisis can help them stem the storm successfully."

Introduction

"No leadership or management in this world can afford or imagine to run a profitable organization with employees feeling mentally disturbed and morally low."

"Major complications that the employees faced, at their personal level, during these unprecedented COVID times, are adjusting to a new work-life situation that includes moving from face-to-face interaction to WFH model, leading to social isolation, deprivation and abandonment."

"Since, employees are the real assets of any organisation, therefore it should become the paramount concern of all the managements in the World to ensure the health and well-being of an employee that should take care of their financial, physical, and emotional issues."

"Albeit, it is reported that many organizations have been proactive in taking control of employee's health and financial issues, howbeit they seem to have failed in attending to their emotional needs which can at times put both the employees and the organization into jeopardy."

Theoretical Framework

"It develops through three stages: cognitive empathy, emotional empathy and compassionate empathy that Paul Ekman refers as empathic concerns."

"A third view called Compassionate or Empathic concern that contains both affective and cognitive components is the kind of empathy that encourages people to act and is the motivation behind reducing the sufferings of another individual."

"Since, the main focus of the current study is to determine the empathic concerns of the leaders towards the well-being of their followers, therefore, the questionnaire so directed to the corporate were based on the Compassionate Empathy theory since a leader is required to display both the cognitive as well as affective empathic skills at the workplace along with related action to that effect to make empathy most valuable attribute."

"In recent years, there has been a shift toward studying employee well-being from the perspective of Self-Determination Theory (SDT) developed by Ryan and Deci [20] since it generates some interesting insights about the work motivation."

Literature Review

"As one of the variable used in this study is empathic leadership, substantial studies on the subject were found to be available in the literature, although most of these studies are dedicated to defining the conceptual understanding of empathy."

"There are some studies done focussing on empathic leadership and a few on the negative aspects of empathy."

"Although the theme of exploring the relationship between compassionate empathic leadership and employee well-being has received attention from the researchers in recent times but, unfortunately there are not substantial studies available on the same."

"In view of its importance, not many studies are found exploring the theme of compassionate empathic leadership and employee well- being post the pandemic."

"In the times of unprecedented crisis, the study on the topic of compassionate empathic leadership and the employee well-being is much required for the survival of an organization."

Research Methodology

"As the study was qualitative in design, therefore, the data so collected to seek answers to the questions so raised was done through interviewing apex leadership from the corporate, representing different business segments from across the world."

"A questionnaire was prepared having 10 statements based on the theories of compassionate empathic leadership and employee well-being."

"The questionnaire was deliberately restricted to ten (10) statements only because of paucity of time and the busy schedules of the apex leadership who would be unwilling and reluctant to answer long list of questions."

"Twenty (20) c-suite executives from different sectors were approached telephonically as well as through e-mails seeking their participation in the said project."

"Once, the leadership from the said sectors were identified and they committed their partaking, a virtual meeting was arranged independently with each one of them where the objective of the study was explained to them."

Data Analysis and Discussion

"Further, some studies that advocated "it is noted that the jobs that require constant empathy can lead to "compassion fatigue"—a state of emotional, mental, physical, and occupational exhaustion, draining one's energy and cognitive resources "also stands rejected "Pandemic or not, this has been the way of life at OLA, hence no emotional fatigue was there for the leaders" (IE4; see annexure pp.")

"The study also unravels during this pandemic crisis, the studied leadership also realized that "a greater degree of empathy was needed as safety (health) and security (job) concerns were high among the employees (IE6; see annexure p. 8), hence they all shared" information in timely and accurate manner, through appropriate internal channels" (IE5; see annexure pp.")

"My challenge was to groom my team into presenting virtually (IE2; see annexure p. 2)"."

Conclusions

"The insights gained from the inputs from top leaders further validates some of the theories as forwarded by earlier studies on leadership communication, compassionate empathic leadership and employee wellbeing and organizational performance."

"The present study also highlights that effective leaders draw upon their ability to identify and express emotions to better understand and influence followers, to convey a compelling vision, to maintain excitement, and to promote interpersonal cooperation the most vital trait for CEOs to manage organizational crisis, especially interpersonal relationships that are changed in new normal times, among many other qualities is empathy."

"The present case study also illustrates that it was emotional faculties and cognitive abilities oKukule (2012) in" Internal communication crisis and its impact on organization's performance" cited that the importance of symmetry has been marked by Gruning and Hunt, describing symmetric communication as a source and a recipient which cannot be separated but are equal participants of a communication process seeking (striving for) mutual understanding and proportional two-way effect (Grunig & Grunig [21])."

The Perceived Well-Being and Health Costs of Exiting Self-Employment [62]

This is a machine-generated summary of:

Nikolova, Milena; Nikolaev, Boris; Popova, Olga: The perceived well-being and health costs of exiting self-employment [62]

Published in: Small Business Economics (2020)

Link to original: https://doi.org/10.1007/s11187-020-00374-4

Copyright of the summarized publication:

The Author(s) 2020

License: OpenAccess CC BY 4.0

This article is licensed under a Creative Commons Attribution 4.0 International License, which permits use, sharing, adaptation, distribution and reproduction in any medium or format, as long as you give appropriate credit to the original author(s) and the source, provide a link to the Creative Commons licence, and indicate if changes were made. The images or other third party material in this article are included in the article's Creative Commons licence, unless indicated otherwise in a credit line to the material. If material is not included in the article's Creative Commons licence and your intended use is not permitted by statutory regulation or exceeds the permitted use, you will need to obtain permission directly from the copyright holder. To view a copy of this licence, visit http://creativecommons.org/licenses/by/4.0/.

If you want to cite the papers, please refer to the original.

For technical reasons we could not place the page where the original quote is coming from.

Machine Generated Summaries 277

Abstract-Summary

"We explore how involuntary and voluntary exits from self-employment affect life and health satisfaction."

"We find that while transitioning from self-employment to salaried employment brings small improvements in health and life satisfaction, the negative psychological costs of business failure (i.e., switching from self-employment to unemployment) are substantial and exceed the costs of involuntarily losing a salaried job."

"Leaving self-employment has no consequences for self-reported physical health and behaviors such as smoking and drinking, implying that the costs of losing self-employment are mainly psychological."

Introduction

"To provide a counterbalance to the well-being literature in entrepreneurship and help examine the potential trade-offs associated with starting and running a business, we pose the following questions: (1) What is the impact of exiting self-employment on perceived health and subjective well-being? (2) How do the perceived health and life satisfaction effects of exiting self-employment compare to losing a salaried job? (3) Is the impact of exiting self-employment persistent, or do people quickly adapt to this adverse event?"

"Transitioning from self-employment to a salaried position can even be beneficial to life and health satisfaction."

"Our results suggest that health and life satisfaction declines associated with business failure persist for 2 or more years after losing self-employment."

"We also compare and contrast the self-reported health and life satisfaction changes of those who involuntarily lose self-employment with those who involuntarily lose a salaried job."

Previous Literature, Theory, and Hypotheses

"Perspective, the unemployment experience after a business exit (i.e., switching from self-employment to unemployment) can be especially damaging to psychological well-being relative to the experience of unemployment due to a loss of salaried employment (i.e., switching from salaried employment to unemployment)."

"Because it is more difficult to separate professional from personal failure, as the identity of the entrepreneur is often closely tied to the business, people who enter unemployment after a business loss may be more likely to fare less well psychologically compared with their counterparts who transition to unemployment from salaried employment."

"The magnitude of the drop in psychological well-being following a self-employment exit may be higher than that of losing a salaried job, even if both groups end up at the same level of subjective well-being as unemployed (Hetschko [22])."

"We expect that: H2a: The negative life and health satisfaction impacts associated with unemployment are stronger for people who transition from self-employment compared with those who transition from salaried employment."

Data

"Our first treated group captures involuntary business exits by those who switch from self-employment to unemployment."

"Respondents in this treated group were full-time self-employed in the previous survey wave but are registered unemployed in the consecutive one."

"The matched comparison group consists of individuals who remain continuously self-employed in both survey years."

"Individuals in this group were salaried employees in the previous wave but in the current survey are registered unemployed due to company closure."

"The matched control group consists of individuals who remain continuously employed in both survey periods."

"Our third treated group includes respondents who voluntarily exit self-employment to become salaried workers."

"This treated group is based on individuals who reported being self-employed in the previous wave but in the current wave work in the private sector as salaried employees."

"The comparison group is based on respondents who remained continuously self-employed in both surveys."

Empirical Strategy

"Our methodology includes two steps: (i) a data pre-processing using entropy balancing to create comparable groups of individuals who are statistically identical except that the treated group experiences a change in their labor market status between two survey waves while the comparison group does not; and (ii) estimating a weighted regression of the treatment (change in labor market status) on the change in perceived life and health satisfaction status based on weights obtained in step 1."

"This ensures that pre-existing psychological or physical health conditions cannot influence the decision to exit self-employment or change salaried jobs in the private sector—i.e., individuals in both the treatment and comparison groups have the same baseline health and psychological well-being levels."

Results

"Switching from self-employment to unemployment significantly reduces life satisfaction and slightly damages health satisfaction (Panel A), which provides support for H1a."

"To our knowledge, we are the first to explore the anticipation and adaptation consequences of losing self-employment and becoming unemployed in terms of both life and health satisfaction."

"The adverse effects of losing self-employment are reflected in both the steeper health and life satisfaction decreases following business failure and the longer adaptation periods."

"They suggest that individuals who voluntarily switch from self-employment to salaried employment enjoy modest increases in life and health satisfaction compared with individuals who stay continuously self-employed (Panel A) and to those who remain in their private sector salaried jobs (Panel B)."

"Changes in life and health satisfaction that follow after exiting from self-employment to unemployment are likely due to worsening mental health."

Limitations and Suggestions for Future Research

"While we document the magnitudes of the health and life satisfaction changes induced by losing self-employment, our paper does not focus on the underlying channels and mechanisms behind them."

"Future research can examine whether the results we document hold across different contexts and countries at varying levels of development while also paying attention to self-selection and causality issues."

"Future research can also compare the physical and mental health costs of different employment transitions and their pecuniary and non-pecuniary implications."

"Given the spillover effects of unemployment within the family (Bubonya & others [23]; Nikolova & Ayhan [24]), future research can also examine how losing a business affects the health and well-being of other family members."

Discussion and Conclusion

"We not only explore involuntary self-employment exits (i.e., transitions from self-employment to unemployment) but also consider how psychological well-being and health satisfaction change after voluntarily transitioning to salaried employment following a business exit."

"Our findings suggest that the life and health satisfaction of the self-employed decrease drastically if the business exit is followed by an unemployment spell."

"Compared with previous studies documenting mental and sometimes physical health gains of switching to self-employment (Nikolova [25]), our results indicate that the potential well-being costs of business failure can be much larger than the benefits from starting a new business venture."

"Our results also suggest that the psychological costs of business failure significantly exceed the costs of involuntary loss of a salaried job, implying that the unemployment experience is particularly psychologically damaging for those losing self-employment."

"This implies that finding alternative salaried employment can cushion the psychological costs of business failure."

Corporate Philanthropy and Employee Wellbeing: Do Types of Corporate Philanthropy Matter? [63]

This is a machine-generated summary of:
Yang, Chih-Hai: Corporate philanthropy and employee wellbeing: do types of corporate philanthropy matter? [63]
Published in: Eurasian Business Review (2022)
Link to original: https://doi.org/10.1007/s40821-022-00211-6
Copyright of the summarized publication:
The Author(s) under exclusive licence to Eurasia Business and Economics Society 2022

Copyright comment: Springer Nature or its licensor (e.g. a society or other partner) holds exclusive rights to this article under a publishing agreement with the author(s) or other rightsholder(s); author self-archiving of the accepted manuscript version of this article is solely governed by the terms of such publishing agreement and applicable law.

All rights reserved.
If you want to cite the papers, please refer to the original.
For technical reasons we could not place the page where the original quote is coming from.

Abstract-Summary

"Dividing donation expenditures into donations to firm-related foundations and donations to unrelated recipients, donations to firm-related foundations have no influence on wage packages."

"Irregular and unscheduled donations, namely, donations to unrelated recipients, have a negative association with employee wage packages."

"The first-stage PSM estimations on the determinants of corporate philanthropy indicate that firm characteristics such as firm size, firm age, earning performance, and stakeholders are factors influencing charitable donations."

Introduction

"Employees may appreciate it if their employers are socially responsible; however, whether and how corporate philanthropy affects their wages and wellbeing is a more practical issue."

"Are actively donating firms also more generous to employees by providing better wage packages than their non-donating counterparts?"

"If firms exhibit responsibility toward employees as ethical employers, they may offer improved wage packages that take care of employees rather than lower their wellbeing."

"This study explores whether and how corporate philanthropy is related to the wage packages offered by Taiwanese manufacturers."

"We discuss various mechanisms regarding how firms' charitable donations are related to wage packages based on a conceptual discussion of their ethical and economic characteristics."

"We discusses the theoretical concepts regarding the relevance of corporate philanthropy to employee wage packages and establishes testable hypotheses."

Literature Review and Hypothesis Development

"Briscese and others [26] examined whether firms' charitable donations attracted and retained talent and demonstrated that CSR played a smaller role in the determination of worker wages."

"By conducting an experiment with 312 participants in which a gift-exchange game designed various combinations of wage offers and donations as a share of the firm's profits to charity, their experiment demonstrated that a firm's donations negatively affect worker earnings, suggesting that CSR initiatives can be costly for workers."

"A company's charitable donations may affect the wage packages that they offer their employees either positively or negatively."

"Charitable donations to firm-related foundations are irrelevant to worker wage packages."

"Workers may appreciate the company's socially responsible behavior and become involved in helping the victims of unexpected natural disasters or accidents by donating a share of their own wages or well-being."

Data Sources and Empirical Specification

"The first is a database maintained by the Taiwan Economic Journal (TEJ) that contains detailed information about basic firm characteristics and production as well as financial statements."

"As this detailed donation information has been available since 2013, we thus constructed an unbalanced panel dataset with 6345 firm observations between 2013 and 2018."

"The reduced-form wage equation to examine whether corporate philanthropy influences employee wellbeing as follows: where Wage_pack represents a wage package that contains wage and non-wage expenditures."

"Controlling for other factors, employees hired by firms that feature a high level of capital intensity should be paid higher wages."

"Young firms in Taiwan, mostly electronics firms, may also provide a competitive wage package to attract high-quality labor."

"We find that employees hired by donation-active firms have significantly higher wages (21.86%) and wage packages (21.20%) than their non-donating counterparts on average, implying that firms undertaking charitable donations tend to treat employees better than non-donating companies."

Empirical Results and Discussion

"This finding indicates that a company's donation activity does not impact employees' wages and wage packages, supporting Hypothesis 1c."

"Combined with the trade-off effects of various motivations, charitable donations do not positively or negatively impact workers' wage packages."

"Relative to donations to unrelated recipients, donations to firm-related foundations may be scheduled and may be one of the most commonly used tax avoidance strategies."

"We separate charitable donations into donations to firm-related foundations (Dona_dum_related) and donations to unrelated recipients (Dona_dum_unrelated)."

"Columns (3)–(5) present a further analysis of donation amounts and demonstrate that donations to firm-related foundations and unrelated recipients have an irrelevant and a negative relationship, respectively, with employees' wage packages."

"Firm-related foundations include charities and cultural and educational foundations established by the donating company or directed by its top managers."

"Younger and exporting firms also provide more reasonable wage packages to workers."

Determinants of Corporate Philanthropy and Robustness Checks

"These analyses indicate that corporate philanthropy is irrelevant to employee well-being, whereas donations to unrelated recipients are negatively related to wage packages."

"To construct a valid control group, Heckman and others [27] suggested that the treatment (donation) should be governed by a latent regression as follows:where β denotes the coefficient and X denotes a vector of the determinants influencing a firm's decision to engage in donation activity."

"The advertising variable is associated with an insignificant coefficient, possibly because the donation activity in this study is concentrated on charitable activities, and donation recipients are not the key consumers of a company's products."

"After the non-random selection of the treatment groups is controlled for, we find no significant differences in the wage packages between donating firms and matched non-donating firms in the current and the subsequent year."

"These results reaffirm that a company's charitable donations do not alter their wage package policy for employees, thereby supporting Hypothesis 1c."

Conclusions and Management Implications

"Based on panel data of publicly listed firms from 2013 to 2018, the panel data model estimations indicate that charitable donations measured by either an engagement dummy or expenditures do not significantly influence employees' wage packages."

"This study starts from the employer's perspective to examine the company philanthropy–worker wage package nexus by using charitable donations as a measure of CSR, unlike previous studies in which the CSR indicators are constructed by the employees' perceptions."

"The first-stage PSM estimations of the determinants of corporate philanthropy find that firm size and firm age are positively associated with the propensity to undertake charitable donations."

"If firms would like to continuously undertake charitable donations, they should consider a better cash management policy."

"An adequate scheme of tax deduction for corporate donation not only facilitates more firms to undertake corporate philanthropy, but also promotes the sustainable operation of charities."

Employee Mindfulness, Innovative Work Behaviour, and IT Project Success: The Role of Inclusive Leadership [64]

This is a machine-generated summary of:

Khan, Jabran; Jaafar, Mastura; Mubarak, Namra; Khan, Abdul Karim: Employee mindfulness, innovative work behaviour, and IT project success: the role of inclusive leadership [64]

Published in: Information Technology and Management (2022)

Link to original: https://doi.org/10.1007/s10799-022-00369-5

Copyright of the summarized publication:

The Author(s), under exclusive licence to Springer Science+Business Media, LLC, part of Springer Nature 2022

All rights reserved.

If you want to cite the papers, please refer to the original.

For technical reasons we could not place the page where the original quote is coming from.

Abstract-Summary

"This study investigates the relationship between project employee mindfulness and project success using innovative work behaviour as a mediator and the project manager's inclusive leadership style as a moderator."

"Project Manager with high inclusive behaviour will strengthen the relationship of employee's mindfulness and innovative work behaviour."

"The study findings validated the proposed model wherein employee personality traits, such as mindfulness, have a key impact on the initiation of project employees' innovative work behaviour."

"The study confirms that innovative work behaviour adds to the project's success."

Introduction

"The current study investigated the role of employee mindfulness' effect on project success directly and indirectly via innovative work behaviour and on the way inclusive leadership moderates this relationship."

"Along with the individual's personality traits, the leadership style of the project manager also plays a key role in shaping the behaviour of project employees [28]."

"Because innovation is the key contributor to project success (Sarwar, Imran & Zahid, 2020), the role of an inclusive leader as a predictor of innovative work behaviour in the case of a mindful employee needs to be determined."

"This study investigates the influence of individual characteristics that can contribute to IT project success (that is, the role of employee mindfulness directly and indirectly via innovative work behaviour to project success) and the role of inclusive leadership as a moderator between mindfulness and innovative work behaviour."

Literature Review and Hypotheses Development

"Hypothesis 2 postulates a positive relationship between employee mindfulness and innovative work behaviour."

"Employee mindfulness is positively associated with innovative work behaviour."

"Hypothesis 3 is postulated: Project employees' innovative work behaviour is positively associated with project success This study suggests that employee mindfulness contributes to the innovative work behaviour of project employees."

"Mindful employees are conscientious [29, 30], and thus display innovative work behaviour that results in project success."

"Based on the above arguments we propose Hypothesis 4: Employees' innovative work behaviour mediates the relationship between employee mindfulness and project success."

"A mindful employee and inclusive leader will contribute positively toward innovative work behaviour."

"Inclusive leadership moderators the relationship between employee mindfulness and innovative work behaviour as this relationship can be stronger when inclusive leadership is employed."

Methodology

"To measure the project employees' innovative work behaviour, the study employed the 9-item scale from Janssen's study (2000) based on Scott and Bruce's study (1994)."

"The proposed model consists of four latent variables: employee mindfulness, innovative work behaviour, IT project success, and inclusive leadership."

"The results suggested that the indirect effect of employee mindfulness on project success through employee innovative work behaviour is stronger at a high level of inclusive leadership (+ 1 SD from the mean value; $\beta = 0.15$, LL 95% CI = 0.08, UL 95% CI = 0.26) and weaker at a low level of inclusive leadership (− 1 SD from the mean value; $\beta = 0.06$, LL 95% CI = 0.02, UL 95% CI = 0.10)."

"The positive and significant moderated mediation index values (Index = − 0.05, LL 95% CI = 0.01, UL 95% CI = 0.10) indicated that inclusive leadership moderates the indirect effect of employee mindfulness on project success via innovative work behaviour."

Discussion

"The interactive effect of project employee mindfulness and project manager inclusive leadership style was investigated to predict employees' innovative work behaviour and project success."

"This study theorised and provided empirical evidence that innovative work behaviour served as an underlying mechanism between employee mindfulness and project success."

"This study established the cumulative effect of employee mindfulness on outcomes, i.e., project success indirectly through innovative work behaviour (as a mediator)."

"The study found that mindful employees nurture and flourish in the form of innovative work behaviour depending on the project managers' inclusive leadership style."

"This study examined) the interactive effect of personality traits (e.g., mindfulness) and leadership style (e.g., inclusive leadership) on project employees' innovative work behaviour."

"The study contributes the ways that mindfulness can help shape project employee behaviour, e.g., innovative work behaviour, and project success."

How Servant Leadership Predicts Employee Resilience in Public Organizations: A Social Identity Perspective [65]

This is a machine-generated summary of:
Peng, Chuanyu; Liang, Yan; Yuan, Guoping; Xie, Mei; Mao, Yanhui; Harmat, László; Bonaiuto, Flavia: How servant leadership predicts employee resilience in public organizations: a social identity perspective [65]
Published in: Current Psychology (2022)
Link to original: https://doi.org/10.1007/s12144-022-04138-z
Copyright of the summarized publication:
The Author(s), under exclusive licence to Springer Science+Business Media, LLC, part of Springer Nature 2022
Copyright comment: Springer Nature or its licensor (e.g. a society or other partner) holds exclusive rights to this article under a publishing agreement with the author(s) or other rightsholder(s); author self-archiving of the accepted manuscript version of this article is solely governed by the terms of such publishing agreement and applicable law.
All rights reserved.
If you want to cite the papers, please refer to the original.
For technical reasons we could not place the page where the original quote is coming from.

Abstract-Summary

"Through the lens of social identity theory, this work aims to investigate the impact of servant leadership on employee resilience during the COVID-19 pandemic and to explore their underlying mechanisms through two types of social identity: organizational identification and professional identity."

"Results yielded from the structural equation modeling analysis via AMOS (24.0) indicated that the effect of servant leadership on employee resilience was fully mediated by organizational identification and professional identity, respectively."

"This study provides the first evidence of the predictive effect of servant leadership on employee resilience through organizational identification and professional identity, highlighting the significance of social identity for building and maintaining employees' resilience in coping with challenges posed by COVID-19."

Introduction

"Our research, conducted under the COVID-19 scenario, aimed to examine the relationship between servant leadership and employee resilience and test their underlying mechanisms by considering two parallel sub-constructs of social identity (i.e., organizational identification and professional identity) based on a social identity approach."

"This study provides a new perspective to explore the potential process through which servant leadership impacts employee resilience by empirically examining the mediating effect of social identity (i.e., organizational identification and professional identity) based on social identity theory. (2) Servant leaders working at public organizations, this group of people who serve their citizens by assisting in combating COVID-19 while also seeking self-protection in coping with such a prevalent pandemic, are more vulnerable to COVID-19."

"Considering the bi-directional impact between organizational identification and professional identity and taking together H2 and H3, we, therefore, propose that: H4: Servant leadership indirectly predicts employee resilience by the sequential mediation effects of organizational identification and professional identity."

Methods

"Data were collected by questionnaire survey among employees from different public organizations (such as government, public schools, hospitals, etc) in southwest China."

"Questionnaire items were prepared online and administered via the URL link and QR (quick response) code to potential employees in public organizations for a pilot test."

"To measure servant leadership in public organizations, we employed a 6-item questionnaire adapted from Sendjaya and others [32] (e.g., "My immediate leaders use power to serve others, not for their ambitions")."

"Two items with factor loadings lower than 0.40 were excluded (Hair & others [33]), and a 4-item organization identification scale was included for further analysis in our study, with adequate internal consistency (Cronbach's $\alpha = 0.796$)."

"We utilized a 5-item scale compiled by London [34] to assess the resilience of employees in the public organization (e.g., "I can build and maintain friendship with people from different departments in my organization")."

Results

"In our hypothesized model, SL was the predictive variable, ER was the dependent variable, and OI and PI were the mediating variables (Model 1: OI and PI as the sequential mediator; Model 2: PI and OI as the sequential mediator)."

"The bootstrapping method via AMOS (24.0) was used to test the significance of the whole mediational model (Shrout & Bolger [35])."

"Besides, the indirect effect of SL on ER through the sequential mediation of OI and PI (H4a: SL—OI—PI—ER) was significant."

"Following, the bootstrapping method via AMOS (24.0) was applied to test the significance of the whole mediational model (Shrout & Bolger [35])."

Discussion

"The present study aimed to investigate the relationship between servant leadership and employee resilience in public organizations by testing a model in which two types of social identity (organizational identification and professional identity) were considered under the COVID-19 challenging context."

"The significant and full mediation effect provided by organizational identification and professional identity emphasized the importance of social identity in the contribution of the relationship between servant leadership and employee resilience, especially in the COVID-19 context."

"This result has added to the leadership and employee resilience literature, and provided evidence for the role of OI and PI as the joint mechanism between SL and ER."

"This study provides a nuanced and comprehensive perspective via social identity (i.e., OI and PI) to understand the SL-ER relationship."

"Through massive strategies, leaders can help improve their employees' organizational identification and professional identity to increase employee resilience in responding to challenges such as the COVID-19 pandemic."

Conclusion

"Our study contributes to the literature in several aspects."

"It sheds light on critical sources of employee resilience with leadership as a crucial driver built on the social identity theory."

"The validated conceptual model demonstrates that the underlying mechanisms between SL and ER are mediated by OI and PI, respectively, and sequentially."

"This study is essential for servant leaders of public organizations to cultivate ER by improving/strengthening their employees' identification with both organizations and professions, especially during COVID-19."

Relationship Conflict and Counterproductive Work Behavior: The Roles of Affective Well-Being and Emotional Intelligence [66]

This is a machine-generated summary of:

Choi, Yongjun; Yoon, David J.; Lee, Joonwhan D.; Lee, Joo Yeon E.: Relationship conflict and counterproductive work behavior: the roles of affective well-being and emotional intelligence [66]

Published in: Review of Managerial Science (2023)

Link to original: https://doi.org/10.1007/s11846-023-00642-z

Copyright of the summarized publication:

The Author(s), under exclusive licence to Springer-Verlag GmbH Germany, part of Springer Nature 2023

Copyright comment: Springer Nature or its licensor (e.g. a society or other partner) holds exclusive rights to this article under a publishing agreement with the author(s) or other rightsholder(s); author self-archiving of the accepted manuscript version of this article is solely governed by the terms of such publishing agreement and applicable law.

All rights reserved.

If you want to cite the papers, please refer to the original.

For technical reasons we could not place the page where the original quote is coming from.

Abstract-Summary

"We examine the mediating role of employees' affective well-being in the relationship between relationship conflict and counterproductive work behavior (CWB) and how this process varies based on their emotional intelligence (EI)."

Theory and Hypotheses

"Although the most direct way for employees to replace losses in positive emotional resources is by seeking people or events that may give them positive emotions (direct replacement; Hobfoll [36]), this may not always be possible in the workplace when employees are experiencing relationship conflict."

"When employees experience relationship conflict, the very people from whom employees first seek positive emotional resources (e.g., supervisors, coworkers) are oftentimes the ones draining these resources by eliciting negative emotions in employees."

"Relationship conflict is likely to be negatively related to affective well-being (i.e., the preponderance of positive emotions over negative emotions), which in turn, leads to CWB."

"Compared to those with low EI, it is likely that emotionally intelligent employees experience lower affective well-being following relationship conflict, which, in turn, may lead them to engage in more CWB."

Method

"Employees' affective well-being was measured using the 20-item version (Fox & others [37]) of the original 30-item Job-related Affective Well-Being Scale (JAWS; Van Katwyk and others [38])."

"Trait EI was measured using 16 items from the Wong and Law Emotional Intelligence Scale (WLEIS; Wong & Law [39]), where four items each are used to measure self emotional appraisal (SEA; $\alpha = .87$), others' emotional appraisal (OEA; $\alpha = .94$), regulation of emotion (ROE; $\alpha = .90$), and use of emotion (UOE; $\alpha = .86$)."

"Of all, based on the three instruments (Aquino & others [40]; Bennett & Robinson [41]; Kelloway & others [42]), 19 common items were derived as a result of discussions with a group of Korean business school graduate students who had previous job experiences (group 1)."

"Using the 12 items, we conducted a pilot test with 59 full-time employees wherein 52 usable surveys were collected."

"Items were measured on a nine-point Likert scale (1 = never, 9 = extremely often)."

Results

"The indirect effect of relationship conflict on CWBO is positive and statistically meaningful (indirect effect = .03, SE = .02, bootstrap 95% confidence interval [CI]: [.002, .065])."

"The indirect effect of relationship conflict on CWBO via affective well-being is positive when EI is high (indirect effect = .04, SE = .03, CI: [.006, .111])."

"When EI is low, there is no significant indirect effect of relationship conflict on CWBO via affective well-being (indirect effect = − .01, SE = .01, CI: [− .045, .015])."

"For CWBI, the conditional indirect effect of relationship conflict via affective well-being was not statistically meaningful for all four dimensions of EI, including SEA (indirect effect = .01, SE = .02, CI: [− .012, .052]), OEA (indirect effect = .02, SE = .02, CI: [− .013, .077]), UOE (indirect effect = .01, SE = .02, CI: [− .018, .049]), and ROE (indirect effect = .00, SE = .01, CI: [− .024, .022])."

Discussion

"Our study shows that although retaliation does occur in both forms of CWB, it is the notable loss of positive emotional resources that pushes those employees experiencing relationship conflict to engage in CWBO, especially in collectivistic cultures such as those in our study."

"When experiencing relationship conflict and the loss of emotional resources that follow, employees try to replenish their lost emotional resources or affective well-being in a circumventing way (i.e., CWBO) without directly addressing the immediate cause of the conflict (i.e., the individuals)."

"Our results extend the COR theory in a team setting: Relationship conflict reduces positive net emotional resources (i.e., affective well-being), which subsequently increases employees' likelihood of withdrawing and disengaging from the work environment."

"Our study extends this line of research by showing that even emotionally intelligent employees engage in CWB, especially in a covert form, (i.e., CWBO) as a response to their low affective well-being resulting from relationship conflict."

[Section 5]

"To unpack how stressors lead to CWB, the roles of negative emotions have received a great deal of attention from scholars (e.g., Spector & Fox [43])."

"Empirical studies found that negative emotions mediate the link between stressors and CWB (e.g., Bruk-Lee & Spector [44]; Fida & others [45]; Fox & Spector [46])."

"Studies also investigated several moderators in the stressor-emotion-CWB process and provided support for the moderating roles of individual traits (e.g., Penney & Spector [47]) and perceived control (e.g., Sprung & Jex [48])."

"We aim to advance our understanding of the stressor-emotion-CWB process and the larger CWB literature."

"Grounded in the classical models of human aggression (e.g., Berkowitz [49]; Dollard & others [50]), previous studies on CWB have focused exclusively on the roles of negative emotions."

"We examine the moderating roles of trait EI, "a constellation of emotion-related self-perceptions and dispositions" (Petrides & Furnham [51, p. 40]), as an important trait in the stressor-affective well-being-CWB process."

Engaging With Intelligent Voice Assistants for Wellbeing and Brand Attachment [67]

This is a machine-generated summary of:

Prentice, Catherine; Loureiro, Sandra Maria Correia; Guerreiro, João: Engaging with intelligent voice assistants for wellbeing and brand attachment [67]

Published in: Journal of Brand Management (2023)

Link to original: https://doi.org/10.1057/s41262-023-00321-0

Copyright of the summarized publication:
The Author(s) 2023

License: OpenAccess CC BY 4.0

This article is licensed under a Creative Commons Attribution 4.0 International License, which permits use, sharing, adaptation, distribution and reproduction in any medium or format, as long as you give appropriate credit to the original author(s) and the source, provide a link to the Creative Commons licence, and indicate if changes were made. The images or other third party material in this article are included in the article's Creative Commons licence, unless indicated otherwise in a credit line to the material. If material is not included in the article's Creative Commons licence and your intended use is not permitted by statutory regulation or exceeds the permitted use, you will need to obtain permission directly from the copyright holder. To view a copy of this licence, visit http://creativecommons.org/licenses/by/4.0/.

If you want to cite the papers, please refer to the original.

For technical reasons we could not place the page where the original quote is coming from.

Abstract-Summary

"The study draws upon the theories of self-determination and motivation of expectancy to examine how intrinsic motives drive consumers to engage with artificial intelligence (AI) powered intelligent voice assistants (IVAs)."

"The study also explores how consumer engagement leads to their wellbeing and attachment to these AI gadgets and their associated brands."

"Engagement in this study refers to consumers' usage and involvement with IVAs."

"Subject wellbeing was modeled as a mediator between consumer engagement and brand attachment."

"Consumer wellbeing also had a significant mediation effect on the relationship between engagement and brand attachment."

"The study is the first to link consumer engagement, individual wellbeing, and brand attachment."

Introduction

"Few studies have attempted to explore the underlying motives of consumer engagement with IVAs and the subsequent outcomes."

"No study to date has attempted to understand the intrinsic drivers of consumer engagement and its relationship with IVAs."

"This study draws upon self-determination theory (Deci & Ryan [52]) to examine how consumers are internally driven to engage with IVAs."

"No study to date has attempted to understand how consumer engagement may result in individual outcomes for the consumer (e.g., wellbeing)."

"Research (e.g., Shank & others [53]) has shown that engaging with AI-powered smart devices (e.g., IVAs) generates positive emotions (e.g., happy, amazed)."

"This discussion leads to the secondary aim of this research to examine how consumer engagement with IVAs affects wellbeing and brand attachment."

"The study contributes to customer engagement and artificial intelligence research by understanding the influence of intrinsic motivations on individual wellbeing and brand attachment."

Literature Review

"The level of engagement depends on the degree of autonomy (the consumer's feeling of control or being controlled by the IVA), the degree of relatedness (how strong is the human self-connection with the IVA), and the consumers competence (the degree of the utilitarian benefits extracted from the relationship)."

"The following hypothesis is offered: The need for autonomy is positively related to consumer engagement with an IVA."

"The following hypothesis is offered: Consumer engagement with an IVA has a positive influence on wellbeing."

"A consumer's engagement with an IVA may lead to attachment with the IVA and its associated brand (e.g., Siri–Apple, Google Home–Google)."

"The following hypothesis is offered: Consumer engagement with an IVA is positively related to IVA attachment."

"The following hypothesis is offered: Subjective wellbeing has a significant mediation effect between consumer engagement and IVA attachment."

Methodology

"The study targeted respondents who had used at least one IVA for more than a year to understand the impact of engagement with the IVA."

"Subjective wellbeing was measured by adapting measures from Van Boven and Gilovich [54] and Bhattacharjee and Mogilner [55], to reflect the authentic happiness as a result of interaction and engagement with IVAs."

"These measures were adapted from existing studies, reliability and validity were assessed by confirmatory factor analysis."

"The measurement items for the different dimensions of a construct were spread throughout the questionnaire and negative wording was used to ensure consistency."

"Prior to conducting the survey, a pilot study was conducted with 15 randomly chosen consumers who had used IVAs to ensure appropriate wording and completion time."

Analysis and Results

"The model was tested using Smart PLS 3.0 and the repeated indicators approach for the second-order reflective-reflective construct (user engagement)."

"Discriminant validity was assessed by two criteria, the Fornell and Larcker criterion and the Heterotrait/Monotrait ratio."

"The Fornell and Larcker criterion indicated that the squared AVE values should be higher than the inter-correlation values (Fornell and Larcker, 1981)."

"Values of AVE higher than 0.5 revealed that the constructs had convergent validity."

"The mediation testing suggests that all indirect effects were significant indicating partial mediation relationships ranging between 0 and 100%, VAF higher than 80% implies full mediation."

Discussion and Implications

"From a psychological and marketing perspective, the study examined how human–IVA interactions affect consumers' subjective wellbeing and brand attachment."

"The significant relationship between self-determination and consumer engagement in this study is consistent with research that found that intrinsic factors drive engagement (Froiland & Worrell [56]; Bhuvanaiah & Raya [57])."

"The study contributes to customer engagement research by identifying the intrinsic factors that are not initiated by the brand firm to engage customers."

"This study examined how self-determination as a personal factor exerts significant influence on brand engagement and attachment."

"This study was the first to examine how personal benefits induce consumer engagement with a product and its associated brand."

"The study contributes to branding research by exploring how self-centric benefits (subject wellbeing) relate to customer engagement and brand attachment."

"In this study, consumers are self-motivated to engage with the brands of their choice."

Limitations and Future Research Directions

"The study acknowledges limitations that may benefit from further research."

"A cross-cultural study may also generate more applicable findings and reveal the role of cultural difference in the use of smart assistants."

"The study also focused on the evaluation of user wellbeing resulting from IVAs."

"A longitudinal study could explore the effect of engagement on happiness over time."

"Future research could also explore moderators such as intimacy, level of interdependence, or level of empathy effects between user engagement and wellbeing."

Conclusion

"The study draws on the theories of self-determination and expectancy of motivation and proposes that intrinsic factors may drive consumers to engage with IVAs."

"The study was undertaken with consumers in the USA who had utilized at least one IVA brand and the results confirmed the proposed relationships."

"Limitations and future research derived from this study conclude the work."

Bibliography

1. Richardson, S., & Best, N. (2003). Bayesian hierarchical models in ecological studies of health–environment effects. *Environmetrics: The Official Journal of the International Environmetrics Society, 14*(2), 129–147. https://doi.org/10.1002/env.571
2. Hobfoll, S. E. (2001). The influence of culture, community, and the nested-self in the stress process: Advancing conservation of resources theory. *Applied Psychology, 50*(3), 337–370.
3. Hobfoll, S. E., Tirone, V., Holmgreen, L., & Gerhart, J. (2016). Conservation of resources theory applied to major stress. In *Stress: Concepts, cognition, emotion, and behavior* (pp. 65–71). Academic Press. https://doi.org/10.1016/B978-0-12-800951-2.00007-8
4. Mishra, S., Lalumière, M. L., & Williams, R. J. (2010). Gambling as a form of risk-taking: Individual differences in personality, risk-accepting attitudes, and behavioral preferences for risk. *Personality and Individual Differences, 49*(6), 616–621. https://doi.org/10.1016/j.paid.2010.05.032
5. Sotardi, V. A., & Dubien, D. (2019). Perfectionism, wellbeing, and university performance: A sample validation of the Frost Multidimensional Perfectionism Scale (FMPS) in New Zealand. *Personality and Individual Differences, 143*, 103–106. https://doi.org/10.1016/j.paid.2019.02.023
6. Spagnoli, P., Buono, C., Kovalchuk, L. S., Cordasco, G., & Esposito, A. (2021). Perfectionism and burnout during the COVID-19 crisis: A two-wave cross-lagged study. *Frontiers in Psychology, 11*, 4087. https://doi.org/10.3389/fpsyg.2020.631994
7. Spagnoli, P., Kovalchuk, L. S., Aiello, M. S., & Rice, K. G. (2021). The predictive role of perfectionism on heavy work investment: A two-waves cross-lagged panel study. *Personality and Individual Differences, 173*, 110632. https://doi.org/10.1016/j.paid.2021.110632
8. Stoeber, J., Hutchfield, J., & Wood, K. V. (2008). Perfectionism, self-efficacy, and aspiration level: Differential effects of perfectionistic striving and self-criticism after success and failure. *Personality and Individual Differences, 45*, 323–327. https://doi.org/10.1016/j.paid.2008.04.021
9. Schunk, D. H. (1991). Self-efficacy and academic motivation. *Journal of Educational Psychology, 26*(3–4), 207–231. https://doi.org/10.1080/00461520.1991.9653133
10. Brand, M., & Altstötter-Gleich, C. (2008). Personality and decision-making in laboratory gambling tasks—Evidence for a relationship between deciding advantageously under risk conditions and perfectionism. *Personality and Individual Differences, 45*(3), 226–231. https://doi.org/10.1016/j.paid.2008.04.003
11. Afthanorhan, A., Awang, Z., Abd Majid, N., Foziah, H., Ismail, I., Al Halbusi, H., & Tehseen, S. (2021). Gain more insight from common latent factor in structural equation modeling. *Journal of Physics: Conference Series, 1793*(1), 012030.
12. Al Halbusi, H., Ruiz-Palomino, P., Jimenez-Estevez, P., & Gutiérrez-Broncano, S. (2021). How upper/middle managers' ethical leadership activates employee ethical behavior? The role of organizational justice perceptions among employees. *Frontiers in Psychology, 12*, 652471. https://doi.org/10.3389/fpsyg.2021.652471
13. Al Halbusi, H., Ruiz-Palomino, P., Morales-Sánchez, R., & Abdel Fattah, F. A. M. (2021). Managerial ethical leadership, ethical climate and employee ethical behavior: Does moral attentiveness matter? *Ethics and Behavior, 31*(8), 604–627. https://doi.org/10.1080/10508422.2021.1937628
14. Preacher, K. J., & Hayes, A. F. (2004). SPSS and SAS procedures for estimating indirect effects in simple mediation models. *Behavior Research Methods Instruments & Computers, 36*(4), 717–731.
15. Preacher, K. J., & Hayes, A. F. (2008). Asymptotic and resampling strategies for assessing and comparing indirect effects in multiple mediator models. *Behavioral Research Methods, 40*(3), 879–891.
16. Weller, J. A., & Thulin, E. (2012). Do honest people take fewer risks? Personality correlates of risk-taking to achieve gains and avoid losses in HEXACO space. *Personality and Individual Differences, 53*(7), 923–926. https://doi.org/10.1016/j.paid.2012.06.010

17. Kruger, P. S. (2011). Wellbeing—the five essential elements. *Applied Research in Quality of Life, 6*(3), 325–328. https://doi.org/10.1007/s11482-010-9127-1
18. Hair, J. F., Hult, G. T. M., Ringle, C. M., & Sarstedt, M. (2017). *A primer on partial least squares structural equation modeling (PLS-SEM)* (2nd ed.). Sage.
19. Henseler, J., Ringle, C. M., & Sarstedt, M. (2015). A new criterion for assessing discriminant validity in variancebased structural equation modeling. *Journal of the Academy of Marketing Science, 43*(1), 115–135. https://doi.org/10.1007/s11747-014-0403-8
20. Ryan, R. M., & Deci, E. L. (2000). Self-determination theory and the facilitation of intrinsic motivation, social development, and well-being. *American Psychologist, 55*(1), 68–78.
21. Grunig, J. E., & Grunig, L. S. (1989). Toward a theory of the public relations behavior of organizations: Review of a program of research. *Journal of Public Relations Research, 1*(1–4), 27–63. https://doi.org/10.1207/s1532754xjprr0101-4_2
22. Hetschko, C. (2016). On the misery of losing self-employment. *Small Business Economics, 47*(2), 461–478. https://doi.org/10.1007/s11187-016-9730-0
23. Bubonya, M., Cobb-Clark, D. A., & Wooden, M. (2017). Job loss and the mental health of spouses and adolescent children. *IZA Journal of Labor Economics, 6*(1), 6. https://doi.org/10.1186/s40172-017-0056-1
24. Nikolova, M., & Ayhan, S. H. (2019). Your spouse is fired! How much do you care? *Journal of Population Economics, 32*(3), 799–844. https://doi.org/10.1007/s00148-018-0693-0
25. Nikolova, M. (2019). Switching to self-employment can be good for your health. *Journal of Business Venturing, 34*(4), 664–691. https://doi.org/10.1016/j.jbusvent.2018.09.001
26. Briscese, G., Slonim, R. L., & Feltovich, N. (2019). Who benefits from corporate social responsibility? Working Papers 2019-18, University of Sydney, School of Economics
27. Heckman, J., Ichimura, H., & Todd, P. (1998). Matching as an econometric evaluation estimator. *Review of Economic Studies, 65*(2), 261–294.
28. Abadiyah, R., Eliyana, A., & Sridadi, A. R. (2020). Motivation, leadership, supply chain management toward employee green behavior with organizational culture as a mediator variable. *International Journal of Supply Chain Management, 9*(3), 981–989.
29. Bodhi, B. (2011). What does mindfulness really mean? A canonical perspective. *Contemporary Buddhism, 12*(1), 19–39.
30. Brown, D. B., Bravo, A. J., Roos, C. R., & Pearson, M. R. (2015). Five facets of mindfulness and psychological health: Evaluating a psychological model of the mechanisms of mindfulness. *Mindfulness, 6*(5), 1021–1032.
31. Al-Omar, H. A., Arafah, A. M., Barakat, J. M., Almutairi, R. D., Khurshid, F., & Alsultan, M. S. (2019). The impact of perceived organizational support and resilience on pharmacists' engagement in their stressful and competitive workplaces in Saudi Arabia. *Saudi Pharmaceutical Journal, 27*(7), 1044–1052. https://doi.org/10.1016/j.jsps.2019.08.007
32. Sendjaya, S., Eva, N., Butar, I. B., Robin, M., & Castles, S. (2017). Slbs-6: Validation of a short form of the servant leadership behavior scale. *Journal of Business Ethics, 156*(4), 941–956. https://doi.org/10.1007/s10551-017-3594-3
33. Hair, J. F., Black, W. C., Anderson, R. E., & Tatham, R. L. (1995). *Multivariate data analysis: With readings.* Prentice Hall.
34. London, M. (1993). Relationships between career motivation, empowerment and support for career development. *Journal of Occupational and Organizational Psychology, 66*(1), 55–69. https://doi.org/10.1111/j.2044-8325.1993.tb00516.x
35. Shrout, P. E., & Bolger, N. (2002). Mediation in experimental and nonexperimental studies: New procedures and recommendations. *Psychological Methods, 7*(4), 422–444.
36. Hobfoll, S. E. (1989). Conservation of resources: A new attempt at conceptualizing stress. *American Psychologist, 44*, 513–524. https://doi.org/10.1037/0003-066x.44.3.513
37. Fox S, Spector PE, Goh A, Bruursema K (2003) Voluntary work behavior: Exploring parallels between counterproductive work behavior and organizational citizenship behavior. In J. Greenberg (Chair) *Vital but neglected topics in workplace research. Symposium conducted at the 18th annual conference of the Society for Industrial and Organizational Psychology.*

38. Van Katwyk, P. T., Fox, S., Spector, P. E., & Kelloway, E. K. (2000). Using the job-related affective well-being scale (JAWS) to investigate affective response to work stressors. *Journal of Occupational Health Psychology, 5*, 219–230. https://doi.org/10.1037/1076-8998.5.2.219
39. Wong, C. S., & Law, K. S. (2002). The effects of leader and follower emotional intelligence on performance and attitude: An exploratory study. *The Leadership Quarterly, 13*(3), 243–274.
40. Aquino, K., Lewis, M. U., & Bradfield, M. (1999). Justice constructs, negative affectivity, and employee deviance: A proposed model and empirical test. *Journal of Organizational Behavior, 20*, 1073–1091. https://doi.org/10.1002/(sici)1099-1379(199912)20:7%3c1073::aid-job943%3e3.0.co;2-7
41. Bennett, R. J., & Robinson, S. L. (2000). Development of measure of workplace deviance. *Journal of Applied Psychology, 85*, 349–360. https://doi.org/10.1037/0021-9010.85.3.349
42. Kelloway, E. K., Loughlin, C., Barling, J., & Nault, A. (2002). Self-reported counterproductive behaviors and organizational citizenship behaviors: Separate but related constructs. *International Journal of Selection and Assessment, 10*, 143–151. https://doi.org/10.1111/1468-2389.00201
43. Spector, P. E., & Fox, S. (2005). A model of counterproductive work behavior. In S. Fox & P. E. Spector (Eds.), *Counterproductive workplace behavior: Investigations of actors and targets* (pp. 151–174). American Psychological Association.
44. Bruk-Lee, V., & Spector, P. E. (2006). The social stressors-counterproductive work behaviors link: Are conflicts with supervisors and coworkers the same? *Journal of Occupational Health Psychology, 11*, 145–156. https://doi.org/10.1037/1076-8998.11.2.145
45. Fida, R., Paciello, M., Tramontano, C., Fontaine, R. G., Barbaranelli, C., & Farnese, M. L. (2015). An integrative approach to understanding counterproductive work behavior: The roles of stressors, negative emotions, and moral disengagement. *Journal of Business Ethics, 130*(1), 131–144.
46. Fox, S., & Spector, P. E. (1999). A model of work frustration–aggression. *Journal of Organizational Behavior, 20*, 915–931.
47. Penney, L. M., & Spector, P. E. (2002). Narcissism and counterproductive work behavior: Do bigger egos mean bigger problems? *International Journal of Selection and Assessment, 10*, 126–134. https://doi.org/10.1111/1468-2389.00199
48. Sprung, J. M., & Jex, S. M. (2012). Work locus of control as a moderator of the relationship between work stressors and counterproductive work behavior. *International Journal of Stress Management, 19*, 272–291.
49. Berkowitz, L. (1989). Frustration–aggression hypothesis: Examination and reformulation. *Psychological Bulletin, 106*, 59–73. https://doi.org/10.1037/0033-2909.106.1.59
50. Dollard, J., Doob, L., Miller, N., Mowrer, O., & Sears, R. (1939). *Frustration and aggression.* Yale University Press.
51. Petrides, K. V., & Furnham, A. (2003). Trait emotional intelligence: Behavioral validation of emotional recognition and reactivity to mood induction. *European Journal of Personality, 17*, 39–57. https://doi.org/10.1002/per.466
52. Deci, E. L., & Ryan, R. M. (2012). Self-determination theory in health care and its relations to motivational interviewing: A few comments. *International Journal of Behavioral Nutrition and Physical Activity.*
53. Shank, D. B., Graves, C., Gott, A., Gamez, P., & Rodriguez, S. (2019). Feeling our way to machine minds: People's emotions when perceiving mind in artificial intelligence. *Computers in Human Behavior, 98*, 256–266.
54. Van Boven, L., & Gilovich, T. (2003). To do or to have? That is the question. *Journal of Personality and Social Psychology, 85*(6), 1193.
55. Bhattacharjee, A., & Mogilner, C. (2014). Happiness from ordinary and extraordinary experiences. *Journal of Consumer Research, 41*(1), 1–17.
56. Froiland, J. M., & Worrell, F. C. (2016). Intrinsic motivation, learning goals, engagement, and achievement in a diverse high school. *Psychology in the Schools, 53*(3), 321–336.
57. Bhuvanaiah, T., & Raya, R. P. (2015). Mechanism of improved performance: Intrinsic motivation and employee engagement. *SCMS Journal of Indian Management, 12*(4), 92.

58. Chuang, Y.-T., Chiang, H.-L., & Lin, A.-P. (2023). Investigating the serial psychological processes of workplace COVID-19 infection risk and employees' performance. *Current Psychology*. https://doi.org/10.1007/s12144-023-04583-4
59. Wang, D., & McGroarty, F. (2022). Does perfectionism influence individual financial risk tolerance and financial well-being? Evidence from an online survey data from the US. *SN Business & Economics*. https://doi.org/10.1007/s43546-022-00339-7
60. Ali, M., Ali, I., Albort-Morant, G., Leal-Rodríguez, A. L. (2020). How do job insecurity and perceived well-being affect expatriate employees' willingness to share or hide knowledge? *International Entrepreneurship and Management Journal*. https://doi.org/10.1007/s11365-020-00638-1
61. Raina, R. (2022). Moving crisis to opportunities: A corporate perspective on the impact of compassionate empathic behaviour on the well-being of employees. *International Journal of Global Business and Competitiveness*. https://doi.org/10.1007/s42943-021-00040-w
62. Nikolova, M., Nikolaev, B., & Popova, O. (2020). The perceived well-being and health costs of exiting self-employment. *Small Business Economics*. https://doi.org/10.1007/s11187-020-00374-4
63. Yang, C.-H. (2022). Corporate philanthropy and employee wellbeing: Do types of corporate philanthropy matter? *Eurasian Business Review*. https://doi.org/10.1007/s40821-022-00211-6
64. Khan, J., Jaafar, M., Mubarak, N., & Khan, A. K. (2022). Employee mindfulness, innovative work behaviour, and IT project success: The role of inclusive leadership. *Information Technology and Management*. https://doi.org/10.1007/s10799-022-00369-5
65. Peng, C., Liang, Y., Yuan, G., Xie, M., Mao, Y., Harmat, L., Bonaiuto, F. (2022). How servant leadership predicts employee resilience in public organizations: A social identity perspective. *Current Psychology*. https://doi.org/10.1007/s12144-022-04138-z
66. Choi, Y., Yoon, D. J., Lee, J. D., Lee, J. Y. E. (2023). Relationship conflict and counterproductive work behavior: The roles of affective well-being and emotional intelligence. *Review of Managerial Science*. https://doi.org/10.1007/s11846-023-00642-z
67. Prentice, C., Loureiro, S. M. C., & Guerreiro, J. (2023). Engaging with intelligent voice assistants for wellbeing and brand attachment. *Journal of Brand Management*. https://doi.org/10.1057/s41262-023-00321-0

Chapter 7
Impact of Emotional Intelligence on Employees Performance

Introduction by the Author

Daniel Goleman Theory and Bar-on model theory of emotional intelligence plays a vital role in measuring employee perception. These theories provide a framework for organizational leaders and managers to find work outcomes as a result of cognitive behavioural outcomes. The theories of emotional intelligence are currently needed in predicting the leadership impact and management. Emotional intelligence is a person's ability to be aware of, but also comprehend, their own feelings and those of others, and then utilise that understanding to govern how they react and respond in social situations. The concept gained popularity in the 1990s, following the publication of Goleman's book "The Emotional Intelligence". Emotional education ought to involve basic instruction that assists individuals in better understanding and managing the emotional exertion required to perform their tasks. Employees with a high level of emotional intelligence will be more satisfied at work, which will lead to increased productivity. Emotional ability manifests itself in various ways, including awareness of oneself, handling relationships, and awareness of others. It impacts the relationship between management and employees. Alsakarneh (2018) studied the relationship between emotional labour and employee performance in insurance industry. Emotional labour may positively affect customer interaction and task effectiveness. Gabriel in (2013) studied the value of smile in emotional performance, employees positive emotional displays showed strongest influence on evaluations.

Being emotionally intelligent is a critical aspect in raising awareness, supporting workers to acquire information from other people, sharing knowledge, and developing confidence and empathy for others. Individual and organisational performance are both influenced by emotional intelligence. Employees with emotional intelligence are adaptable in their confidence, allowing them to shift their attention from fault-finding to dispute resolution. EI should be part of the selection and recruiting process because it will help the company reach its goals and increase production.

Employees that use EI often enhance their careers and the organisation. A workforce comprised of emotionally aware employees promotes team interactions and contributes to the creation of a pleasant work culture. Employees that are emotionally inept struggle to control their emotions. As a result, individuals frequently behave impulsively, believing that the repercussions of their actions would not affect them or dose around them. Developing EI can help people better understand themselves by providing them with the tools they need to direct their future cognitive processes and actions.

The exploration of relationship between emotional intelligence and job performance was conducted in police organizations by Al Ali (2011). This study argues that EI is an exceptional incremental value in predicting police job performance. The Schutte EI test was used to measure emotional intelligence of police officers. This helps in building constructive communication and to meet demands of the organisation. The emotional Machiavellianism between leaders and employees are measured by Liyanagamage in (2022). These leaders use the knowledge gained from empathy to influence the followers positively and to support corporate goals. Some of the better ways to implement EI in workplace includes providing constructive feedback rather than individual criticism and challenging behaviour rather than persons in job settings. Providing assistance to co-workers by understanding their emotions and helping them to decrease stress will improve the harmony of workplace. Staying cool and productive under pressure and helping employees to resolve team member conflicts will enable productivity.

The impact of emotional intelligence and personality traits in managing team performance was studied by Murmu (2022). This study compares EI with Five Big Personality traits in creating trust and understanding emotions. The finding of this study reveals that EI has a positive significance on virtual team effectiveness. The emotional AI at workplace was studied by Mantello (2021) which learns about sociodemographic and cross cultural determinants of attitude in workplace. This study reveals that individuals with higher cross-cultural awareness show ethical and social implications towards emotional EI.

Machine Generated Summaries

Disclaimer: The summaries in this chapter were generated from Springer Nature publications using extractive AI auto-summarization: An extraction-based summarizer aims to identify the most important sentences of a text using an algorithm and uses those original sentences to create the auto-summary (unlike generative AI). As the constituted sentences are machine selected, they may not fully reflect the body of the work, so we strongly advise that the original content is read and cited. The auto generated summaries were curated by the editor to meet Springer Nature publication standards. To cite this content, please refer to the original papers.

Machine generated keywords: display, five, leadership, emotional, service, organisation, chinese, emotional display, supervisor, workplace, success, service performance, subordinate, signal, big five

How Emotional Intelligence Promotes Leadership and Management Practices [131]

This is a machine-generated summary of:
  Gransberry, Christopher K.: How Emotional Intelligence Promotes Leadership and Management Practices [131]
  Published in: Public Organization Review (2021)
  Link to original: https://doi.org/10.1007/s11115-021-00550-4
  Copyright of the summarized publication:
  The Author(s), under exclusive licence to Springer Science+Business Media, LLC, part of Springer Nature 2021
  Copyright comment: corrected publication 2021
  All rights reserved.
  If you want to cite the papers, please refer to the original.
  For technical reasons we could not place the page where the original quote is coming from.

Abstract-Summary

"This study sought to determine the relationship between leadership and managerial practices from over 615,395 respondents at 83 U.S. Federal agencies."
  "The research established the mean for the respondent's views on leadership and managerial practices was 51.53."
  "Revealing an increase in positive responses among employees and identified that EI improves leadership and managerial practices."

Introduction

"As FEVS- Federal Employee Viewpoint Survey (1) puts it, the U.S. OPM has been committed to annually implement a viewpoint survey to assess the Federal workers' insight on the level of "conditions that characterize the successful organization.""
  "The U.S. OPM names the study 'Federal Employee Viewpoint Survey' (FEVS)."
  "The associated 2019 codebook focusses on the participating 83 different agencies, across the Federal government, which includes department-level to large and small independent agencies (FEVS- Federal Employee Viewpoint Survey [1])."

"The 2019 OPM FEVS was a self-administered survey web survey that attracted a significant number of respondents from different departments (FEVS- Federal Employee Viewpoint Survey [1])."

"In the 2019 version, the 101-item survey consists of 85 items that assess Federal employees' perception of personal work experiences, work unit, agency, supervisor, leadership, performance, partial government shutdown, work-life programs, satisfaction, and demographics (FEVS- Federal Employee Viewpoint Survey [1])."

Research Questions

"To what extent are the leadership and management practices impacted by a leader's EI score?"

"How does the impact of a leader's EI on performance impact employee perception of them?"

"How does employee perception of leadership and management practices signal their the EI of leaders/managers in the organization they work?"

"What is the relationship between employee perception of leadership and management practices in an organization and employee satisfaction?"

Literature Review

"Employee perception with EI as measured variable is the focus of this research, it draws upon two major theories of emotional intelligence to understand EI plays to enhance leadership and management: Daniel Goleman's theory and The Bar-On model theory of emotional intelligence (Drigas & Papoutsi [2])."

"The theories' relevance is that they provide a framework for managers and organizational leaders to perceive work as a subject of cognitive and behavioral outcomes that impact employee and organizational performance."

"Managers, and particularly those operating in a global context and interacting in multicultural environments prefer working with emotionally competent personnel because they are better at forming relationships, fostering social cohesion, controlling their emotions, and understand how to alphabetize different poignant states that overall impacts organizational performance, as Pastor [3] avers."

"According to Norboevich [4], theories on EI are currently relevant in predicting the impact of leadership and management on employee behavior and perceptions that directly affect the overall performance of any organization, whether a company or a government agency."

Research Methods

"The data used to inform this study is derived from conducting surveys through the FEVS survey questionnaire consisting of 71 questions targeted to over 615,395 respondents from 83 U.S. Federal agencies."

"In 2019 U.S. OPM, the FEVS survey consists of 71 questions from five different items."

"According to FEVS- Federal Employee Viewpoint Survey [1], the questions can be categorized into two perspectives that involve functional and conditional leadership and managerial practices perspectives."

"The FEVS administrators sent invitations to 1,443,152 staff to complete the survey; therefore, the 2019 OPM FEVS targeted a significant number of participants (FEVS- Federal Employee Viewpoint Survey [1])."

"Out of the 1,443,152 invited respondents, only 615,395 workers completed the survey successfully, accounting for a low response rate of 42.6% (FEVS- Federal Employee Viewpoint Survey [1])."

"As illustrated in 2019 OPM FEVS, the process for collecting responses and converting data used a 5-point Likert-type response scales (FEVS- Federal Employee Viewpoint Survey [1])."

Results

"The mean of the respondents' data was calculated as follows: Therefore, the simple average of the positive respondents on the impact of leadership and managerial practices on agencies performance is 51.53."

"The study established that the mean for the respondent's views on leadership and managerial practices was 51.53."

"The standard deviation for the respondents was 11.78."

"The study found that the respondents' answers concerning leadership and managerial practices were diverse because the standard deviation shows that the investigated data sets were not concentrated around the mean."

Discussion and Conclusion

"Although the standard deviation can be difficult to interpret in a single figure, the study found a significant relationship between respondents' views on leadership and managerial practices between 2015 and 2019."

"Although the 2019 OPM FEVS does not mention a specific theory, the selected items reflect some components of EI that led to an increase in employees' positive views on leadership and managerial practices."

"The study has evaluated the relationship between leadership and managerial practices using data sets from the 2019 OPM FEVS."

"The study identified that EI improves leadership and managerial practices; therefore, it increases positive responses among employees."

"EI impacts the relationship between leaders and employees, and also the management and leadership practices they employ in an organization."

"The research contributes to the understanding of leadership by introducing the necessary need for researchers to explore EI for both employees as potential organizational leaders and managers/leaders as agents of the organization."

Exploring the Relationship Between the Emotional Labor and Performance in the Jordanian Insurance Industry [132]

This is a machine-generated summary of:

Alsakarneh, Asaad Ahmad Abdelqader; Hong, Shen Chao; Eneizan, Bilal Mohammad; AL-kharabsheh, Kamel A.: Exploring the relationship between the emotional labor and performance in the Jordanian insurance industry [132]

Published in: Current Psychology (2018)

Link to original: https://doi.org/10.1007/s12144-018-9935-2.

Copyright of the summarized publication:

Springer Science+Business Media, LLC, part of Springer Nature 2018

All rights reserved.

If you want to cite the papers, please refer to the original.

For technical reasons we could not place the page where the original quote is coming from.

Abstract-Summary

"The present study explores the relationship between emotional labor and employee performance."

"This research analyses whether human resource practices, such as service training, can moderate the effect of emotional labor on the performance of employees."

"Results indicated the negative relationship of surface acting with the performance of employees and job satisfaction."

"Deep acting has a positive relationship with the performance of employees but exhibits a negative relationship with job satisfaction."

"Service training mediated the relationship between emotional labor and the performance of employees."

"The perspective of customer services and theories on emotional labor were used to discuss the theoretical and practical implications of this research."

Introduction

"Emotional labor may likewise positively affect the performance of employees, such as by facilitating customer interaction and task effectiveness (Ashforth and Humphrey [5]; Kluemper and others [6])."

"This research mainly endeavors to analyses how two emotional labor stratagems, namely, surface acting (faking or suppressing emotions) and deep acting (cognitive change to feel the appropriate emotions), affect job satisfaction and performance and how they relate to strain and service performance on a daily basis."

"We explore how the emotional labor strategies of surface and deep acting correspond to two critical results: job satisfaction and employee performance."

"The relationship between emotional labor and employee performance in the Jordanian insurance industry is the main aim of this paper."

"This paper will examine the effect of moderating variable service training on the affiliation between emotional labor and employee performance."

Literature Review

"Emotional labor has been a popular research topic among service academics because of the nature of service jobs requiring responding to guests with a smile at all times."

"Research of the past three decades has shown that emotional labor may influence employee performance positively, for example, by smoothening the interaction with the client and facilitating task effectiveness (Ashforth and Humphrey [5]; Kluemper and others [6])."

"In filling this research gap, there is a need to study the relationship between emotional labor and employee's performance."

Theoretical Background and Hypothesis Development

"Emotional labor strategies, including surface and deep acting, are mainly essential in customer service because clients frequently perceive employee behaviour in the provision of services (e.g. empathy, friendliness and responsiveness) as the most crucial facet of service quality (Bitner and others [7])."

"The centrality and the monotony of employee emotional labor that evokes negative customer response prompts us to suggest the negative relationship between the extent of employee participation in emotional labor and their task-related performance (Goodwin and others [8])."

"We foresee surface and deep acting having negative and positive relationships, respectively, with employee performance."

"We posit that surface acting, which involves such emotional suppression, has a negative relationship with employee performance."

"We theorise the differences in the relationships between surface and deep acting and employee performance."

Effect of Emotional Labor on Job Satisfaction

"Numerous studies have established the negative correlation between emotional labor and job satisfaction."

"Employees who are immersed in emotional labor are likely to experience job dissatisfaction than those who do not perform emotional labor."

"Emotional labor entails organisational display rules despite the felt emotions of an individual and requires employees to use strategies that regulate emotions at work (Gosserand and Diefendorff [9])."

"The significant influence of emotional labor on employee job satisfaction was demonstrated in certain private hospitals in Punjab."

"Emotional labor, which is negatively related to job satisfaction, has various dimensions; deep acting and emotional consonance are identified as major causes of job satisfaction (Kaur and Malodia [10])."

"Several studies have centred on two emotional labor strategies (i.e. surface and deep acting), which are commonly used to regulate emotional displays at work."

"Deep acting involves low-level cognitive dissonance, in which employees display emotions that approximate their true feelings."

Effect of Job Satisfaction on Employee Performance

"We theorise how service training and the mentoring programs of employers function as beneficial job resources that moderate the relationship between emotional labor and employee performance."

"Effective service training programs can enhance employee job-related resources by increasing their expertise and skills on customer interactions and service delivery processes (Chuang and Liao [11])."

"The preceding arguments indicate that although surface acting drains the energy and cognitive resources of employees to assist customers and address their needs, service training can support employees to deliver services and handle customer needs appropriately even while employees engage in surface acting."

"Such finding suggests that service training can buffer the detrimental effects of employee surface acting on their performance."

"We propose the following hypothesis: Hypothesis 3a: Service training moderates the effect of surface acting on employee performance."

"We used the preceding arguments to posit the following hypothesis: Hypothesis 3b: Service training moderates the effect of deep acting on employee performance."

Method

"We assessed the surface and deep acting of the respondents using a 15-item scale."

"Surface and deep acting were measured by 10 items and 5 items (1 = seldom; 5 = always) as proposed by Diefendorff and others [12]."

"For surface acting, sample items include 'I hide my true feelings about a situation'."

"Sample items for deep acting include 'I try to actually experience the emotions that I must show to customers'."

"Sample items for this measure include 'I am extremely proud to tell people that I work for this organisation' and 'I am very satisfied with my job'."

"Service training was measured using a five-item scale developed by the Questionpro website [13]."

"We measured employee performance using a 10-item scale developed by Brayfield and Crockett [14] and the Survey Monkey website [15]."

"Sample items include 'The performance of employees is high' and 'Employees in the company are effective' (1 = seldom; 5 = always)."

Results

"A negative and significant relationship is determined ($r = -0.181$, $p < 0.05$) between deep acting and low employee performance, whilst a negative effect is revealed between surface acting and employee performance."

"A significant and negative effect is established between job satisfaction and low employee performance ($r = 0.471$, $p < 0.01$)."

"Despite a negative and significant relationship ($r = -0.242$, $p < 0.01$) between service training and employee performance, no significant relationship is determined when service training moderates the effect of surface acting on employee performance."

"We included surface and deep acting as independent variables and employee performance as the dependent variable because we measured emotional labor using two different sources."

"To test H3a and H3b, the main and moderating effects were included to evaluate the unique effects of service training and emotional labor on employee performance."

Discussion

"This study aimed to explore the relationship between emotional labor and employee performance and determine the manner by which service training moderates the effect of surface and deep acting on employee performance."

"The results indicated that surface acting significantly and positively affects employee performance (P-value = 0.001)."

"The present study also confirms that service training does not moderate the effect of surface acting (P-value = 0.081) and deep acting (P-value = 0.133) on employee performance."

"Consistent with these suggestions, we determined that service training support enhances the positive effects of deep acting and alleviates the negative effects of surface acting on employee performance."

"Empirical findings indicate that service training strengthens the positive relationship between deep acting and employee performance, but such training does not moderate the association between surface acting and employee performance."

Limitations and Future Research Implications

"Although we focused on the relationships between employee choices of display strategies (i.e. surface and deep acting) and their inner feelings (i.e. job satisfaction and employee performance), future studies should broadly consider employee ratings or customer perceptions of employee emotional displays."

"Of examining the display of true emotions when employees are in a bad mood, future research should also focus on the potential positive effect of surface acting."

"The research design can be utilised to test the possibility of a controversial relationship where deep acting may lead to high levels of employee performance, which could be why an employee will use surface acting as a low investment approach to meet the required display emotions (Grandey [16])."

"This study also provides evidence of the importance of training employees in deep acting, which outperforms surface acting in the delivery of services (Chen and others [17])."

Conclusion

"Emotional labor studies are predominantly focused on the negative effects of surface acting on employee performance."

"Investigations into the relationship between emotional labor and employee performance on a daily basis remain scarce."

"This study provides crucial theoretical and methodological contributions to the emotional labor literature by offering evidence of direct and indirect links between emotional labor strategies and organisational outcomes, particularly employee performance and job satisfaction."

"The current study argues that the concept of emotional labor should be related to employee performance and job satisfaction simultaneously."

Managers' Conflict Management Styles and Employee Attitudinal Outcomes: The Mediating Role of Trust [133]

This is a machine-generated summary of:
 Chan, Ka Wai; Huang, Xu; Ng, Peng Man: Managers' conflict management styles and employee attitudinal outcomes: The mediating role of trust [133]

Conclusion

Published in: Asia Pacific Journal of Management (2007)
Link to original: https://doi.org/10.1007/s10490-007-9037-4.
Copyright of the summarized publication:
Springer Science+Business Media, LLC 2007
All rights reserved.
If you want to cite the papers, please refer to the original.
For technical reasons we could not place the page where the original quote is coming from.

Abstract-Summary

"This study examines the mediating effects of trust on the relationships between manager's conflict management styles (CMS) and employee attitudinal outcomes, as well as identifies the potential deviations in the areas of CMS and trust from the west in Chinese culture."

"As predicted, Integrating CMS of managers is found significantly correlated to trust and subordinates' job satisfaction and turnover intention."

"Trust fully mediates the link between Integrating CMS and subordinates attitudinal outcomes."

Conflict Management Styles

"Rahim [18] used a similar conceptualization to create five conflict management styles based on two dimensions—concern for self and concern for others which portray the motivational orientation of a given individual during conflict."

"Among the five conflict management styles, the ones in which a moderate to high level of concern for the other party is shown, namely integrating, obliging and comprising, are considered as "cooperative conflict management styles"; while the ones in which little concern is shown for the other party, namely avoiding and dominating, are considered as "uncooperative conflict management styles" (Rahim, Magner, & Shapiro [19]; Song, Xie, & Dyer [20])."

"As previous literature has found that cooperative CMS generally produces positive job outcomes, we believe that a cooperative CMS (integrating, obliging, and compromising), which focuses on satisfying the concerns of others, will lead to a positive job attitude among subordinates, including high job satisfaction and low turnover intention."

Potential Deviations of Conflict Management Styles in the Chinese Context

"While Western conflict management literature suggests that people tend to react more positively to cooperative CMS and more negatively to uncooperative CMS, the link between the uncooperative CMS of managers and negative subordinate attitudinal outcomes may not be supported in Chinese context."

"We argue that in dealing with conflict situations in the workplace in the Chinese context, the uncooperative CMS of leaders (dominating and avoiding), which ignores the work autonomy of subordinates, open communication, and participative decision making, may not necessarily lead to negative consequences, such as low trust in leadership, low job satisfaction, or high turnover intention."

"Although studies conducted in the West have consistently found a negative relationship between the uncooperative CMS (dominating and avoiding) of managers and the job outcomes of their subordinates, we argue that this negative relationship may not be supported in the Chinese context."

Mediating Role of Trust on Conflict Management Styles (CMS)

"It is argued that interactional justice involves the degree of respect with which a leader treats his/her followers, and thus sends a strong signal about the nature of the relationship by which subordinates would make inferences about their degree of trust towards the manager (Dirks & Ferrin [21])."

"We can conclude that managerial behavior that shows care and respect for subordinates, as well as open communication, are important factors in fostering trust in the relationship, which are found in transformational leadership, interactional justice and participative decision-making."

"Based on social exchange theory, when employees perceive that the cooperative CMS of a manager (integrating, obliging, and compromising) shows that they are being valued and cared for, their trusting relationship will be enhanced."

"Discussion, we propose that: Trust mediates the positive relationship between the cooperative CMS of a manager and subordinate job satisfaction."

Materials and methods

"Of the 148 questionnaires distributed, 126 employees responded, yielding a response rate of 85.14%."

"Employees were instructed to indicate the extent to which they agreed that each item described the way in which their immediate supervisor handled interpersonal conflicts with them on a 5-point Likert-type scale, ranging from strongly disagree (1) to strongly agree (5)."

"Responses to these 11 items were measured on a 5-point Likert-type scale, ranging from strongly disagree (1) to strongly agree (5)."

"The three-item job satisfaction scale was based on a measure developed by Cammann, Fichman, Jenkins, and Klesh [22]."

"The responses were on a 5-point Likert-type scale, ranging from strongly disagree (1) to strongly agree (5)."

Conclusion 311

"The turnover intention variable was operationalized as a three-item scale adapted from Cammann, Fichman, Jenkins, and Klesh [23] on a 5-point Likert-type scale, ranging from strongly disagree (1) to strongly agree (5)."

Results

"Since uncooperative CMS is not related to subordinate job satisfaction and turnover intention in the result of multiple regression analyses, the argument concerning potential deviations of CMS in the relationship between managerial uncooperative CMS and subordinates' trust and attitudinal outcomes in the Chinese context is fully supported."

"To test the mediating effects of trust, the three-step process described by Baron and Kenny [24] was used to test whether trust in supervisor is a mediator of the relationships between the cooperative CMS of managers and subordinates' job satisfaction and turnover intention."

"When we enter the mediator trust in Model 3, integrating CMS becomes insignificant on both job satisfaction and turnover intention, whereas the beta of trust remains significant ($\beta = 0.62$ and -0.63, $p < 0.05$, respectively; $\Delta R^2 = 0.11$ and 0.02, respectively)."

"Hypotheses 2a and 2b, which propose that trust in supervisors mediates the relationships between cooperative CMS and the attitudinal outcomes of subordinates in job satisfaction and turnover intention, are only partially supported."

Discussion

"This paper attempts to achieve two goals: to investigate the role of trust in the relationships between the CMS of manager and subordinate attitudinal outcomes; and to identify the potential deviations in the areas of CMS and trust in Chinese culture."

"This study once again confirmed that the use of Integrating CMS by manager leads to positive subordinate outcomes."

"The results of this study further illustrate the mediating role of trust in the relationships between integrating CMS and subordinate positive attitudinal outcomes."

"Under this kind of paternalistic leadership style in Chinese culture, uncooperative CMS becomes more acceptable and does not affect trust in leadership."

"This result also suggests a salient feature of trust in the supervisor–subordinate relationship under the paternalistic leadership style of Chinese culture."

Implications for Practice

"An implication for practice is that cooperative CMS, especially an integrating CMS, is desirable to ensure positive attitudinal outcomes for subordinates in the workplace."

"To build a better work environment and to win the trust of employees, managers should show more concern towards their employees when dealing with conflicts in the workplace and should focus on solving the problems in a win-win situation."

"As the mediating role of trust has been supported in this study, managers should improve their managerial effectiveness by augmenting levels of trust and should work on different ways to build trust with subordinates."

"Organizations should provide more training opportunities for managers to promote trustworthy behavior in the areas of leadership, human resources, communication, and conflict management."

Limitations and Areas for Future Study

"Several limitations of this study that need further attention in the future should be noted."

"This study only focused on the individual level to investigate the relationship between CMS and individual outcomes; future studies should focus on different levels, such as the team level, to investigate the relationships among CMS, trust, and team outcomes."

"Future research is also needs to examine the influence of national or corporate culture on the proposed relationships, and other mediators, such as trust in the organization or trust in co-workers, should also be explored."

"Future research in this area is necessary to enhance our understanding of trust in leadership."

[Section 9]

"Other studies show that CMS of managers is related to various outcomes of subordinates, such as job satisfaction, supervision satisfaction, supervisor–subordinate relationships, long-term cooperation, and attitudinal and behavioral compliance (Alexander [25]; Blake & Mouton [26]; Follett [27]; Rahim [28]; Thomas & Kilmann [29]; Weider-Hatfield & Hatfield [30])."

"It is likely that managers using cooperative conflict management styles enhance social exchange process and earn trust from subordinates which lead to positive outcomes."

"The primary purpose of this study is to examine the mediating role of trust in the relationship between the conflict management styles of superiors and the work attitudes (job satisfaction and turnover intention) of subordinates."

Conclusion 313

"We suspect that while Western conflict management literature suggests that people tend to react more positively to cooperative CMS and more negatively to uncooperative CMS, Chinese employees are more tolerant of uncooperative CMS and thus less likely to have discussions or direct confrontations with their superiors in conflict situations."

Building Emotional Principal–Teacher Relationships in Chinese Schools: Reflecting on Paternalistic Leadership [134]

This is a machine-generated summary of:
Qian, Haiyan; Walker, Allan: Building Emotional Principal–Teacher Relationships in Chinese Schools: Reflecting on Paternalistic Leadership [134]
Published in: The Asia–Pacific Education Researcher (2021)
Link to original: https://doi.org/10.1007/s40299-021-00563-z.
Copyright of the summarized publication:
De La Salle University 2021
All rights reserved.
If you want to cite the papers, please refer to the original.
For technical reasons we could not place the page where the original quote is coming from.

Abstract-Summary

"Relationships between leaders and followers entail building emotional connections."

"Using data collected from 101 primary school principals from six Chinese provinces, this paper explores how principals build reciprocal relationships with teachers via the display and enactment of paternalistic leadership."

"The principals adopted a paternal leadership approach where they provided protection and care for teachers' professional and personal lives while maintaining high expectations of quality teaching and cultivating a shared understanding of what teachers should and should not do."

"The study provides an empirical basis to reflect and revisit the concept of paternalistic leadership and relationship between culture, leadership and emotional relationships."

Introduction

"One widely practiced leadership style among political and business leaders in Confucian heritage societies is paternalistic leadership (Farh & Cheng [31]; Tan & Dimmock [32])."

"The purpose of this article is to explore how school principals in China enact paternalistic leadership and the leadership practices they employ to build strong emotional relationships with teachers."

"As we have written elsewhere (Author 2020), the principals involved in the study tended to adopt a form of paternalistic leadership."

"Few studies have explored principals' perspectives about gearing paternalistic leadership toward building emotional relationships between principals and teachers in schools in China."

"This article therefore attempts to understand how principals interpret the three key dimensions of paternalistic leadership—authoritarianism, benevolence and morality (Aycan [33]; Farh & Cheng [31]; Farh and others [34]), and how these leadership practices intentionally shape strong emotional bonds with teachers."

"It provides empirical insights extracted from principals' views of how to build and maintain emotional relationships with teachers in Chinese schools."

Literature Review

"In the school context, school leaders, particularly principals, indirectly influence student learning through a direct impact on teacher motivation, ability, emotions and working conditions (Leithwood and others [35]; Zheng and others [36])."

"Such a climate is dependent on leaders building strong emotional connections and harmonious relationships with teachers (Day and others [37]; Hallinger [38])."

"Paternalistic leaders can induce various emotional reactions from followers, as they do from their own families; these may include respect, liking, gratitude, or fear (Chen and others [39]; Farh and others [34])."

"A number of empirical studies have examined the relationship between principals' paternalistic leadership and the level of trust or performance of teachers in the Chinese school context (e.g., Shi and others [40]; Zheng and others [36])."

"Most of these studies collected survey data from teachers and did not explore how school principals endeavor to build emotional relationships with teachers through exerting paternalistic leadership."

Method

"The data for this article were drawn from a qualitative study that involved interviews with 101 primary school principals in selected regions in China, including Shanghai (SH), Beijing (BJ), Guangdong (GD, South China), Hubei (HB, central China), Liaoning (SY, Northeast China) and Guizhou (GZ, Southwest China)."

Conclusion 315

"The primary purpose of the data collection was to understand the perception and practice of Chinese school principals' instructional leadership."

"A Chinese instructional leadership model was posited from the data."

"One of the strongest patterns of Chinese instructional leadership practices was the robust focus on understanding and developing teachers."

"Many of the practices adopted by the Chinese principals involved in the study were relationally oriented and focused on engendering emotional reactions through emphasizing conformity, care and role modeling (Walker & Qian [41])."

"The next section will present how principals interpreted these three dimensions in their leadership practices and how they influenced their relationships with teachers."

Findings—Paternalistic Leadership Practices of Chinese Principals

"Principals claimed that teachers were the most important assets of the schools and that they needed to value and appreciate each individual teacher as a whole person (ren)."

"For schools with larger numbers of younger teachers, the principal might need to deal with conflicts they had with their parents."

"As one Liaoning female principal shared: In our schools we have a lot of young teachers."

"Principals cared about the well-being of teachers."

"Seeing themselves as parents in their schools, principals felt they were responsible for protecting teachers."

"A Shanghai principal believed that teachers at her school "feel happy in spite of the high workload.""

"Another Liaoning principal believed that she was trusted by her teachers."

"Principals believed that if they treated teaches as family members, teachers would reward them with more than they expected."

Discussion

"The data showed an array of strategies used by paternalistic principals to develop positive relationships with teachers."

"If we examine these leadership strategies in relation to Popper's [42] framework of three types of emotional relations (regressive, symbolic and developmental relations), some initial conclusions include: The adoption of paternalistic leadership and the deep-rooted perception of the leader as a parent already creates conditions for regressive relations in Chinese schools."

"If principals can display and demonstrate their teaching expertise before teachers, these will boost leaders' personal charisma and authority."

"Chinese principals adopt various strategies to develop teachers' capacities; this is a key part of Chinese instructional leadership (Qian & Walker [43])."

"New principals can work on maintaining a nuanced balance between caring about both teachers' professional and personal development and respecting teachers' autonomy and independence."

Limitation and Future Research

"The purpose of this paper was to explore how school principals in China enact paternalistic leadership and the leadership practices they employ to build strong emotional relationships with teachers."

"The data showed how a diverse group of principals influenced, perhaps unconsciously, by traditional cultural values demonstrate a belief in and commitment to a form of paternalistic leadership."

"Deeper research in this area which also taps into teacher and community perspectives is needed to further understand the emotional component of paternalistic leadership; such investigation would be most worthwhile."

"Future research may target the following areas: Collecting data from school teachers to understand whether and how they perceive principals' paternalistic leadership; Collecting data from multiple sources to delineate the correlation between the exercise of paternalistic leadership and emotional bonds between principals and teachers at schools; Conducting comparative studies which investigate how principals in different cultures craft empathetic beliefs and practices to improve school performance and foster leader-teacher relationships."

The Value of a Smile: Does Emotional Performance Matter More in Familiar or Unfamiliar Exchanges? [135]

This is a machine-generated summary of:

Gabriel, Allison S.; Acosta, Jennifer D.; Grandey, Alicia A.: The Value of a Smile: Does Emotional Performance Matter More in Familiar or Unfamiliar Exchanges? [135]

Published in: Journal of Business and Psychology (2013)

Link to original: https://doi.org/10.1007/s10869-013-9329-2.

Copyright of the summarized publication:

Springer Science+Business Media New York 2013

All rights reserved.

If you want to cite the papers, please refer to the original.

For technical reasons we could not place the page where the original quote is coming from.

Abstract-Summary

"In Study 1, we assessed whether service familiarity (as rated by employees) moderated the relationship of employee-reported positive emotional displays and coworker ratings of service performance."

"In Study 2, through observed employee–customer exchanges, we tested whether customer-reported familiarity with the service context moderated the relationship between third-party-observed employee positive emotional displays and customer ratings of transaction satisfaction and employee friendliness."

"Employee positive emotional displays had the strongest influence on evaluations of performance under low familiarity contexts."

"Service performance evaluations may be less influenced by employee positive emotional displays when the customer has a familiar relationship, suggesting that such displays from the employee are not always necessary."

Service Familiarity as a Boundary Condition

"Studies on employee positive emotional displays and performance have primarily been conducted in contexts where customers and employees tend to be less familiar with each other (e.g., food service, shoe stores)."

"Our primary objective is to determine whether nonverbal behaviors from employees (i.e., positive emotional displays) function differently as signals of good performance under different levels of service familiarity."

"Central to the focus of the current study, we propose that employees' frequency of displaying positive emotions to customers is more strongly linked to service performance evaluations when customers tend to be less familiar compared to more familiar."

"Both (a) employee positive emotional displays and (b) service familiarity have unique positive relationships with service performance ratings."

"Service familiarity moderates the relationship between employee positive emotional displays and service performance ratings: the relationship is stronger when customer interactions tend to be less familiar rather than more familiar."

Study 1 Method

"For our preliminary test of these ideas, we took a between-person approach to assess the variability of an employee's familiarity with customers in general (i.e., across all of an employee's customers) and frequency of displaying positive emotions with customers, and whether they interactively predicted a coworker's rating of service performance."

"We needed to measure employee-level variation in familiarity, or variation in the proportion of customers with whom an employee has more relationship-based interactions as opposed to encounters; this variation is likely driven by both employee behaviors (i.e., actively learning customers' names) and work characteristics (i.e., location of store, nature of work)."

"Coworkers are able to observe repeated interactions between the focal employees and customers, they can provide a service performance evaluation that is less deficient than supervisors and less biased than self-ratings (Grandey [44])."

"High service familiarity occupations (coded 1) are occupations where employees almost always interact repeatedly with customers to share knowledge or expertise."

Study 1 Results

"To reduce the risks associated with the inclusion of extraneous variables (Spector & Brannick [45]), only employee gender and occupational service familiarity were retained as control variables."

"Supporting Hypotheses 1a and 1b, employee positive emotional displays (b = .16, P < .05; Hypothesis 1a) and service familiarity (b = .12, P < .001; Hypothesis 1b) positively and uniquely related to coworker ratings of service performance."

"In support of Hypothesis 2, the interaction between employee positive emotional displays and service familiarity was significant (b = −.12, P < .05), accounting for an additional 3 % of the variance in coworker service performance ratings."

"but were positively related to judgments in low-familiarity contexts (1 SD below the mean; b = .35, P < .01)."

Study 1 Discussion and Limitations

"Study 1 demonstrated that coworkers rated performance higher for employees who reported (a) displaying more positive emotions toward customers and (b) having more familiar relationships with customers."

"These effects were found controlling for occupational service familiarity, suggesting the possibility that the performance value of employee emotional displays may be attributable to employee variations in familiarity with customers."

"To explore this, we tested whether the interaction between occupational service familiarity and employee positive emotional displays predicted coworker service performance ratings; the results were null."

"Study 2 was designed to more directly test our signaling hypothesis by observing positive emotional displays (i.e., smiling, eye contact, vocal quality) of employees toward a single customer during a service transaction, and surveying that customer's evaluation of the transaction as well as his or her level of familiarity with the employee and store."

Conclusion

Study 2 Method

"Out of 208 observed transactions, we received 164 customer evaluations that could be matched to employee observation data (79 % response rate)."

"Since positive emotional displays create impressions of employee friendliness, a key part of service performance (Parasuraman and others [46]), we also asked customers to rate employee friendliness with one item ("In your opinion, to what extent was the service provider friendly?") on a five-point scale (1 = "not at all;" 5 = "extremely")."

"To our two focal dependent variables, we asked for a rating of efficiency with one item ("In your opinion, to what extent was the service provider efficient/timely?") on a five-point scale (1 = "not at all;" 5 = "extremely") given that it is also a key part of employee service performance (Parasuraman and others [46]) and to avoid focusing the customer on our focal variables."

Study 2 Results

"Responding to this call, we integrated separate literatures on the relationship between the employee and customer (Gutek [47]) and signaling theory (Bangerter and others [48]), and proposed that service familiarity changes the meaning of observable behaviors or cues (e.g., positive emotional displays) performed by employees toward customers."

"In the service context, positive emotional displays signal motivation to cooperate and help others; these behaviors matter especially for new customers who lack previous information about the employee (i.e., "typical" emotional performance)."

"This is one of the first studies to consider both the social-relational context (i.e., service familiarity) and behaviors (i.e., employee positive emotional displays to customers) simultaneously."

"In service contexts, positive emotional displays are part of achieving performance goals (i.e., customer service); thus, displays may be unrelated to how an employee actually feels (see also Pugh [49])."

Conclusion

"As the service sector continues to be a dominant part of the U.S. and global economy (Ryan & Ployhart [50]), understanding how to provide excellent service is increasingly important."

"Our research advances knowledge by demonstrating that the relational context combined with employee positive emotional displays plays a critical role in service exchanges."

"Service familiarity is not only linked to better quality service, but also determines whether employee positive emotional displays are important for performance-related judgments."

"Our research suggests that employee positive emotional displays are not as necessary for effective service delivery in established service relationships, suggesting a critical boundary condition for managers and employees alike to consider."

[Section 8]

"We suggest that the relational context—the familiarity of the customer with the employee and service provided—moderates the influence of employee positive emotional displays on performance evaluations."

"Considering the ideas of signaling theory in the impression management literature (Bangerter and others [48]; Barrick and others [51]; Kacmar and others [52]), we posit that employee positive emotional displays matter more in low-familiarity contexts (e.g., service encounters) than in high-familiarity settings (e.g., service relationships)."

"In Study 1, we used a multi-source survey of employees from a variety of service occupations to provide an initial test of whether the relationship between an employee's positive emotional displays toward customers and a coworker's performance rating was moderated by the tendency for the employee to interact with familiar customers on the job."

"In Study 2, we conducted an observational study of food service transactions to more formally test how variability in customer-reported service familiarity moderates the relationship between observed employee positive emotional displays and customer performance evaluation."

An Exploration of the Relationship Between Emotional Intelligence and Job Performance in Police Organizations [136]

This is a machine-generated summary of:
Al Ali, Omar Ebrahim; Garner, Iain; Magadley, Wissam: An Exploration of the Relationship Between Emotional Intelligence and Job Performance in Police Organizations [136]
Published in: Journal of Police and Criminal Psychology (2011)
Link to original: https://doi.org/10.1007/s11896-011-9088-9.
Copyright of the summarized publication:
Springer Science+Business Media, LLC 2011
All rights reserved.
If you want to cite the papers, please refer to the original.
For technical reasons we could not place the page where the original quote is coming from.

Abstract-Summary

"The results show significant correlations between EI levels and police job performance."

"After controlling for general mental abilities and personality traits, EI has been found to explain additional incremental variance in predicting police job performance."

Introduction

"Several researchers (e.g., Daus & Ashkanasy [53]) have argued that EI is important for effective police performance, given that there is a high need for officers to manage their own and others' emotions as part of their job."

"EI may contribute significantly for police effectiveness in communicating with the public in that officers who possess the ability to appraise and express emotion may be able to create environments that support the development of people trust and collaboration which will support their performance in fighting against crime."

"Notwithstanding that very few studies have studied the validity of EI in policing, police officers appear logically to require a high level of EI since their work is based on human contact, need effective teamwork, and need high ability to deal with negative affect."

"The main goal of the present study, therefore, is to examine the validity of EI in predicting job performance among a sample of police officers."

Method

"EI was measured by a self-report emotional intelligent test that developed by Schutte and others (The SREIT 1998)."

"Job performance tests used to evaluate participants were implemented by the Abu Dhabi Police force."

"To test the incremental validity of EI in predicting job performance over cognitive ability and personality traits, participants completed the Arabic version of the NEO-FFI (Alansari [54]) as a measure of the five-factor model of personality."

"This was important in order to help the researcher collect their annual official job performance evaluations from the Human Resources Department at the Abu Dhabi Police (in order to match the results of the tests and criteria measurements)."

Results

"Hypothesis Two proposes that EI explains additional variance in the prediction of police job performance over cognitive ability and personality traits."

"This hypothesis was tested using hierarchical regression analysis, with cognitive ability entered at Step 1, personality traits at Step 2, and EI at Step 3."

"The hierarchical regression results demonstrate that after cognitive ability and personality traits were controlled for, EI accounted for a statistically significant portion of variance (R2 Change = .039) in the prediction of police performance."

Discussion

"The aim of the current study was to explore the relationship between EI and job performance in a sample of police officers."

"These explanations may justify the current results of the positive correlation between EI and police officers' job performance."

"Argument, it would appear that high levels of EI (officers' abilities to manage their own and others' emotions) may play a significant role in building constructive communication practices with other people and agencies within a community (such as in schools) to meet these demands, which in turn would aid in predicting other aspects of police officer performance."

"The current research shows that for police work in the UAE, which is likely to be similar worldwide, EI is more likely to predict job performance."

"Despite these limitations, the results of this study may contribute to existing literature by providing additional evidence regarding the validity of EI in predicting job performance within police organization in the UAE."

The Emotional Machiavellian: Interactions Between Leaders and Employees [137]

This is a machine-generated summary of:

Liyanagamage, Nilupulee; Fernando, Mario; Gibbons, Belinda: The Emotional Machiavellian: Interactions Between Leaders and Employees [137]

Published in: Journal of Business Ethics (2022)

Link to original: https://doi.org/10.1007/s10551-022-05233-8.

Copyright of the summarized publication:

The Author(s) 2022

License: OpenAccess CC BY 4.0

This article is licensed under a Creative Commons Attribution 4.0 International License, which permits use, sharing, adaptation, distribution and reproduction in any medium or format, as long as you give appropriate credit to the original author(s) and the source, provide a link to the Creative Commons licence, and indicate if changes were made. The images or other third party material in this article are included in the article's Creative Commons licence, unless indicated otherwise in a credit line to the material. If material is not included in the article's Creative Commons licence and

Conclusion   323

your intended use is not permitted by statutory regulation or exceeds the permitted use, you will need to obtain permission directly from the copyright holder. To view a copy of this licence, visit http://creativecommons.org/licenses/by/4.0/.

If you want to cite the papers, please refer to the original.

For technical reasons we could not place the page where the original quote is coming from.

Abstract-Summary

"This paper examines the emotional processes in Machiavellian leadership."

"This study explores Machiavellian emotional processes at multiple levels—within-persons and relational levels (between-persons and interpersonal interactions in organisations)."

"Emotions and leadership are not explored in isolation but as social processes that occur in relationships between leaders and employees in evolving organisational settings."

"The findings suggest that Machiavellianism influences leader and employee emotional processes."

"The emotional processes, influenced by Machiavellianism, appear to facilitate the development of leader and employee relationships and emotional experiences at within-persons and relational levels in organisations."

Introduction

"Machiavellianism in organisations relates to unethical actions, employee dissatisfaction, distress, emotional exhaustion, turnover and other negative workplace consequences (Bagozzi & others [55]; Belschak & others [56]; Den Hartog & Belschak [57])."

"Although much research has considered the outcomes of Machiavellian leaders on employee performance, satisfaction, well-being and organisational goals (Belschak & others [58]; Castille & others [59]; Koo & Lee [60]), to our knowledge, no published study explicitly explores why Machiavellians engage in unethical actions in organisations."

"To consider the why, in this research, we explore the relational processes of Machiavellian leadership –specifically the emotional processes."

"Since leaders and employees frequently experience obstacles in the workplace, it is important to explore the emotional processes of Machiavellians in relation to others."

"We explore the multiple levels of emotions at within-persons and relational levels (including between-persons and interpersonal interactions) in organisations, among leaders and employees with varying levels of Machiavellianism."

"We highlight various emotional processes of Machiavellian leaders, employees and dyads in different situations in natural workplace settings."

Literature Review

"Leadership is inherently an emotional process (Ashkanasy [61]; George [62]; Humphrey & others [63])."

"Scholars further study how emotions affect leaders' decision-making (Ashkanasy & Daus [64]) and leaders' capacity to empathise (George [62]), that is, the capacity to understand another's feelings and re-experience them."

"At an interpersonal interactions level, leadership studies concentrate on the emotions of group members: the spread of emotions through a group (i.e. emotional contagion) (Ashkanasy & Dorris [65]) and emotions in dyadic partnerships (Herman & others [66])."

"There have only been a limited number of studies on Machiavellianism and emotions (Austin & others [67, 68]; O'Connor & Athota [69]), and even fewer on Machiavellian leadership and emotions (Gkorezis & others [70]; Stradovnik & Stare [71])."

"To address the evident gap in research, this paper explores the emotional processes in Machiavellian leadership."

"Machiavellian leaders can use the knowledge gained from their sense of empathy to understand and positively influence followers' emotions and attitudes, to support corporate goals."

"High Machiavellian employees in unethical leadership settings are likely to exhibit increased knowledge hiding and emotional manipulation (Belschak & others [58])."

"We explore the emotional processes in Machiavellian leadership."

Machiavellianism, Leadership and Emotions in the Global South

"The review of literature is led by considering cross-cultural implications."

"Research shows that emotions associate differently in the Global South compared to the Global North (Hafen & others [72])."

"This study acknowledges cultural differences and that conceptual differences may arise with applying Global North origin constructs to the Global South."

"Western literature considers Sri Lanka a collectivist nation with strong family values and a feminine culture with emotional, caring and sympathetic people (Hofstede [73])."

"What these ideologies mean in terms of Machiavellianism, leadership, and emotions is yet to be considered in academic literature."

"The implications of this study are not only relevant to Sri Lanka, but for countries with growing migrant Sri Lankans in prominent leadership positions, other similar developing countries deprived of a platform in the Global North literature, and, more importantly, cross-cultural literature."

Study Context: Construction Industry in Sri Lanka

"The construction industry is transitionary and project-based."

"Construction firms in developing countries are challenged with both organisational and country-level uncertainties."

"Leadership research in construction industries (Graham & others [74]) in developing countries (Yap & others [75]) is scarce."

"This study seeks to understand an important social process: emotional processes in leadership, specifically 'dark' Machiavellian leadership in the Sri Lankan construction industry."

"Developing countries are rarely considered in studies of Machiavellianism, yet uncertain national and organisational contexts in developing contexts have important implications for leadership (Yap & others [75])."

"The highly masculine nature of the construction industry has important implications on emotions and leadership (George & Loosemore [76])."

"We consider the construction industry in a developing country, an important yet neglected context, to highlight the emotional processes in Machiavellian leadership."

Methodology

"This study uses qualitative research methods to explore the emotional processes in Machiavellian leadership in four construction organisation sites in Sri Lanka."

"To examine the within-person and between-persons levels of emotions in leaders and followers, we questioned the participants on (i) their perspectives on expressing emotions in the workplace, (ii) coping with negative or positive emotions, (iii) the role of emotions in decision-making and (iv) their knowledge about the impact of emotional expressions in the workplace (i.e. consequences of emotions)."

"To examine the relational dimensions, that is, between-persons emotions and interpersonal interactions at the organisational level, we question the participants on (i) how their leader/employee makes them feel (i.e. emotion contagion), (ii) their expressions of emotions in relationships and (iii) their sharing of emotions with others in the organisation (i.e. emotional sharing)."

"The interview data analysis drew on the thematic analysis technique by Braun and Clarke [77], which helped systematically identify, organise, and develop insights into patterns of meaning in the data."

Emotional Processes of Machiavellians

"The interviews show that Machiavellian leaders and employees experience complex negative emotions in the workplace."

"Stuart, a low Mach leader's approach to coping with negative emotional experiences and his understanding of emotions differ from high Machs."

"If I'm getting that responsibility, then I can take that risk... Vivian, a low Mach employee, explains that she refrains from expressing negative emotions towards labourers because they have more bargaining power."

"The interviews suggest that high Mach leaders try to control the employees by evoking specific emotional experiences."

"The interviews suggest that high Mach employees may be more vocal and expressive about their negative emotional experiences in the workplace than low Mach employees."

"There is nothing [we can] do... Mike, a low Mach employee, also explains that Uday expresses many negative emotions in the workplace."

Implications

"This study explored emotions in Machiavellian leadership from within-person to relational levels by considering both leader and employee experiences."

"The interviews with Machiavellians in this study suggest various facets of explicit emotion regulation operating at within-persons and relational levels."

"Time and Machiavellian personality may influence mutual trust in leader and employee relationships and, consequently, the evolving emotional experiences in the workplace."

"This study identifies contextual elements at organisational, industrial and national levels that may have influenced the emotional processes in Machiavellian leadership: power distance, respect culture, and industrial expectations."

"This study suggests that followers with fewer interactions with the leader because of power distance within the workplace may experience more negative emotions."

"The cultural understanding of time may frame how mutual trust in the Machiavellian leader and employee relationships develop and consequently their evolving emotional experiences."

Directions for Future Research

"This study has a disproportionate number of high and low Machiavellians."

"Although this may be a natural occurrence in this context, future studies could seek to balance high and low Machiavellians in their study."

"Future research could study the emotions of Machiavellian females or compare the emotional processes of male and female Machiavellians."

"This research is an initial endeavour to explore the emotional processes of Machiavellian leaders and employees from a relational perspective."

Conclusion

Impact of Emotional Intelligence and Personality Traits on Managing Team Performance in Virtual Interface [138]

This is a machine-generated summary of:
 Murmu, Susan; Neelam, Netra: Impact of emotional intelligence and personality traits on managing team performance in virtual interface [138]
 Published in: Asian Journal of Business Ethics (2022)
 Link to original: https://doi.org/10.1007/s13520-022-00154-1.
 Copyright of the summarized publication:
 The Author(s), under exclusive licence to Springer Nature B.V. 2022
 Copyright comment: Springer Nature or its licensor holds exclusive rights to this article under a publishing agreement with the author(s) or other rightsholder(s); author self-archiving of the accepted manuscript version of this article is solely governed by the terms of such publishing agreement and applicable law.
 All rights reserved.
 If you want to cite the papers, please refer to the original.
 For technical reasons we could not place the page where the original quote is coming from.

Abstract-Summary

"This research paper explores the implications of emotional intelligence and the Big Five personality model on virtual team effectiveness."

"It illustrates how emotional intelligence and Big Five personality traits help team members better understand interpersonal relationships and develop constructive virtual teams."

"The relationship between personality traits and team effectiveness is mediated by emotional intelligence."

"It is explored that having control over emotional intelligence or developing emotional intelligence would improve team performance while managing and working with a diverse group of people."

Introduction

"One main factor in mitigating these obstacles and improving team performance is creating trust and by understanding emotions and personality of individual team members by motivating them for the formation of individual members of teams as leaders (interested to hold on leadership roles) which would ultimately build trust and create virtual effectiveness."

"Since conversations between emotionally intelligent individuals (Mayer & others [78]) can accrue the advantages of EI by focusing on communication skills and self-involvement while working in teams, EI could be an essential aspect in positive outcomes for virtual effectiveness."

"The goal in this project aims to empirically determine the impact of emotional intelligence and model Big Five variables as inputs within virtual teams to analyse individual performance and team problem-solving process that in addition, governs each structure of group personalities and virtual group effectiveness success experiences."

"The research also investigates whether emotional intelligence (EI) and Big Five variables boost the efficiency of team members in virtual settings."

Literature Review

"Virtual collaboration can be defined as the use of technology-mediated tools to enable geographically dispersed employees or work teams to communicate and collaborate on the same project."

"Although effective virtual team collaboration may be built on a number of pillars, one of the most important of these is the relationship between the tasks being performed as well as tools and teams, as well as trust and the depth of relationships between the members of the team. (Peters & Manz [79]; Zhang & others [80])."

"Mysirlaki and Paraskeva [81] observed that in virtual collaboration with remote workers emotional intelligence has been a major indicator of group effectiveness, and employee participation activities as one mechanism whereby intellectual ability affects the effectiveness of groups in team performance."

"In virtual team study, the relevance regarding personality and emotional intelligence as a comprehensive construction variable has attracted considerable interest and there is currently no empirical evidence of measures to achieve improved results during the resolution of virtual conflicts."

Research Model and Hypothesis Development

"Emotional intelligence acts as a mediating effect on the impact of personality traits on team effectiveness in a virtual setting, with emotional intelligence having a positive influence on the results."

"Of these considerations, the following is the first hypothesis of the research: H1: Big Five personality traits will have a positive significance on Virtual Team Effectiveness While emotional intelligence tests various personality traits and intellectual functioning, the additional assessments for emotional intelligence include measuring a few specific characteristics of emotional competence."

"Of these considerations, the following is the third hypothesis of the research: H3: Emotional Intelligence will have a positive significance on Virtual Team Effectiveness As per Mayer and Salovey [82], emotional intelligence (EI) is composed of four skill sets: observation, utilisation, interpretation, and management of one's emotions."

"The following is hypothesised: H4: Emotional Intelligence will act as a mediator on the impact of Big Five personality traits on Virtual Team Effectiveness"

Research Methodology

"The proposed research model was tested in this quantitative study by analysing primary survey data, which was conducted as part of the investigation."

"Participants' acquaintance with virtual teams was tested in order to determine their level of comfort."

"24 per cent of participants have solely participated in virtual teams, while 23 per cent have participated in virtual teams as well as physically present groups."

"The information was gathered through an online questionnaire that includes questions about the Big Five Personality Inventory (BFI), emotional intelligence (EI), and the effectiveness of virtual teams (VTE)."

"Each individual and groups' emotional intelligence was tested with the help of the Brief Emotional Intelligence Scale (BEIS-10; Davies & others [83]), which has a reliability score of ($\alpha = 0.865$) and was used in this study."

Results

"A statistical significance and positive (p 0.01) relationship was discovered between observed members' overall Big Five personality qualities and Emotional Intelligence (r = 0.285), Virtual Team Collaboration (r = 0.520), and Trust (r = 0.109)."

"The direct relationship between emotional intelligence and virtual team effectiveness has been demonstrated to be positive and statistically significant (B = 0.648, S.E. = 0.088, p = 0.000)."

"It can be concluded that the mediation is highly favourable due to the fact is that interaction between the personality traits of the Big Five qualities and emotional intelligence has demonstrated insignificant and significant relations on all areas of virtual team efficiency respectively."

"The study's findings support the hypotheses, revealing that there is a significant positive relationship between individuals' Big Five personality traits and virtual team effectiveness, with emotional intelligence acting as a mediator that can control personalities who respond negatively."

Discussions

"Of these concerns, the study aims to evaluate the effect of the personality traits of five dimensions characteristics as well as emotional intelligence of individuals in a virtual environment while they execute any work in a group."

"It was discovered in this research, based on the results of the first hypothesis, that an individual's personality alone cannot create a good connection between team effectiveness and group members while working in a virtual interface with other people."

"By doing so, it illustrates the significant goal of this research, which is to comprehend emotional intelligence (EI) as a mechanism in investigating the association between the personality traits of the Big Five qualities as well as team efficiency required in groups in the virtual interface, as stated in hypothesis 4."

"The findings of the study suggest that emotional intelligence (EI) serves as a mediating factor that enhances communication between personalities and the success of virtual teams."

Conclusion

"The findings of the study may be useful to any business that is already utilising virtual teams or remote working programmes, or that is evaluating the possibility of implementing such groups in the future."

"The results of the study might potentially be used to identify the kind of persons who would be better suited for collocated teams rather than virtual teams."

"The studies revealed statistically significant results demonstrating that virtual team members believed that EI features contributed to the success of the project."

"Of the research, it can be concluded that people with high emotional intelligence and have demonstrated in a manner that shows they have faith in others, feel good about themselves, and are willing to try new things, have a greater tendency to comply to culturally approved norms, and are capable of managing significant doubt and negative emotions will be much more effective in virtual interface teams than others."

Bosses Without a Heart: Socio-Demographic and Cross-Cultural Determinants of Attitude Toward Emotional AI in the Workplace [139]

This is a machine-generated summary of:

Mantello, Peter; Ho, Manh-Tung; Nguyen, Minh-Hoang; Vuong, Quan-Hoang: Bosses without a heart: socio-demographic and cross-cultural determinants of attitude toward Emotional AI in the workplace [139]

Published in: AI & SOCIETY (2021)

Link to original: https://doi.org/10.1007/s00146-021-01290-1.

Copyright of the summarized publication:

The Author(s), under exclusive licence to Springer-Verlag London Ltd., part of Springer Nature 2021

Conclusion 331

All rights reserved.
If you want to cite the papers, please refer to the original.
For technical reasons we could not place the page where the original quote is coming from.

Abstract-Summary

"Biometric technologies are becoming more pervasive in the workplace, augmenting managerial processes such as hiring, monitoring and terminating employees."

"However, a new generation of biometric devices has emerged that can sense, read, monitor and evaluate the affective state of a worker."

"More popularly known by its commercial moniker, Emotional AI, the technology stems from advancements in affective computing."

"Whereas previous generations of biometric monitoring targeted the exterior physical body of the worker, concurrent with the writings of Foucault and Hardt, we argue that emotion-recognition tools signal a far more invasive disciplinary gaze that exposes and makes vulnerable the inner regions of the worker-self."

"While this emerging technology is driven by neoliberal incentives to optimize the worksite and increase productivity, ultimately, empathic surveillance may create more problems in terms of algorithmic bias, opaque decisionism, and the erosion of employment relations."

"This paper nuances and extends emerging literature on emotion-sensing technologies in the workplace, particularly through its highly original cross-cultural study."

Introduction

"Although there exists a growing body of literature on digital surveillance in the workplace (Ball [84]; Marciano [85]; Rosenblat [86]; Manokha [87]; Moore & Woodcock [88]), the impact of EAI on workers, managers and the labor process is understudied apart from Andrew McStay's seminal book, Emotional AI: The Rise of Empathic Media."

"EAI vendors claim that their technologies can assist human managers to find better ways of understanding and supervising employees as well as lead to greater levels workplace satisfaction (Gal & others [89])."

"The intention of the survey is to better understand how socio-demographic, cultural, gender and economic factors influence perception and attitude toward three aspects of the AI-enabled human resources (HR) management: job entry gatekeeping, workplace monitoring, and the threat to a worker's sense of agency, thus enabling a comprehensive and cross-culturally informed discussion of AI ethics and governance in the age of the quantified workplace."

Literature Review

"The idea that emotions could not be quantified were largely premised on and supported by the fact that besides scientific laboratory settings, medical institutions, or focus groups, no technologies existed in the workplace to measure a person's affective state (Davies [90])."

"Of the few studies on the perception of AI in the modern workplace, it is clear that the research methods to measure awareness of AI, especially EAI, and its effects are still in an early stage."

"Our current study can be situated within two relevant bodies of literature: (i) technological adoption in the workplace; and (ii) AI-augmented management practice."

"This section reviews relevant studies on various factors that influence the perception of AI in the workplace, namely, socio-demographic, behavioral, and cross-cultural."

"The absence of studies on the impact of emotion-sensing technologies in the workplace calls for further research to fill the intellectual vacuum."

Research Design

"The Remarks/Survey questions column contains information on the measurement instrument, i.e., the survey questions and how they are combined to create a measurement for a variable."

"For the outcome variables, the Cronbach's alpha values for Attitude and Familiarity were calculated to check for whether the questions measured the same construct."

"Following the recent guidelines on conducting Bayesian inference (Aczel & others [91]; Vuong & others [92]), twelve models are constructed which gradually expand the number of variables and levels."

"Equation No.1 models the linear relationship between attitude towards the use of EAI for automated HR management, the dependent variable, and four independent (exploratory) socio-demographic variables: income level, school year, biological sex, and school major."

"Model 10 is the most complex as it is a multi-level model where the Region variable functions as the varying-intercept and there present all other variables."

Results

"Attitude toward EAI-enabled HR management is a very multi-faceted issue, as it is best predicted from a host of factors: not only socio-demographic and behavioral factors, but also cultural and political factors (religion, religiosity, and region) (Model 10)."

Conclusion 333

"Students with higher income, men, business majors, and higher school year are likely to have a less-worried outlook toward EAI-enabled HR management, thus validating H1–4."

"Model 10 shows that students who have higher self-rated familiarity with AI tend to view the EAI-enabled HR management more positively (rejecting H5)."

"This result contradicts a Saudi Arabian study of medical students (Bin Dahmash & others [93]), which found anxiety toward using AI was correlated with a higher self-perceived understanding of this technology."

"Our analyses show religiosity indeed negatively correlates with attitude toward EAI-enabled HR management, supporting H6."

Discussion

"Besides being among the few cross-cultural empirical studies on the perception of EAI tools in HR management, the paper discovers that being managed by AI is the greatest AI risk perceived by the international future job-seekers, which answers RQ1 on the concerns of future job-seekers regarding AI as managers versus AI as their replacement."

"In exploring the effects of various factors on the attitude toward automated management (RQ3,4,5) via the Bayesian MCMC approach, this study also highlights various cross-cultural and socio-demographic discrepancies in concern and ignorance about the EAI-enabled management of the workplace that must be bridged to bring more equalities to the AI-augmented workplace."

"RQ3 and RQ4 are inquiries into the effects of socio-demographic and cross-cultural factors on self-rated knowledge regarding AI and attitude toward automated management."

Conclusions

"Our study suggests three fundamental concerns for future job-seekers who will be governed and assessed in either small or large ways by non-human resource management."

"At a deeper biopolitical level, EAI represents an emerging era of automated governance where Foucauldian strategies and techniques of control are relegated to software systems."

"Of physically monitoring and confining individuals in brick-and-mortar enclosures or enacting forms of control based on the body's exteriority, the 'algorithmic governmentality' of emotion-sensing AI ultimately targets the mind and behavioral processes of workers to encourage their productivity and compliance (Mantello [94])."

"The empirical cross-cultural and socio-demographic discrepancies observed in this paper seek to promote awareness and discussion as well as serve as a platform for further intercultural research on the ethical and social implications of EAI as an emerging tool in non-human resource management."

The Joint Influence of Supervisor and Subordinate Emotional Intelligence on Leader–Member Exchange [140]

This is a machine-generated summary of:
  Sears, Greg J.; Holmvall, Camilla M.: The Joint Influence of Supervisor and Subordinate Emotional Intelligence on Leader–Member Exchange [140]
  Published in: Journal of Business and Psychology (2009)
  Link to original: https://doi.org/10.1007/s10869-009-9152-y.
  Copyright of the summarized publication:
  Springer Science+Business Media, LLC 2009
  All rights reserved.
  If you want to cite the papers, please refer to the original.
  For technical reasons we could not place the page where the original quote is coming from.

Abstract-Summary

"The purpose of this study was to investigate the relationship between supervisor and subordinate levels of emotional intelligence (EI) and leader–member exchange (LMX)."

"Results of both hierarchical moderated multiple regression and difference score analyses showed that supervisor–subordinate EI similarity was significantly associated with LMX."

"Our results temper recent findings supporting direct effects of EI on various workplace outcomes, and reinforce a dyadic approach to studying individual difference variables in LMX development."

"This is one of the first studies to examine EI in relation to LMX, and in particular, the joint influence of supervisor and subordinate EI on LMX."

Introduction

"Drawing on theoretical frameworks of LMX (Dienesch & Liden [95]; Graen & Scandura [96]; Graen & Uhl-Bien [97]) and interpersonal similarity (e.g., Byrne [98]; Schaubroeck & Lam [99]), we posit that supervisor and subordinate EI will jointly contribute to LMX development, such that supervisor–subordinate similarity on EI will be significantly associated with LMX quality."

"Given both the affective and performance-based underpinnings of EI (e.g., Law & others [100]; Mayer & Salovey [101]; Sy & others [102]), we propose that subordinate EI and the level of EI of one's supervisor will play an integral role in LMX development."

"Drawing on two conceptual models of interpersonal similarity—the similarity-attraction paradigm (e.g., Byrne [98]) and behavioral integration theory (e.g., Hambrick [103]; Schaubroeck & Lam [99])—we posit that supervisor–subordinate similarity on EI will be associated with higher levels of LMX."

"In line with behavioral integration theory (Hambrick [103]; Schaubroeck & Lam [99]), supervisors and subordinates with similar levels of EI should be more likely to develop clear role expectations, more effective interpersonal communication processes, and improved role definition."

Method

"Consistent with prior research on LMX (e.g., Bauer & Green [104]; Bernerth & others [105]; Green & others [106]; Liden & others [107]), we also tested several demographic variables as potential control variables in our analysis, including supervisor and subordinate gender (0 = male; 1 = female), age, and education levels (0 = junior high school diploma to 5 = graduate degree), as well as supervisor–subordinate differences on these variables."

"The overall relationship between EI similarity and LMX was tested by computing a partial correlation between the EI difference score index and LMX, controlling for supervisor and subordinate differences on conscientiousness and core self-evaluations."

"Our use of different rating sources (supervisors and subordinates), which minimizes potential component intercorrelations (and potential measurement error), coupled with the appreciable reliabilities yielded for the EI Scale ($\alpha = .90$ subordinates; $\alpha = .81$ supervisors), provide conditions that render the use of the difference score measure appropriate in this study (e.g., Tisak & Smith [108])."

Results

"Results from the difference score analysis examining the relationship between supervisor and subordinate EI similarity and LMX indicated that the partial correlation between the EI difference score index and LMX, controlling for differences on the personality variables, was $r = -.50$ ($p < .01$)."

"Greater differences between supervisors and subordinates on EI were associated with lower LMX quality."

"On step 2, we entered the (centered) main effect terms for supervisor and subordinate EI."

"To tease apart the interaction further, we used the procedures outlined by Aiken and West [109] to examine the simple effect of supervisor EI at high and low levels of subordinate EI."

"There was a significant effect of supervisor EI at high levels of subordinate EI (b = 1.01, p < .01, one-tailed)."

"There was also a significant effect of supervisor EI at low subordinate EI (b = −.65, p < .05, one-tailed)."

Discussion

"While the effects of EI similarity on LMX appeared to be strongest when supervisors and subordinates were both high on EI, our pattern of findings also signals that similarity at lower levels of EI may result in relatively high levels of LMX."

"In line with behavioral integration theory, this common perspective regarding the importance of expressing and attending to emotion in workplace interactions may result in low EI supervisors and subordinates sharing similar expectations surrounding their work roles, which may, in turn, enable clearer role communication, improved behavioral coordination (Hambrick [103]), and the development of higher LMX."

"This greater relative emphasis on task-oriented behaviors that facilitate role-making processes, as opposed to socio-emotional behaviors that more directly contribute to the development of a strong affective bond, may explain why supervisor–subordinate similarity at lower levels of EI yields appreciable levels of LMX, but not to the same extent as similarity at higher levels of EI."

A Thematic Analysis on "Employee Engagement in IT Companies from the Perspective of Holistic Well-being Initiatives" [141]

This is a machine-generated summary of:

Rajashekar, S.; Jain, Alka: A Thematic Analysis on "Employee Engagement in IT Companies from the Perspective of Holistic Well-being Initiatives" [141]

Published in: Employee Responsibilities and Rights Journal (2023)

Link to original: https://doi.org/10.1007/s10672-023-09440-x.

Copyright of the summarized publication:

The Author(s), under exclusive licence to Springer Science+Business Media, LLC, part of Springer Nature 2023

Copyright comment: Springer Nature or its licensor (e.g. a society or other partner) holds exclusive rights to this article under a publishing agreement with the author(s) or other rightsholder(s); author self-archiving of the accepted manuscript version of this article is solely governed by the terms of such publishing agreement and applicable law.

All rights reserved.

If you want to cite the papers, please refer to the original.

For technical reasons we could not place the page where the original quote is coming from.

Abstract-Summary

"Attaining sustainable competitive advantage in changing paradigms of the business world is possible through highly engaged employees, and holistic well-being is considered one of employee engagement's most important drivers (Ryder, G., & Director-General, I. (2020)."

"World employment and social outlook—trends 2020."

"As per the (ILO) International Labour organization's World Employment and Social Outlook report of 2020, there are more than 630 million workforces worldwide."

"The aim of this qualitative research is investigating employee engagement practices from the perspective of holistic well-being initiatives impacting employee engagement."

"The research design employed is Thematic Analysis (Braun and Clarke, Qualitative Research in Psychology 3:77–101, 2006), in which interviews conducted over calls were transcribed and coded, leading to the development of themes."

"The five dimensions are; Physical, Psychological (Mental & Emotional), Social, Financial, and Spiritual."

"The findings of this study accentuate substantial focus on physical, psychological, and social aspects of well-being with inadequate attention towards the spiritual dimension."

"It is suggested that organizations evaluate the present status of the well-being of employees through specific tools, identify gaps, and formulate strategies that encompass a holistic well-being approach to enhance employee engagement positively."

Introduction

"The need to enhance employee engagement is growing across all sectors and more so in the IT industry, owing to the low levels of employee engagement worldwide (Gallup Inc & Pendell [110, 111])."

"As per the latest report, only 21% of employees are engaged in the workplace, meaning most of the workforce worldwide needs to be more engaged."

"Considering the ill effects of low employee engagement levels, corporations allocate considerable budgets to enhance employee engagement."

"Past research suggests that strengthening the holistic well-being of employees can improve employee engagement (Bureau [112])."

"In response to the significant changes in the workplace following COVID-19, organizations are now focusing on holistic employee wellness, according to a report from Advantage Club, a global provider of employee benefits."

"This study aims at investigating various holistic well-being initiatives undertaken by IT and ITES companies in Bangalore city, as a strategy to enhance Employee Engagement, identifying relevant gaps and suggesting suitable interferences to improve employee engagement."

Literature Review and Research Gap

"Engaged staff members are not only content with their positions but are continuously thinking of ways to advance the company (Grace [113]). American psychological Association undertook a study in 2016 which showcased 89 percent of employees mentioned their company culture was in place and 91 percent said they were motivated to work better because the company undertook workplace wellness programs."

"The results show that Psychological Capital positively impacts employee engagement levels to General wellbeing and Control at work."

"Employees exhibited high levels of engagement, job happiness, and overall well-being when they had higher Perceived Organizational Support and Psychological Capital."

"The researcher has found out that in the Irish Private Sector employers are undertaking health and wellbeing initiatives, and it has an impact on Employee Engagement, especially on Generation Y Employees."

"The impact of holistic wellbeing initiatives can have on the organization are it increases productivity, increases employee engagement, reduces absenteeism, reduces stress, and improves employee morale."

Research Gap

"A dearth of studies indicates a linkage or relationship between employees' holistic well-being and employee engagement."

"Limited studies have measured the linkages between khan's employee engagement and well-being in the context of organizational studies."

"None examined the various employee engagement initiatives of Information Technology (IT) companies in Bangalore city from the point of view of holistic well-being and its impact on employee engagement."

Purpose of the Study

"This qualitative research aims at investigating various employee engagement initiatives undertaken by the IT companies of Bangalore city concerning holistic wellness and understanding its impact on employee engagement."

"Through this thematic analysis, the study intends to examine the gaps and suggest efficient strategies that are important to overall employees' wellbeing, eventually leading to efficient employee engagement."

Methodology

"Thematic Analysis is one of the several qualitative research methodologies employed in this study (Braun & Clarke [114])."

"Thematic analysis (TA) is a methodological approach for locating, examining, and summarising themes or patterns within data."

"Unlike statistical software, CAQDAS does not actually perform analysis; it only helps manage the data, codes them, and performs specific functions such as word frequency calculation, auto codes, etc, which aids research."

"Hybrid coding was used; the study began with a deductive approach keeping employee engagement and the five dimensions of Holistic well-being (Physical, psychological, social, financial, and spiritual) as a framework which was derived from the literature review and working through the data new codes were added in an inductive approach."

"A total of 164 initial codes were generated, and during this phase, the analysis was concentrated on themes at a more general level."

Results and Discussion

"The codes generated from the transcripts were deductively assigned to these overarching themes for holistic well-being and employee engagement."

"The interviews elicit participants' views about the concept of holistic well-being, the considered dimensions, and its effect on employee engagement."

"Employees were aware of the activities conducted in their respective organizations regarding employee engagement and its importance."

"Also, the equally important, if not more for me, will be the human-related aspects, like how the people's culture is, Employee Engagement in the company, is employee wellbeing is taken care of, etc, I believe holistic well-being covers all aspects of life."

"In my view, when you feel satisfied with your life and company, you concentrate on yourself, your health, and especially your mental Wellness is essential, and that is what contributes to holistic wellbeing."

Discussions

"There are multiple studies on all the determinants except the well-being aspect where minimum studies are done; hence in this study, the focus is only on holistic wellbeing as a determinant of employee engagement."

"Past research suggests that spiritual well-being is critical in one's life and, more importantly, in the workplace, companies have yet to have any specific initiatives to uplift this crucial dimension of holistic well-being."

"There are studies concerning employee engagement and its drivers such as remuneration, work environment, leadership, rewards, recognition, etc There is dearth of studies on the impact of wellbeing on employee engagement and very minimum studies on holistic wellbeing with all the dimensions and employee engagement."

"This study provides an overview of holistic wellbeing initiatives undertaken by the IT companies in Bangalore city."

"This study emphasizes on impact of holistic wellbeing on employee engagement."

Conclusion

"This qualitative research contributes conceptually and theoretically to the field of holistic wellbeing and employee engagement."

"The results of this thematic analysis can be used not only by the management of IT companies but across sectors to develop holistic wellbeing initiatives as a tool to enhance employee engagement."

"The holistic wellbeing of employees ensures a high level of job satisfaction and employee engagement."

"This study has a few limitations; the data was collected only from ten employees, and the insights gathered may not represent the whole population."

"Future studies can include other dimensions such as occupational well-being, Societal well-being, etc Future researchers can include other sectors to investigate holistic well-being initiatives and employee engagement."

Paying Close Attention to Strengths Mindset: The Relationship of Employee Strengths Mindset with Job Performance [142]

This is a machine-generated summary of:

Ding, He; Liu, Jun: Paying close attention to strengths mindset: the relationship of employee strengths mindset with job performance [142]

Published in: Current Psychology (2022)

Link to original: https://doi.org/10.1007/s12144-022-03400-8.

Copyright of the summarized publication:

Conclusion

The Author(s), under exclusive licence to Springer Science+Business Media, LLC, part of Springer Nature 2022

All rights reserved.

If you want to cite the papers, please refer to the original.

For technical reasons we could not place the page where the original quote is coming from.

Abstract-Summary

"This study investigated the relationship between employee strengths mindset and positive affect and job performance (i.e., task performance and innovative behavior), and considered the mediating role of positive affect in the strengths mindset-job performance relationship."

"Analytical results illustrated that strengths mindset positively relates to positive affect and job performance."

"Positive affect was found to significantly mediate the relationship of strengths mindset with task performance and innovative behavior."

"This study contributes to advancing strengths mindset theory and research, and identifies a new pathway for improving employee job performance."

Introduction

"Strengths mindset may be the most important influencing factor of employee outcomes, in that Walsh and Charalambides [115] pointed out that individuals' mindsets determine the way that individuals collect and interpret new information, which in turn, influences individuals' attitudes, emotions, behaviors, and performance."

"Based on the above findings, it is feasible to believe that employee strengths mindset is positively related to job performance."

"By so doing, this study contributes to enriching the empirical research on effect of strengths mindset and identifying a new pathway of promoting employee job performance."

"Based on the aforementioned arguments, strengths mindset might be associated with improved positive affect and in turn, job performance."

"This study also empirically examines the mediating role of positive affect in the relationship between strengths mindset and job performance."

"This study contributes to revealing the emotional mechanism through which strengths mindset positively relates to job performance."

Theory and Hypothesis Development

"Strengths mindset may also boost individual's positive affect that, in turn, leads to greater job performance."

"This study utilized strengths theory as a rationale explaining the mediation model regarding strengths mindset, positive affect, and job performance."

"Based on the above reasoning, we formulate the following hypotheses: Positive affect mediates the relationship between strengths mindset and task performance."

"Positive affect mediates the relationship between strengths mindset and innovative behavior."

"We proposed a mediation model concerning strengths mindset, positive affect, and job performance (i.e., task performance and innovative behavior) in which strengths mindset positively relates to task performance, innovative behavior, and positive affect, and positive affect mediates the relationship of strengths mindset with task performance and with innovative behavior."

Methods

"Participants were asked to complete questionnaire regarding demographic variables and strengths mindset scale."

"Strengths mindset was evaluated with a twelve-item scale developed for the current study."

"We surveyed 350 employees from diverse enterprises (e.g., IT and manufacturing industries) using a questionnaire including demographic variables and strengths mindset scale, and received 296 respondents (84.57% response rate)."

"We recruited 380 employees working in different Chinese organizations (e.g., retail industry, education and training industry) using a questionnaire regarding demographic variables and the scales of strengths mindset, growth mindset (Heslin & others's [116] four-item scale), humility (Owens & others's [117] nine-item scale), and strengths use (Ding & Yu's [118] five-item scale)."

"We also conducted CFA to test the strengths mindset scale's construct validity."

"In terms of dataset comprising 407 employees in the current study, Cronbach's α of the strengths mindset scale was 0.94."

Results

"We first adopted CFA to test the discriminant validity between strengths mindset, positive affect, task performance, and innovative behavior."

"One common method factor was created and loaded on all items of strengths mindset, positive affect, task performance, and innovative behavior."

"The five-factor measurement model containing the common factor and the four focal research variables ($\chi^2 = 1199.90$, df $= 488$, χ^2/df $= 2.46$, RMSEA $= 0.06$, CFI $= 0.93$, TLI $= 0.93$, SRMR $= 0.05$) exhibited a better fit to the data than the four-factor model comprising the four focal research variables, but the common factor only explained 15.92% of variance less than 25% suggested by Williams and others [119]."

Conclusion 343

"We constructed a SEM (Model 1) in which strengths mindset predicts task performance and innovative behavior while controlling for age and gender."

Discussion

"This study of 407 employees working in various Chinese organizations investigated strengths mindset and its relationship with job performance (i.e., task performance and innovative behavior), and considered positive affect as a mediator between strengths mindset and job performance."

"This study found that strengths mindset is positively related to job performance (i.e., task performance and innovative behavior), which provides a new insight into improving employee performance."

"This study revealed the affective mechanism underlying the relationship of strengths mindset with job performance by considering the mediational effect of positive affect."

"This study is the first to investigate why strengths mindset positively relates to job performance, which contributes to deepening our understanding of potential mechanisms underlying the relationship of strengths mindset with job performance."

"Future research should attempt to conduct longitudinal or experimental research to test the causality of the relationships between strengths mindset, positive affect, and job performance."

Conclusions

"Since mindsets dominate individuals' attitudes, behaviors, emotions, and performance, and the greatest room of personal growth and development is the areas of strengths, it is quite essential to deeply investigate strengths mindset."

"This study provided a clear and comprehensive definition of strengths mindset, developed and validated the 12-item strengths mindset scale, and authenticated that strengths mindset positively relates to positive affect and job performance."

"We also found that positive affect mediates the positive relationship between strengths mindset and job performance."

"This study is conductive to advancing strengths mindset theory and research."

The Effects of Perceived Supervisor Incivility on Child-Care Workers' Job Performance: The Mediating Role of Emotional Exhaustion and Intrinsic Motivation [143]

This is a machine-generated summary of:
Han, Youjin; Kim, Yeonshin; Hur, Won-Moo: The effects of perceived supervisor incivility on child-care workers' job performance: The mediating role of emotional exhaustion and intrinsic motivation [143]
Published in: Current Psychology (2019)
Link to original: https://doi.org/10.1007/s12144-019-0133-7.
Copyright of the summarized publication:
Springer Science+Business Media, LLC, part of Springer Nature 2019
All rights reserved.
If you want to cite the papers, please refer to the original.
For technical reasons we could not place the page where the original quote is coming from.

Abstract-Summary

"The authors examined how perceived supervisor incivility negatively affected the performance of child-care workers, focusing on emotional exhaustion and intrinsic motivation as underlying mediators."

"Data were collected from 321 child-care workers at 43 daycare centers in South Korea."

"Perceived supervisor incivility emotionally exhausted child-care workers, decreased their intrinsic motivation, and reduced their overall performance."

Introduction

"Prior studies of incivility management have focused on human services that require intense interpersonal involvement in institutions devoted to healthcare (e,g., Bunk & Magley [121]; Cortina & others [122]; Laschinger & others [123]) and education (Bibi & others [124]; Sulea & others [125]), but have overlooked the occupational consequences of incivility to workers in the child care sector."

"The child care sector is highly relevant for observing the negative impact of incivility, as indicated by high turnover rates that deplete service quality (e.g., Cortina & others [126]; Phillips & others [127])."

"Fact, there is a scarcity of empirical evidence on the relationship between perceived incivility and work outcomes among child-care workers."

"To fill the gap, we studied how experiencing incivility in the workplace influences occupational and psychological outcomes for child-care providers."

"Environment, the performance of child-care workers greatly depends on their perceived relationships with supervisors (Park & Kim [128])."

Theoretical Background and Hypotheses

"Based on the extant research and the combined rationale of AET and COR theory, we propose that experiencing incivility from a supervisor does not directly affect employees' job performance, but rather that emotional exhaustion and intrinsic motivation sequentially mediate the effect of perceived supervisor incivility on the performance of child-care workers."

"We argue that emotional exhaustion and intrinsic motivation mediate the relationship between perceived supervisor incivility and child-care workers' job performance."

"Our serial-mediation model better explains how supervisor-initiated incivility damages employee performance: child-care workers who are the targets of uncivil supervisor behavior are likely to feel emotional exhaustion from their efforts to deal with negative affective responses."

"We hypothesize: H4: Emotional exhaustion and intrinsic motivation sequentially mediate the effect of perceived supervisor incivility on the job performance of child-care workers."

Research Method

"The study participants were South Korean child-care workers employed by multiple daycare centers identified through the primary investigator's personal contacts."

"The average number of child-care workers per center participating in this study was 7.47 (Min)."

"According to a recent child care center and teacher census conducted by the Korea Institute of Childcare and Education [129], the overall demographic characteristics of the child-care teachers can be described as mostly females (98.3%), with an undergraduate college or university degree (78.7%), and an average of 38.4 years old."

"Since the 321 child-care teachers were nested in 43 child-care centers, we conducted multilevel structural equation modeling (MSEM) using M-plus 8.0 software to accurately capture the effects of individual-level variables while accounting for the non-independence of observations within the daycare center (Bliese & Hanges [130])."

Data Analysis and Results

"Although the χ^2 value was significant ($\chi^2_{(168)} = 301.81$, $p < .05$), the other indices yielded good fit to the data ($\chi^2/df = 1.80$, TLI $= .95$, CFI $= .96$, SRMR$_{(within)} = .04$, RMSEA $= .05$)."

"The results of confirmatory factor analysis indicated that the one-factor model ($\chi^2_{(90)} = 2028.83$; $p < .05$, CFI $= .42$, TLI $= .32$, RMSEA $= .26$, SRMR $= .19$) was a worse fit than our measurement model."

"Our proposed research model offers an acceptable fit to data ($\chi^2_{(218)} = 395.59$, $p < .05$: CFI $= .96$, TLI $= .95$, RMSEA$_{(within)} = .05$, SRMR $= .05$)."

"Hypothesis 4 predicted that emotional exhaustion and intrinsic motivation are significant mediators in the relationship between perceived supervisor incivility and job performance."

"The results for H4 showed that emotional exhaustion and intrinsic motivation fully and sequentially mediated the relationship between experienced supervisor incivility and job performance ($b = -.031$, 99% CI $[-.056, -.007]$)."

Discussion

"Based on the related AET and COR theory research, we hypothesized that emotional exhaustion and intrinsic motivation sequentially mediate the negative relationship between perceived supervisor incivility and performance."

"Serial mediation analysis confirms that emotional exhaustion and intrinsic motivation sequentially mediate the relationship between perceived supervisor incivility and performance in child-care workers (H4)."

"Owners and management are urged to consider the mediating effect of emotional exhaustion between supervisor incivility and performance factors (i.e., intrinsic motivation and job performance) and to find ways to mitigate emotional exhaustion in child-care workers."

"Future studies are recommended to use a random sampling technique and to investigate child-care workers in other countries or service employees in other industries (e.g., flight attendants, long-term caregivers, social workers, etc.) to see if perceived supervisor incivility has an influence on employee outcomes such as psychological well-being and employee performance similar to the findings of this research."

Bibliography

1. FEVS—Federal Employee Viewpoint Survey. (2019). Retrieved December 8, 2019, from https://www.opm.gov/fevs/public-data-file/
2. Drigas, A. S., & Papoutsi, C. (2018). A new layered model on emotional intelligence. *Behavioral Sciences, 8*(5), 45.
3. Pastor, I. (2014). Leadership and emotional intelligence: The effect on performance and attitude. *Procedia Economics and Finance, 15*(2014), 985–992. Retrieved February 26, 2021, from https://core.ac.uk/download/pdf/82112799.pdf
4. Norboevich, T. B. (2020). Analysis of psychological theory of emotional intelligence. *European Journal of Research and Reflection in Educational Sciences, 8*(3), 99–104.
5. Ashforth, B. E., & Humphrey, R. H. (1993). Emotional labor in service roles: The influence of identity. *Academy of Management Review, 18*(1), 88–115.
6. Kluemper, D. H., DeGroot, T., & Choi, S. (2013). Emotion management ability: Predicting task performance, citizenship, and deviance. *Journal of Management, 39*(4), 878–905.
7. Bitner, M. J., Booms, B. H., & Tetreault, M. S. (1990). The service encounter: Diagnosing favorable and unfavorable incidents. *Journal of Marketing, 54*, 71–84.
8. Goodwin, R. E., Groth, M., & Frenkel, S. J. (2011). Relationships between emotional labor, job performance, and turnover. *Journal of Vocational Behavior, 79*(2), 538–548. https://doi.org/10.1016/j.jvb.2011.03.001
9. Gosserand, R. H., & Diefendorff, J. M. (2005). Emotional display rules and emotional labor: The moderating role of commitment. *Journal of Applied Psychology, 90*(6), 1256–1264.
10. Kaur, S., & Malodia, L. (2017). Influence of emotional labor on job satisfaction among employees of private hospitals: A structural equation modelling approach. *Journal of Health Management, 19*(3), 456–473.
11. Chuang, C. H., & Liao, H. U. I. (2010). Strategic human resource management in service context: Taking care of business by taking care of employees and customers. *Personnel Psychology, 63*(1), 153–196.
12. Diefendorff, J. M., Croyle, M. H., & Gosserand, R. H. (2005). The dimensionality and antecedents of emotional labor strategies. *Journal of Vocational Behavior, 66*(2), 339–357.
13. Questionpro, website. (2018). https://www.questionpro.com/. Accessed 1 Dec 2018.
14. Brayfield, A. H., & Crockett, W. H. (1955). Employee attitudes and employee performance. *Psychological Bulletin, 52*(5), 396.
15. Survey Monkey.com, LLC. (n.d.). Retrieved March 4, 2013, from www.surveymonkey.com.
16. Grandey, A. A. (2003). When "the show must go on": Surface acting and deep acting as determinants of emotional exhaustion and peer-rated service delivery. *Academy of Management Journal, 46*(1), 86–96.
17. Chen, Z. G., Sun, H. W., Lam, W., Hu, Q., Huo, Y. Y., & Zhong, J. A. (2012). Chinese hotel employees in the smiling masks: Roles of job satisfaction, burnout, and supervisory support in relationships between emotional labor and performance. *International Journal of Human Resource Management, 23*(4), 826–845.
18. Rahim, M. A. (1983). *Rahim organizational conflict inventory-II*. Consulting Psychologists Press.
19. Rahim, M. A., Magner, N. R., & Shapiro, D. L. (2000). Do justice perceptions influence styles of handling conflict with supervisors? What are justice perceptions, precisely? *The International Journal of Conflict Management, 11*, 9–31.
20. Song, X. M., Xie, J., & Dyer, B. (2000). Antecedents and consequences of marketing managers' conflict-handling behaviors. *Journal of Marketing, 64*, 50–66.
21. Dirks, K. T., & Ferrin, D. L. (2002). Trust in leadership: Meta-analytic findings and implications for research and practice. *Journal of Applied Psychology, 87*(4), 611–628.
22. Cammann, C., Fichman, M., Jenkins, D., & Klesh, J. (1983). Assessing the attitudes and perceptions of organizational members. In S. E. Seashore, E. E. Lawler, P. H. Mirvis, & C. Cammann (Eds.), *Assessing organizational change: A guide to methods, measures, and practices* (pp. 71–138). Wiley.

23. Cammann, C., Fichman, M., Jenkins, D., & Klesh, J. (1979). *The Michigan organizational assessment questionnaire* [Unpublished manuscript]. University of Michigan, United States.
24. Baron, R. M., & Kenny, D. A. (1986). The moderator–mediator variable distinction in social psychological research: Conceptual, strategic, and statistical considerations. *Journal of Personality and Social Psychology, 51*(6), 1173–1182.
25. Alexander, D. C. (1995). *Conflict management styles of administrators in schools for the deaf: Teacher perceptions of job satisfaction* [Unpublished doctoral dissertation]. Gallaudet University, United States.
26. Blake, R. R., & Mouton, J. S. (1964). *Managerial grid*. Gulf.
27. Follett, M. P. (1940). Constructive conflict. In H. C. Metcalf & L. Urwick (Eds.), *Dynamic administration: The collected papers of Mary Parker Follett* (pp. 30–49). Harper & Row (originally published 1926).
28. Rahim, M. A. (1986). *Managing conflict in organizations*. Praeger.
29. Thomas, K. W., & Kilmann, R. H. (1974). *The Thomas-Kilmann conflict MODE instrument*. Xicom.
30. Weider-Hatfield, D., & Hatfield, J. D. (1996). Superiors' conflict management strategies and subordinate outcomes. *Management Communication Quarterly, 10*, 189–208.
31. Farh, J. L., & Cheng, B. S. (2000). A cultural analysis of paternalistic leadership in Chinese organisations. In J. T. Li, A. S. Tsui, & E. Weldon (Eds.), *Management and organisations in the Chinese context* (pp. 94–127). Macmillan.
32. Tan, C. Y., & Dimmock, C. (2014). How a 'top-forming' Asian school system formulates and implements policy: The case of Singapore. *Educational Management Administration & Leadership, 42*(5), 743–763.
33. Aycan, Z. (2006). Paternalism: Towards conceptual refinement and operationalization. In K. S. Yang, K. K. Hwang, & U. Kim (Eds.), *Scientific advances in indigenous psychologies: Empirical, philosophical, and cultural contributions* (pp. 445–466). Cambridge University.
34. Farh, J., Cheng, B., Chou, L., & Chu, X. (2006). Authority and benevolence: Employees' responses to paternalistic leadership in China. In A. S. Tsui, Y. Bian, & L. Cheng (Eds.), *China's domestic private firms: Multidisciplinary perspectives on management and performance* (pp. 230–260). M.E. Sharpe.
35. Leithwood, K., Sun, J., & Pollock, K. (2017). *How school leaders contribute to student success: The four paths framework*. Springer.
36. Zheng, X., Shi, X., & Liu, Y. (2020). Leading teachers' emotions like parents: Relationships between paternalistic leadership, emotional labor and teacher commitment in China. *Frontiers in Psychology, 11*, 519. https://doi.org/10.3389/fpsyg.2020.00519
37. Day, C., Sammons, P., Leithwood, K., Hopkins, D., Gu, Q., Brown, E., & Ahtaridou, E. (2011). *School leadership and student outcomes: Building and sustaining success*. Open University Press.
38. Hallinger, P. (2011). Leadership for learning: Lessons from 40 years of empirical research. *Journal of Educational Administration, 49*(2), 125–142.
39. Chen, X. P., Eberly, M. B., Chiang, T. J., Farh, J. L., & Cheng, B. S. (2014). Affective trust in Chinese leaders: Linking paternalistic leadership to employee performance. *Journal of Management, 40*(3), 796–819.
40. Shi, X., Yu, Z., & Zheng, X. (2020). Exploring the relationship between paternalistic leadership, teacher commitment, and job satisfaction in Chinese schools. *Frontiers in Psychology, 11*, 1481. https://doi.org/10.3389/fpsyg.2020.01481
41. Walker, A., & Qian, H. (2020). Developing a model of instructional leadership in China. *Compare: A Journal of Comparative and International Education*. Advance online publication. https://doi.org/10.1080/03057925.2020.1747396
42. Popper, M. (2004). Leadership as relationship. *Journal for the Theory of Social Behaviour, 34*(2), 107–125.
43. Qian, H. Y., & Walker, A. (2020). Creating conditions for professional learning communities (PLCs) in schools in China: The role of school principals. *Professional Development in Education*. Advance online publication. https://doi.org/10.1080/19415257.2020.1770839

44. Grandey, A. A. (2003). When 'the show must go on'. Surface acting and deep acting as determinants of emotional exhaustion and peer-rated service delivery. *Academy of Management Journal, 46*(1), 86–96.
45. Spector, P. E., & Brannick, M. T. (2011). Methodological urban legends: The misuse of statistical control variables. *Organizational Research Methods, 14*(2), 287–305.
46. Parasuraman, A., Zeithaml, V. A., & Berry, L. L. (1985). A conceptual model of service quality and its implications for future research. *Journal of Marketing, 49*(4), 41–50.
47. Gutek, B. A. (1995). *The dynamics of service: Reflections on the changing nature of customer/provider interactions.* Jossey-Bass.
48. Bangerter, A., Roulin, N., & Köing, C. (2012). Personnel selection as a signaling game. *Journal of Applied Psychology, 97*, 719–738. https://doi.org/10.1037/a0026078
49. Pugh, S. D. (2001). Service with a smile: Emotional contagion in the service encounter. *Academy of Management Journal, 44*(5), 1018–1027.
50. Ryan, A. M., & Ployhart, R. E. (2003). Customer service behavior. In W. C. Borman, D. R. Ilgen & R. J. Klimoski (Eds.), *Handbook of psychology: Industrial and organizational psychology* (Vol. 12, pp. 377–397). Wiley. https://doi.org/10.1002/0471264385.wei1215 .
51. Barrick, M. R., Shaffer, J. A., & DeGrassi, S. W. (2009). What you see may not be what you get: Relationships among self-presentation tactics and ratings of interview and job performance. *Journal of Applied Psychology, 94*(6), 1394.
52. Kacmar, K. M., Delery, J. E., & Ferris, G. R. (1992). Differential effectiveness of applicant impression management tactics on employment interview decisions. *Journal of Applied Social Psychology, 22*, 1250–1272. https://doi.org/10.1111/j.1559-1816.1992.tb00949.x
53. Daus, C. S., & Ashkanasy, N. M. (2005). The case for the ability-based model of emotional intelligence in organizational behavior. *Journal of Organizational Behavior, 26*, 453–466.
54. Alansari, B. M. (2002). *Sourcebook of objective personality scales: Standardization for Kuwaiti society.* The New Book Home Co.
55. Bagozzi, R. P., Verbeke, W. J. M. I., Dietvorst, R. C., Belschak, F. D., van den Berg, W. E., & Rietdijk, W. J. R. (2013). Theory of mind and empathic explanations of Machiavellianism: A neuroscience perspective. *Journal of Management, 39*(7), 1760–1798.
56. Belschak, F. D., Muhammad, R. S., & Den Hartog, D. N. (2018). Birds of a feather can butt heads: When Machiavellian employees work with Machiavellian leaders. *Journal of Business Ethics, 151*(3), 613–626.
57. Den Hartog, D. N., & Belschak, F. D. (2012). Work engagement and Machiavellianism in the ethical leadership process. *Journal of Business Ethics, 107*(1), 35–47.
58. Belschak, F., Den Hartog, D., & De Hoogh, A. (2018). Angels and demons: The effect of ethical leadership on Machiavellian employees' work behaviors. *Frontiers in Psychology, 9*, 1082. https://doi.org/10.3389/fpsyg.2018.01082
59. Castille, C. M., Buckner, J. E., & Thoroughgood, C. N. (2018). Prosocial citizens without a moral compass? Examining the relationship between Machiavellianism and unethical pro-organizational behavior. *Journal of Business Ethics, 149*(4), 919–930.
60. Koo, B., & Lee, E.-S. (2021). The taming of Machiavellians: Differentiated transformational leadership effects on Machiavellians' organizational commitment and citizenship behavior. *Journal of Business Ethics*, 1–18.
61. Ashkanasy, N. M. (2003). Emotions in organizations: A multi-level perspective. In *Multi-level issues in organizational behavior and strategy.* Emerald Group Publishing Limited.
62. George, J. M. (2000). Emotions and leadership: The role of emotional intelligence. *Human Relations, 53*(8), 1027–1055. https://doi.org/10.1177/0018726700538001
63. Humphrey, R. H., Burch, G. F., & Adams, L. L. (2016). The benefits of merging leadership research and emotions research. *Frontiers in Psychology, 7*, 1022.
64. Ashkanasy, N. M., & Daus, C. S. (2002). Emotion in the workplace: The new challenge for managers. *Academy of Management Perspectives, 16*(1), 76–86.
65. Ashkanasy, N. M., & Dorris, A. D. (2017). Emotions in the workplace. *Annual Review of Organizational Psychology and Organizational Behavior, 4*, 67–90. https://doi.org/10.1146/annurev-orgpsych-032516-113231

66. Herman, H. M., Troth, A. C., Ashkanasy, N. M., & Collins, A. L. (2018). Affect and leader-member exchange in the new millennium: A state-of-art review and guiding framework. *The Leadership Quarterly, 29*(1), 135–149.
67. Austin, E., Farrelly, D., Black, C., & Moore, H. (2007). Emotional intelligence, Machiavellianism and emotional manipulation: Does EI have a dark side? *Personality and Individual Differences, 43*(1), 179–189. https://doi.org/10.1016/j.paid.2006.11.019
68. Austin, E. J., Saklofske, D. H., Smith, M., & Tohver, G. (2014). Associations of the managing the emotions of others (MEOS) scale with personality, the Dark Triad and trait EI. *Personality and Individual Differences, 65*, 8–13.
69. O'Connor, P. J., & Athota, V. S. (2013). The intervening role of agreeableness in the relationship between trait emotional intelligence and Machiavellianism: Reassessing the potential dark side of EI. *Personality and Individual Differences, 55*(7), 750–754.
70. Gkorezis, P., Petridou, E., & Krouklidou, T. (2015). The detrimental effect of Machiavellian leadership on employees' emotional exhaustion: Organizational cynicism as a mediator. *Europe's Journal of Psychology, 11*(4), 619–631. https://doi.org/10.5964/ejop.v11i4.988
71. Stradovnik, K., & Stare, J. (2018). Correlation between Machiavellian leadership and emotional exhaustion of employees. *Leadership and Organization Development Journal, 39*(8), 1037–1050. https://doi.org/10.1108/lodj-06-2018-0232
72. Hafen, C. A., Singh, K., & Laursen, B. (2011). The happy personality in India: The role of emotional intelligence. *Journal of Happiness Studies, 12*(5), 807–817.
73. Hofstede, G. (2011). Dimensionalizing cultures: The Hofstede model in context. *Online Readings in Psychology and Culture, 2*(1), 2307–2919.
74. Graham, P., Nikolova, N., & Sankaran, S. (2020). Tension between leadership archetypes: Systematic review to inform construction research and practice. *Journal of Management in Engineering, 36*(1), 03119002.
75. Yap, J. B. H., Chow, I. N., & Shavarebi, K. (2019). Criticality of construction industry problems in developing countries: Analyzing Malaysian projects. *Journal of Management in Engineering, 35*(5), 04019020.
76. George, M., & Loosemore, M. (2019). Site operatives' attitudes towards traditional masculinity ideology in the Australian construction industry. *Construction Management and Economics, 37*(8), 419–432.
77. Braun, V., & Clarke, V. (2012). Thematic analysis. In H. Cooper, P. Camic, D. Long, A. T. Panter, D. Rindskopf, & K. Sher (Eds.), *APA handbook of research methods in psychology* (pp. 57–71). American Psychological Association.
78. Mayer, J. D., Roberts, R. D., & Barsade, S. G. (2008). Human abilities: Emotional intelligence. *Annual Review of Psychology, 59*(1), 507–536.
79. Peters, L. M., & Manz, C. C. (2007). Identifying antecedents of virtual team collaboration. *Team Performance Management: An International Journal.*
80. Zhang, Y., Sun, J., Yang, Z., & Wang, Y. (2018). Mobile social media in inter-organizational projects: Aligning tool, task and team for virtual collaboration effectiveness. *International Journal of Project Management, 36*(8), 1096–1108.
81. Mysirlaki, S., & Paraskeva, F. (2020). Emotional intelligence and transformational leadership in virtual teams: Lessons from MMOGs. *Leadership & Organization Development Journal.*
82. Mayer, J. D., & Salovey, P. (1997). What is emotional intelligence. *Emotional Development and Emotional Intelligence: Educational Implications, 3*, 31.
83. Davies, K. A., Lane, A. M., Devonport, T. J., & Scott, J. A. (2010). Validity and reliability of a brief emotional intelligence scale (BEIS-10). *Journal of Individual Differences.*
84. Ball, K. (2010). Workplace surveillance: An overview. *Labor History, 51*(1), 87–106.
85. Marciano, A. (2019). Reframing biometric surveillance: From a means of inspection to a form of control. *Ethics and Information Technology, 21*(2), 127–136.
86. Rosenblat, A. (2018). *Uberland: How algorithms are rewriting the rules of work.* University of California Press.
87. Manokha, I. (2020). The implications of digital employee monitoring and people analytics for power relations in the workplace. *Surveillance & Society, 18*(4), 540–554. https://doi.org/10.24908/ss.v18i4.13776

88. Moore, P. V., & Woodcock, J. (Eds.). (2021). *Augmented exploitation: Artificial intelligence, automation, and work.* Pluto Press.
89. Gal, U., Jensen, T. B., & Stein, M.-K. (2020). Breaking the vicious cycle of algorithmic management: A virtue ethics approach to people analytics. *Information and Organization, 30*(2), 100301. https://doi.org/10.1016/j.infoandorg.2020.100301
90. Davies, W. (2015). *The happiness industry: How the government and big business sold us well-being.* Verso Books.
91. Aczel, B., Hoekstra, R., Gelman, A., Wagenmakers, E.-J., et al. (2020). Discussion points for Bayesian inference. *Nature Human Behaviour, 4*(6), 561–563. https://doi.org/10.1038/s41562-019-0807-z
92. Vuong, Q.-H., Bui, Q.-K., La, V.-P., et al. (2018). Cultural additivity: Behavioural insights from the interaction of Confucianism, Buddhism and Taoism in folktales. *Palgrave Communications, 4*(1), 143. https://doi.org/10.1057/s41599-018-0189-2
93. Bin Dahmash, A., Alabdulkareem, M., Alfutais, A., Kamel, A. M., Alkholaiwi, F., Alshehri, S., Al Zahrani, Y., & Almoaiqel, M. (2020). Artificial intelligence in radiology: Does it impact medical students preference for radiology as their future career? *BJR Open, 2*(1), 20200037. https://doi.org/10.1259/bjro.20200037
94. Mantello, P. (2016). The machine that ate bad people: The ontopolitics of the precrime assemblage. *Big Data & Society, 3*(2), 2053951716682538. https://doi.org/10.1177/2053951716682538
95. Dienesch, R. M., & Liden, R. C. (1986). Leader-member exchange model of leadership: A critique and further development. *Academy of Management Review, 11*, 618–634.
96. Graen, G. B., & Scandura, T. A. (1987). Toward a psychology of dyadic organizing. In L. L. Cummings & B. M. Staw (Eds.), *Research in organizational behavior* (Vol. 9, pp. 175–208). JAI Press.
97. Graen, G. B., & Uhl-Bien, M. (1995). Relationship-based approach to leadership: Development of leader-member exchange (LMX) theory of leadership over 25 Years: Applying a multi-level multi-domain perspective. *Leadership Quarterly, 6*, 219–247.
98. Byrne, D. (1971). *The attraction paradigm.* Academic Press.
99. Schaubroeck, J., & Lam, S. S. K. (2002). How similarity to peers and supervisor influences organizational advancement in different cultures. *Academy of Management Journal, 45*, 1120–1136.
100. Law, K. S., Wong, C.-S., & Song, L. J. (2004). The construct and criterion validity of emotional intelligence and its potential utility for management studies. *Journal of Applied Psychology, 89*(3), 483–496. https://doi.org/10.1037/0021-9010.89.3.483
101. Mayer, J. D., & Salovey, P. (1997). What is emotional intelligence? In P. Salovey & D. Sluyter (Eds.), *Emotional development and emotional intelligence: Implications for educators* (pp. 3–31). Basic Books.
102. Sy, T., Tram, S., & O'Hara, L. A. (2006). Relation of employee and manager emotional intelligence with satisfaction and performance. *Journal of Vocational Behaviour, 68*(3), 461–473.
103. Hambrick, D. C. (1994). Top management groups: A conceptual integration and reconsideration of the "team" label. In B. M. Staw & L. L. Cummings (Eds.), *Research in organizational behavior* (Vol. 16, pp. 171–213). JAI Press.
104. Bauer, T. N., & Green, S. B. (1996). Development of leader-member exchange: A longitudinal test. *Academy of Management Journal, 39*, 1538–1567.
105. Bernerth, J. B., Armenakis, A. A., Field, H. S., Giles, W. F., & Walker, H. J. (2008). The influence of personality differences between subordinates and supervisors on perceptions of LMX. *Group and Organization Management, 33*, 26–40.
106. Green, S. G., Anderson, S. E., & Shivers, S. L. (1996). Demographic and organizational influences on leader-member exchange and related work attitudes. *Organizational Behavior & Human Decision Processes, 66*(2), 203–214.
107. Liden, R. C., Wayne, S. J., & Stilwell, D. (1993). A longitudinal study on the early development of leader-member exchanges. *Journal of Applied Psychology, 78*, 662–674.

108. Tisak, J., & Smith, C. S. (1994). Defending and extending difference score methods. *Journal of Management, 20*, 675–682.
109. Aiken, L. S., & West, S. G. (1991). *Multiple regression: Testing and interpreting interactions*. Sage.
110. Gallup Inc, & Pendell, R. (2022a). *The world's $7.8 trillion workplace problem*. Gallup.Com. https://www.gallup.com/workplace/393497/world-trillion-workplace-problem.aspx. Accessed 22 June 2022.
111. Gallup Inc, & Pendell, R. (2022b). *Why leaders must address the employee wellbeing deficit*. Gallup.Com. https://www.gallup.com/workplace/393524/why-leaders-address-employee-wellbeing-deficit.aspx. Accessed 22 June 2022.
112. Bureau, B. M. (2022). Corporates increasingly prioritise holistic employee wellness: Report. *The Hindu Business-Line*. https://www.thehindubusinessline.com/info-tech/corporates-increasingly-prioritise-holistic-employee-wellness-report/article65397329.ece. Accessed 30 June 2022.
113. Anitha, J. (2014). Determinants of employee engagement and their impact on employee performance. *International Journal of Productivity and Performance Management, 63*(3), 308–323. https://doi.org/10.1108/IJPPM-01-2013-0008
114. Braun, V., & Clarke, V. (2006). Using thematic analysis in psychology. *Qualitative Research in Psychology, 3*(2), 77–101. https://doi.org/10.1191/1478088706qp063oa
115. Walsh, J. P., & Charalambides, L. C. (1990). Individual and social origins of belief structure change. *The Journal of Social Psychology, 130*(4), 517–532. https://doi.org/10.1080/00224545.1990.9924614
116. Heslin, P. A., Vandewalle, D., & Latham, G. P. (2006). Keen to help? Managers' implicit person theories and their subsequent employee coaching. *Personnel Psychology, 59*, 871–902. https://doi.org/10.1111/j.1744-6570.2006.00057.x
117. Owens, B. P., Johnson, M. D., & Mitchell, T. R. (2013). Expressed humility in organizations: Implications for performance, teams, and leadership. *Organization Science, 24*(5), 1517–1538. https://doi.org/10.1287/orsc.1120.0795
118. Ding, H., & Yu, E. (2021). Followers' strengths-based leadership and strengths use of followers: The roles of trait emotional intelligence and role overload. *Personality and Individual Differences, 168*, 110300. https://doi.org/10.1016/j.paid.2020.110300
119. Williams, L. J., Cote, J. A., & Buckley, M. R. (1989). Lack of method variance in self-reported affect and perceptions at work: Reality or artifact? *Journal of Applied Psychology, 74*(3), 462–468.
120. Preacher, K. J., & Hayes, A. F. (2004). SPSS and SAS procedures for estimating indirect effects in simple mediation models. *Behavior Research Methods, Instruments, & Computers, 36*, 717–731.
121. Bunk, J. A., & Magley, V. J. (2013). The role of appraisals and emotions in understanding experiences of workplace incivility. *Journal of Occupational Health Psychology, 18*, 87–105.
122. Cortina, L. M., Kabat-Farr, D., Leskinen, E. A., Huerta, M., & Magley, V. J. (2013). Selective incivility as modern discrimination in organization evidence and impact. *Journal of Management, 39*(6), 1579–1605.
123. Laschinger, H., Leiter, M., Day, A., & Gilin, D. (2009). Workplace empowerment, incivility, and burnout: Impact on staff nurse recruitment and retention outcomes. *Journal of Nursing Management, 17*, 302–311.
124. Bibi, Z., Karim, J., & Din, S. (2013). Workplace incivility and counterproductive work behavior: Moderating role of emotional intelligence. *Pakistan Journal of Psychological Research, 28*(2), 317–334.
125. Sulea, C., Filipescu, R., Horga, A., Orțan, C., & Fischmann, G. (2012). Interpersonal mistreatment at work and burnout among teachers. *Cognition, Brain, Behavior: An interdisciplinary Journal, 16*(4), 553–570.
126. Cortina, L. M., Magley, V. J., Williams, J. H., & Langhout, R. D. (2001). Incivility in the workplace: Incidence and impact. *Journal of Occupational Health Psychology, 6*, 64–80.

127. Phillips, D., Mekos, D., Scarr, S., McCartney, K., & Abbott-Shim, M. (2000). Within and beyond the class-room door: Assessing quality in child care centers. *Early Childhood Research Quarterly, 15*, 475–496.
128. Park, H. S., & Kim, J. J. (2010). Relations among the professional learning environment, organizational commitment and awareness of professionalism in child care teachers. *The Journal of Child Education, 19*(2), 87–102.
129. Korea Institute of Childcare and Education. (2016). *2015 National Census Survey of Childcare Centers (Korean).* http://www.kicce.re.kr/kor/publication/02_04.jsp?mode=view&idx=20060&startPage=0&listNo=7&code=report03&search_item=subject&search_order=2015&order_list=10&list_scale=10&view_level=0. Accessed 1 August 2018.
130. Bliese, P. D., & Hanges, P. J. (2004). Being both too liberal and too conservative: The perils of treating grouped data as though they were independent. *Organizational Research Methods, 7*, 400–417.
131. Gransberry, C. K. (2021). How emotional intelligence promotes leadership and management practices. *Public Organization Review.* https://doi.org/10.1007/s11115-021-00550-4
132. Alsakarneh, A. A. A., Hong, S, C., Eneizan, B. M., & AL-kharabsheh, K. A. (2018). Exploring the relationship between the emotional labor and performance in the Jordanian insurance industry. *Current Psychology.* https://doi.org/10.1007/s12144-018-9935-2
133. Chan, K. W., Huang, X., Ng, P. M. (2007). Managers' conflict management styles and employee attitudinal outcomes: The mediating role of trust. *Asia Pacific Journal of Management.* https://doi.org/10.1007/s10490-007-9037-4
134. Qian, H., & Walker, A. (2021). Building emotional principal–teacher relationships in Chinese Schools: Reflecting on paternalistic leadership. *The Asia-Pacific Education Researcher.* https://doi.org/10.1007/s40299-021-00563-z
135. Gabriel, A. S., Acosta, J, D., Grandey, A. A. (2013). The value of a smile: Does emotional performance matter more in familiar or unfamiliar exchanges? *Journal of Business and Psychology.* https://doi.org/10.1007/s10869-013-9329-2
136. Al Ali, O. E., Garner, I., & Magadley, W. (2011). An exploration of the relationship between emotional intelligence and job performance in police organizations. *Journal of Police and Criminal Psychology.* https://doi.org/10.1007/s11896-011-9088-9
137. Liyanagamage, N., Fernando, M., & Gibbons, B. (2022). The emotional Machiavellian: Interactions between leaders and employees. *Journal of Business Ethics.* https://doi.org/10.1007/s10551-022-05233-8
138. Murmu, S., & Neelam, N. (2022). Impact of emotional intelligence and personality traits on managing team performance in virtual interface. *Asian Journal of Business Ethics.* https://doi.org/10.1007/s13520-022-00154-1
139. Mantello, P., Ho, M.-T., Nguyen, M.-H., & Vuong, Q.-H. (2021). Bosses without a heart: Socio-demographic and cross-cultural determinants of attitude toward Emotional AI in the workplace. *AI & SOCIETY.* https://doi.org/10.1007/s00146-021-01290-1
140. Sears, G. J., & Holmvall, C. M. (2009). The joint influence of supervisor and subordinate emotional intelligence on leader–member exchange. *Journal of Business and Psychology.* https://doi.org/10.1007/s10869-009-9152-y
141. Rajashekar, S., & Jain, A. (2023). A thematic analysis on "employee engagement in IT companies from the perspective of holistic well-being initiatives". *Employee Responsibilities and Rights Journal.* https://doi.org/10.1007/s10672-023-09440-x
142. Ding, H., & Liu, J. (2022). Paying close attention to strengths mindset: The relationship of employee strengths mindset with job performance. *Current Psychology.* https://doi.org/10.1007/s12144-022-03400-8
143. Han, Y., Kim, Y., & Hur, W.-M. (2019). The effects of perceived supervisor incivility on childcare workers' job performance: The mediating role of emotional exhaustion and intrinsic motivation. *Current Psychology.* https://doi.org/10.1007/s12144-019-0133-7

Chapter 8
Emotional Intelligence on Customer Experience in Service Domain

Introduction by the Author

Emotional intelligence is essential in customer experience because it allows us to engage with clients on a level that is more intimate and personal. It's additionally about addressing their issues; comprehending their emotions, recognising their sentiments, and ultimately demonstrating that we truly care for them. Research conducted by Chowdhary in (2022) about emotional intelligence and consumer ethics. In virtual collaboration, emotional intelligence of remote workers acts as a major indicator in group effectiveness and employee participation. According to Mayer and Salovey emotional intelligence contains four skill sets: observation, managing emotion, interpretation and utilisation. A study undergone by Sears in 2009 about the supervisor and subordinate emotional intelligence on leader- follower management in an organisation proves that the greater the emphasis on task oriented

Here are a few of the most fundamental explanations why emotional intelligence remains vital in customer service: Compassion is the foundation of emotional intelligence, which is what allows us to connect with clients on a personal level. We can better comprehend their wants, expectations, and disappointments when we are able to place ourselves in their position. Customers are more inclined to trust us and stay loyal to our business when they feel heard and understood. Take, for example, a melodramatic customer. It becomes easier to discover a solution that actually satisfied them after learning to empathise with their feelings and frustrations, Miao [90].

Emotionally intelligent people are competent at adapting their method of communication to meet the state of mind of the person with whom they are talking. In the context of the client experience, this is being sensitive to a client's emotions and changing our approach accordingly. Consider attempting to appease an irate customer by blasting them with some facts and data Hur [91]. It's roughly as successful as using petrol to put up a fire. Before plunging into problem-solving mode, the skill of emotional intelligence educates us to recognise and acknowledge the customer's feelings. As a result, our encounters become smoother, more productive.

© The Author(s), under exclusive license to Springer Nature Singapore Pte Ltd. 2024
R. Mekhala (ed.), *Emotional Intelligence Matters*,
https://doi.org/10.1007/978-981-99-7727-7_8

Working in customer service may be a roller coaster of emotions. On certain days, you may feel like a super heroes, easily sweeping in to safeguard the day for appreciative customer. Then there are times when everything seems to go right and we feel trapped in a never-ending downward spiral of irritation and disappointment. Emotional intelligence is a skill that gives us the tools we need to manage our emotions, especially in high-stress situations. We may keep a cool and collected attitude when confronting difficult or angry consumers by recognising and controlling our emotions. Following all, if anybody're anxious and worried, the manner in which can we possibly hope to help someone else effectively? For me, learning to understand my emotions proved to be a game changer.

Emotional intelligence enables to connect with customers on an emotional level, allowing to create rapport, Majeed [93]. Customers are more inclined to trust and be loyal to company when they feel like they are treated like people instead of just another transaction. The organizations may establish a setting where consumers are acknowledged and appreciated by asking intelligent inquiries, paying close attention, and demonstrating real interest in their issues. Consumers are more ready to overlook modest glitches and stay loyal in the midst of challenges when they experience that kind of closeness, Zhou [92].

I encourage you to investigate the field of emotional intelligence. You might well find it to be the hidden ingredient that elevates your client encounters from ordinary to outstanding. Remember, dear reader, logic is our dependable sidekick, but emotional intelligence is the real superhero cape. Through it, you can rise to fresh levels in the realm of customer service, leaving a path of happy, devoted consumers in our wake.

Machine Generated Summaries

Disclaimer: The summaries in this chapter were generated from Springer Nature publications using extractive AI auto-summarization: An extraction-based summarizer aims to identify the most important sentences of a text using an algorithm and uses those original sentences to create the auto-summary (unlike generative AI). As the constituted sentences are machine selected, they may not fully reflect the body of the work, so we strongly advise that the original content is read and cited. The auto generated summaries were curated by the editor to meet Springer Nature publication standards. To cite this content, please refer to the original papers.

Machine generated keywords: consumer, brand, customer, marketing, consumption, emotion, product, attachment, quality, miao, interaction, csr, response, service provider, artificial

Emotional Intelligence and Consumer Ethics: The Mediating Role of Personal Moral Philosophies [86]

This is a machine-generated summary of:
 Chowdhury, Rafi M. M. I.: Emotional Intelligence and Consumer Ethics: The Mediating Role of Personal Moral Philosophies [86]
 Published in: Journal of Business Ethics (2015)
 Link to original: https://doi.org/10.1007/s10551-015-2733-y
 Copyright of the summarized publication:
 Springer Science+Business Media Dordrecht 2015
 All rights reserved.
 If you want to cite the papers, please refer to the original.
 For technical reasons we could not place the page where the original quote is coming from.

Abstract-Summary

"These abilities, which are components of emotional intelligence (Davies and others, J Person Soc Psychol [1]), are examined as antecedents to consumers' ethical beliefs in this study."

"Five hundred Australian consumers participated in this study by completing an online questionnaire that included measures of emotional intelligence, consumers' ethical beliefs and personal moral philosophies (idealism and relativism, Forsyth, J Person Soc Psychol [2])."

"Results demonstrate that the ability to appraise and express emotions in oneself is directly negatively related to beliefs regarding actively benefiting from illegal actions as a consumer, passively benefiting at the expense of the seller and actively benefiting from questionable but legal actions as a consumer."

"The ability to appraise and express emotions in oneself is directly positively related to beliefs regarding 'doing-good' (pro-social) actions."

"The effects of the different components of emotional intelligence on consumers' ethical beliefs are (in most cases) mediated by personal moral philosophies."

"This study demonstrates the relationship between emotional intelligence and consumer ethics and highlights the interplay of affect and cognition in consumers' ethical decision-making."

Introduction

"The lack of studies on the role of emotions in consumers' ethical decision-making is an important gap in the literature on consumer ethics as current research in moral psychology indicates that emotions have a strong influence on ethical decision-making (e.g. Haidt [3]; Hardy [4])."

"In a recent review on ethical decision-making by consumers, Vitell and others [5] has also highlighted the significant role of emotions in this domain."

"The current research also goes beyond the extant research by examining whether the various components of emotional intelligence have direct effects on consumer ethics or whether these effects are mediated through cognitive belief systems, e.g. personal moral philosophies (i.e. idealism and relativism, Forsyth [6])."

"This is the first study to examine the relationship between emotional intelligence and consumer ethics."

"Testing the relationships of emotional intelligence with ethics in a consumer behaviour context is important, as the study of the ethical decision-making of consumers has theoretical and managerial implications."

Moral Emotions and Ethical Decision-Making

"Tangney and others [7] divide moral emotions into two categories: self-conscious moral emotions (e.g. shame, guilt, embarrassment and pride) and other-focused moral emotions (e.g. empathy and compassion)."

"Self-conscious moral emotions include shame, guilt, embarrassment, pride, etc Moral emotions affect moral behaviour through action tendencies that arise when the emotion is experienced."

"Beer ([8, p. 53]) states that "The negative flavours of self-conscious emotions such as embarrassment, shame, and guilt that arise from social misdeeds are sufficiently unpleasant that, once given a taste, people are highly motivated to regulate their behaviour so as to avoid experiencing them.""

"Tangney and others [7] note that the self-conscious moral emotion of pride provides reward and reinforcement for being committed to ethical actions."

"Apart from empathy, the other-focused moral emotions of elevation and gratitude are also positively related to moral behaviour (Haidt [3]; McCullough and others [9])."

Emotional Intelligence and Morality

"In describing the dimensions of emotional intelligence as proposed by Davies and others [1], Law and others [10, p. 484] state that the ability to appraise and express emotions in oneself "relates to an individual's ability to understand his or her deep emotions and to be able to express emotions naturally", whereas the ability to appraise and recognise emotions in others "relates to an individual's ability to perceive and understand the emotions of the people around them"."

"Some scholars consider emotional intelligence as a requirement for ethicality, e.g. Goleman [11, p. 286] states "emotional literacy goes hand in hand with education for character, for moral development, and for citizenship"."

"Recent research, particularly in business ethics, supports the view that emotional intelligence is related to ethical decision-making."

"Most of the studies that have examined emotional intelligence and its relationship with ethics have not considered the (possible) different effects of the various components of emotional intelligence."

Dimensions of Consumer Ethics

"These are based on the relative ethicality of various types of consumer actions."

"Of these four dimensions, the first three are clearly unethical actions and are rated as unethical by consumers (e.g. Chowdhury & Fernando [12]; Lu & Lu [13] etc)."

"The fourth dimension of consumer ethics ('no harm, no foul' actions) is not considered unethical by many, and in many studies that have empirically examined responses to the consumer ethics scale, the scores associated with this dimension are near the middle of the range on the scale related to unethicality (e.g. Chan & others [14]; Chowdhury & Fernando [12]; Lu & Lu [13] etc)."

"As these actions are ethically neutral from a consumer point of view, this study does not examine the relationship of EI with this type of consumer action."

"The current research examines the relationship of emotional intelligence with ethically positive and ethically negative consumer actions."

The Relationship of Emotional Intelligence and Consumer Ethics

"The following hypothesis is provided: The ability to appraise and experience one's own emotions (SEA) is negatively related to beliefs regarding actively benefiting from illegal actions as a consumer."

"The following hypothesis is proposed: The ability to regulate one's own emotions (ROE) is negatively related to beliefs regarding actively benefiting from illegal actions as a consumer."

"The following hypotheses are provided: The ability to appraise and experience one's own emotions (SEA) is negatively related to beliefs regarding actively benefiting from legal but questionable actions as a consumer."

"The ability to appraise and experience others' emotions (OEA) is negatively related to beliefs regarding actively benefiting from legal but questionable actions as a consumer."

"The ability to regulate one's own emotions (ROE) is negatively related to beliefs regarding actively benefiting from legal but questionable actions as a consumer."

The Mediating Role of Personal Moral Philosophies

"It can be predicted that the effects of SEA, OEA and ROE on beliefs regarding actively benefiting from illegal actions will be mediated by idealism and relativism."

"Idealism and relativism can be predicted to mediate the effects of SEA, OEA and ROE on beliefs regarding the passive dimension of consumer ethics."

"It can be predicted that the effects of SEA, OEA and ROE on beliefs regarding actively benefiting from legal but questionable actions will be mediated by idealism and relativism."

"These hypotheses are proposed: The effect of SEA on beliefs regarding actively benefiting from legal but questionable actions as a consumer is mediated through idealism."

"The effect of OEA on beliefs regarding actively benefiting from legal but questionable actions as a consumer is mediated through idealism."

"Idealism and relativism can be predicted to mediate the effects of the different components of emotional intelligence on beliefs regarding 'doing-good' actions as a consumer."

Method

"In order to assess the convergent and discriminant validity of the measures, a confirmatory factor analysis (CFA) was conducted with the items measuring self-emotions appraisal (SEA), OEA, ROE, idealism, relativism and the relevant dimensions of consumer ethics."

"The relativism scale was purified by eliminating the four items and using six items to measure this construct in line with the recommendation of Cui and others [15]."

"In the final model, SEA, OEA, ROE were each measured using four items, idealism was measured using ten items, relativism was measured using six items, actively benefiting from illegal actions as a consumer was measured with six items, passively benefiting at the expense of the seller and actively benefiting from legal but questionable actions as a consumer was measured with nine items, 'doing-good' actions was measured with five items and pro-environmental buying actions was measured with three items."

Results

"A multiple regression analysis was conducted with SEA, OEA, ROE, age and education qualification as independent variables and beliefs regarding the passive/'active legal' dimension as the dependent variable."

"A series of multiple mediation models were utilised that use bootstrapping (n = 1000) to generate bias-corrected confidence intervals to test for the indirect effects of the various components of emotional intelligence on beliefs regarding the 'active illegal' dimension through idealism and relativism (Hayes [16])."

"A series of multiple mediation models were utilised that use bootstrapping (n = 1000) to generate bias-corrected confidence intervals to test for the indirect effects of the various components of emotional intelligence on beliefs regarding the passive/ 'active legal' dimension through idealism and relativism (Hayes [16])."

"A series of multiple mediation models were utilised that use bootstrapping (n = 1000) to generate bias-corrected confidence intervals to test for the indirect effects of the various components of emotional intelligence on beliefs regarding pro-environmental buying through idealism and relativism (Hayes [16])."

Discussion

"The key findings of this research are discussed below: The ability to appraise and express one's own emotions is negatively related to beliefs regarding unethical consumer actions and is positively related to beliefs regarding 'doing-good' actions."

"The results from this study indicate that the ability to appraise and recognise others' emotions is positively related to beliefs regarding both 'doing-good' actions and pro-environmental buying actions."

"Although the items measuring pro-environmental buying have been utilised as part of the 'doing-good' dimension in prior studies (e.g. Vitell & others [17]), the results from this study indicate that the effects of the various components of emotional intelligence on beliefs regarding pro-environmental buying are not always the same as the effects related to 'doing-good' actions."

"Personal moral philosophies mediate the effects of emotional intelligence on beliefs regarding the 'active illegal' dimension, passive/'active legal' dimension and 'doing-good' actions."

Limitations and Future Research

"Although the effects of emotional intelligence on various domains of consumer ethics were in some cases significant, these effects were not extremely strong."

"Future research can use ability-based measures of EI to examine the relationship between emotional intelligence and consumer ethics and compare whether the results are similar to this study."

"Future studies should further examine the factor structure of the consumer ethics scale."

"This study has examined emotional intelligence as an antecedent to consumer ethics as a step in reducing this gap in the consumer ethics literature."

"The research has built upon the framework of moral emotions to make a case for the role of emotional intelligence in the ethical decision-making of consumers."

"The role of specific moral emotions in consumers' ethical decision-making has not been directly examined in this study."

"Future research can examine the specific effects of these moral emotions on consumers' ethical decision-making."

Implications and Conclusion

"As emotionally intelligent consumers have more positive beliefs regarding ethical consumer actions and more negative beliefs regarding unethical consumer actions, public policy should be crafted that encourages the development of emotionally intelligent consumers."

"A path to developing emotional intelligence in individuals is through supporting social and emotional learning (SEL) programmes in educational institutions."

"Research shows that emotional intelligence has positive influences on the ethical behaviour of employees (Fu [18]), and thus, such training will help develop both ethical employees and consumers."

"This research is the first to examine emotional intelligence in relation to consumer ethics."

"The ability to appraise and express emotions in oneself is the most important component of emotional intelligence in terms of its effects on consumer ethics, as self-emotions appraisal is positively related to beliefs regarding ethical consumer actions and negatively related to beliefs regarding unethical consumer actions."

Enhancing International Buyer–Seller Relationship Quality and Long-Term Orientation Using Emotional Intelligence: The Moderating Role of Foreign Culture [87]

This is a machine-generated summary of:

Leonidou, Leonidas C.; Aykol, Bilge; Larimo, Jorma; Kyrgidou, Lida; Christodoulides, Paul: Enhancing International Buyer–Seller Relationship Quality and Long-Term Orientation Using Emotional Intelligence: The Moderating Role of Foreign Culture [87]

Published in: Management International Review (2021)

Link to original: https://doi.org/10.1007/s11575-021-00447-w

Copyright of the summarized publication:

The Author(s), under exclusive licence to Springer-Verlag GmbH Germany, part of Springer Nature 2021

All rights reserved.

If you want to cite the papers, please refer to the original.

For technical reasons we could not place the page where the original quote is coming from.

Abstract-Summary

"Building on Emotion Regulation Theory, we examine the role of an exporter's emotional intelligence (EI) in enhancing the quality and boosting the long-term orientation of the working relationship with its import buyers."

Introduction

"Although psychology research has repeatedly confirmed the role of EI in improving relationships between interacting individuals (e.g., Lopes & others [19]), its examination within a business context has been confined mainly to the sphere of relationships between supervisors-employees (e.g., Jordan & Troth [20]), salespersons-customers (e.g., Delpechitre & others [21]), and service providers-consumers (e.g., Matute & others [22])."

"One summary conclusion that can be derived from these studies is that the proper use of EI between parties in an interpersonal working relationship can indeed improve various positive dimensions of their interactive behavior, such as trust, satisfaction, and loyalty."

"In light of the above gaps in the literature, this article explores the role of EI in influencing the quality of the exporter-importer relationship (taking into consideration the idiosyncrasies of foreign cultures) and how this in turn contributes to the adoption of long-term orientation."

"Our study contributes to the international business literature by: (a) extending the EI knowledge accumulated on interpersonal relationships to cross-border business relationships, with a particular focus on enhancing the quality of interactions between exporters and importers, which is a core issue in achieving international business success (Leonidou & others [23]); (b) highlighting the importance of cultural contingencies in the importer's country in influencing the favorable effect of an export manager's EI on the quality of the working relationship at the inter-organizational level (Miao & others [24]); and (c) stressing the conducive role of achieving high levels of relationship quality (through the proper use of EI) in cultivating a long-term oriented spirit between interacting parties, which is vital in protecting their relationship against factors that may lead to its discontinuity (Barnes & others [25])."

Research Background

"An individual with high levels of EI is usually very selective in activating his/her emotional ability to develop relationships with others."

"With regard to the latter case, there are indications in the management literature (e.g., Krishnakumar & others [26]; Shih & Susanto [27]) that emotionally intelligent people are in a better position than their counterparts who do not possess such ability to effectively handle existing relationships in a way to improve their quality and performance outcomes."

"Emotionally intelligent expatriate managers were also found to deliver better performance results (Gabel & others [28]) and higher levels of organizational commitment (Lii & Wong [29]) compared to their counterparts with low EI levels."

"Lillis and Tian [30] also concluded that business students with high levels of EI were in a better position to recognize context-based emotion patterns and adapt to intercultural contexts, compared to those with low levels of EI."

Theory, Model, and Hypotheses

"We can hypothesize that: Hypothesis 2: The existence of high levels of trust in the working relationship between the exporter and the import buyer will enhance its long-term orientation."

"This leads us to the following hypothesis: Hypothesis 4: The existence of high levels of cooperation in the working relationship between the exporter and the import buyer will enhance its long-term orientation."

"We can hypothesize that: Hypothesis 9: Uncertainty avoidance positively moderates the association between EI and (a) trust, (b) commitment, (c) cooperation, and (d) satisfaction in the relationship between the exporter and its import buyer. (National) long-term orientation refers to the promotion of virtues by people—especially perseverance and thrift—oriented toward future rewards (Hofstede & Hofstede [31])."

"We can propose the following: Hypothesis 10: (National) long-term orientation positively moderates the association between EI and (a) trust, (b) commitment, (c) cooperation, and (d) satisfaction in the relationship between the exporter and its import buyer."

Research Method

"Our key informant was the individual in charge of export operations, who was contacted by telephone to explain the objectives of the study, explore his/her willingness to participate, and clarify his/her postal/electronic contact details."

"Firms that declined to participate in the survey did so mainly on the basis of company policy not to disclose internal information, lack of available time to fill in the questionnaire, or termination of their export activity."

"The various model constructs and their operationalized scales were incorporated in a questionnaire in three different sections, with each corresponding to emotional intelligence, relationship quality, and long-term orientation."

"The questionnaire also included a section seeking information on the firm's exporting activities (e.g., export experience, nature of products exported, export destination countries), while another section requested information about business experience, number of employees, and sales turnover."

Data Analysis and Findings

"In support of H_{10a-d}, our findings show that in the case of importers living in countries high in long-term orientation, the positive effect of EI on trust ($\beta = 0.29$, t = 5.73, p = 0.00), commitment ($\beta = 0.44$, t = 9.52, p = 0.00), cooperation ($\beta = 0.43$, t = 7.86, p = 0.00), and satisfaction ($\beta = 0.52$, t = 9.68, p = 0.00) is amplified."

"We also tested an alternative model in which EI was set as a moderating variable between relationship quality (which was treated as a higher-order construct) and long-term orientation ($\chi^2 = 47.39$, p = 0.00, df = 26; NFI = 0.92; NNFI = 0.93; CFI = 0.93; RMSEA = 0.09)."

Discussion

"This study has amply demonstrated the substantial role of the exporter's EI in creating a high-quality business relationship with the import buyer, which in turn will help to increase its long-term orientation."

"The fact that we found high levels of EI by the exporter to boost satisfaction levels in the relationship with the importer corroborates previous study findings within the services context (e.g., Kernbach & Schutte [32]; Tsaur & Ku [33]) that the EI of service providers enhances customer satisfaction."

"With regard to the moderating role of import customer's culture on the association between EI and the various elements of relationship quality, our findings resemble those of Miao & others [24] meta-analysis, indicating that a leader's EI has a stronger positive effect on the organizational citizenship behavior of subordinates in more collectivistic, more feminine, higher uncertainty avoidance, and high (national) long-term orientation cultures."

Study Implications

"One key implication of our study is that EI is an important construct that can be usefully employed to better understand inter-organizational working relationships in an international business context."

"Although extant research on seller-buyer relationships in general and exporter-importer relationships in particular analyzed working relationships at the firm level, only a few studies (e.g., Gu & others [34]; Sousa & others [35]) attempted to stress the role of specific individuals in the interacting organizations in influencing the behavioral and/or economic dimensions of these relationships."

"Our finding that the influence of the exporter's EI on the quality of the working relationship with the import buyer is moderated by cultural factors implies that there should be a clear understanding of the specific cultural nuances of the importer's country, through, for example, the acquisition of relevant information, participation in educational seminars, and involvement in cultural assimilation exercises."

Limitations and Future Research

"To make the analysis more complete, it is also necessary to have the views of the import buyer on how s/he perceives the exporter's EI, each of the four dimensions of relationship quality, and long-term orientation."

"In relation to this, it would be interesting to see how different combinations of EI possessed by each party in the working relationship will affect different quality dimensions."

"Fifth, we measured the moderating role of culture on the association between an exporter's EI and the various quality constructs describing its relationship with the import buyer, using Hofstede and Hofstede's [31] dimensions at the national level."

"Psychic distance has been extensively used in the exporting literature (e.g., Skarmeas & others [36]) as having a predicting role on exporter-importer relationships, and, as such, it would be illuminating to examine its moderating effect on the association between EI and relationship quality."

Consumer Emotional Intelligence and Its Effects on Responses to Transgressions [88]

This is a machine-generated summary of:
Ahn, Hongmin; Sung, Yongjun; Drumwright, Minette E.: Consumer emotional intelligence and its effects on responses to transgressions [88]
Published in: Marketing Letters (2015)
Link to original: https://doi.org/10.1007/s11002-014-9342-x
Copyright of the summarized publication:
Springer Science+Business Media New York 2015
All rights reserved.
If you want to cite the papers, please refer to the original.
For technical reasons we could not place the page where the original quote is coming from.

Abstract-Summary

"This research suggests that consumer emotional intelligence (CEI) is an important construct in explaining why some consumers react destructively to conflicts in consumer-brand relationships whereas others approach them constructively."

Introduction

"Why do some consumers respond to disappointments and conflicts in brand relationships destructively and terminate relationships, while others respond constructively and maintain their relationships with the brands?"

"Consumer emotional intelligence (CEI) is a relatively new concept that provides a unique, useful lens through which one understands why consumers vary dramatically in their ability to deal with negative emotions and choose appropriate coping strategies in consumption contexts."

"The purpose of this study is to provide a better understanding of the effect of CEI on coping responses in consumer-brand relationship conflicts."

"It also investigates the influence of consumer perceptions of a company's intentions on the relationship between CEI and coping responses."

"Another goal is to explore a broader set of consumer responses to conflicts than the dichotomous responses, maintaining or exiting a brand relationship, that have characterized many studies of brand relationships."

Theoretical Background and Hypotheses

"High CEI individuals may possess the ability to choose appropriate strategies for coping with conflicts when a brand transgression threatens the relationship."

"H1: When consumers experience a brand transgression, high CEI consumers are less likely to respond with destructive responses (exit and neglect), and more likely to respond with constructive responses (voice and loyalty) than low CEI consumers."

"H2: The effect of CEI on coping responses is stronger when a brand transgression threatens a consumer's self-interest rather than society's interests."

"H3: Consumers' perceptions of a company's intention mediate the effect of CEI on coping responses."

"High CEI consumers were less likely to exit the relationship in response to the transgression (M = 4.50) than low CEI consumers (M = 4.98)."

"High CEI consumers were less likely to neglect the relationship in response to the transgression (M = 3.71) than low CEI consumers (M = 4.19)."

Discussion and Implications

"It provides empirical evidence that CEI is an important explanatory variable in predicting consumers' coping responses to brand relationship transgressions."

"For destructive coping, consumers might focus on managing the elicited negative emotions rather than solving the problem, thereby drawing on CEI to control their emotions."

"The effect of CEI would be stronger when consumers use destructive coping strategies vs. constructive strategies."

"This study supports the notion that consumers' perceptions of a brand's intention (i.e., cognitive appraisal) are important mediators in the relationship between CEI and their responses."

"The finding that low CEI consumers tend to attribute negative intentions to a company provides useful insights."

"For low CEI consumers, a full-apology approach that highlights the company's good intentions will be more effective than a defensive approach, which focuses on minimizing the company's responsibility for the transgression."

Modeling Brand Immunity: The Moderating Role of Generational Cohort Membership [89]

This is a machine-generated summary of:
Saju, B.; Harikrishnan, K.; Joseph Jeya Anand, S.: Modeling brand immunity: the moderating role of generational cohort membership [89]
Published in: Journal of Brand Management (2017)
Link to original: https://doi.org/10.1057/s41262-017-0063-3
Copyright of the summarized publication:
Macmillan Publishers Ltd 2017
All rights reserved.
If you want to cite the papers, please refer to the original.
For technical reasons we could not place the page where the original quote is coming from.

Abstract-Summary

"This research proposes an augmented conceptual model which traces the role of perceived brand trustworthiness (PBT) and emotional attachment to the brand (EAB) on the formation of brand immunity (BI) and tests it for the moderating influence of generational cohort membership."

"Test results of the model with an Indian sample of Gen Y and Gen X consumers validate all the propositions except one, thereby enriching BI theory in the backdrop of generational differences."

"We contribute to the branding literature by showing that the proposed model holds good for consumers belonging to both Gen X and Y, though the strength of the relationships varies based on the specific cohort membership."

Introduction

"The extant literature leaves gaping holes in explaining how consumers having membership in different generational cohorts develop brand immunity."

"We investigate the formation of brand immunity and the way it is influenced by generational cohort membership with a consumer sample from India."

"As Indian cohorts are shaped by unique Indian socioeconomic events, it is worthwhile to examine if generational differences influence brand relationships in the Indian context."

"This study narrows down onto two significant Indian cohorts, Gen Y and Gen X, for examining the generational difference on brand attitude and behavior."

"These relationships are tested with a moderating factor, generational cohort membership, or the consumers' age-based categorization which makes them belong to Gen X or Gen Y. We propose that the strength of the hypothesized relationships culminating in brand immunity significantly differs between these two groups."

Literature Review and Conceptual Framework

"There exist diverse perspectives on the nature of attachment consumers have with brands in marketing literature, we focus on the emotional bonding (Malär & others [38]) aspects of consumer–brand relationship."

"Extant literature provides ample evidence for defining emotional attachment to brands as an "emotion-laden bond with consumers and commercial objects, primarily brands" (Jiménez & Voss [39])."

"The surveyed literature on the broad domain of brand devotion provides insights also into a state of extreme brand commitment which makes a consumer immune to even negative word of mouth (Arruda-Filho & others [40]; Batra & others [41]; Ortiz & others [42]; Mikulincer & Shaver [43]; Whan Park & others [44])."

"It is very much possible that some consumers with high brand commitment may be insular toward even negative word of mouth against their preferred brand."

"Indian Gen Y consumers have high purchasing power and are highly aware of brands compared to other cohorts (Viswanathan & Jain [45])."

Hypothesis Development

"Previous studies have empirically established that consumers' perception of a brand's believability or trustworthiness has a significant positive impact on affective feelings, a concept very close to emotional brand attachment (Kim & others [46])."

"Brands would be greatly benefited if they could strengthen consumers' emotional attachment to the brand as a result of enhanced trustworthiness."

"We propose that perceived brand trustworthiness has a positive impact on emotional brand attachment."

"Perceived brand trustworthiness (PBT) has a positive effect on emotional attachment to the brand (EAB)."

"Building on the previous arguments, we posit that that perceived brand trustworthiness not only has a direct effect on BI but has an indirect effect also through emotional attachment resulting in brand immunity."

"Emotional attachment to the brand (EAB) mediates the relationship between perceived brand trustworthiness (PBT) and brand immunity (BI)."

Methodology

"Smartphones are ubiquitous, an important accessory for most people, relatively durable, and appeared to be an appropriate category for branding research (Cheng & others [47])."

"Previous studies have also reported mobile phones as one of the most loved brand categories for consumers (Karjaluoto & others [48]), a testimonial to the importance of social and affective benefits of the category making it appropriate to investigate the proposed constructs and relationships (Chaudhuri & Holbrook [49])."

"The respondents were required to choose a brand of smartphone they have ever purchased or had been used for at least 6 months."

"All the subsequent questions were based on this focal brand given by the respondents, in line with the previous branding studies (Batra & others [41]; Xie & others [50])."

"Data across brands were pooled in the subsequent analysis."

"Perceived brand trustworthiness (PBT) was measured using a five-item scale developed by Erdem and Swait [51]."

"Emotional attachment to the brand (EAB) was measured using four-item semantic differential scale originally developed by Jiménez and Voss [39]."

Results

"For the model with the path PTR → EAB constrained with equivalence for Gen Y and Gen X, the fit statistics were found as follows: $\chi^2 = 164.32$ with 125 degrees of freedom, p = 0.014."

"The model with the path PBT → BI constrained for both Gen X and Gen Y groups provided fit as $\chi^2 = 163.931$ with 125 degrees of freedom, p = 0.012."

"Moderation effect could not be established on the third proposed link EAB → BI as the constrained path model did not produce significant worsening of fit ($\chi^2 = 160.49$ with 125 degrees of freedom, p = 0.018; $\Delta\chi^2 = 0.479$ with 1 degree of freedom, p = 0.489)."

Discussion and Implications

"We empirically documented the formation of brand immunity through different routes and demonstrated the differences in relationship strength for Gen Y and Gen X consumers."

"Another important observation is that though Gen X group has a stronger effect on the formation of EAB and BI, it does not discount the fact that the proposed model of brand immunity is valid for Gen Y consumers too."

"This implies that Gen Y consumers are also moved by perceived trustworthiness of the brand, end up making meaningful emotional connections with the brand, and stay immune to negative word of mouth."

"Since a strong emotional bond with a brand leads to high commitment in terms of continued patronage withstanding negative information, brand managers need to make investments to build such bonds both with Gen X and Gen Y consumers."

Emotional Intelligence and Service Quality: A Meta-Analysis with Initial Evidence on Cross-Cultural Factors and Future Research Directions [90]

This is a machine-generated summary of:

Miao, Chao; Barone, Michael J.; Qian, Shanshan; Humphrey, Ronald H.: Emotional intelligence and service quality: a meta-analysis with initial evidence on cross-cultural factors and future research directions [90]

Published in: Marketing Letters (2019)

Link to original: https://doi.org/10.1007/s11002-019-09495-7

Copyright of the summarized publication:
Springer Science+Business Media, LLC, part of Springer Nature 2019
All rights reserved.

If you want to cite the papers, please refer to the original.

For technical reasons we could not place the page where the original quote is coming from.

Abstract-Summary

"Selecting employees who are high on emotional intelligence (EI), and training employees in emotional competencies, may be ways to improve service quality."

"This meta-analysis tests the claims that EI improves service quality."

"The findings indicate that EI is significantly and positively related to service quality and that this relationship is stronger (1) for cultures that are short (versus long) term oriented and that are indulgent (versus restrained), and (2) for professional services and service shops than for mass services."

Introduction

"Such research shows that service employees who display high levels of EI during service interactions can improve customer outcomes (Kernbach & Schutte [52]), perhaps because EI aids in building relationships that are important to the customer experience (Kim & Drumwright [53])."

"It is also important to investigate the effects of EI on service quality insofar as the value of EI to performance is often disputed."

"The major purpose of this study is to investigate the importance of EI to service quality by obtaining the best estimate of its effect size."

"Such evidence would serve to not only facilitate future academic research but to also inform firms as to when investing in EI selection and training may improve service quality perceptions (Gelbrich & Roschk [54])."

"Another objective of this meta-analysis is to test how different conceptual and methodological moderators may accentuate or attenuate the relationship between EI and service quality, providing a more contextualized understanding of when employee EI increases service quality perceptions (Bijmolt & Pieters [55])."

Theoretical Development and Hypotheses

"This relationship may arise because employees who are high (versus low) in EI should be better able to identify and manage the specific emotions customers experience during service encounters, as suggested by Golder and others [56, p. 14]: "Service providers who monitor customer emotions during their service delivery are more likely to adapt their service's attributes and improve experienced attribute quality.""

"EI should therefore have a larger impact on service quality perceptions in feminine cultures that encourage paying attention to the needs of others than in masculine cultures emphasizing competition (Bolino & others [57]). H2: The EI–service quality relationship is stronger in feminine versus masculine cultures."

"Service representatives from long- (versus short-) term-oriented cultures should therefore be more likely to leverage EI as a means of increasing service quality evaluations and boosting their future career prospects."

Method

"Eligible studies must have been empirical in nature and had to report at least one correlation coefficient for the relation between EI and service quality (or offer results that could be converted into effect sizes (Lipsey & Wilson [58]; Peterson & Brown [59]))."

"Based on these procedures, 19 eligible studies (denoted with an asterisk in the References section) were identified with a sample size of 4625 subjects for inclusion in the present meta-analysis."

"To effect sizes, we coded each study with regard to the EI measure that was used (see Miao & others [60]; O'Boyle & others [61])."

"We corrected measurement errors for the independent and dependent variables for each effect size using the reliabilities (coefficient alphas) reported in primary studies, and constructed corrected 95% confidence intervals to assess the statistical significance of effect sizes."

Results

"The relationship between EI and service quality was significant and strongly positive ($\rho = .67$), supporting hypothesis 1; this same pattern of results held for all three types of EI (ability EI: $\rho = .82$; self-report EI: $\rho = .66$; mixed EI: $\rho = .67$)."

"The $\text{Var}_{\text{art}}\%$ value which reflects the percentage of variance in ρ explained by statistical artifacts of the meta-analytic distribution of EI–service quality was 6%, allowing for the test of potential moderators (Schmidt & Hunter [62])."

"The results also indicate that the EI–service quality relationship does not differ between masculine and feminine cultures (hypothesis 2) or between low and high uncertainty avoidance cultures (hypothesis 4)."

Discussion

"A second contribution involves our integration of cross-cultural research with the EI and service quality literatures to identify theoretically relevant moderators involving national cultural dimensions."

"Rather, this finding suggests that individuals from short-term-oriented cultures may be more likely to use their EI to improve service quality in order to enjoy the immediate gratification that is associated with high service quality evaluations (e.g., praise from supervisors, peers, and customers)."

"Our results support the notion that EI is a consistently strong predictor of service quality in general and across all cultural dimensions, although the effects of EI are stronger in some cultures than in others."

"Based on findings indicating that EI has a stronger influence on service quality in short-term-oriented and indulgent cultures as well as in professional services and service shops, retailers operating in such cultures and selling these types of services would also be wise to add EI into service delivery strategies."

When Does Customer CSR Perception Lead to Customer Extra-Role Behaviors? The Roles of Customer Spirituality and Emotional Brand Attachment [91]

This is a machine-generated summary of:
Hur, Won-Moo; Moon, Tae-Won; Kim, Hanna: When does customer CSR perception lead to customer extra-role behaviors? The roles of customer spirituality and emotional brand attachment [91]
Published in: Journal of Brand Management (2020)
Link to original: https://doi.org/10.1057/s41262-020-00190-x
Copyright of the summarized publication:
Springer Nature Limited 2020
All rights reserved.
If you want to cite the papers, please refer to the original.
For technical reasons we could not place the page where the original quote is coming from.

Abstract-Summary

"The first objective of this study is to test the mediating role of emotional brand attachment in the relationship between customers' perception of corporate social responsibility (CSR) and two types of customer extra-role behavior: customer participation behavior and customer citizenship behavior."

"The second objective is to examine the moderating effects of customer spirituality on the customer CSR perception–emotional brand attachment relationship and the indirect relationship between customer CSR perception and customer participation/citizenship behavior through emotional brand attachment."

"Emotional brand attachment partially mediated the relationship between customer CSR perception and customer participation/citizenship behavior."

"Customer spirituality further moderated the indirect effect of customer CSR perception and customer participation/citizenship behavior through emotional brand attachment."

Introduction

"We expect that emotional brand attachment would mediate the relationship between customers' CSR perceptions and their extra-role behaviors."

"The primary purpose of our study is to investigate the mediating effect of emotional brand attachment on the relationship between customers' CSR perceptions and their extra-role behaviors."

"We investigate the moderated mediation effects of customer spirituality on the relationship between customers' CSR perceptions and their extra-role behaviors as mediated by emotional brand attachment."

"We suggest that the treatment effect of customers' CSR perceptions on extra-role behaviors via emotional brand attachment differs depending on customer spirituality."

"The current study complements and extends the extant research on customers' CSR perceptions by providing an empirical framework for the process by which consumers' CSR perceptions affect their extra-role behaviors, which incorporates the mediating variables of emotional brand attachment."

Literature Review and Hypotheses Development

"On the basis of AET, we predict that customers' emotional perceptions regarding the extent to which their organization engages in CSR activities (i.e., work events) will influence their emotional brand attachment (i.e., affective reactions), leading to extra-role behaviors (i.e., changes in work attitudes and behaviors)."

"Since spirituality not only promotes an individual's ethical decision-making but also develops social responsibility contributions (Fry & Slocum [64]; Pawar [65]), customers equipped with higher levels of spirituality respond more keenly to a company's CSR activities, leading to a stronger affective attachment toward its brand."

"Drawing on the H-V theory of ethics, we further suggest that customers' spirituality performs a role as a moderator in the mediating effect of emotional brand attachment on the relationship between customers' CSR perceptions and extra-role behavior."

"By positively influencing their decision-making when faced with ethical dilemmas and ethics-laden situations, customers' spirituality is likely to strengthen the indirect effect of customer CSR perception on extra-role behavior through emotional brand attachment."

Method

"In line with such CSR research in the banking sector (e.g., Pérez & Del Bosque [66, 67]), we asked subjects two screening questions to select appropriate customers."

"Using transaction duration question (e.g., more than 1 year or not), we recruited customers to use one of five South Korean banks as a main bank."

"To assess customer participation behavior, we used four-item scales from Chan and others [68], measuring the extent to which a customer invests time and effort in sharing information, making suggestions, and being involved in the decision-making process of their bank."

"Sample items are "I spent a lot of time sharing information about my needs and opinions with the staff during XXX's service process" and "I have a high level of participation in XXX's service process" (Cronbach's α = .90)."

"To measure social desirability bias, we used five items from Hays and others' [69] scale."

Data Analysis and Results

"When emotional brand attachment was included in the model, the direct effect of customer CSR perception on CPB was not statistically significant (b = .074, 95% CI ([− .073, .234])), which indicates the full mediation effect of emotional brand attachment on the relationship between customer CSR perception and CPB."

"We detected no significant relationship customer CSR perception and emotional brand attachment when customers reported mean and low level of customer spirituality (mean: b = .17, 95% CI [− .01, .36]; low: b = .08, 95% CI [− .02, .32]), lending support to Hypothesis 3."

"Our results showed that the conditional indirect effect of customer CSR perception and CPB through emotional brand attachment was strengthened by customer spirituality (b = .030, 95% CI [.005, .081])."

"The test for Hypothesis 5 indicated that the conditional indirect effect of customer CSR perception and CCB via emotional brand attachment was also strengthened by customer spirituality (b = .084, 95% CI [.017, .166])."

Discussion

"Customer spirituality moderated the indirect effect of customer CSR perception and customer extra-role behavior through emotional brand attachment."

"The results of this study support affective events theory (AET) by explaining the mediating effects of emotional brand attachment in the relationship between CSR and customer extra-role behavior."

"The findings here prove that the direct and indirect effects differ between the two behaviors when emotional brand attachment mediates the relationship between customers' CSR perceptions and extra-role behaviors."

"The results of our study show that customer spirituality strengthens the indirect effect of customer CSR perceptions on extra-role behavior mediated by emotional brand attachment."

"While we proved the mediating effect of emotional brand attachment as a brand-related variable, it would be useful for future research to prove the effects of brand familiarity or brand image on the relationship between customer CSR perception and customer extra-role behavior for better branding implications."

How Does Topic Consistency Affect Online Review Helpfulness? The Role of Review Emotional Intensity [92]

This is a machine-generated summary of:
Zhou, Chuanmei; Yang, Shuiqing; Chen, Yuangao; Zhou, Shasha; Li, Yixiao; Qazi, Atika: How does topic consistency affect online review helpfulness? The role of review emotional intensity [92]

Published in: Electronic Commerce Research (2022)

Link to original: https://doi.org/10.1007/s10660-022-09597-x

Copyright of the summarized publication:

The Author(s), under exclusive licence to Springer Science Business Media, LLC, part of Springer Nature 2022

Copyright comment: Springer Nature or its licensor holds exclusive rights to this article under a publishing agreement with the author(s) or other rightsholder(s); author self-archiving of the accepted manuscript version of this article is solely governed by the terms of such publishing agreement and applicable law.

All rights reserved.

If you want to cite the papers, please refer to the original.

For technical reasons we could not place the page where the original quote is coming from.

Abstract-Summary

"Despite many scholars have devoted to understanding the effects of manager response on review helpfulness, the mechanism of how the topic consistency between manager responses and corresponding reviews affect review helpfulness remains unclear, especially in different conditions of review emotional intensity."

"Based on the uncertainty reduction theory, a research model reflected the impacts of topic consistency on review helpfulness in different conditions of review emotional intensity was developed."

"In terms of the negative discrete emotions, anxiety has a negative moderating effect on the relationship between topic consistency and review helpfulness."

Introduction

"Managers' inappropriate response to consumers reviews may even cause negative effects [71]."

"How does the topic consistency between managers response and consumer reviews affects review helpfulness?"

"More topic-related responses indicate that the hotel manager provided more related information and solutions to the specific issues mentioned in the review [72, 73]."

"The present study investigated the following questions: (1) Does topic consistency between manager responses and consumer reviews affect consumers' perception of the review helpfulness? (2) Whether the intensity of positive and negative emotions (e.g., anger, anxiety, and sadness) embedded in the reviews may affect the relationship between topic consistency and review helpfulness?"

"Unlike many previous researches usually explain online review helpfulness from a single consumer review perspective, the present study explored the impacts of topic consistency between manager responses and the corresponding reviews on the review helpfulness."

Literature Review

"On online review platforms, potential consumers may read review information and manager responses to reduce the uncertainty caused by other consumer decision-making behavior."

"We expect that the appropriate manager response will be effective against helping consumers understand the review text, thereby reducing the uncertainty caused by the product itself."

"Besides, Kwok and Xie [74] argue that reviews with manager responses contain more information and help potential consumers reduce uncertainty, and they found that reviews with manager responses received more helpfulness votes."

"Previous research has not deeply explored what kind of response can help the review receive more helpfulness votes and help potential consumers reduce the uncertainty of the product."

"We integrate manager responses and reviews from the perspective of topic consistency to examine whether manager responds to the topics involved in reviews can help potential consumers to understand reviews and thus reduce perceived uncertainty."

Research Model and Hypotheses

"In order to obtain more useful decision-making information to reduce uncertainty, potential consumers may be more concerned about whether the manager communicates with the consumer about the topics involved in the reviews when they focus on reviews with high intensity of positive emotions."

"Compared reviews embedded with other emotions, potential consumers have already received enough certain information to reduce uncertainty about products when reading anger-reviews, and they do not need excessive additional information (e.g., manager responses) to help them understand the review text."

"We consider that a response strategy with high topic consistency for reviews with high anxiety may cause potential consumers to attribute the negative review to other aspects rather than the service or product itself, thus reducing their perception of the review helpfulness."

Research Methodology

"In this dataset, in addition to the review helpfulness votes, it includes review information (e.g., review rating, title text, review text and review posted time), reviewer information (e.g., number of badges owned by the reviewer, number of followers and total helpfulness votes), and the manager response information (e.g., response text and responder information)."

"We obtained the topic probability distribution of each response text based on the LDA model trained by the review text set, and calculated the similarity between the two probability distributions by Hellinger distance to represent the topic consistency between the review text and the response text."

"Through the prediction process of LDA model, we can obtain the words and weights under each topic, and represent each review text by topic probability distribution."

"We used Hellinger Distance to calculate the similarity between the topic probability distributions of the response text and review text."

Data Analysis and Results

"The interaction terms between emotional intensity and topic consistency were incorporated into the Model 1.4."

"Model 1.4 indicates the moderating effects of positive emotional intensity and negative emotional intensity on the influence of topic consistency on review helpfulness."

"The coefficient of the interaction term between topic consistency and positive emotional intensity is positively significant ($\beta = 0.21$, $p < 0.001$)."

"The coefficient of the interaction term between topic consistency and negative emotional intensity is negatively significant ($\beta = -0.21$, $p < 0.05$)."

"In Model 2.2, similar result was found for the coefficient of the interaction term between positive emotional intensity and topic consistency ($\beta = 0.22$, $p < 0.001$)."

"Consistent with the regression results of Model 1.4, anxiety is a category of negative emotions, which weakens the positive effect of topic consistency on review helpfulness."

Discussion and Conclusion

"Based on uncertainty reduction theory, the present study examined the impacts of topic consistency between manager responses and corresponding reviews on review helpfulness."

"The present study found that the intensity of positive emotions in reviews moderated the relationship between topic consistency and review helpfulness."

"The present study found that topic consistency between manager responses and reviews has positively influences on review helpfulness."

"The present study also found that the emotional intensity of reviews also moderated the impact of the topical consistency between manager response and corresponding reviews on review helpfulness."

"Considering manager responses to the positive discrete emotion are usually non-personalized which are not commonly analyzed in previous related studies, the present study thus did not examine the moderating effects of the different positive discrete emotions on the relationships between topic consistency between manager responses and corresponding reviews on review helpfulness."

Want to Make Me Emotional? The Influence of Emotional Advertisements on Women's Consumption Behavior [93]

This is a machine-generated summary of:

Majeed, Salman; Lu, Changbao; Usman, Muhammad: Want to make me emotional? The influence of emotional advertisements on women's consumption behavior [93]

Published in: Frontiers of Business Research in China (2017)

Link to original: https://doi.org/10.1186/s11782-017-0016-4

Copyright of the summarized publication:

The Author(s). 2019

License: OpenAccess CC BY 4.0

This article is distributed under the terms of the Creative Commons Attribution 4.0 International License (http://creativecommons.org/licenses/by/4.0/), which permits unrestricted use, distribution, and reproduction in any medium, provided you give appropriate credit to the original author(s) and the source, provide a link to the Creative Commons license, and indicate if changes were made.

If you want to cite the papers, please refer to the original.

For technical reasons we could not place the page where the original quote is coming from.

Abstract-Summary

"The objective of this study is to better conceptualize how women emotionally respond to emotional advertisements (EAs)."

"This empirical study examines women's emotional response using data from 240 Chinese women respondents."

"The study participants were invited to develop ACE mix based advertisements and fill out questionnaires."

"PLS-SEM analysis, a novel approach in ACE advertisement development and its applicability to consumer behavior, was used."

"The results show that showbiz celebrities expressing the emotion of happiness with music and color make the most effective ACE mix to influence the consumption behavior of women."

"The study also calls for further research with different ACE mixes in different contexts and on different audiences."

Introduction

"Although marketing professionals and other stakeholders are convinced about the effectiveness of celebrity endorsers, yet little is known about what kind of celebrity endorsement is a good fit with EAs, under emotions and appeal drivers, to influence consumers' attention, buying and consumption behavior (Erdogan & others [75]; Agrawal & Kamakura [76])."

"Although much of the research examines the behavior and profitable relationship with consumers, the industry and academic literature is silent about the prioritized combination of ACE mixes and attention levels in advertisement and their ultimate effect on consumers' behavior."

"Since some studies suggest that women express emotions three times, on average, more than the men do (Vigil [77]), the results presented in this study may provide some guidelines to Chinese marketing and advertising professionals to effectively boost business volumes in China by influencing Chinese women's consumption and contagion behavior."

Literature Review

"The literature discussed in this study has illuminated the concepts of emotional advertising stimuli, with a focus on appeal drivers (A), celebrity endorsement (C), and emotions (E), and their likely associative influence on women's consumption behavior."

"The featuring of celebrities and their exhibited emotions in tandem with the advertising execution factors have been discussed by researchers in order to explain their impact on women's attention and consumption behavior (Solomon [78]; Agrawal & Kamakura [76]; Stoeckel & others [79]; Park & Young [80]; Klaus & Bailey, 2008; Lwin & Phau [81])."

"The present study's ACE model, which is theoretically embedded within the ARM and AIDA premises where exposure to advertisement is presented and its ultimate impact on the audience's behavior is documented integrates the subordinate levels of human emotions (i.e., happiness, pride, sadness, and fear), appeal drivers (i.e., message, picture quality, music, and colors), and celebrity endorsement (i.e., showbiz and sports) constructs in order to show their influence on women's responses (modeled with attention, interest, and consumption behavior)."

Methodology

"The scenario allowed the respondents to choose the best combination of ACE variables, and develop their own advertisement, which would capture their attention and possibly convince them to buy the product (consumption behavior) if a product is advertised with the developed ACE mix."

"To measure the interest and attention levels of the study respondents towards the ACE variables, the participants were asked to rate their response on a 7-point Likert scale (ranging from strongly disagree to strongly agree)."

"The suitability of PLS-SEM was determined due to certain reasons, for example, (1) this research work's scope is extended to predict and explain the variance levels in certain target constructs, (2) the study's research paradigm is complex, and, (3) the interaction of emotions, appeal drivers, and celebrity endorsement in the advertisement with attention level and consumption behavior is a new element that can add to theory development and thus provides an opportunity to shed light on new processes."

Results

"The ranking analysis shows that overall the participants positively preferred music and color appeal drivers over the other appeal drivers being tested in the present study with the highest mean values (i.e., $Mean_{music} = 5.46$, $Mean_{colors} = 4.55$) and lowest standard deviation values comparatively (i.e., $S.D_{music} = 1.53$, $S.D_{colors} = 1.79$) as compared to the other appeal drivers ($Mean_{picture} = 4.38$, $S.D_{picture} = 1.82$; $Mean_{message} = 3.34$, $S.D_{message} = 1.88$)."

"The study respondents positively preferred the emotions of happiness and pride over the other emotions being tested with the highest mean values (i.e., $Mean_{happiness} = 5.86$, $Mean_{pride} = 4.43$) and the lowest standard deviation values (i.e., $S.D_{happiness} = 1.52$, $S.D_{pride} = 1.80$) as compared to the other emotional stimuli ($Mean_{fear} = 4.31$, $S.D_{fear} = 1.87$; $Mean_{sadness} = 3.28$, $S.D_{sadness} = 1.90$)."

Discussion

"The antecedents to women's consumption behavior are depicted to study the proposed hypotheses while highlighting some new insights in the spheres of emotional responses to ACE-based advertising."

"It has been found that, as expected, interesting and eye catchy advertisements may hold the attention levels of Chinese women which also mediates the direct effect of ACE constructs on their consumption behavior."

"Although all the ACE variables (appeal drivers, celebrity endorsements, and emotions) show their influence on Chinese women's consumption behaviors, however, the resulting robustness suggests that Chinese women are attracted to advertisements based on happy emotions with showbiz celebrities' endorsement, music, and the colors themes."

"The age cohorts of Chinese women were found to have a significant and pervasive impact on their ACE choice and consumption behavior, followed by their work status."

Contribution and Implications

"This research work contributes to the growing knowledge of marketing and advertisement theory that investigates the relationship between emotions, appeal drivers, celebrity endorsement, attention levels and consumption behavior."

"The study shows that women's response, particularly Chinese women's response, was primarily driven by their interest and attention levels induced by a specific ACE combination (comprised of showbiz celebrity endorsers showing happy emotions with music and colors) in the advertisement."

"This research work provides empirical grounding for some of the theoretical assumptions surrounding EAs and its developments and measures the magnitude of consumer response."

"The results and findings of the study need to be treated with skepticism while measuring real market mechanisms and consumers' emotional behaviors."

"Consumers feel that they are study objects during experiments (Tsai [82]), and may feel differently than in a real market environment."

Conclusion

"The resulting robustness notes that a better understanding of ACE combinations to develop EAs may generate the desired emotional response among Chinese women and influence their consumption behavior."

"The findings provide support to the arguments that emotional responses are predicted by the attention levels generated by EAs and how well the ACE combination is developed."

"The methods incorporated to map the antecedents to Chinese women's emotional responses generalize it to measure the response of consumers across different business marketing and advertising realms, and hence fuel the notions of Guerilla Marketing."

"Further research is needed to develop the insights into other niches in the business world by incorporating ACE combinations and engaging different target audiences with different demographic combinations."

Artificial Empathy in Marketing Interactions: Bridging the Human-AI Gap in Affective and Social Customer Experience [94]

This is a machine-generated summary of:

Liu-Thompkins, Yuping; Okazaki, Shintaro; Li, Hairong: Artificial empathy in marketing interactions: Bridging the human-AI gap in affective and social customer experience [94]

Published in: Journal of the Academy of Marketing Science (2022)

Link to original: https://doi.org/10.1007/s11747-022-00892-5

Copyright of the summarized publication:

The Author(s) 2022

License: OpenAccess CC BY 4.0

This article is licensed under a Creative Commons Attribution 4.0 International License, which permits use, sharing, adaptation, distribution and reproduction in any medium or format, as long as you give appropriate credit to the original author(s) and the source, provide a link to the Creative Commons licence, and indicate if changes were made. The images or other third party material in this article are included in the article's Creative Commons licence, unless indicated otherwise in a credit line to the material. If material is not included in the article's Creative Commons licence and your intended use is not permitted by statutory regulation or exceeds the permitted use, you will need to obtain permission directly from the copyright holder. To view a copy of this licence, visit http://creativecommons.org/licenses/by/4.0/.

Copyright comment: corrected publication 2022

If you want to cite the papers, please refer to the original.

For technical reasons we could not place the page where the original quote is coming from.

Abstract-Summary

"Addressing this issue, this article argues that artificial empathy needs to become an important design consideration in the next generation of AI marketing applications."

"Drawing from research in diverse disciplines, we develop a systematic framework for integrating artificial empathy into AI-enabled marketing interactions."

"We elaborate on the key components of artificial empathy and how each component can be implemented in AI marketing agents."

"We further explicate and test how artificial empathy generates value for both customers and firms by bridging the AI-human gap in affective and social customer experience."

Introduction

"These studies point to a significant gap between AI-enabled marketing interactions and those managed by humans, impeding the effective use of AI technologies and the consistent management of firm-customer interactions."

"We argue that artificial empathy is key to bridging the human-AI gap on affective and social customer experience and should become an important consideration in future AI-enabled firm-customer interactions."

"Despite the technological promise and growing realization that artificial empathy is important to effective AI applications, detailed examination of artificial empathy as it applies to marketing is lacking."

"Drawing from diverse disciplines such as computer science, psychology, robotics, and communications, we explicate artificial empathy, its key components, and how it can be implemented in marketing interactions through the latest empathic AI technologies."

"By considering most recent technological advances and best practices, our research offers practical guidance on when and how marketing practitioners should realize artificial empathy in their AI applications."

What Is Artificial Empathy?

"From the human empathy literature, a commonly adopted approach to empathy is a hierarchical three-layer structure of empathic development, from more unconscious emotional empathy to more conscious cognitive empathy (de Waal [83])."

"Built upon the perception-action mechanism, the next layer of empathy consists of empathic concern, which refers to the ability to intuit others' emotional state and to express concern toward others (Wieseke & others [84])."

"While the core layer of empathy, emotional contagion, is natural and automatic in humans, it is challenging to embed such a process into a computational machinery (Asada [85])."

"Based on machine algorithms' capability for handling cognitive versus emotional tasks, we believe that the hierarchy of human empathy should be reversed in artificial empathy, with perspective-taking at its core, followed by empathic concern, and emotional contagion as the outmost layer."

What Are the Dimensions of Artificial Empathy?

"In the case of AI-enabled marketing interactions, the AI agent needs to formulate an appropriate response to the consumer's emotions identified in the first step to create the impression of empathic concern."

"After the appraisal routine determines that it is appropriate for the AI agent to mimic the consumer's emotion, the next step involves actually expressing that emotion."

"An AI agent taking the perspective of a consumer does not need to involve the mimicking of the consumer's emotions."

"In the example above, being able to take the consumer's perspective and understand his/her innate needs and goals may help the AI agent better detect the consumer's emotional state and subsequently identify the optimal response."

"By integrating the hidden reward function discovered via perspective-taking into emotion detection and appraisal, an AI agent can anticipate a consumer's emotional reaction (e.g., frustration) before the emotion is explicitly manifested by the consumer."

How Does Artificial Empathy Create Value?

"We propose that the gap in affective customer experience quality between AI- and human-based marketing interactions can be mitigated through artificial empathy, by amplifying positive emotions and regulating negative emotions."

"The ability of artificial empathy to amplify positive emotions and regulate negative emotions should enhance the quality of AI-enabled affective customer experience, bringing it closer to a human-based interaction."

"P2 Artificial empathy will moderate the effect of agent type on social customer experience activation such that the gap in the activation of social customer experience between AI-enabled and human-based marketing interactions will be smaller at a higher level of artificial empathy."

"P3 Artificial empathy will moderate the effect of agent type on social customer experience quality such that the gap in the quality of social customer experience between AI-enabled and human-based marketing interactions will be smaller at a higher level of artificial empathy."

The Effect of Artificial Empathy on Customer Experience: A Pilot Study

"To test P1 ~ P3, we conducted a MANCOVA with these three customer experience ratings as the dependent variables and empathy condition, agent identity, and their interaction as the independent variables."

"When empathy was high, the difference in affective experience quality between the human and AI agents was no longer significant ($M = 6.10$ vs. 5.96, $F_{1,519} = 1.49$, $p = .22$)."

"Participants under the low-empathy condition considered the customer experience with the human agent more social than that with the AI chatbot ($M_{social\ activation} = 5.44$ vs. 4.62, $F_{1,519} = 19.72$, $p < .001$)."

"Further contrasts between high- and low-empathy conditions within each agent type suggest that empathy significantly improved all three customer experience outcomes for the AI agent but not for the human agent."

When Does Artificial Empathy Create Value?

"P4 The ability of artificial empathy to bridge the human-AI gap in affective customer experience is contingent on the availability of high-quality emotional signals."

"P5 The ability of artificial empathy to create value by bridging the human-AI affective experience gap depends on consumers' need for affect."

"These findings suggest that in an instrumental context, the value of improved affective customer experience due to artificial empathy is contingent on the AI agent's functional competence in helping consumers to achieve their goal (e.g., recommending the right product to meet a consumer's need)."

"P10 The ability of artificial empathy to bridge the human-AI gap in social customer experience is contingent on the anthropomorphic design of the AI agent."

"P12 The ability of artificial empathy to create value by bridging the human-AI social experience gap is higher for brands with high anthropomorphism than for those with low anthropomorphism."

Conclusion, Limitations, and Further Research

"Addressing these divergent views of AI from firms and consumers, we argue that artificial empathy needs to become an important consideration in the next generation of AI-enabled marketing interactions."

"Filling these gaps, we draw from research in diverse disciplines to create a conceptual framework of artificial empathy in the context of AI-enabled marketing interactions."

"The results confirmed the ability of artificial empathy to bridge the customer experience gap between AI and human agents."

"This difference disappeared under high empathy, such that interaction with a human agent vs. an AI agent brought about comparable levels of affective and social customer experience quality."

"How consumer awareness of the AI identity interacts with artificial empathy is a worthwhile question for future research."

"Even though artificial empathy has the potential to bridge the AI-human gap in customer experience, its implications for consumer privacy may be quite different and need to be examined in future research."

Bibliography

1. Davies, M., Stankov, L., & Roberts, R. D. (1998). Emotional intelligence: In search of an elusive construct. *Journal of Personality and Social Psychology, 75*(4), 989–1015.
2. Gardner, H. (1985). *Frames of mind: The theory of multiple intelligences.* Basic Books.
3. Haidt, J. (2003). The moral emotions. In R. J. Davidson, K. R. Scherer, & H. H. Goldsmith (Eds.), *Handbook of affective sciences* (pp. 852–870). Oxford University Press.

4. Hardy, S. A. (2006). Identity, reasoning and emotion: An empirical comparison of three sources of moral motivation. *Motivation and Emotion, 30*(3), 205–213.
5. Vitell, S. J., King, R. A., & Singh, J. J. (2013). A special emphasis and look at the emotional side of ethical decision-making. *AMS Review, 3*(2), 74–85.
6. Forsyth, D. R. (1980). A taxonomy of ethical ideologies. *Journal of Personality and Social Psychology, 39*(1), 175–184.
7. Tangney, J. P., Stuewig, J., & Mashek, D. J. (2007). Moral emotions and moral behaviour. *Annual Review of Psychology, 58*, 345–372.
8. Beer, J. S. (2007). Neural systems for self-conscious emotions and their underlying appraisals. In J. L. Tracy, R. W. Robins, & J. P. Tangney (Eds.), *The self-conscious emotions: Theory and research* (pp. 53–67). Guilford Press.
9. McCullough, M. E., Kilpatrick, S. D., Emmons, R. A., & Larson, D. B. (2001). Is gratitude a moral affect? *Psychological Bulletin, 127*(2), 249–266.
10. Law, K. S., Wong, C.-S., & Song, L. J. (2004). The construct and criterion validity of emotional intelligence and its potential utility for management studies. *Journal of Applied Psychology, 89*(3), 483–496. https://doi.org/10.1037/0021-9010.89.3.483
11. Goleman, D. P. (1995). *Emotional intelligence: Why it can matter more than IQ*. Bantam Books.
12. Chowdhury, R. M. M. I., & Fernando, M. (2013). The role of spiritual well-being and materialism in determining consumers' ethical beliefs: An empirical study with Australian consumers. *Journal of Business Ethics, 113*(1), 61–79.
13. Lu, L. C., & Lu, C. J. (2010). Moral philosophy, materialism, and consumer ethics: An exploratory study in Indonesia. *Journal of Business Ethics, 94*(2), 193–210.
14. Chan, A., Wong, S., & Leung, P. (1998). Ethical beliefs of Chinese consumers in Hong Kong. *Journal of Business Ethics, 17*(11), 1163–1170.
15. Cui, C. C., Mitchell, V., Schlegelmilch, B. B., & Cornwell, B. (2005). Measuring consumers' ethical position in Austria, Britain, Brunei, Hong Kong and USA. *Journal of Business Ethics, 62*(1), 57–71.
16. Hayes, A. F. (2013). *Introduction to mediation, moderation, and conditional process analysis: A regression-based approach*. Guilford Press.
17. Vitell, S. J., Singh, J. J., & Paolillo, J. G. (2007). Consumers' ethical beliefs: The roles of money, religiosity and attitude toward business. *Journal of Business Ethics, 73*(4), 369–379.
18. Fu, W. (2014). The impact of emotional intelligence, organizational commitment, and job satisfaction on ethical behaviour of Chinese employees. *Journal of Business Ethics, 122*(1), 137–144.
19. Lopes, P. N., Salovey, P., & Straus, R. (2003). Emotional intelligence, personality, and the perceived quality of social relationships. *Personality and Individual Differences, 35*(3), 641–658.
20. Jordan, P. J., & Troth, A. (2011). Emotional intelligence and leader member exchange: The relationship with employee turnover intentions and job satisfaction. *Leadership & Organization Development Journal, 32*(3), 260–280.
21. Delpechitre, D., Beeler-Connelly, L. L., & Chaker, N. N. (2018). Customer value co-creation behavior: A dyadic exploration of the influence of salesperson emotional intelligence on customer participation and citizenship behavior. *Journal of Business Research, 92*(November), 9–24.
22. Matute, J., Palau-Saumell, R., & Viglia, G. (2018). Beyond chemistry: The role of employee emotional competence in personalized services. *Journal of Services Marketing, 32*(3), 346–359.
23. Leonidou, L. C., Samiee, S., Aykol, B., & Talias, M. A. (2014). Antecedents and outcomes of exporter-importer relationship quality: Synthesis, meta-analysis, and directions for further research. *Journal of International Marketing, 22*(2), 21–46.
24. Miao, C., Humphrey, R. H., & Qian, S. (2018). A cross-cultural meta-analysis of how leader emotional intelligence influences subordinate task performance and organizational citizenship behavior. *Journal of World Business, 53*(4), 463–474.
25. Barnes, B. R., Leonidou, L. C., Siu, N. Y. M., & Leonidou, C. N. (2010). Opportunism as the inhibiting trigger for developing long-term-oriented Western exporter–Hong Kong importer relationships. *Journal of International Marketing, 18*(2), 35–63.

26. Krishnakumar, S., Perera, B., Hopkins, K., & Robinson, M. D. (2019). On being nice and effective: Work-related emotional intelligence and its role in conflict resolution and interpersonal problem-solving. *Conflict Resolution Quarterly, 37*(2), 147–167.
27. Shih, H., & Susanto, E. (2010). Conflict management styles, emotional intelligence, and job performance in public organizations. *International Journal of Conflict Management, 21*(2), 147–168.
28. Gabel, R. S., Dolan, S. L., & Cerdin, J. L. (2005). Emotional intelligence as predictor of cultural adjustment for success in global assignments. *Career Development International, 10*(5), 375–395.
29. Lii, S., & Wong, S. (2008). The antecedents of overseas adjustment and commitment of expatriates. *The International Journal of Human Resource Management, 19*(2), 296–313.
30. Lillis, M. P., & Tian, R. G. (2009). Cross-cultural communication and emotional intelligence: Inferences from case studies of gender diverse groups. *Marketing Intelligence & Planning, 27*(3), 428–438.
31. Hofstede, G., & Hofstede, G. J. (2005). *Cultures and organizations: Software of the mind*. McGraw Hill.
32. Kernbach, S., & Schutte, N. S. (2005). The impact of service provider emotional intelligence on customer satisfaction. *Journal of Services Marketing, 19*(7), 438–444.
33. Tsaur, S., & Ku, P. (2019). The effect of tour leaders' emotional intelligence on tourists' consequences. *Journal of Travel Research, 58*(1), 63–76.
34. Gu, F. F., Wang, J. J., & Wang, D. T. (2019). The role of sales representatives in cross-cultural business-to-business relationships. *Industrial Marketing Management, 78*(April), 227–238.
35. Sousa, C. M. P., Ruzo, E., & Lozada, F. (2010). The key role of managers' values in exporting: Influence on customer responsiveness and export performance. *Journal of International Marketing, 18*(2), 1–19.
36. Skarmeas, D., Katsikeas, C. S., Spyropoulou, S., & Salehi-Sangari, E. (2008). Market and supplier characteristics driving distributor relationship quality in international marketing channels of industrial products. *Industrial Marketing Management, 37*(1), 23–36.
37. Podsakoff, P. M., Mackenzie, S. B., & Podsakoff, N. P. (2012). Sources of method bias in social science research and recommendations on how to control it. *Annual Review of Psychology, 63*(1), 539.
38. Malär, L., Krohmer, H., Hoyer, W. D., & Nyffenegger, B. (2011). Emotional brand attachment and brand personality: The relative importance of the actual and the ideal self. *Journal of Marketing, 75*(4), 35–52.
39. Jiménez, F. R., & Voss, K. E. (2014). An alternative approach to the measurement of emotional attachment. *Psychology & Marketing, 31*(5), 360–370.
40. Arruda-Filho, E. J., Cabusas, J. A., & Dholakia, N. (2010). Social behavior and brand devotion among iPhone innovators. *International Journal of Information Management, 30*(6), 475–480.
41. Batra, R., Ahuvia, A., & Bagozzi, R. P. (2012). Brand love. *Journal of Marketing, 76*(2), 1–16.
42. Ortiz, M. H., Reynolds, K. E., & Franke, G. R. (2013). Measuring consumer devotion: Antecedents and consequences of passionate consumer behavior. *Journal of Marketing Theory and Practice, 21*(1), 7–30.
43. Mikulincer, M., & Shaver, P. R. (2001). Attachment theory and intergroup bias: Evidence that priming the secure base schema attenuates negative reactions to out-groups. *Journal of Personality and Social Psychology, 81*(1), 97.
44. Whan Park, C., MacInnis, D. J., Priester, J., Eisingerich, A. B., & Iacobucci, D. (2010). Brand attachment and brand attitude strength: Conceptual and empirical differentiation of two critical brand equity drivers. *Journal of Marketing, 74*(6), 1–17.
45. Viswanathan, V., & Jain, V. (2013). A dual-system approach to understanding "generation Y" decision making. *Journal of Consumer Marketing, 30*(6), 484–492.
46. Kim, J., Morris, J. D., & Swait, J. (2008). Antecedents of true brand loyalty. *Journal of Advertising, 37*(2), 99–117.
47. Cheng, S. Y., White, T. B., & Chaplin, L. N. (2012). The effects of self-brand connections on responses to brand failure: A new look at the consumer–brand relationship. *Journal of Consumer Psychology, 22*(2), 280–288.

48. Karjaluoto, H., Karjaluoto, H., Munnukka, J., Munnukka, J., Kiuru, K., & Kiuru, K. (2016). Brand love and positive word of mouth: The moderating effects of experience and price. *Journal of Product & Brand Management, 25*(6), 527–537.
49. Chaudhuri, A., & Holbrook, M. B. (2001). The chain of effects from brand trust and brand affect to brand performance: The role of brand loyalty. *Journal of Marketing, 65*(2), 81–93.
50. Xie, Y., Batra, R., & Peng, S. (2015). An extended model of preference formation between global and local brands: The roles of identity expressiveness, trust, and affect. *Journal of International Marketing, 23*(1), 50–71.
51. Erdem, T., & Swait, J. (1998). Brand equity as a signaling phenomenon. *Journal of consumer Psychology, 7*(2), 131–157.
52. Kernbach, S., & Schutte, N. S. (2005). The impact of service provider emotional intelligence on customer satisfaction. *Journal of Services Marketing, 19*, 438–444.
53. Kim, E., & Drumwright, M. (2016). Engaging consumers and building relationships in social media: How social relatedness influences intrinsic vs. extrinsic consumer motivation. *Computers in Human Behavior, 63*, 970–979.
54. Gelbrich, K., & Roschk, H. (2011). Do complainants appreciate overcompensation? A meta-analysis on the effect of simple compensation vs. overcompensation on post-complaint satisfaction. *Marketing Letters, 23*, 31–47.
55. Bijmolt, T. H. A., & Pieters, R. G. M. (2001). Meta-analysis in marketing when studies contain multiple measurements. *Marketing Letters, 12*, 157–169.
56. Golder, P. N., Mitra, D., & Moorman, C. (2012). What is quality? An integrative framework of processes and states. *Journal of Marketing, 76*, 1–23.
57. Bolino, M. C., Hsiung, H. H., Harvey, J., & LePine, J. A. (2015). "Well, I'm tired of tryin'!" Organizational citizenship behavior and citizenship fatigue. *Journal of Applied Psychology, 100*, 56–74.
58. Lipsey, M. W., & Wilson, D. B. (2001). *Practical meta-analysis*. Sage.
59. Peterson, R. A., & Brown, S. P. (2005). On the use of beta coefficients in meta-analysis. *Journal of Applied Psychology, 90*, 175–181.
60. Miao, C., Humphrey, R. H., & Qian, S. (2017). A meta-analysis of emotional intelligence and work attitudes. *Journal of Occupational and Organizational Psychology, 90*, 177–202.
61. O'Boyle, E. H., Humphrey, R. H., Pollack, J. M., Hawver, T. H., & Story, P. A. (2011). The relation between emotional intelligence and job performance: A meta-analysis. *Journal of Organizational Behavior, 32*, 788–818.
62. Schmidt, F. L., & Hunter, J. E. (2015). *Methods of meta-analysis: Correcting error and bias in research findings*. Sage.
63. Thomson, M., MacInnis, D. J., & Park, C. W. (2005). The ties that bind: Measuring the strength of consumers' emotional attachments to brands. *Journal of Consumer Psychology, 15*(1), 77–91.
64. Fry, L. W., & Slocum, J. W. (2008). Maximizing the triple bottom line through spiritual leadership. *Organizational Dynamics, 37*(1), 86–96.
65. Pawar, B. S. (2009). Workplace spirituality facilitation: A comprehensive model. *Journal of Business Ethics, 90*(3), 375–386.
66. Pérez, A., & Del Bosque, I. R. (2014). Customer CSR expectations in the banking industry. *International Journal of Bank Marketing, 32*(3), 223–244.
67. Pérez, A., & Del Bosque, I. R. (2017). Personal traits and customer responses to CSR perceptions in the banking sector. *International Journal of Bank Marketing, 35*(1), 128–146.
68. Chan, K. W., Yim, C. K., & Lam, S. S. (2010). Is customer participation in value creation a double-edged sword? Evidence from professional financial services across cultures. *Journal of Marketing, 74*(3), 48–64.
69. Hays, R. D., Hayashi, T., & Stewart, A. L. (1989). A five-item measure of socially desirable response set. *Educational and Psychological Measurement, 49*(3), 629–636.
70. Guo, B., & Zhou, S. (2016). What makes population perception of review helpfulness: An information processing perspective. *Electronic Commerce Research, 17*(4), 585–608.

71. Xu, Y., et al. (2020). Effects of online reviews and managerial responses from a review manipulation perspective. *Current Issues in Tourism, 23*(17), 2207–2222.
72. Zhang, X., et al. (2020). Exploring the impact of personalized management responses on tourists' satisfaction: A topic matching perspective. *Tourism Management, 76*(2), 103953.
73. Wang, Y., & Chaudhry, A. (2018). When and how managers' responses to online reviews affect subsequent reviews. *Journal of Marketing Research, 55*(2), 163–177.
74. Kwok, L., & Xie, K. L. (2016). Factors contributing to the helpfulness of online hotel reviews. *International Journal of Contemporary Hospitality Management, 28*(10), 2156–2177.
75. Erdogan, B. Z., Baker, M. J., & Tagg, S. (2001). Selecting celebrity endorsers: The practitioner's perspective. *Journal of Advertising Research, 41*, 39–48.
76. Agrawal, J., & Kamakura, W. A. (1995). The economic worth of celebrity endorsers: An event study analysis. *Journal of Marketing, 59*, 56–62.
77. Vigil, J. M. (2009). A socio-relational framework of sex differences in the expression of emotion. *Behavioral and Brain Sciences, 32*, 375–428.
78. Solomon, M. (2002). *Consumer behaviour: Buying, having, and being* (5th ed.). Prentice Hall.
79. Stoeckel, L. E., Cox, J. E., Cook, E. W., & Weller, R. E. (2007). Motivational state modulates hedonic value of food images differently in men and women. *Appetite, 48*, 139–144.
80. Park, W., & Young, M. S. (1986). Consumer response to television commercials: The impact of involvement and background music on brand attitude formation. *Journal of Marketing Research, 23*(1), 11–24.
81. Lwin, M., & Phau, I. (2013). Effective advertising appeals for websites of small boutique hotels. *Journal of Research in interactive Marketing, 7*(1), 18–32.
82. Tsai, J. (2010). Are you smarter than a neuromarketer. *Customer Relationship Management, 14*, 19–20.
83. de Waal, F. B. M. (2008). Putting the altruism back into altruism: The evolution of empathy. *Annual Review of Psychology, 59*, 279–300.
84. Wieseke, J., Geigenmüller, A., & Kraus, F. (2012). On the role of empathy in customer-employee interactions. *Journal of Service Research, 15*, 316–331.
85. Asada, M. (2015). Development of artificial empathy. *Neuroscience Research, 90*, 41–50.
86. Chowdhury, R. M. M. I. (2015). Emotional intelligence and consumer ethics: The mediating role of personal moral philosophies. *Journal of Business Ethics*. https://doi.org/10.1007/s10551-015-2733-y
87. Leonidou, L. C., Aykol, B., Larimo, J., Kyrgidou, L., & Christodoulides, P. (2021). Enhancing international buyer-seller relationship quality and long-term orientation using emotional intelligence: The moderating role of foreign culture. *Management International Review*. https://doi.org/10.1007/s11575-021-00447-w
88. Ahn, H., Sung, Y., Drumwright, M. E. (2015). Consumer emotional intelligence and its effects on responses to transgressions. *Marketing Letters*. https://doi.org/10.1007/s11002-014-9342-x
89. Saju, B., Harikrishnan, K., Joseph Jeya Anand, S. (2017). Modeling brand immunity: The moderating role of generational cohort membership. *Journal of Brand Management*. https://doi.org/10.1057/s41262-017-0063-3
90. Miao, C., Barone, M. J., Qian, S., Humphrey, R. H. (2019). Emotional intelligence and service quality: A meta-analysis with initial evidence on cross-cultural factors and future research directions. *Marketing Letters*. https://doi.org/10.1007/s11002-019-09495-7
91. Hur, W.-M., Moon, T.-W., Kim, H. (2020). When does customer CSR perception lead to customer extra-role behaviors? The roles of customer spirituality and emotional brand attachment. *Journal of Brand Management*. https://doi.org/10.1057/s41262-020-00190-x
92. Zhou, C., Yang, S., Chen, Y., Zhou, S., Li, Y., Qazi, A. (2022). How does topic consistency affect online review helpfulness? The role of review emotional intensity. *Electronic Commerce Research*. https://doi.org/10.1007/s10660-022-09597-x
93. Majeed, S.; Lu, C., & Usman, M. (2017). Want to make me emotional? The influence of emotional advertisements on women's consumption behavior. *Frontiers of Business Research in China*. https://doi.org/10.1186/s11782-017-0016-4

94. Liu-Thompkins, Y., Okazaki, S., Li, H. (2022). Artificial empathy in marketing interactions: Bridging the human-AI gap in affective and social customer experience. *Journal of the Academy of Marketing Science.* https://doi.org/10.1007/s11747-022-00892-5

Printed in the USA
CPSIA information can be obtained
at www.ICGtesting.com
CBHW061029090924
14265CB00004B/203

9 789819 977260